Jacob Srampickal - Giuseppe Mazza - Lloyd Baugh
(edd.)

Cross Connections

*Interdisciplinary communications studies
at the Gregorian University*

Saggi celebrativi per il
XXV anniversario del CICS

EDITRICE PONTIFICIA UNIVERSITÀ GREGORIANA
ROMA 2006

IMPRIMI POTEST
Romae, die 16 ianuarii anni 2006
R.P. FRANCISCO J. EGAÑA, S.J.
Vice Rector Universitatis

IMPRIMATUR
Dal Vicariato di Roma, 14 febbraio 2006
Mons. MAURO PARMEGGIANI
Prelato Segretario Generale

© 2006 – E.P.U.G. – ROMA
ISBN 88-7839-061-5

EDITRICE PONTIFICIA UNIVERSITÀ GREGORIANA
Piazza della Pilotta, 35 - 00187 Roma, Italia

TABLE OF CONTENTS

EDITORIAL NOTE 9

FELICITATIONS

1. Messaggio del Cardinale Carlo Maria Martini 17
2. "A distinguished quarter-century history"
   Archbishop John P. Foley,
   President of the Pontifical Council for Social Communications 19
3. Il CICS al servizio della Chiesa universale
   Peter-Hans Kolvenbach, SJ,
   Superior General of the Society of Jesus 21
4. Saluto del Rettore Magnifico
   Gianfranco Ghirlanda, SJ 23

INTRODUCING A CICS VISION

5. Communications training
   for the Church today: the CICS approach
   Jacob Srampickal, SJ, *Director of the CICS* 27
6. Alle origini del CICS: l'interdisciplinarietà
   S.E. Mons. Peter Henrici, *Founder-Director of the CICS* 37
7. A celebration of interdisciplinarity: my twenty-two years at the
   Pontificia Università Gregoriana and in the Centro Interdisciplinare sulla Comunicazione Sociale
   Lloyd Baugh, SJ 41

THE LANGUAGE OF THE MEDIA

8. Press journalism: a search for the truth
   Mary Wilsey 55
9. La información religiosa. Hacia una naturalización
   del periodismo religioso en los medios
   Miriam Diez Bosch 67

10. La radio come comunicatore
    Paolo Prato 77
11. Gli studi sulla televisione
    Michele Sorice 89
12. L'insegnamento di Internet in un'Università Pontificia
    Xavier Debanne 103

THE THEOLOGICAL-PASTORAL DIMENSION

13. Recent work in communication and theology
    Paul A. Soukup, SJ 121
14. Verso una teologia pastorale della comunicazione nell'era globale
    Giuseppe Mazza 147
15. Comunicar a Palavra da Cruz
    Nuno Brás Martins 159
16. Communication theology in priestly formation
    Joseph Palakeel, MST 171

THE SPIRITUAL DIMENSION

17. The spirituality of the Christian communicator
    Franz-Josef Eilers, SVD 187
18. Maybe angels: glimpses of spirituality in popular culture
    Jim McDonnell 199
19. La lettura come realtà virtuale: tra letteratura,
    spiritualità e *media* elettronici
    Antonio Spadaro, SJ 211

THE ETHICAL-PHILOSOPHICAL DIMENSION
AND OTHER HUMAN SCIENCES

20. Wieso braucht Kommunikation Philosophie?
    Johannes Ehrat, SJ 227
21. Semiotica ai media
    Sante Babolin 241
22. "And they have seen his glory": aesthetic communications
    David Eley, SJ 249
23. Media accountability challenges in sub-Saharan Africa:
    the limits of self-regulation in Tanzanian newsrooms
    Bernardin F. Mfumbusa 259
24. A social psychology of communication
    Augustine Savarimuthu, SJ 271

The Socio-Cultural Dimension

25. Communalistic approach to communication with examples from the Yorùbá of Nigeria
    Joseph Oládèjo Fáníran 287
26. La educación para los medios en tempos de secularización
    José Martínez de Toda, SJ 297
27. Discovering a theory and methodology for studying media and religion: the "Media, Religion and Culture" perspective
    Robert A. White, SJ 313
28. Communication for education and development as a key to formation: development communication studies at CICS in perspective
    Jacob Srampickal, SJ 343

From the Beginning to a Future

29. Communicating with the world?
    Maria Way 363
30. Some twenty-first century challenges facing Catholics in communication formation
    William E. Biernatzki, SJ 375
31. Verso una comunicazione partecipativa. L'opera del CICS in un'esperienza di vita e insegnamento
    Robert A. White, SJ 385

Contributors 399

EDITORIAL NOTE

On the occasion of the 25th anniversary of the Interdisciplinary Centre for Social Communications (CICS) at the Pontifical Gregorian University in Rome, as we reflect on the way communication study and formation have been developed here, we can see that the experience has been both challenging and fruitful. In the late 1970s, while universities elsewhere in the world were establishing faculties of communications with Bachelor's, Master's and Doctorate degrees, the visionaries who established the program in Social Communication at the Gregorian University promoted another approach.

These men – Pedro Arrupe, SJ, then Superior General of the Jesuits, Carlo Maria Martini, SJ, then Rector of the University (now, Cardinal Martini), Peter Henrici, SJ, then Dean of Philosophy at the Gregorian and the founding Director of the CICS (now Bishop Henrici), and others like Robert White, SJ, John E. O'Brien, SJ, Stephan Bamberger, SJ, and Franz Josef Eilers, SVD – believed that communications should be taught with an interdisciplinary approach, relating to the major disciplines taught at the University, such as theology, philosophy, missiology and social sciences. The Jesuits wanted the program at the Gregorian to make a specific contribution to the Church and they understood the importance of linking the discipline of communications with other Church-related disciplines. Their vision was far ahead of its time.

On this 25th anniversary we want to re-affirm this vision of the pioneers who reached out to other faculties at the Gregorian with an approach that focussed on a number of dimensions of the study of communication: the theological-pastoral dimension, the spiritual dimension, the philosophical and ethical dimension, and the socio-cultural dimension.

In this volume, we who have followed in their footsteps and struggled to keep their vision alive and clear, celebrate these twenty-five years of courageous and fruitful intellectual ministry. For the most part the contributors are professors and former students of the CICS, and the volume is divided according to above-mentioned dimensions. We present these papers in several languages in order to highlight the multinational and multicultural nature of studies and teaching at the Gregorian, and the universality of our outreach. Clearly, the papers vary in style and format, underlining the variety of thinking and topics dealt within the area of communications.

The CICS vision

Jacob Srampickal, the present Director of the Interdisciplinary Centre, elaborates a vision for the future of the CICS, based on conversations with some of the pioneers of the program. Peter Henrici highlights the origins and the basic vision of the Centre; he describes the interdisciplinary approach as elaborating the relationship between communications and the traditional classical subjects, suggesting how the classical disciplines can be enriched by developing the implicit communication dimension in them. Lloyd Baugh reflects on his experience of interdisciplinary studies, research, teaching and thesis direction in the CICS, work in which he bridges the disciplines of film studies, theology, philosophy, spirituality and interreligious dialogue.

The language of the media

In the vast area of the languages of the various media, the contributors focus on the importance of their medium, on the particular way it is taught in the CICS and on how our training contributes to equip the student to meet the challenges of the media world today. Mary Wilsey and Miriam Diez Bosch focus on different dimensions of print journalism, proposing an ongoing primacy for this medium in spite of the technological advances made by other media. Paolo Prato, on the other hand, centers his reflections on the medium of radio, commenting on its ongoing universal popularity and on its particular relevance to the students of the CICS. Michele Sorice discusses the medium of television, relating it to cultural studies and reception theory. Xavier Debanne speculates on the many possibilities offered to the field of Church communication by Internet.

Communication and theology

One of the major contributions of the CICS has been to develop the relationship between communication and theology. Paul Soukup reviews the various categories to which recent studies in communication and theology belong and notes common themes and some general weaknesses in the writings on these subjects. Giuseppe Mazza studies the possibilities of a link between fundamental theology and communications, outlining the resources for developing a modern concept of pastoral theology of communication, and the difficulties of such a task in the face of today's challenges. Nuno Martins investigates the communication dimension in Christian revelation and analyses the notion of Christ as the perfect communicator, through the "scandalous" event in which all communications appear to fail, the Cross. Joseph Palakeel argues that communication is a constituent dimension of Christian theology, proclamation and praxis, and so that any major change in communication media and culture demands a rethinking of theology and pastoral praxis. For him, the seminary should become a school of communication where critical informing alone can lead to genuine formation.

The spiritual dimension

Communication and spirituality and the spirituality of the communicator are an important dimension of the work we do in the CICS. Franz Josef Eilers does a wide investigation of this theme; with the thought of Carlo Maria Martini as his foundation, Eilers points out that the spirituality of the Christian communicator must be grounded in biblical considerations and must be based on a solid communication theology which sees the whole of theology under the perspective of communication. Thus communication becomes a theological principle, and clearly this has consequences for the personal spirituality of the communicator. Jim McDonnell's paper highlights this aspect of communication and spirituality in popular culture and media. For him the entertainment media are responding to and nourishing what might be called a spirituality of "openness to possibilities". Antonio Spadaro investigates how literature and even virtual realities help in developing a spirituality for the contemporary world. He demonstrates a formal analogy between the virtual reality of the videogame and the experience of the Spiritual Exercises of Ignatius of Loyola.

The philosophical-ethical and human sciences dimension

Philosophy and the human sciences have tried to articulate the richness of the science of communications. Johannes Ehrat traces the importance of philosophical reflection in understanding communication, pointing out certain tacit philosophical assumptions behind communication research, in order to prove the necessity of posing the question of communication as a philosophical problem. Sante Babolin highlights how semiotics becomes an important element in mediated communication. Showing a connection between semiotics and culture, the author distinguishes the concepts of sign and symbol. In his paper on aesthetics, David Eley establishes the aesthetic foundations of the communicative act, as it is enlightened by contemporary communication studies and through the Christian elements of the Creed, the Cross and the Christ.

Ethics is a privileged theme in the work we do in the CICS. Michael Traber, a mainstay in the area of media ethics in the world, and one who has, in his teaching in the CICS, contributed immensely to develop clear paradigms and ethical norms, had accepted our invitation to contribute an essay to this volume, but unfortunately, due to prolonged illness, he was unable to complete the piece. Bernardin Mfumbusa investigates some of the credibility problems facing media systems in sub-Saharan Africa and discusses how self-regulation, effected through the use of codes of ethics, among other self-regulation mechanisms can restore media ethics.

Working in the area of psychology, Augustine Savarimuthu argues for a model of communication in which the interactants keep generating, maintaining and renewing themselves and their relationships, thus providing clues to the understanding of self and the nature of human relationships.

The socio-cultural dimension

The cultural studies dimension has always been another major interest in the CICS. Joseph Faniran demonstrates how an innovative theory of ritual drawn from African philosophies, and from Turner and Rothenbuhler, leads towards communal patterns of communication, learned through life-cycle rituals of socialisation. Media and audience interactions remained a mainstay in media education studies and José Martínez de Toda argues how genuine media education can help people discover God in an ever-more secularized world. The interactions between media and religion aimed at formulating a new culture of peace is the theme of Robert White's essay. He points out that in understanding the role of media in spiritual and religious development, a number of elements are helpful: an ethnographic description of meaning construction in the holistic contexts of lifetimes, the use of multiple forms of information in response to personal crises, the process of subcultural identity formation, the historical development of rituals, and the comparison of belief systems. Jacob Srampickal points out why communication for education and development is of paramount importance in a world where media are widely considered as entertainment and as agents of commercial gain. Focussing on the plight of the developing world, he underlines current concerns in development communication.

Looking to the future

Maria Way looks at the problems and successes of Jesuits in communication and considers possible ways for future efforts. William Biernatzki traces some of the challenges the Church must face if it is to make a useful contribution to communications formation. He argues that the future Church communicators will need both theological and secular expertise to supply the modern world with truly Christian approaches, which demands high professionalism and a well-honed sense of journalistic ethics. In the final article, Robert White poses the challenges of participatory communications. He argues that a clear vision for participatory communication formation needs to focus on the idea of the human person, the social teaching of the Church, education for freedom, affirmation of cultural rights and models of socio-economic development based on networks of popular grassroots organizations.

Our thanks

Besides the contributors who made this volume possible, there are others whom we wish to thank for their generous commitment to this project. Gerald O'Collins, Norman Tanner, Mark Henninger and Robert Araujo, all Jesuits teaching at the Gregorian, generously helped with editing texts. Carlo Valentino of the Pontifical Biblical Institute and Tiziano Repetto, a Jesuit and second year student of communications, put much care and expertise with the electronic technologies into giving this book its final form. Our own professor of graphic arts, Gianfranco Caldarelli, furnished the front cover, for which we are grateful. We wish also to thank the Gregorian University Press for having completed the project so well and on time.

For their financial support of our various Anniversary celebrations, which includes this book, we are grateful to Porticus, Missio, Misereor and the Jesuits of Upper Canada.

Finally, dear reader, our effort is in your hands. We hope that our publication will help you understand how we, in the Interdisciplinary Centre for Social Communications at the Gregorian University in Rome, are developing an understanding of communications and communication formation designed for the Church in the 21st century.

The Editors
Jacob Srampickal, Giuseppe Mazza, Lloyd Baugh

FELICITATIONS

Messaggio del Cardinale Carlo Maria Martini

Gerusalemme, 3 gennaio 2006

Caro Padre Jacob Srampickal, SJ, Direttore del CICS,

sono lieto che si voglia celebrare il XXV anniversario del Centro Interdisciplinare sulla Comunicazione Sociale presso la Pontificia Università Gregoriana. Io stesso fui strettamente connesso con le origini di tale Centro e me ne occupai direttamente nel periodo del mio rettorato, precisamente verso la fine degli anni Settanta. Godo ora nel vedere gli sviluppi assunti da questa istituzione, che attraverso offerte tematiche e specializzazioni mediatiche abilita a orientarsi nel mondo spesso confuso e un po' caotico della comunicazione sociale odierna.

L'importanza di questo tema per la Chiesa si può cogliere già nel fatto che la "comunicazione" costituisce l'ottava ed ultima specializzazione della teologia, secondo la divisione proposta dal filosofo Bernard Lonergan, SJ, che fu anche professore alla Gregoriana. Egli nota quanto la cura per la "comunicazione" debba essere particolarmente pressante, perché è in questo stadio finale che la riflessione teologica porta il suo frutto. Senza quest'ultima funzione, tutte le precedenti (come la ricerca, l'interpretazione, la storia, la dialettica, la sistematica, ecc.) sarebbero vane e inconcludenti.

Ma anche al di là della riflessione teologica e della trasmissione del messaggio cristiano, la comunicazione resta una realtà che pervade un po' tutto il vivere sociale delle persone e dei gruppi. È anche compito della Chiesa educare e formare a una retta comunicazione, soprattutto ad una retta percezione dei segnali lanciati dai mass media. Negli anni in cui sono stato Arcivescovo a Milano, mi sono interessato molto di questo ambito, anche perché avevo modo di constatare ogni giorno quanto fosse necessario un buon rapporto coi mass media e quanto fosse utile un'adeguata ermeneutica al riguardo. Ho poi voluto lanciare per la diocesi di Milano (ma la cosa si è estesa anche oltre i confini della diocesi) un programma triennale proprio sul "comunicare". Esso partiva dalle regole fondamentali del comunicare umano, derivate a loro volta anche dalle coordinate del comunicare di Dio all'uomo, per considerare poi la comunicazione a livello di ambiti sociali e infine le caratteristiche specifiche della comunicazione di massa. In questa rassegna, avevo modo anche di confutare alcuni luoghi comuni che spesso emergono quando si parla di questi problemi, come ad esempio quello del rapporto tra degrado dei mass media e degrado della società o quello dell'illusione di una comunicazione perfetta e sempre luminosa. Facevo notare, un po' polemicamente, che una comunicazione pubblica degradata è anzitutto effetto e non causa di una società degradata, e che quindi occorre anzitutto guarire la società per guarire le deviazioni dei mass media. Inoltre sottolineavo che spesso è il desiderio di troppo comunicare, fino a schiacciare l'altro, che guasta la relazione comunicativa, assai più di quanto faccia una comunicazione mediocre, ma comunque discreta e rispettosa dell'altro.

Ho ricordato queste cose per dire quanto mi stia a cuore il problema della comunicazione e quanto dunque mi rallegri che l'Università Gregoriana abbia deciso di dedicare anche ad essa le sue energie, investendo molto in tale programma, che ora è giunto felicemente al suo primo giubileo di venticinque anni e al quale auguriamo un sempre maggiore sviluppo.

Suo cordialmente

Carlo Maria card. Martini, SJ

"A distinguished quarter-century history"

Archbishop John P. Foley
President of the Pontifical Council for Social Communications

The Interdisciplinary Centre for Social Communications has had a distinguished quarter-century history.

In 1980, when I was English-language press secretary for Synod of Bishops on the Family, I recall speaking to the late Bishop Agnellus Andrew, OFM, then vice president of our then Pontifical Commission for Social Communication, about the new initiative in communications formation at the Gregorian University, started with the sponsorship and encouragement of the then Rector of the Gregorian, Father (now Cardinal) Carlo Maria Martini, SJ. Bishop Andrew was enthusiastic about the fact that the Jesuit pontifical university had begun such a Centre, even though some professors in more traditional disciplines might have considered the university's involvement in communications as a frivolous distraction from more serious studies!

The past twenty-five years have proven Cardinal Martini and Bishop Andrew to have been correct in their positive assessment of what the Interdisciplinary Centre for Social Communications (CICS) might do for the Church – especially in the developing world.

First, under Father (now Bishop) Peter Henrici, SJ, and then under Father Robert White, SJ, and his successors CICS has prepared hundreds of men and women, clergy, religious and lay people, to animate the work of the Catholic Church in communications around the world.

Fathers White, Martínez de Toda and Srampickal have kindly invited me as President of the Pontifical Council for Social Communications to pray and meet with the students of CICS many times during my more than twenty years in Rome, and it has always been an inspiration and a sign of hope.

It is almost impossible to believe that Father White is now entering retirement, because he has truly been a dynamo in promoting the communications apostolate of the Church, literally in some of the most remote areas of the world. Father White is learned, kind, approachable and dedicated to helping to form and assist Catholic communicators wherever they may be found. He is known and loved around the world. For me, it has always been a pleasure and an inspiration to work with him – and to learn from him.

I feel sure that the most precious gift that could be given to Father White at this moment in his life is the assurance that his work – and CICS – might continue for many more years with continuing adaptation to the new communication realities in the world and to the needs of the Church. To CICS and to Father White, "ad multos annos!"

Il CICS al servizio della Chiesa universale*

Peter-Hans Kolvenbach, SJ
Preposito Generale della Compagnia di Gesù

È con vivo piacere che ho risposto all'invito di intervenire a questo Simposio celebrativo dei 25 anni del CICS e dei 75 anni di padre Robert White. Partecipo al Rettore Magnifico dell'Università, padre Ghirlanda, al Direttore del CICS, padre Srampickal, e a tutti voi, professori e studenti qui convenuti, il mio cordiale augurio per tale ricorrenza.

È mia gioia esprimere anzitutto il più convinto apprezzamento nei riguardi del Centro sulla Comunicazione Sociale, distintosi sin dagli inizi per l'innovativo programma interdisciplinare, unico su scala internazionale. La sua peculiare insistenza su teologia, Chiesa e comunicazione e la specifica attenzione alle dinamiche della comunicazione religiosa ne fanno un'istituzione all'avanguardia nell'attuale panorama accademico. Considero un pregio aver concentrato nella proposta di un unico corso di studi i fondamenti della teologia e della filosofia della comunicazione, le più aggiornate acquisizioni della sociologia dei media e il tirocinio nell'apprendimento e nella pratica dei diversi linguaggi della comunicazione mediatica. Interdisciplinarietà vuol dire proprio questo: impegno congiunto, di professori e studenti, nella ricerca e nell'approfondimento di temi cruciali secondo molteplici prospettive. Non posso che esortare vivamente il contributo di tutto il corpo docente verso quest'opera, dalla quale tutta l'Università trarrà sicuro giovamento. La comunicazione influenza ogni settore disciplinare, senza eccezioni: sarà un bene che nel prossimo futuro le varie facoltà ed il Centro per le comunicazioni sappiano lavorare in perfetta sinergia cooperativa, così da ottenere un duplice vantaggio: il Centro si avvantaggerà di una sempre più ricca proposta formativa, impreziosita dal contributo di tutte le altre discipline insegnate in Gregoriana; di ritorno, un altrettanto

---

* Intervento tenuto in occasione del Simposio celebrativo dei 25 anni del CICS (17 novembre 2005), sul tema "Comunicare e (è) partecipare – Dai mass media alla comunicazione partecipativa: quali sfide per la Chiesa?".

prezioso arricchimento giungerà alle diverse altre facoltà, la cui apertura al mondo della comunicazione non può ormai tollerare ritardi.

A voi, carissimi studenti, mi sento di dire: siete fortunati a studiare le comunicazioni con questo respiro interdisciplinare! Ciò che l'Università Gregoriana ed il CICS vi offrono non è solo un percorso orientativo tra le innumerevoli tecniche di comunicazione, ma una solida formazione nei fondamenti teoretici delle stesse. Una volta che sarete tornati nei vostri paesi di provenienza, sarà proprio questo che farà la differenza. Il vostro compito è lo stesso che il CICS si prefigge da 25 anni: dare peso e spessore alla comunicazione cristiana in seno alla società e – specialmente – in seno alle stesse istituzioni ecclesiali cui apparteniamo.

Come ricordavamo in occasione della XXXIV Congregazione Generale della Compagnia di Gesù, la comunicazione non può più essere considerata "un settore dell'attività apostolica, un campo riservato ad alcuni specialisti, che si sono spesso sentiti soli o al margine del corpo apostolico". Piuttosto, è oggi una priorità di tutta la Compagnia – e quindi anche della Gregoriana – quella di "riconoscere che la comunicazione non è un settore ristretto ad alcuni [...] che se ne occupano per professione, ma è una dimensione apostolica fondamentale di ogni nostro ministero" (Decreto 15, n. 3). Il vostro impegno di riflessione risponde perfettamente a questa preoccupazione della Compagnia di Gesù: la comunicazione che vogliamo testimoniare ed insegnare dovrà integrare uomini e donne, con un linguaggio "inclusivo" che sappia superare barriere e discriminazioni. In questo senso, sono davvero lieto di sapere che c'è un numero significativo di laiche e laici che studiano al CICS: anche a loro guardiamo con serena fiducia, come a protagonisti determinanti per la realizzazione di quella comunicazione partecipativa cui avete felicemente scelto di dedicare questa giornata.

Nella circostanza odierna, ci preme ricordare che nulla di ciò che stiamo celebrando sarebbe stato possibile senza l'impareggiabile contributo di padre Robert White, già direttore del Centro per ben undici anni. Ciò che il CICS oggi rappresenta è dovuto, in larga parte, alla sua infaticabile opera di progettazione e di accompagnamento. A lui va il mio personale augurio. Il suo impegno continua oggi nell'opera del CICS, e soprattutto nello sforzo continuo di promozione della comunicazione oltre i limiti dei settori elitari che spesso ne hanno il monopolio.

Saluto del Rettore Magnifico*

Molto Reverendo Padre Generale,
Decani, Professori, Colleghi, studenti, ospiti, amici.

Sono lieto di porgervi il benvenuto in questa sede, in occasione del Simposio celebrativo del XXV Anniversario del CICS, nato con l'idea di promuovere un momento di confronto sui grandi temi connessi alla comunicazione e agli strumenti di cui si avvale, che, come sostenuto nel Decreto *Inter mirifica*, promulgato il 4 dicembre 1963, "[...] sono in grado di raggiungere e muovere non solo i singoli uomini, ma le stesse moltitudini e l'intera umanità".

Dalla promulgazione di questo documento la Chiesa ha cercato e cerca la collaborazione con il vasto mondo della comunicazione sociale, ma – come sottolineava Sua Santità Benedetto XVI, rivolgendosi ai rappresentanti dei mezzi di comunicazione sociale il 25 aprile 2005 – "perché gli strumenti di comunicazione possano rendere un positivo servizio al bene comune, occorre l'apporto responsabile di tutti e di ciascuno".

La ricerca della verità, la salvaguardia della centralità della persona umana e della sua dignità, pongono responsabilità etiche molto profonde e serie, soprattutto nella società odierna, che vive in un'epoca di comunicazione globale dove tanti momenti della vita umana si realizzano attraverso processi mediatici, o sono chiamati a confrontarsi continuamente con essi, come sostenuto da Giovanni Paolo II, nella sua lettera apostolica del 24 gennaio 2005.

Come Università Pontificia che da 25 anni si impegna per formare i futuri operatori delle comunicazioni sociali, abbiamo una grande responsabilità: formare i comunicatori di domani, che, nell'esercizio della loro missione, dovranno essere sempre fedeli alla verità e all'autenticità

---

* Intervento tenuto in occasione del Simposio celebrativo dei 25 anni del CICS (17 novembre 2005), sul tema "Comunicare e (è) partecipare – Dai mass media alla comunicazione partecipativa: quali sfide per la Chiesa?".

dei messaggi di cui si faranno portavoce, memori della responsabilità individuale della formazione delle coscienze e della pubblica opinione.

Per questo l'etica delle comunicazioni è e deve restare il centro del nostro programma di formazione e della missione a cui la Chiesa stessa ci ha chiamati e ci chiama.

Ringrazio sentitamente tutti i relatori che hanno accolto il nostro invito, offrendo i loro contributi su temi di grande attualità, e soprattutto portandoci la propria testimonianza. Ringrazio in modo particolare il reverendo padre Peter-Hans Kolvenbach, Preposito Generale della Compagnia di Gesù, che ci onora della sua presenza.

Ringrazio ognuno di voi, infine, per la vostra presenza qui, oggi, perché se è vero che comunicare è partecipare, è vero anche che la partecipazione, la presenza, la disponibilità all'ascolto e alla comprensione sono alla base di ogni comunicazione.

Gianfranco Ghirlanda, SJ
Rettore della Pontificia Università Gregoriana

INTRODUCING A CICS VISION

Communications training for the Church today: the CICS approach

Jacob Srampickal, SJ

L'articolo inizia con un elenco delle caratteristiche specifiche della formazione sulle comunicazioni offerta presso il Centro Interdisciplinare sulla Comunicazione Sociale dell'Università Gregoriana, e procede con una elaborazione del concetto di formazione interdisciplinare sviluppato dal medesimo Centro nei suoi venticinque anni di attività. L'autore considera l'approccio del Centro come d'avanguardia, in virtù del suo intento di collegare la disciplina della comunicazione ad altre discipline più tipiche della Gregoriana, come la teologia, la filosofia, la missiologia e le scienze sociali. Per progettare corsi che concretizzino questi collegamenti sono stati necessari docenti esperti nelle diverse discipline, benché gran parte dei corsi interdisciplinari siano stati sviluppati all'interno del Centro stesso. L'autore indica inoltre quanto sia importante che persone che si preparano a compiere la missione della Chiesa nel mondo traggano beneficio da una solida formazione interdisciplinare nelle comunicazioni.

Today communications have become an essential element in the active and effective functioning of any social body. In the Church, people with some awareness of mass media speak of the importance of these media for communicating more effectively the truth and values of the Kingdom of God; they also propose the use of group media, participative techniques, audio-visual presentations etc. to make the catechetics, teaching, liturgies and seminars more appealing and more effective. These positions indicate the Church's traditional understanding of the power and potential of the media and there is much truth here.

The Church has also realized that any attempt to be present and participate in the secular media has to be highly professional, or else it is counterproductive. The need for trained professionals with a clear understanding of the Church's position on the media and with a thorough knowledge of communication theory, analysis and practice is what prompted the Jesuits to establish and promote a communications studies program at the Gregorian University since the early 1980s, a program which blends theory and practice, and adapts itself to the changing needs of the times.

1. A new understanding and new approach to media

As a matter of fact, the understanding of communications around the world has changed dramatically over the past twenty-five years, and clearly requires new responses and new approaches. But unfortunately, in many parts of the world and in many centers for education in the media, both in universities and other professional institutes, communications studies are often limited to the technological dimensions of the media: audio, video and now Internet. Encouraged by the enormous business development and job possibilities opened up by the new information communications technologies, training in the media has gained paramount economic importance and social status. Naturally enough, in these circles, the focus on mastering the tool of the technology dominates.

Regarding the way religious groups have reacted to the challenges of the contemporary media, the Protestant Churches have focussed on a direct proclamation of the Word of God through the media and often enough, their principal proponents end up proposing a rather fundamentalistic message, as is the case with the televangelists. On the other hand, the Catholic Church has been preoccupied with only using the tools of the various media, projecting an inoculation method of media criticism and often not equipping Catholics to face the challenges of the new cultures generated by the media. It is however of crucial importance to have very clear perspectives on communications so that Church communicators can adapt immediately, smoothly and effectively to the rapidly-changing situations in which it finds itself. This constant vigilance and readiness to adapt to new times and challenges seems to be difficult for the Church, as is evidenced by the incontrovertible fact that the most Church people – high officials and lesser authorities – feels most comfortable with the oldest mass medium, print.

2. Major challenges

One of the major challenges for those working with communications in the Church is the lack of enlightened support and encouragement of their efforts. Classically-trained personnel who have become bishops, superiors, rectors, and seminary professors show little in-depth understanding of why and how communications can and should function in the Church. Often people in authority in the Church have been trained in systems and traditions that tend to isolate them from the realities they have to face in the world today, and sometimes these people can see no reason for giving any priority to the communications apostolate in the mission of the Church. Often they still see education in communications as being mostly about correctly handling the hardware, "pushing the right buttons". There are also those who consider media as mere entertainment, for relaxing and enjoyment. Of course, it is also true that some media moguls and clever businessmen use media to manipulate audiences seeking *"panem et circences"*, turning the desire for mere entertainment into major profits. It should not be forgotten, however, that healthy entertainment does play a major role in individual character formation and social formation, neither of which should be ignored by responsible educators.

Another major challenge for Church people working in communications is that the authorities heading communication structures in dioceses have little or no training in this field or the wrong kind of training. In fact proper training with a clear vision of the realities facing humankind and the Church in the contemporary world is what is needed today. In this article I attempt to develop a synthesis of what really constitutes good and solid training for Church people in communications. As an example I speak of the kind of training provided by the Interdisciplinary Centre for Social Communications (CICS) at the Gregorian University in Rome, a program that envisages clear perspectives on communications that can adapt well to the changing needs and situations in the Church. In fact, reaching beyond the confines of any specific local church or culture or nation, communication studies in the CICS stresses the following dimensions:

- a cultural studies approach and a design of media studies to promote local cultures;
- a participatory, community media approach;
- a view of communications as an interdisciplinary discipline linked to theology, philosophy, social sciences, spirituality, interreligious dialogue;
- the role of mass media for justice and democratization, proposing an analytical and critical attitude to the media, imbued with a strong grasp of media ethics;
- a research orientation that takes into serious consideration the sociological and ecclesial dimension of the presence of media.

With these dimensions as the foundation of its program, the CICS prepares students for administrative, policy-planning and university-teaching positions in the Church's communication work in any country of the world. As part of a Jesuit institution, the CICS focuses on preparing future Church leaders, who think closely with the Church and who are committed to help the Church face the major challenges brought about by the explosion of mediated messages in the modern world. Taking a cue from the Church document, *Redemptoris Missio*, people trained in media in Church institutions need to be "evangelisers of the media", which, among other things, means that their media products must be of high professional caliber and they must display the following qualities:

- be capable of creatively using and producing media to promote human rights and human values;
- be capable of working seriously and with commitment in the secular media, contributing to and positively influencing their policies for the welfare of society, rather like the leaven of the Gospel, that spreads hope;
- be capable of and willing to give voice to the voiceless, to empower the weaker sectors of society, the poor, the marginalised, oppressed women, minorities, etc.;
- as committed Christians, be ready and willing to stand up for the real and critical issues of society today, without getting caught up in the superficial glamour, glitz and glory that the media world sometimes offers;
- be watchdogs and promoters of democracy, contributing to the development of egalitarian and just societies, not influenced by the interests of the rich and powerful;
- be respectful of indigenous cultures with a clear and sympathetic understanding of their richness and uniqueness.

As the Puebla document of the Latin American Church emphasized, "media training must equip professionals to adopt a critical attitude toward the bombardments launched by mass media and to counteract the impact of media's alienating messages — be they ideological, cultural, or promotional".

3. The interdisciplinary nature of communications formation in the CICS

The licentiate and doctoral programs in the CICS are *interdisciplinary in nature*. Clearly, communications as a fundamental aspect of human life cannot be separated from other vital considerations and forces influencing life in its varied forms. Hence the CICS moves students to discover the link between communications and other disciplines such as theology, philosophy, social sciences, missiology, spirituality and inter-religious and inter-cultural dialogue.

The link between communications and these other disciplines has a reciprocal effect: it strengthens the communications component, making the one doing the studies more versatile and effective in the work of the Church, and it adds a critical dimension to those other disciplines. A major element of the CICS program is the dimension of cultural adaptability – coming from the idea of inculturation – which when well-understood and put into practise, makes the media products informed by it much more acceptable to and effective with an audience, and renders the Good News of the Kingdom proposed by Christian communicators more palatable and attractive to young people in diverse cultures.

The CICS, without downplaying the importance of technological training as a useful tool for good communication, insists that students acquire in-depth understanding of the major social, cultural, spiritual, theological and philosophical issues in the contemporary world. All students are given some exposure to interdisciplinary study and thought; some register for course in other faculties at the Gregorian, and some do a combined degree in communications and another discipline. Students, for example, from countries with high Muslim, Hindu or Buddhist populations find it useful to combine communications with the disciplines of missiology and/or inter-religious dialogue. Students specializing in journalism, documentary video or radio may choose to do courses in the social sciences – the social teaching of the Church, social analysis, economics, political science, cultural anthropology and psychology, etc. Above and beyond these dimensions of interdisciplinarity, all CICS students must write a thesis which combines communications and another discipline.

4. Communications and other disciplines

The links between the various other disciplines and communications are many and varied.

Theology: The disciplines of theology and communication offer many points of contact. Revelation, for example, a critical notion in theology, is understood as God's communication with human beings through the ages. The Holy Scriptures too are the written documents, inspired by the Spirit, which communicate the many and varied ways by which God communicates his saving love to the world. The Church is expression of God's ongoing communication of love and truth in history. The sacraments are experiences of symbolic communication through sacred rituals developed and perpetuated in the Christian community and liturgy is a mode of celebration perpetuated through ritual and can be interpreted as the communicative responses of the people of God to God's communication to them.

Philosophy is a science that deals with the study of knowledge. Languages, signs, symbols, codes, etc. help communicate knowledge. The various theories of philosophy shed light on the way people comprehend and interpret messages and the philosophies of major thinkers like Marx, Sartre, Kafka and others have been recreated by the media, either in fictional or in audio visual, popular forms.

Social Sciences like anthropology and sociology supply the framework for a mediated society. Certainly the development of the media of communication through constantly evolving technology has effects on human beings and human society that are noted and studied by the sociological and anthropological sciences. The evolution of humans is closely related to the evolution of language and the quality of communication.

Missiology studies the proclamation of the Good News in different cultures, amidst diverse religions. Obviously, the way the Gospel is communicated in different cultures is a very important dimension of communication studies. The sharing of the Good News by word and action, by teaching and example, is itself a loving act of communication, which involves the giving of one's life in love after the example of Jesus the "perfect communicator".

Spirituality: Media experiences replete with cultural nuances have often proved to be the sources of deep spiritual experiences. Artistic representations and cultural symbols have often led human beings to go beyond themselves and reach for the Absolute.

Students in programs in the CICS may choose any of the above disciplines for deeper study at the licentiate or doctoral levels. Clearly the combination of disciplines is a most fruitful way of coming to understand and appreciate the importance of media in the contemporary world.

5. Objectives of the CICS program

Communication studies at the Gregorian proposes five principal objectives or "capacities" for its graduates.

1. *The capacity to plan and evaluate a program of communications that supports the pastoral priorities of a diocese or Episcopal conference.*

Following the guidelines of the Church documents *Communio et Progressio* and *Aetàtis Novae*, a graduate of the CICS program is able to analyze, with the bishop and diocesan leadership, the major communication problems and pastoral priorities in a given constituency and to organize a communication program that responds to these necessities. Graduates of the CICS have an understanding of some typical dimensions of diocesan programs:

- public relations and presence in the public media;
- the organization of diocesan media units, such as programming for local radio or television, writing for local newspapers, managing a website, preparing a media education program relevant to the local Church etc.;
- the training of pastoral personnel in communication for work with youth, families, etc.;
- the guidance of Catholics in the use of media;
- the integration of media into the work of human and social development and justice, clearly ever-more-critical areas;
- working with media professionals, especially in the area of media ethics;
- helping to improve communication within parish communities;
- providing workshops in all these areas for the training of seminarians, priests and religious;

– the ability to use the various group media in BBCs and other group animation programs of the diocese, and to teach others to do the same.

Students coming from the Third World, where dioceses have development projects and where radio or video must contribute to social and human development, are given a very strong grounding in communication and development and in the sociology of communications.

Much emphasis is given to learning skills as a *facilitator*, who can then help diocesan offices of catechetics, education, health care, youth ministry etc., analyze the causes of communication problems and guide them towards the resources that will help them solve these problems. The formation in the CICS also emphasizes working not as an individual but as part of a *diocesan team*, i.e., with parish priests, with diocesan lay organizations, with seminaries.

2. *An understanding of what is high quality* in radio, television and print media and of how to produce this high quality.

Graduates of the CICS are prepared to be media *producers* rather than technicians. All students must select a specialization in a particular medium (radio, television, print or Internet) and must take a minimum of four production courses, plus an major, hands-on internship in a media organization. Emphasis is given to the writing and evaluation of effective scripts and on religious media. For example, students specializing in video/television, in their final year, take a year-long course to produce a religious documentary, ten to twenty minutes in length. Each student is personally responsible for the script writing, casting, producing, filming and editing of their religious documentary.

Within the CICS, students have access to state-of-the-art equipment for radio and video production, and for graphic design and Internet work. The Centre also has a well-developed program in film- and television-analysis, supported by a film viewing facility with a collection of over 3.000 feature films in VHS and DVD.

3. *An understanding of how media and communication contribute to religious faith*, to the development of ecclesial community, and to personal and public morality.

The assumption is that since CICS graduates will assume leadership and administration roles in communications in the *Church*, virtually all the decisions they will make will either be directly *theological* or will have *theological implications*, for example regarding the issue of how a diocesan radio station will best contribute to a deeper understanding of the truths of the faith, to linking faith to a more integrated life with the family or within society. CICS students therefore are given a solid grounding in theology and communication, in the nature of religious communication, and in the effective use of media for evangelization.

This preparation is accomplished through a range of seminars which discuss typical problems of diocesan communication from the perspective of Church's documents on communication, ecclesiology, moral theology, the theology of inter-religious dialogue and biblical studies. Also very important, virtually all CICS courses in production, in film analysis, in public relations, in audience analysis etc. include theological analysis as an essential dimension. For example, in a seminar on media and audience, a central question considered is not just the impact of media on audience but how media contribute to faith development in that audience.

Further, group media and participatory approaches in learning allow students to experience communications as something intensely communitarian in which lives, hopes and visions of the future can be shared.

4. *A strong professional capacity in the sciences of religious communication.*

Graduates of the CICS are prepared to analyze the *causes* of communication problems in a diocese or in a media organization and come up with creative solutions, a skill based on their extensive study of theories of communications and of evangelization. For example, to understand how to develop and increase audiences for Church media products, one must have a good understanding of the theories of audience from the perspective of faith communication. To develop and support diocesan programs in catechetics and evangelization, one must understand, for example, the role of symbol and story telling in faith commitment.

For the development of this creative, analytic capacity, our students are given a solid grounding in audience theory, the theory of relation of media and culture, and the foundations of media ethics. Equally important in the CICS is an appropriate pedagogy, that is, a teaching method that includes a great deal of discussion in class and the writing of essays on various issues. Students are given typical problems to solve and then the various and alternative solutions are discussed together. Students are taught to defend their positions with an understanding of current communication theory and in the discussions, students who have developed an interdisciplinary approach to theology or philosophy can offer their valuable perspectives. Courses in media, religion and culture offer students valuable opportunities to reflect on these areas.

5. *A multimedia approach to communication problems.*

Typically dioceses or other religious organizations employ a variety of media in their communications: newspapers, magazines, radio, television, Internet, group media and, of course, interpersonal media. Each of these media has its own way of impacting the public. Radio has the advantage of instant presence while print media offer the possibility of re-reading and deepening the understanding of what is written. Group media are most indicated for more authentic exchanges of diverse values and attitudes. Interpersonal communication is useful for more personal contact and problem solving. Video, on the other hand, contributes a strong symbolic, iconic dimension to communications. Very successful educational systems such as the British Open University and the Radio Schools in Latin America have employed a *combined, multimedia* approach.

A *multimedia* approach is particularly important for the development of the kind of deeper faith commitment expected in the work of evangelization. For evangelical Christians, for example, the mass media are important points of identification, but in fact conversions to these communities are effected through print media, interpersonal contact and group discussions. Training and formation in the CICS stress not only mass media but also interpersonal and group communication. The ability to bring media together in a mutually reinforcing process is considered a priority and is developed in various courses.

Alle origini del CICS: l'interdisciplinarietà
S.E. Mons. Peter Henrici, SJ
Già Direttore e Fondatore del CICS
Presidente del Comitato Episcopale Europeo per i Media (CEEM)

Si sta pure lavorando per l'istituzione di una cattedra sulla comunicazione sociale, il cui scopo sarebbe di aiutare tutti gli studenti delle varie Facoltà a familiarizzarsi con la problematica della comunicazione sociale, in quanto nuova dimensione del vivere umano e sfida per la missione della Chiesa. Dal momento che oggi i cosiddetti "mass media" costituiscono un fattore culturale di prima importanza, è necessario, con l'aiuto dei migliori mezzi tecnici oggi disponibili, studiarne concretamente l'impatto nella mentalità della gente, cercando di comprendere le conseguenze che ne derivano per la comunicazione della fede.

Con queste parole programmatiche l'allora Rettore, padre Carlo Maria Martini, in occasione dell'inaugurazione dell'anno accademico 1979-80 dava il primo annuncio di quello che sarebbe diventato il Centro Interdisciplinare sulla Comunicazione Sociale. Il programma è rimasto lo stesso, la sua realizzazione doveva invece passare per diverse vicissitudini. Già da alcuni anni, nella stessa epoca in cui promuoveva la fondazione di un Centro di Ricerca sulla comunicazione sociale – che sarebbe divenuto nel 1976 il "Centre for the Study of Communication and Culture" (CSCC) a Londra –, il padre Generale Pedro Arrupe aveva auspicato che la Gregoriana istituisse per i suoi alunni un Centro di formazione alle comunicazioni sociali. Per mancanza di fondi e di personale specializzato, il progetto tardava ad essere realizzato. Solo l'Istituto di Scienze Religiose poteva offrire agli studenti laici sin dal 1972 un ben nutrito indirizzo di specializzazione in "Pastorale della Comunicazione sociale".

Nel corso dell'anno 1978 la situazione cambiava. Grazie all'interessamento dell'economo generale, padre Eugen Hillengass, la Fidel Goetz Stiftung a Vaduz si dichiarò disponibile a contribuire con 100.000 franchi svizzeri ai costi di fondazione di un Centro, e il nuovo Rettore, padre Martini, incaricò il sottoscritto, che aveva appena lasciato la carica di decano della facoltà di filosofia, di promuovere l'istituzione della nuova entità accademica, desiderata dal padre Vice Gran Cancelliere, e mi conferiva pieni poteri a quel fine.

Mi mancava però la competenza professionale. Cercai pertanto un contatto con il Centro di Londra, con il quale si instaurò presto una fruttuosa e intensa collaborazione. Si convocò una Commissione internazionale di esperti, tra cui il futuro Vice Presidente della Pontificia Commissione per le Comunicazioni Sociali, padre Agnellus Andrew, OFM, e l'allora Direttore della Radio Vaticana, padre Roberto Tucci, SJ. A questa Commissione, che si riunì poi regolarmente per alcuni anni, si deve il disegno della struttura e dei programmi del futuro Centro. Al fine di inserirlo bene nelle strutture accademiche già esistenti della Gregoriana, una delle prime cose da fare fu la definizione della sua figura accademica. Si conveniva presto che la sua prima caratteristica doveva essere l'interdisciplinarietà, vale a dire che i suoi insegnamenti dovevano essere accessibili a tutti gli studenti delle varie facoltà della Gregoriana, contemporaneamente con il loro piano di studi principale. Per questa ragione non si pensò alla costituzione di un nuovo istituto o persino di una facoltà, dal momento che tali unità, secondo le regole accademiche, avrebbero escluso una doppia iscrizione. Si pensò invece soltanto ad una "cattedra" (che diventò poi un Centro) in grado di conferire agli studenti un Diploma di specializzazione aggiunto al loro grado di Licenza o di Dottorato.

Ma il significato della parola "interdisciplinare" (assai di moda nel mondo accademico di quegli anni) non si limitava a tali formalità organizzative. Era anche e soprattutto un programma di insegnamento. Dato che a Roma funzionavano già due istituzioni di formazione all'uso dei mezzi di comunicazione sociale, gestiti rispettivamente dai padri Paolini e dall'Università Salesiana, con i quali si era preso contatto sin dagli inizi, non sembrava sensato fondare una terza istituzione, concorrenziale, dello stesso tipo. Ci voleva qualcosa di nuovo e di diverso, di tipo più teoretico che immediatamente pratico. Una tale impostazione – si poteva supporre – si sarebbe anche meglio inserita tra gli altri insegnamenti che impartivano le facoltà. Infatti quello a cui si mirava in primo luogo era di sensibilizzare gli studenti che si preparavano ad un ministero pastorale per il fenomeno e la cultura dei "mass media", sensibilizzazione sorretta da una solida e fondata conoscenza di questi. In questo modo, si pensava, alcuni degli studenti piu specializzati avrebbero poi potuto diventare responsabili per le communicazioni sociali nelle proprie diocesi. Il primo passo che si fece per la realizzazione di tale programma fu l'inserimento di regolari corsi opzionali sulla comunicazione sociale nei programmi delle facoltà di filosofia e di teologia. In breve tempo, fino a 300 studenti fecero richiesta di iscrizione a quei corsi.

Ma più ancora – e questa era la vera novità – con l'interdisciplinarietà si intendeva mettere in luce, tanto nell'insegnamento quanto nella ricerca, fino a che punto il fenomeno delle comunicazioni sociali realizzasse e modificasse la dimensione comunicativa dell'oggetto formale sia della filosofia che della teologia ed evidentemente anche delle scienze sociali. Il problema della comunicazione, infatti, è sotteso a quasi tutta la storia della filosofia, e la comunicazione tra Dio e gli uomini è uno degli oggetti principali della ricerca teologica. Nonostante questo, tutto ciò parve allora un terreno quasi completamente ancora da esplorare. Per questo, in stretta collaborazione con il Centro di Londra e in particolare con padre Robert White, si organizzò una serie di seminari interdisciplinari tra teologi e/o filosofi e specialisti delle scienze delle comunicazioni di varie nazioni. Questi seminari, consistenti in otto e più giorni di "clausura" nell'ameno ambiente autunnale di Villa Cavalletti (Grottaferrata) dovevano servire ad una prima esplorazione del terreno di ricerca comune e a marcare alcuni punti fermi per un ulteriore lavoro interdisciplinare.

La serie fu iniziata nell'ottobre 1981 con un seminario sulla "Integrazione della comunicazione negli studi pastorali" e proseguì nel 1983 con un seminario su "Teologia fondamentale e comunicazione". Seguirono poi nel 1985 un terzo seminario su "Filosofia e comunicazione", nel 1987 uno su "La formazione del giudizio morale in una cultura condizionata dai mass-media", nel 1989 su "The communication issues in contemporary ecclesiology" e nel 1991 su "Gesù Comunicatore". La serie si concluse nel 1993 con un ulteriore seminario su "The new image of religious film". Con il ricco materiale elaborato in occasione di questi incontri, pubblicato purtroppo soltanto in parte, e grazie anche ai talvolta accesi dibattiti tra gli specialisti, si acquisirono non soltanto un solido fondamento per l'insegnamento interdisciplinare nel Centro, ma anche stimoli e prospettive per la prosecuzione di simili ricerche tanto da parte del corpo docente quanto da parte dei diplomandi e dottorandi.

Ancora oggi il programma di interdisciplinarietà, iscritto nella struttura del Centro sin dalla sua origine, dovrà concretizzarsi secondo due direttive, l'una negativa e l'altra positiva, di orientamento sia per i professori quanto per gli studenti del Centro. Negativamente, si dovrà escludere un approccio puramente strumentalista ai media, tanto in fase di apprendimento quanto e soprattutto nel loro uso pratico, prescrivendo invece di tenere sempre conto anche e principalmente della loro dimensione antropologica, sociale e culturale. Positivamente, l'interdisciplinarietà dovrà ricordare che i mass-media, come tutti i nuovi mezzi che le tecnologie nel loro "rapido sviluppo" ci daranno ancora, rimangono pur sempre espressioni e realizzazioni della profonda struttura comunicativa, iscritta da Dio nella struttura stessa dell'essere umano: una struttura comunicativa di cui Dio si è voluto servire per la propria autocomunicazione al genere umano e ad ogni singola persona. Perciò è altamente auspicabile che gli studenti del CICS combinino il loro studio delle comunicazioni sociali con altri studi teologici, filosofici o di scienze sociali.

Possa il CICS in questa maniera essere un po' di lievito nella Chiesa, per una migliore consapevolezza del fatto che da sempre essa ha vissuto in una cultura di comunicazione, che oggi è anche e forse soprattutto mediatica, cultura nella quale la Chiesa non solo si trova inserita, ma che essa contribuisce anche – lo voglia o no – a formare e a trasformare: una cultura che, in altre parole, la Chiesa deve evangelizzare come tutte le altre culture umane.

Roma, ottobre 2005

A celebration of interdisciplinarity: my twenty-two years at the Pontificia Università Gregoriana and in the Centro Interdisciplinare sulla Comunicazione Sociale

Lloyd Baugh, SJ

> *L'autore, gesuita ed ex alunno della Gregoriana e del Centro Interdisciplinare, dove svolge la sua attività di docente, esamina diverse sfaccettature della dimensione dell'interdisciplinarietà, principale caratteristica della natura e delle attività del Centro. Basandosi sulla propria esperienza nel creare "ponti" tra cinematografia e teologia, filosofia ed altre discipline, egli dimostra quanto l'interdisciplinarietà, così come viene proposta dal Centro Interdisciplinare, abbia conferito e conferisca tuttora un marchio particolare e un valore notevole alle proprie attività di studio, di ricerca, di insegnamento e di pubblicazione, oltre che alle attività accademiche e scientifiche di molti altri.*

When I arrived in Rome and at the Gregorian in September 1984, it was as a student, a newly-ordained Jesuit priest missioned to study theology and communications. Already my life and my academic thrust was being marked by interdisciplinarity, though at that time I had no way of knowing where this new direction would lead me in the succeeding twenty-two years. Now, looking back on those years, almost the quarter of a century of the *Centro Interdisciplinare*, I am deeply grateful for my mission and career as an academic doing interdisciplinary work among the disciplines of art, cinema, theology, philosophy, spirituality and interreligious dialogue. I am also grateful for the fact that from the beginning my interdisciplinary studies and later my interdisciplinary academic work have been encouraged, nurtured and supported at the Gregorian and in the *Centro Interdisciplinare*, by the academic structures and by individual Jesuit administrators and teachers within those structures, to many of whom I will refer in this short essay.

It is with joy and gratitude that I accepted the invitation to contribute to this book in honor of the *Centro Interdisciplinare sulla Comunicazione Sociale*, an academic unit that has formed me academically and in which I have been able to develop an exciting and fruitful professional life. A brief aside: we are two Jesuit graduates of the Gregorian and the *Centro Interdisciplinare*, who are now teaching here; Augustine Savarimuthu, though working in a different field from me, is as committed to interdisciplinary work as I am, as his essay in this volume makes clear.

In this article I intend to focus on the word "*interdisciplinare*" in the name of the *Centro*, that is, on the dimension of interdisciplinarity that gives this Centre at the Gregorian its uniqueness and value and that gives to studies at the Gregorian a valuable dimension not available in any other of the Pontifical universities in Rome. The article necessarily will be somewhat autobiographical – I will speak largely of my own experience, direct and indirect, as I attempt to do justice to the wide range of elements of academic interdisciplinarity that I have encountered and continue to encounter in my experience here at the Gregorian and in the CICS.

1. Interdisciplinary studies at the Gregorian in the 1980s

To begin, as they say, at the beginning, in my first year in Rome, I was doing courses in two separate programs, that of the Licentiate in fundamental theology and that of the Diploma in communications. Several of my courses encouraged me to bring things together from each department. For example, an interdisciplinary theology course team-taught by Jos Janssens SJ and Heinrich Pfeiffer SJ focussing on the image of Jesus in art, an exciting adventure in itself, became the inspiration of a course I later developed and of a book I wrote. The film esthetics classes of Virgilio Fantuzzi SJ, both in that first year and in the succeeding years, often focussed on films and themes of notable religious, spiritual or theological significance. And when, in the major seminar directed by Gerald O'Collins SJ, I proposed as theme of my Licentiate thesis to do a study of the evidently Christian/Catholic anthropology operative in Ermanno Olmi's masterpiece *The Tree of the Wooden Clogs* (1978), a film which had won universal critical acclaim and also the top prize, the "Palme d'Or" at the Cannes Film festival, not only was O'Collins willing and enthusiastic to guide the thesis but he insisted that this same paper could serve for my Diploma in social communications: a powerful, concrete and very fruitful first experience of interdisciplinarity at the Gregorian.

When I came to the Gregorian in 1984, it was to be for a terminal Licentiate, but then, on the basis of the recognized success of my interdisciplinary Licentiate thesis on that one film of Olmi, my superiors assigned me to stay on at the Gregorian and do a Doctorate in Fundamental Theology. For my thesis, and under the guidance of the then Don Rino Fisichella – now Bishop and Rector of the Lateran University here in Rome – I expanded the Licentiate study to cover the development of Olmi's Christian anthropology of human transcendence in his first eight feature films, ending with *The Tree of the Wooden Clogs*. This very long Doctoral thesis at first raised a little nervous comment in the University – some were suspicious of its interdisciplinary nature and approach – but it was strongly defended as a prophetic work, an example interdisciplinary studies as the way of the future, by the then *Rettore Magnifico* Giuseppe Pittau SJ – later Archbishop at the Congregation for Catholic Education – who took the very unusual and symbolically-significant step of presiding at the doctoral defense, and by its director and by Robert White, the second reader of the thesis.

2. Interdisciplinary teaching at the Gregorian

Before the thesis was completed, Pittau had hired me – and Superiors had assigned me – to teach in the *Centro Interdisciplinare* with Robert White, and my mission of interdisciplinary teaching and research at the Gregorian was launched. In the first couple of years, in addition to teaching some basic communications material, I developed two courses that bridged theology and film studies, "The Notion and Esthetics of the Religious Film", and "Images of Jesus in Film". The courses were listed among the offerings of the *Centro Interdisciplinare* and almost immediately, also in the program of the Faculty of theology. Within three or four years those two courses had grown into a cycle of four theology courses which I now teach over four semesters, the two additional courses being: "The Fundamental Moral Discourse in the Films of Kieslowski" and "The Experience of God in World Cinema"; the latter considers eight films from the Western Christian tradition and eight from other religious/cultural traditions. Beyond that four-course cycle, whose courses have been cross-listed also in the Faculty of Missiology, in the Institute of Religious Sciences and in the Institute for the Cultural Heritage of the Church, I have also directed a seminar for the Institute of Spirituality, on "The Spirituality of Sainthood in the Cinema", and one for the Centre for the Study of Cultures and Religions, on "World Cinema: An Intercultural and Interreligious Dialogue".

Beyond my own interdisciplinary courses, other professors of the Gregorian have called on the *Centro Interdisciplinare*, and on my experience, for support in their courses. I have arranged screenings and directed discussions of films for visiting and regular professors in the Institute for Studies of Religions and Cultures, the Institute of Psychology and the Institute of Spirituality. For a number of years I worked with Maria La Vecchia in Philosophy, screening films and directing discussions on the critical philosophical-anthropological theme of the "wild child" in cinema: Francois Truffaut's *L'enfant sauvage* (1969), Arthur Penn's *The Miracle Worker* (1962) and Werner Herzog's *The Enigma of Kaspar Hauser* (1974).

Recently, I have "custom-developed" two series of films for philosophy seminars of Paul Gilbert SJ. In this experiment not only in interdisciplinarity but also in team-teaching – by no means the norm at the Gregorian – I introduced each film, giving pointers regarding how its themes are expressed both in narrative content and in a variety of formal and stylistic choices of its director. After the screening, Gilbert and I directed the discussion-dialogue.

In 2004, on the theme of "Evil, Forgiveness and Hope", the films screened were: *Dogville* by Lars von Trier (2003), *Doctor Strangelove* by Stanley Kubrick (1963), *Decalogue Two* by Kieslowski (1988), *I'm Not Scared* by Gabriele Salvatores (2003) and *Babette's Feast* by Gabriel Axel (1998). In 2005, on the theme of "The Body, The Senses, in Contemporary Philosophical Phenomenology", the films were: *Room with a View* by James Ivory (1985), *Like Water for Chocolate* by Alfonso Arau (1991), *The Girl with the Pearl Earring* by Peter Webber (2003), *The Miracle Worker* by Arthur Penn (1962) and *The Wings of Desire* by Wim Wenders (1987). The value and the success of this interdisciplinary venture can be measured by the fact that the screenings and discussions, held during the lunch-hour break, attracted not only Gilbert's students but many students – usually a "full house, SRO" – from the *Centro Interdisciplinare* and from other faculties in the University.

3. Interdisciplinary Doctorate and Licentiate theses

These interdisciplinary courses and the corresponding generous acquisitions in the Gregorian library naturally and happily have led to a number of Doctorate and Licentiate theses. I here mention only a few of these interdisciplinary studies with which I was involved and which were connected with the *Centro Interdisciplinare* at the Gregorian. One of the most original and most interesting is a doctoral dissertation by an Italian Franciscan, Angelo Saporiti, bridging theology and cinema, with the title, "The Representation of Death in Recent Cinema as a Provocation to Fundamental Theology" (1996).

Another groundbreaking interdisciplinary doctoral dissertation, this time bridging Social Sciences, Womens' and Gender Studies and Film Studies, is by a Ugandan Religious Sister of Mary, Mother of the Church (MMC), Dominica Dipio, with the title: "The Representation of Women and Changing Gender Roles in African Film Narrative: A Feminist Critical Approach" (2002).

Dipio is now professor at Makerere University in Kampala. Currently I am co-directing a doctoral dissertation at the Pontifical Salesian University (Rome) in Theology and Film Studies; Pedro Sanchez Rodriguez, a Spanish priest already teaching theology in Barcelona, is writing on the very timely theme of "The Death of God in Contemporary Cinema".

Among the more interesting interdisciplinary Licentiate theses I have directed are several concerned in one way or another with the films of Kieslowski, an area of my own particular interest and research. Two of these papers bridge theology and film studies: "Conversion and Personal Existence: A Dialogue Between Fundamental Theology and Kieslowski" by an Italian layman, Marco Cardinali, and "Faith: A New Mode of Knowing: *The Eyes of Faith* of Pierre Rousselot and *A Short Film about Love* of Kieslowski", by a Spanish priest and now-professor of fundamental theology, Juan Jesus Garcia Morales. Other theses bridging the areas of philosophy, psychology, sociology and film studies are: "The Representation of Transcendent Truth in the Formal and Esthetic Project of Kieslowski's *Decalogue* Films", by Thomas Kycia, a German layman; "A Psycho-Social Study of the 'Mystery Man' in Kieslowski's *Decalogue* Films", by Elisabetta Marangon, an Italian laywoman; "The Rwandan Genocide: The Historical-Social Reality and Two Cinema Versions: Terry George's *Hotel Rwanda* (2004) and Peter Raymont's *Shake Hands with the Devil* (2004)" by Francis Mwangoyva, a layman from Kenya.

4. Interdisciplinary research and publications

As in any University, professors at the Gregorian and in the *Centro Interdisciplinare* have, as an essential dimension of their mission, the enterprise of scholarly research and publication. In my case, the university has been very generous in encouraging and supporting my research, with a teaching schedule that permits time and energy for research during the school year, and time and financial support during breaks between semesters and in the summertime; I have been fortunate, too, to have made good contacts at the British Film Institute in London where I go regularly to work. Three scholarly publications have also been very supportive of my research and writing: *Gregorianum*, the University's flagship journal – traditionally it has been a publication of "straight" theological and philosophical scholarship – first under the editorship of Jacques Dupuis SJ and more recently under Paul Gilbert, has shown enthusiasm and support for my theology-film interdisciplinary studies; *Landas*, the journal of the Loyola School of Theology in Manila, Philippines, publishes my material too. *Consacrazione e Servizio*, the widely-distributed journal of the USMI research centre in Rome, in effect has given me regular contributor status, and over the years they have published twenty-five of my interdisciplinary essays, for which support and encouragement I am most grateful.

Over the years, and often in conjunction with courses I have taught, my research and scholarship has moved in diverse directions. One area of interest for me has been the clearly interdisciplinary issue of the representation of Jesus and of the Christ-Event in film texts: it is the subject of a book-length study, *Imaging the Divine: Jesus and Christ Figures in Film* (1996), and of a number of long articles since then, updating the book by considering the Jesus films that have come out since 1996, and by refining things that I wrote in new directions.

Another area of my interest is the identification and analysis of theological dimensions and themes – mystery, openness to mystery, salvation/redemption, incarnation, *kenosis*, resurrection-promise – in classical and contemporary films, the use of theological categories and themes as hermeneutical tools for better understanding film texts, and the consideration of how, in these texts, the sacred and the profane meet and are reciprocally modulated and enriched. The meeting of and dialogue between cultures and religions in and through film texts is another very fertile area for research, especially since I am doing this work at the Gregorian, known as "The University of the Nations" for its international faculty and student-body and for its role as a *carrefour* of cultures and religious traditions.

As students in my courses quickly learn from my abundant use of the terms "extradiegetical" and "intradiegetical", perhaps the clearest hallmark of my research – learned from my Jesuit mentor, Marc Gervais, from the Canadian media-prophet, Marshall McLuhan and from studies such as Paul Schrader's seminal *Transcendental Style in Film: Ozu, Bresson, Dreyer* (1972) – is that the formal and stylistic elements of the medium of film impinge decisively on the content of any film, that the final communication of a film text is determined not only, and at times not mainly, by its content, but by formal and stylistic choices of the director. To make a Jesus-film in black and white rather than in color, to represent the passion of Jesus in extreme-close-up shots, to use a simple cut rather than digital effects to represent a miracle, to privilege silence over a swelling music score, to combine apochryphal and fictional material with canonical biblical material in a script: all these are choices that impact the way a film is received by the viewer and so on the final communication of theological or religious truth effected by the film.

Another area in which I have done considerable teaching, research and writing has been the recent films of the Polish director Krzysztof Kieslowski, *The Decalogue* (1988) and after. A course taught yearly, a book-manuscript and a number of articles testify to the importance I have given to studying these remarkable films from an interdisciplinary – theological-philosophical-films studies – perspective. Kieslowski's films, in spite of the director's denial of personal religious belief, are dense with metaphysical, theological and moral meaning and implications, and certainly I am only at the beginning of my work on him.

A further area of interdisciplinary research to which I continue to devote time and publication is the practical-experimental area of the use of film texts, usually but not always, entire films, for meditation and prayer experiences, and so, by extension, in retreat work. I began this research in a very restricted way, offering films in VHS cassettes to people with whom I was doing monthly spiritual direction, and suggesting they be used in the context of prayer exercises, but always, and only, as a supplement to texts from Scripture which, of course, remain primary. The results were quite surprising, with people reporting enthusiastic satisfaction and some quite remarkable breakthroughs in their spiritual lives.

When in 1998, while still doing full-time teaching, I was appointed founding director of the campus ministry program – *Cappella Universitaria* – at the Gregorian, one of the priorities the pastoral team set was, in keeping with our Ignatian charism, to organize regular weekend retreats and at least one eight-day retreat each year. From the beginning the retreat teams have taken films-in-video with them and used them very fruitfully for group-viewings during the prayer days. This practise, coming out of an academic interest, has led to the writing and publication of a series of articles, theoretical and practical – I have developed detailed *schemata* for one-, two-, three-, four-, and seven-day prayer/retreat experiences using an "interdisciplinary" biblical text-film text approach – as I attempt to understand better the possibilities and limits of this practical exercise in interdisciplinarity, and how to move forward with the practice.

5. Interdisciplinarity in co-curricular and extra-curricular outreach

My experience of interdisciplinarity at the Gregorian and in the CICS goes beyond the strictly academic sphere. In collaboration with the *Cappella Universitaria*, our campus ministry program, the *Centro Interdisciplinare* organizes regularly, once or twice a semester, cycles of films on themes of theological, spiritual or moral interest to our students. Usually the films are screened during the three-hour break at lunch time; sometimes the films are shown two or three days in a row and sometimes once a week for several weeks. The screenings are preceded by a brief introduction and are followed by an open discussion. One of the more recent cycles we have offered has been on the theme of religious intolerance in the Christian, Jewish and Moslem traditions, for which the films screened were Liliana Cavani's *Galileo* (1968), Amos Gitai's *Kadosh* (1999) and Youssef Chahine's *Destiny* (1997). Christian responsibility in the face of genocide has been another theme, with four-days-in-a-row showings of Claude Lanzmann's monumental four-part series *Shoah* (1985) and more recently, regarding the genocide in Rwanda, two-days-in-a-row showings of *Hotel Rwanda* and *Shake Hands with the Devil*. When Mel Gibson's *The Passion of the Christ* (2004) came out, we presented it twice, back-to-back with Pasolini's *The Gospel According to Saint Matthew* (1964). By all accounts, and especially by the numbers attending and by the quality and vivacity of the discussions, these exercises in co-curricular interdisciplinarity are popular and fruitful activities.

Another version of this activity, an outreach beyond the Gregorian, has been a very fruitful series of cineforums sponsored by the *Centro Interdisciplinare* and held in some of the residential colleges here in Rome, always at the request of the Colleges. I myself have run cineforums, with cycles of three to six films each time, at the Seminario Romano at the Lateran University, at the Collegio Lombardo and the Collegio Capranica, and at the Irish, Portuguese and Ukranian Colleges. The value of these para-academic exercises is twofold: they encourage the interdisciplinary approach to the theological studies that most of the student-viewers are doing, and they serve as models for ministerial activities in parishes and with young people, in which many of these seminarians/deacons/priests are already involved.

6. Exporting theology-film interdisciplinarity

Though interdisciplinary study is a well-established tradition in many universities worldwide, the particular variety of interdisciplinarity we have undertaken at the Gregorian and in the *Centro Interdisciplinare* – bridging film studies and theology/spirituality/religious studies – is quite rare and so we have begun exporting it beyond the classrooms and viewing labs of this 450-year-old institution, and with considerable good fruit. I have adapted theology-and-film courses from the Gregorian to programs in theology faculties and departments in Universities in Canada, at Regis College, University of Toronto and at Campion College, University of Regina; in the United States, at Notre Dame University and at Loyola Marymount in Los Angeles; in the Philippines, at the Loyola School of Theology, Ateneo de Manila University and at the Ateneo de Naga University; in the near future I will be taking some of our courses to Madagascar and to francophone Africa.

My experience with this "exportation" is that the courses we teach here in Rome need little adaptation elsewhere, and, in fact, the theology-film, interdisciplinary approach seems to have a universal appeal, perhaps because – here I am referring to statements made by students in course evaluation surveys – it serves a perceived need in students of theology for "the narrative approach" to theological truth; for "texts which incarnate theological significance in characters, narratives and human conflicts", for "concrete stories and dramas through which the viewer is invited to participate in the search and the struggle for meaning, for God". These film texts are not at all meant to replace the traditional philosophical-theological discourse, the propositional approach, but their concreteness, their dramatic structure, their sensual imagery – students often refer to some films texts as "parables for today" – their ability to evoke mystery and to invite participation in that mystery, to encourage in the viewer an active role in the discovery, formation and appreciation of theological and religious meaning, clearly adds a significant dimension to the theological enterprise.

7. ... and other things ... interdisciplinary

Another dimension of work in the interdisciplinary field at the Gregorian is that we professors are, whether we like it or not, much in demand by the mass media and by other groups. For example, I and a couple of other colleagues of mine have been members of the juries at a number of international film festivals that have religious films in the competition. Our ability to talk convincingly, and on the professional level, about both cinema and film texts and theological and spiritual issues is a not-very-common skill.

My most dramatic experience of this media-interest was in the spring of 2004. I was on a sabbatical year, teaching in the theology department at Loyola Marymount University, when Mel Gibson's controversial *Passion of the Christ* film was released. The local, national and international media were very much interested in talking to priests, with a formation in Scripture study and theology; better, of course, if that priest were also trained in film studies. Those were a busy couple of months for me – radio and television interviews, live and taped; round table discussions in the university; talks given at several Los Angeles synagogues; eight articles published on the *Passion* film and the *Passion* phenomenon – and perhaps the most satisfying thing about all that activity was the clear realization that it was the interdisciplinary nature of my training and work made me a sought-after speaker and commentator.

8. Looking towards the future

At fifty-nine years of age, and so, with eleven and perhaps up to sixteen years of teaching left, I have a number of interdisciplinary projects in mind. One would be some research and a course or a seminar on the issue of the faith/non-faith of a few selected filmmakers, as evidenced in their films: Fellini, Antonioni, Scorsese, Coppola, Wenders, Arcand, Kieslowski and others. Another project would be a research-and-book project on the representation of saints in film, saints already canonized and saints not canonized and perhaps not even in the Catholic tradition. Certainly, I would like also to bring my *Imaging the Divine* book up to date, either with a second edition or a monograph that would include a number of new Jesus-films that have been released since the early 1990s. More work needs to be done on the use of film texts for prayer and retreat experiences; on the use of religious and even Christological images in popular film; on how "New Age" ideas and pseudo-religious imagery are threatening more traditional and more authentic religious imagery in cinema; and on the representation of moral issues in film.

A project that I hope to bring to fruition in the short term is a course that would study significant shifts in the moral, religious and theological positions of selected film directors, as suggested by couples of films by each director, for example: Wenders: *Paris, Texas* (1984) and *The Wings of Desire* (1988); Arcand: *The Decline of the American Empire* (1986) and *Jesus of Montreal* (1989); Liliana Cavani: *Francis of Assisi* (1966) and *Francesco* (1989); Pasolini: *The Gospel According to St. Matthew* and *Teorema* (1968); Fellini: *La strada* (1954) and *La dolce vita* (1960). Another project, some elements of which are already part of existing courses I teach, is a course that couples films on religious themes, with the written texts on which they are based: the two treatments of *The Last Temptation of Christ*, by Kazantzakis (1955) and Scorsese (1988); the two treatments of *The Diary of a Country Priest*, by Georges Bernanos (1936) and Robert Bresson (1951); the text of Matthew's gospel and Pasolini's film; the autobiography of Therese de Lisieux and Alain Cavalier's film, *Therese* (1986); the historical accounts of Joan of Arc's trials and the films by Dreyer (1928) and Bresson (1962).

Twenty-two years of interdisciplinary study and teaching at the Gregorian University and in the *Centro Interdisciplinare sulla Comunicazione Sociale*: they have been interesting, challenging, fruitful, enjoyable, fulfilling and reassuring years, and for this mission, and for the many Jesuits and others who have supported my work, I am most grateful. The future of interdisciplinary study and research at the Gregorian and in the *Centro Interdisciplinare* indeed looks very good.

THE LANGUAGE OF THE MEDIA

Journalism: a search for the truth

Mary Wilsey

Il giornalismo è importante oggi per la Chiesa? E la Chiesa è importante per i giornalisti? In un'era dominata dai media, le due parti hanno molto da guadagnare da una certa fiducia e cooperazione reciproca. Gli studenti del Centro Interdisciplinare sulla Comunicazione Sociale della Gregoriana – tecnicamente parlando – non vengono preparati ad essere giornalisti; tuttavia, con una buona conoscenza di come funzioni la professione giornalistica, dei suoi punti forti e delle sue debolezze, essi sono messi in grado di servire come intermediari vitali tra i giornalisti e la Chiesa, potendo quindi promuovere una maggiore cooperazione e conoscenza reciproca nella ricerca della verità.

1. Introduction

Near the summit of a hill in central Italy, there is a small, ill-built house. It is made of the local tufo, only a few of its windows have glass and over one of them is a shabby piece of canvas to keep out the summer sun. There is a hand-dug well beside the tin-roofed barn.

The house stands on a few hectares and the owners have about 10 sheep, a pig, an olive grove and a vineyard. A battered old car stands at the door. The inhabitants don't need to move far; they have probably never been to Rome, which is only about 40 kms away. There is everything they need in the nearby village: a school, a hospital and several churches. Almost all their food is homegrown.

The house, a legacy from another age, would probably be condemned as unsanitary if the health inspectors were ever called in. But it does have one sign of the 21st century. It displays a satellite dish on its crumbling walls. At the push of a button the inhabitants can watch constant and near-instant coverage of natural disasters, armed conflicts and terrorist attacks across the world; they can watch political debates, they can tune into religious programmes, cartoons for their grandchildren, sports that they had never heard of only a couple of years ago, they can learn about scientific discoveries they never imagined possible and they can watch a large choice of films (if they pay extra).

2. The speed of change

When the Interdisciplinary Centre for Social Communications (CICS) was founded at the Pontifical Gregorian University 25 years ago, these same inhabitants would have had the choice of only two national, state-run television channels. News programmes on the state-controlled RAI television were scheduled about three times a day and colour broadcasting was only three years old. Italy's first privately-owned television network had just started nation-wide transmission.

About a century ago the formative influence on the inhabitants of such houses would have been the parish priest, the local landowner and perhaps the village doctor. A quarter of a century later the local politician, the leaders of agricultural co-operatives and the village schoolteacher would have been their references points. By the mid-20th century the political parties and the local trades union activists would have been added to the list.

At the beginning of the 21st century these influences still exist but to a much lesser degree; there is a lack of vocations to the religious life, the doctors have left to work for hospitals in the big cities, the profession of teacher is no longer held in such high esteem as previously, political parties and trades unions have ceased to be as important as they once were.

Into the space walks the journalist, with news of what is happening across the world, with advice on health, family life, economics, finance, science, sport, offering every conceivable type of entertainment, and with the ability to chat to listeners and viewers about their daily lives and worries on numerous shows throughout the day and well into the night.

3. The figure of the journalist

Today there is hardly an aspect of daily life that is not invaded by the journalist. Once defined as someone who writes for newspapers and magazines or who prepares news for radio or television, journalists are fast trespassing on the role of priest, doctor, educator, financial advisor, companion, entertainer and ombudsman.

It is all the more surprising therefore that these new gurus of the modern age lack several of the key characteristics of the authorities of the past. Although almost every country has different training schemes it is still possible for a journalist to rise to the height of the profession without a university degree or a diploma in journalism, perhaps even without a period of apprenticeship, other than on-the-job-training. While priests, doctors and teachers have to undergo a long period of preparation for their work, for journalists there is no official period or universal standard of training.

Furthermore, unlike politicians and union leaders, journalists never have to stand for election. The closest a radio or television journalist comes to being called to popular account is by the audience ratings. Print journalists may never have to answer to their readers; once employed, unless they make numerous factual errors, they can hold that position for life.

There are few modern figures so loved and so hated, so admired and so scorned, held responsible for so much that is good and so much that is evil in the modern age.

Journalists are at once the heroes of modern society and the villains. They are the people who uncover scandals and corruption, who keep watch over the politicians and the leaders of business and finance, who rescue the weak from exploitation and who espouse the cause of the downtrodden in societies that no longer care. They are the people who call governments to account, who help stop unjust wars and topple unpopular despots.

At the same time they are seen as responsible for the decadence in society, the disenchantment with modern democracy, the disregard into which political and economic life has fallen, for the pervading sense of mistrust in modern life. In almost the same breath people will say: "Never trust what you read in the press", and: "I wonder what the papers will say tomorrow?". Journalists are considered both too powerful or not powerful enough, they are criticized as opinionated and arrogant. But they are also sought-after and courted when convenient. "No-one ever talks to a journalist without a reason", is a common attitude among people who have to deal with the media. Journalists are useful when there is a job to be done; when there isn't, they are often considered a nuisance, maybe even a danger. Journalists are the people everyone loves to love and loves to hate.

4. The Church and journalism

With this potential for both good and bad it is of great importance that there should be an understanding of both the possibilities and the limitations of journalism in the Church today. The Pontifical Gregorian University was at the forefront of understanding these needs when CICS was founded in 1980. That the specialization of journalism should have been included in the CICS curriculum was far-sighted indeed. It is worth remembering today, now that there are numerous schools, centres, institutes of social communications and journalism all over Italy, that there were few such bodies in 1980. The degree in social communications at La Sapienza University in Rome, for example, was not available until 1992.

If it was important a quarter of a century ago for the Catholic Church to understand how journalists work, it is even more important now when the influence of the media is even stronger than it was then. Six reasons why this is so are worth a mention here.

1. The Church is itself one of the most extensive sources of information about the world today. In any city, in any rural area throughout the world the Catholic Church probably has more information at its fingertips in its parishes and dioceses than any other single organisation, religious or lay. The network is vast and it is universal. It can be accessed either locally (within a country or region) or internationally (from Rome). It is therefore important that the Church should know how to put the information it has to wider and better use.

At present much of the information that reaches the media comes from the centres of political and economic power. The information produced is either heavily centralized (in the case of governments) and therefore controllable, or only partial (in the case of large multinational corporations) and therefore incomplete. If instead information were to flow from the grass roots of a country, from the disenfranchised, the poor, the ill, the disabled, the old, to local papers, radio and television stations and from there into international channels, it is conceivable that much more information about poverty, disease, political repression, social injustice, genocides, would gain international attention more quickly. In other words the Church should be working to provide alternative channels of information. If foreign correspondents in a country were to visit the parishes as quickly as they make appointments to see the heads of the big corporations or the political parties they might have a very different story to suggest to the foreign editor back home. How many journalists do this, and how many clerics think that this type of dialogue is important?

2. The Catholic Church is now a part of the news story that interests the world today. Pope John XXIII was perhaps the first modern Pope to have captured the attention of the mass media, but the relationship of the media and the Church came of age under the pontificate of Pope

John Paul II. During his 27 years as Pope the Church became one of the world's major news stories.

Anyone who was in Rome throughout the months that led up to Pope John Paul II's death in April 2005 will have seen one of the largest media operations of modern times in action. That complicated process by which public interest generates news coverage, which in turn generates more public interest, which produces more media coverage, in an ever-widening circle, was nowhere more evident than in those three weeks in April from the death of one Pope to the election of the next. The intense and close interaction of journalists and clergy in those days was beneficial for all concerned.

However it is also true that adverse events in the Church's life, such as the paedophilia scandals in the United States, Ireland and the United Kingdom, demonstrate that the Church can become the centre of media interest in an entirely different way. As journalists, alerted by a public outcry, brought to light deviant parts of the Church organization, the Church was obliged to make reforms in its codes of conduct, in its management and finances that would not have been imagined even a few decades ago.

3. It is probably safe to say that most priests, and certainly most bishops, will now come into contact with journalists in the course of their work. Whether or not the experience turns out to be enriching or damaging will often depend on the sort of communication the two sides manage to establish with each other.

4. At some time during their lives many priests and religious will have to make use of the communicative skills that are employed by journalists. This may be only at the level of the parish bulletin, or increasingly the parish internet site, but the way in which they communicate the news about the parish to the parishioners, as well as to the larger outside community, is of importance to the well-being of the Church.

5. Many priests and religious will be called to work for Catholic newspapers, magazines, radio and television stations in their missionary work. Furthermore increasing numbers of religious are being called to work with the international media on all sorts of topics, not just religious ones.

To understand the extent of the developments that have taken place in the last 25 years one has only to reflect on the number of cardinals who called press conferences both before going into the conclave to elect the successor to Pope John Paul II and after they had elected Pope Benedict XVI.

6. At a time when vocations and church attendance are declining in western Europe there has been an increasing in religious affairs. When CICS started it would be safe to say that there were only a handful of journalists reporting on religious affairs. Now religious affairs correspondent are more prominent than education or the science correspondents. Often special correspondents, journalists at the height of the profession, also report on the workings of the Church. Paradoxically in a secular western world religion has become newsworthy. Therefore it is more important than ever that the Catholic Church should have the knowledge to benefit from this newsworthiness.

5. CICS and the journalism

The courses on journalism at CICS were not designed to form and train journalists but to give students a greater understanding of the way journalism works, of its strengths and its weaknesses.

One of the ways of achieving this was to give students a real-life experience, both in and outside the classroom, of what it is like to be a journalist. At the same time other important aspects of the journalists' profession, sometimes in direct contrast with those of the religious life, were demonstrated and explained.

1. The importance of timing. This is vital to journalists, especially if they are working for a 24-hour news organization, but also if they are part of an organization or programme that has a weekly or monthly schedule. Deadlines have to be respected and information often has to be obtained with speed. These timings may often be in contrast, if not conflict, with the timings of the Church, which are by their nature much slower; the hours or minutes that a journalist may have to develop a story compare with the decades, centuries or millennia in which the Church measures its history.

2. Space, whether it is measured in words (in the print media) or minutes (in radio and broadcasting) is also crucial to journalists. What may take many hours, days or months to research, has to be condensed into a comparatively small space either on the page or on the airwaves. This contrasts directly with the academic and contemplative life, and a lack of understanding of these constrictions often leads to misunderstanding and at worst accusations of superficiality.

3. Information is the basic material with which the journalist works. It has to be obtained from a variety of sources and it must be verifiable. The closed, centralized and diffuse nature of the Church community often makes information difficult to obtain and difficult to verify.

4. Information forms the foundation of news but it is not news. The production of news is dependent on a large number of factors, such as the social and cultural context, timing, internal media management, external market competition and other events competing for the same space or time.

5. Press offices and public relations operators are all useful for journalists but they are only a part of the network of other, perhaps conflicting sources, that journalists need for their work. Eye-witnesses, independent sources of information, archives, balance sheets, extensive on-the-spot investigation, are all tools the journalist uses to provide accurate news.

6. Journalism may be something of a vocation but it is also a job; journalists are employees within an organization that has as much of a career hierarchy as any other. This offers both invaluable controls (there is nothing more conducive to accuracy than peer group pressure) as well as potential restrictions (the adverse pressures of ownership bias and commercial competition).

6. Trust and truth

Among all the many skills that a journalist must have – accuracy, discipline, observation, curiosity, narrative ability, a sense of composition, imagination, organizational capacity, honesty and integrity – there are two more that are essential to the work of a good journalist; the ability in inspire trust and the capacity to discover and then reveal the truth. Journalists must be able to trust their sources of information, just as the sources must be able to trust the journalists. Trust is a narrow two-way street.

There is nothing more that journalists welcome more than a reliable source of local information. Can the Church provide such information and if so can journalists respect the trust that the Church places in them?

Is such a dialogue between journalists and the Church possible? Journalists need new sources of information and the Church needs new outlets to communicate with the world today. Perhaps, as both sides learn to understand what each has to offer, it may be possible to work more closely together in the search for the truth.

7. The search for the truth

"What is truth?", asked Pontius Pilate of our Lord into St. John's Gospel, a question that has been asked ever since.

What might journalists at the time have made of the events that took place in Jerusalem over 2.000 years ago? Would they have arrived at the "truth"? The chances are that they would not, for a series of reasons and circumstances, which are as applicable today as they might have been 2.000 years ago.

What might people in Jerusalem have read the day after the crucifixion in news reports of the time?

"Blasphemer Meets Just Reward", might have been front page news in the Sanhedrin-financed "Jewish Morning Echo".

"Rebellion Averted" could have been the headlines in the Roman garrison's "Jerusalem News".

"No Miracle for the Miracle Worker" could have been the interpretation that the "Galilean Chronicle" gave to the death of its native son.

And what would have come from the dwindling followers of Jesus himself? Too disorganized to be able to think, too busy following the final hours of the Christ, too desperate, too afraid of both the Jewish and Roman authorities, they would not have had the organization, the time, the inclination, or the know-how to write news, let alone search out journalists to give them their version of what happened.

Are the above headlines too sensational? Are they a distorted version of the facts? Would they be dismissed as biased reporting? Yes, probably the headlines could be dismissed for all these reasons. But they also contain a certain degree of "truth" for both the owners and the readers of these imaginary papers. Put them in the context of their time, their culture and their readership and all these headlines are a reflection of what was happening at that moment. But none of them arrive at the truth.

So how was the hypothetical journalist to get to the truth of the matter? Where was the key to the story? What were the sources of information available that night? There was precious little available to our hypothetical reporter. Only if he (or she) had walked through the crowds, listened to the people, followed the man who was to be crucified and stood at the foot of the cross might our hypothetical journalist have arrived at the truth.

While the above scenario is a somewhat fantastic tale of what might have happened that night some 2.000 years ago it raises a number of considerations that are of importance in any debate on journalism today.

1. Journalists work within an organization and therefore work within a context of expectations and a defined culture. The journalists working for the hypothetical Roman and Jewish papers would have used different concepts and assumptions. But if journalists write with their readers and their employers in mind can they ever arrive at the truth?

2. In a moment of political turmoil is it possible to source all the facts of an event? The Jerusalem of the hours before and after the crucifixion would have been the centre of what in modern jargon is called "a fast moving story". There were, according to the Gospels, less than 24 hours between the arrest of Jesus and his death, most of them during the night. Would Jewish reporters have had access to the Roman authorities during those crucial hours? What sort of story would Roman journalists have had from their own authorities about those events? Would Roman reporters have received a true picture if they had listened to what the Jewish hierarchy had to say? Where would Jewish or Roman reporters have found the followers of the crucified man in order to check their facts? Would the followers of Christ have had the courage to speak up during that desperate night?

3. If it is possible to report the conflicting points of view of two (or more) powerful organizations that have access to the media, how is it possible to arrive at those small and persecuted movements, those who often know the truth of so many stories in the world today, but who are too afraid, too persecuted or just not available to speak out?

8. The search for sources

Journalists work with the sources available. Without sources there is no news. According to the rules of the most reliable news organizations, facts must be verifiable by three separate sources of information to form the basis of news. While this generally acts as a powerful check on the accuracy of news reporting, it can also prevent crucial events ever being reported. How long does it take ethnic cleansing to be verified by three separate sources, how long to verify cases of torture, how long does it take cases of child abuse to be verified if three separate sources of information are required to confirm such events? In this light it is perhaps understandable why it sometimes takes a long time to uncover injustice and wrong-doing. Should journalists therefore cut corners to speed up the process? Should they report events even if they have not been checked in this painstaking way? Should they lower their standards in the search for the truth? This is just one of the many controversial issues facing journalists today.

It takes courage to confirm stories of ethnic cleansing, of torture, of child abuse, of corruption. But unless there is courage on the part of the sources of information, of which the Church is one, journalists have no news to provide their editors, and the editors have no news that is fit to print or broadcast.

9. Looking ahead to the next 25 years

What will the next 25 years bring? Maybe it is too early to tell, but two opposing trends are discernable.

On the one hand there are the growing demands of 24-hour, non-stop news. The time it takes to produce and transmit news is decreasing at the same time as the quantity of news provided is increasing. News programmes on television and the radio are now available on the hour every hour, often more frequently. Updating is constant and the news is related almost as quickly as the events unfold. The time to check the facts gets shorter and shorter. The speed at which news is now produced requires increasing reliance on sophisticated and expensive equipment for transmission (anyone who has ever seen a broadcast team in action will know this). There is also an increasing use of official news sources because they are the most readily available (it is quicker and easier to use a press release than to pick up the phone and ask for information. It is easier and cheaper to fill prime-time with press conferences of presidents and prime ministers than to produce a political feature programme). At the same time there is also a greater reliance on what are now known as the celebrity journalists (the anchor men and women in the studio and the special correspondents out in the field), stars in their own right, who sometimes command (and demand) as much attention and interest as the events that they are following.

On the other hand there is the rapid expansion of the new decentralized, and increasingly inexpensive, means of communication such as the Internet and cell phones. It was cell phones that first brought the news of the death of Pope John Paul II to the waiting world, and it was cell phones that spread the first news that a new Pope had been elected in April 2005, even before the news organizations could confirm the events. During the terrorist bombings in London in July 2005 it was once again cell phones and photos taken with cell phones that supplied first-hand information about what was happening across the city.

The Internet is also changing the way news is produced and distributed. News can now be delivered at low-cost and with great speed across the globe in a way that is not possible for either the traditional print or broadcasting media. News can also be accessed by end-users more cheaply and more rapidly than ever before and it can also be stored and recalled indefinitely, as well as being cross-linked to other similar happenings across the world.

Where will these trends lead? With space no longer an issue (as it is in the traditional magazine or newspaper) and with time no longer a factor (as it is in broadcast journalism) some of the key barriers to the flow of information have been removed. The public (the audience) is now involved in the supply of information in a way that has not been possible before, making it an active participant in the making of news.

It is however the evaluating and making sense of that information that will be the challenge for the modern journalist.

Will today's journalists be up to the task or are they already superfluous in a world of instant information that is easily accessed almost anywhere in the world at anytime of the day or night?

Much will depend on the profession itself. Should news become too uniform (which is the danger of the 24/7 non-stop broadcasting age), should it prove unreliable (if journalists come to rely on too few sources of information), should it cease to be critical and analytical of the society in which it operates (if journalists are too close to the centres of political and economic power to be independent) then journalism will lose it standing and credibility.

This would be a loss in an age where there is now a danger of an information free-for-all. The standards of research, accuracy, reliability, discipline, timing, imagination, the ability to communicate complex subjects in the common idiom (whether in words or images), quality control, all of which are the tools of the journalists' profession, are as essential today in the search for the truth as they were in the past.

In this search for the truth both the Church and journalists stand to benefit if they learn to know, respect and to trust each other. CICS can be a small but a valuable way to achieving that trust. If one were to dream dreams and see visions for a CICS of the future what would they be? That diocesan communications centres might become as much a part of a foreign correspondent's itinerary on arrival in a foreign country as the headquarters of the political parties or the offices of the multinational corporations. A vision indeed.

La información religiosa.
Hacia una naturalización del periodismo religioso en los medios

Miriam Diez Bosch

Understanding "religious information" from a Catholic perspective, the article underlines how the different conceptions of religious information coincide with other types of journalism in its professional demands, while the aspect of the journalist's personal religious adherence remains a secondary element. The author observes how conflict is not a specific aspect of religious journalism but of journalism in general, and argues that its effectiveness moves between the journalist's perception of reality and his/her capacity to take a critical distance from that same reality. Underlining that religious journalism is gaining a relevance parallel to the increasing importance of religion in the public sphere, the author shows how the marginalization of religion is transforming into a new awakening of interest in religious issues and, consequently, in religious information.

Estamos en un momento de "retorno a lo religioso" (Graf, 2004: 15) en el que la información religiosa se configura como una materia altamente sensible. "Informar sobre hechos religiosos es sumamente arduo", afirma con buen conocimiento de causa el cardenal Carlo Maria Martini, y añade: "Y porqué es arduo, es fascinante, es un discurso en diagonal" (Martini, 1991: 107). La cobertura de la religión sigue algunas convenciones y prejuicios ya señalados por Stewart M. Hoover que comprenden desde considerar la religión como una "categoría residual de la vida" hasta la más extendida, que ve a la religión como "asunto privado" (Hoover, 1994: 15). Una de las críticas que recibe la información religiosa – entenderemos aquí información religiosa aquella información sobre la Iglesia Católica – es que no es verificable con los métodos empíricos usados comúnmente por los periodistas (Biernatzki, 1995: 13). Esta visión positivista ha dominado la teoría periodística y sigue en boga.

Su presencia – prescindible en muchos medios – no es inocua. Requiere sujetos responsables y formados que sepan detectar que es la noticia religiosa y logren hacerla pasar a través de los medios. La información religiosa se ve no pocas veces marginada por clichés: un encuentro con casi un millón de personas del Papa no alcanza la primera página de un periódico, mientras una decena de manifestantes que se encadenan ante una multinacional sí. Aquí intervienen ya elementos de derecho a la información, que lamentablemente se vulneran con facilidad cuando se trata de cubrir la religión.

1. La información religiosa: una delimitación del terreno

No existe un acuerdo tácito sobre que es, y que no es, información religiosa. Para algunos es la información que hace referencia a experiencias y realidades de una religión, ya sea institucionalmente como desde la periferia. Otros consideran que la información religiosa es "toda" la información, pues ven el mundo sacralizado y detectan en cada realidad la presencia divina. La información sobre el Papa no es nunca totalmente religiosa, pero ciertamente tampoco es enteramente política (Pirard, 1987: 331). Así, los toros serían también un tipo de información religiosa, o la energía nuclear, los desfiles de moda o la gastronomía. Lo que los convierte en información religiosa, según el criterio totalizante, es su relación con la institución religiosa, su dependencia de un sujeto religioso (una modelo cristiana, un manjar budista, un torero católico). Tal vez una definición más apropiada sea la propuesta por el maestro de periodistas José Luis Martín Descalzo, según el cual la información religiosa sería una "parcela de la actualidad" y por lo tanto el informador religioso sería un "profesional" que "informa de una parcela de la actualidad: la religiosa" (Martín Descalzo, 1990: 119). Añadiríamos que este profesional se mueve en un contexto cultural determinado. Esta premisa insiste en la labor profesional del informador religioso (Donaire Martín, 1994: 294) y presupone que el informador no hablará de modo abstracto ni hará sermones o comentarios frívolos. Donaire Martín se atreve a hablar de un "informador religioso ideal" cuando exista un profesional, no necesariamente creyente (aunque debe tener cierta sintonía con las manifestaciones religiosas) que informe sobre lo religioso con una debida preparación y que pueda lanzar puentes hacia otras realidades sociales (Donaire Martín, 1994: 295).

Por esta precisa presencia social de factor religioso como tal no estamos de acuerdo con la afirmación según la cual la información religiosa consiste en la realización del periodismo natural por parte de los cristianos verdaderamente creyentes y coherentes (Galdón López, 2001: 131). A nuestro modo de ver, la información religiosa es religiosa por el tema que trata, no por el sujeto que la realiza.

Otra definición considera que la información religiosa es "toda información que emana de la Iglesia Católica o de cualquier otra Iglesia" (Bosque Orero, 1997: 181). Para el autor, sus protagonistas pueden ser su jerarquía o sus miembros individual o colectivamente. Este tipo de información también puede centrarse en el culto o en las celebraciones.

Tomamos como definición válida la propuesta por la UCIP (Unión Católica Internacional de la Prensa) en su texto *La religión en los Medios: un Desafío Profesional*. Según los criterios asumidos por la UCIP, información religiosa es substancialmente "una información periodística como las demás, donde la investigación, la selección, el tratamiento y la publicación giran en torno al interés del público y no de una fuente de información". Añade que "las informaciones religiosas son aquellas que se refieren a diversas sociedades religiosas o a las relaciones entre estas y la sociedad civil: tales noticias asumen lo religioso como un hecho social, ligado a la historia de los hombres y no como un hecho profundo ligado a la historia del alma" y por tanto "en su calidad de noticia, la información religiosa informa sobre los nuevos acontecimientos que son de actualidad para el público al que se dirige: hechos inesperados, incluso impactantes; anuncios de acontecimientos programados, declaraciones, documentos, publicaciones, informaciones útiles...". Es menester que esta información, como cualquier otra, para llegar a un estándar de excelencia sea "exacta, objetiva, completa y comprensible". La UCIP presupone que "para hacerla comprensible y considerando que el público dispone de escasos conocimientos y cultura religiosa, la información religiosa debe ser adecuadamente explicada". A diferencia del comentario, "la explicación es parte integrante de la información: esta consiste en complementos informativos necesarios para la comprensión de la noticia". Asumimos y subrayamos la afirmación de la UCIP según la cual

> en materia religiosa, como en cualquier otra, la distinción clásica entre información y comentario se hace imprescindible para los periodistas y debe ser clara para los lectores. La información religiosa es una cosa, el comentario religioso – que puede aplicarse tanto a las noticias religiosas como a las demás – es otra.

Como apuntábamos en el título, esta información es delicada. La UCIP la define "sensible" pues se refiere a valores sagrados, que son percibidos y vividos como tal tanto por las fuentes como por los lectores interesados (UCIP, 1998).

2. Las deficiencias del periodismo religioso

Cubrir la información religiosa, la Iglesia, comporta dificultades. Contreras ilustra tres niveles de dificultades objetivas: natural, cultural y instrumental. La natural parte de la constatación que es difícil comprender lo que es la Iglesia, puesto que no existen puntos de referencia válidos. La cultural es que subyacen dificultades añadidas por los planteamientos ideológicos más difundidos en la cultura dominante de una época y lugar determinados y la instrumental es la dificultad provocada por el uso contingente que se hace de ella, por ejemplo políticamente. Estas dificultades pueden facilitar, sin justificarlas, las distorsiones a la hora de informar sobre la Iglesia (Contreras, 2005: 6).

La Iglesia recibe críticas por su hermetismo, poca destreza comunicativa o silencios. Pero también el periodista religioso suele ser objeto de numerosas críticas. Por parte del medio en el que trabaja achaca incomprensión profesional y a veces un cierto menosprecio por dedicarse "a esas cosas". Los lectores también se lamentan y a menudo se sienten ofendidos por informaciones que no les satisfacen, a veces por demasiado críticas o demasiado blandas. Hay una queja generalizada, elevada ya a tópico, de la "insuficiente formación de los periodistas religiosos". También existen insatisfacciones cuantitativas: se habla poco de religión, y mal. Algunos medios se han dado cuenta que no pueden permitirse la negligencia frente al dato religioso, sencillamente porqué hace noticia y porqué tiene un mercado. Por otro lado, el público tiene derecho a recibir información también de la realidad religiosa, y los medios son conscientes de este deber social. Una clara insatisfacción en lo que concierne la información religiosa es que se delega casi o exclusivamente a clérigos, que si por una parte se ganan la confianza del lector y de la fuente – propia, al menos – por otra parte necesitan desarrollar aptitudes profesionales periodísticas de las que normalmente carecen. Por fortuna, esta tendencia está comenzando a transformarse con el acceso de laicos preparados para la función de informador religioso y con el auge de escuelas y centros de formación en este sentido. Porque el informador religioso es antes que nada un informador. Tiene que conocer la estructura de la noticia y tener sensibilidad para captar dónde se esconde la noticia religiosa.

Los elementos que configuran la noticia son múltiples, siendo la novedad, el impacto en la vida pública o la proximidad al lector algunos de ellos (Randall, 2000: 23). Por encima encontramos el conflicto. La conflictividad, advierta Contreras, no se manifiesta sólo en la información religiosa, sino que caracteriza a la actividad periodística en su conjunto (Contreras, 2001: 98). Lo mismo ocurre con el campo religioso. La polémica y el conflicto son características esenciales de la noticia y forman parte como tales también de la noticia religiosa. Aunque a menudo la religión es sólo noticia cuando el conflicto aparece (Haynes, 2000: 82). Si no "hace conflicto", este tipo de noticia acaba siendo tratado como una historia de interés humano y termina en la sección local o en la página religiosa – si la hubiera – del domingo.

3. La religión en los medios, un sujeto incómodo

La presencia de la religión en los medios seculares registra un aumento considerable en los últimos tiempos. Esto no significa que la religión cuente con secciones especializadas o con profesionales que se dediquen a ello. Las secciones especializadas no son tan urgentes como la profesionalidad. Es discutible si es aconsejable que la religión tenga una sección fija, pues su versatilidad y transversalidad la convierten *a priori* en objeto de muchas y distintas secciones. La religión cuenta y tiene su lugar junto a deportes, economía o política internacional. El problema es cómo indexar la religión. Si el Papa asiste a un partido de fútbol, ¿la noticia es deportiva?. Si la Federación Luterana Mundial emite un comunicado contra el hambre ¿estamos en religión, política internacional o sociedad?. La respuesta a estas preguntas se decide habitualmente con un criterio flexible que no siempre juega a ventaja de los asuntos religiosos, pues si estos no tienen una sección fija es posible que acaben no teniendo espacio y se pierdan en la nada. La religión se ha movido en este terreno de nadie durante muchas décadas. El momento presente, especialmente desde el 11 septiembre del 2001, ha cambiado el panorama. Los medios habían ignorado las noticias de matriz religiosa en la guerra de los Balcanes y es ahora cuando se dan cuenta que quizá algo de religioso había, en el conflicto. El problema de la información religiosa y su cabida en los medios generalistas está directamente relacionado con la cuestión de la religión en la vida pública y por ende con la libertad religiosa. Todo y esto, resulta evidente que la religión también influye en la configuración de muchos conflictos contemporáneos (Röhrich, 2004: 267).

Esta marginalización y dificultad para tratar adecuadamente la religión no es atribuible sólo a la responsabilidad de los medios. Haynes indica que durante al menos la última mitad del siglo XX han sido otras instituciones dominantes en la arena pública las que han tratado la religión como residual, marginándola de la vida pública, de las entidades educativas y culturales y del discurso dominante (Haynes,

2000: 83). La consecuencia de esta marginalización de la religión es que se termina con tener un cuadro del mundo mutilado, en el que falta una de las dimensiones – la religiosa – más fundamental. Pongamos un ejemplo. Se celebra la Feria del Libro de Frankfurt. Si los responsables de la sección de cultura no saben que existe una ingente producción literaria religiosa, no la van a destacar ni la incluirán en sus crónicas. El gran obstáculo es cómo la casa editorial llega al informador cultural. Porqué si el único referente de la casa editorial es el periodista religioso – si lo hay –, las novedades editoriales religiosas se quedarán siempre en un artículo breve en la hipotética sección de religión del periódico. La religión importa y es necesaria hacerla visible en todos los campos. También en la ciencia, especialmente en cuestiones bioéticas, se está empezando a vislumbrar una voz creyente en los debates. Este esfuerzo para estar transversalmente presente no puede quedar sólo en la responsabilidad del informador religioso, que se convertiría en un puente hacia todas las realidades que configuran un medio (tendría que estar en reuniones editoriales, tener acceso a sociedad, cultura, internacional, ciencia, educación, sanidad, deportes etc). Aquí entra un cambio de mentalidad por parte de los editores para incluir en sus debates la componente religiosa. Para ello son todavía necesarios muchos encuentros, comidas de trabajo y confianza mutua entre ellos y el mundo de la religión en general y de la Iglesia en particular. Lo que importa, en definitiva, no es que crezca el número de piezas religiosas en un medio (que también es deseable) sino que se acreciente la calidad y la variedad. Lo importante, en el fondo, es cómo se cubre la religión.

4. La información religiosa, entre el apego y la distancia

El informador religioso no debe ser, forzosamente, creyente. Sin embargo, es una obviedad que se informa con más conocimiento de causa sobre aquello que se conoce. El hecho de ser creyente puede ser un aliciente. El informador religioso católico, por ejemplo, tendrá más destreza en el lenguaje propio de la religión que maneja, sabrá entender los silencios, las frases hechas, los tiempos y los ritos. Gozará de la confianza del ambiente eclesiástico y tendrá un interés más agudo por lo que acaece en la Iglesia Católica. Pero lo más importante es que sea un periodista apasionado por la información, con olfato por la noticia y con talento para explicarla.

El informador religioso desarrolla en su labor periodística dos aspectos no siempre fácilmente conciliables: la proximidad, casi apego, al tema que le ocupa (la religión, la Iglesia) y la distancia crítica necesaria para no convertirse en un militante acrítico de la misma.

La proximidad es esencial y tiene una dirección directa con el buen acceso a las fuentes. El periodista debe cuidar sus fuentes de información, pero no caer en ellas. Debe ser allí donde están también los otros periodistas, pero ser lo suficientemente hábil para ser presente en otras realidades olvidadas. Y ser consciente que él no crea, ni inventa las noticias: las explica. El periodista religioso también necesita distancia. Cuanto más se implique en la realidad que explica, el informador se verá más comprometido. Tendrá más experiencia, pero también menor libertad de movimiento. Es por tanto muy importante que el informador religioso no baje nunca la guardia y no se identifique hasta confundirse con la realidad que explica. En este sentido, es vital recordar que este punto es imprescindible en la información. Un artículo de opinión, una editorial o un comentario son otro género que permite más personalización.

Los medios seculares no son esencialmente el lugar ideal para la transmisión del Evangelio y el periodista religioso debe tenerlo en cuenta. Que no sean el lugar ideal no significa de ningún modo que no sean un lugar privilegiado para evangelizar, lo que ocurre es que los medios seculares tienen como objetivo primordial ganar dinero, y no salvar almas. El periodista religioso no es un predicador, ni debe serlo. Debe cubrir la noticia, la noticia religiosa. Esto no exime a los cristianos a estar presentes en los medios seculares, pero siendo siempre conscientes que no son el órgano ideal para transmitir el mensaje cristiano (Dulles, 1993).

5. La información religiosa católica: las fatigas de la Iglesia para comunicar

El cardenal Carlo Maria Martini reconoce que la Iglesia tiene ciertas dificultadas para expresarse, lo cual es una cruz y al mismo tiempo un estímulo para un examen de conciencia incesante (Martini, 1991: 106). Él mismo confiesa sentirse "descontento" de casi todo lo que comunica, y señala tres motivos. El primero, que hay un contenido indecible. Como solución alude al lenguaje simbólico y parabólico. El segundo problema es la gran fatiga de la Iglesia a la hora de expresarse, y por tanto, la fatiga de la información religiosa. Martini alude a un riesgo de la información religiosa: convertirse en citación de citaciones. Se recurre a citaciones del Evangelio, de San Pablo, del Papa, de las *auctoritates*, en el sentido antiguo de la palabra. Y de ahí que no haya espacio para la vida, para el testimonio. El tercer motivo de insatisfacción aducido por Martini es que la atmósfera del lenguaje religioso es sobretodo aquella de la oración y la liturgia, y no el de la mundanidad.

De estas insatisfacciones destacamos dos aspectos: a veces la información religiosa es insuficiente por pereza, incompetencia o conformismo del mismo periodista. Acostumbrado a beber siempre de las mismas fuentes, no se esfuerza en contrastar las noticias, en buscar nuevos o distintos puntos de vista y no se mueve de su entorno. El periodista no puede pretender que su trabajo sea sólo recibir comunicados de prensa de instituciones eclesiales y de ahí sacar su trabajo. Necesita moverse, no sólo físicamente sino mentalmente: estudiar, asesorarse, buscar contexto, escuchar voces discordantes, comprar periódicos que no le gusten y asistir a charlas que no le produzcan paz interior. Es importante que el periodista religioso no esté en manos de algunos grupos o sectores. Es vital que se haga siempre la pregunta: ¿y si no fuera así?, y que mantenga aquella distancia sana y crítica que requieren los acontecimientos. El periodista religioso, lejos de ser un perezoso burócrata delante de un ordenador, debería tender a ser un buscador de noticias en la inmensa parcela del mundo de la religión, que no es otra que la del mundo.

Aparte de esta incompetencia o falta de estímulo por parte del periodista, queremos destacar otro aspecto de la insatisfacción en la información religiosa, y es la de la misma institución religiosa, en nuestro caso la Iglesia. Exponentes de ésta se lamentan, casi por tradición, de la poca profesionalidad de los informadores religiosos. Sin eximir nada de la responsabilidad del periodista de formarse para informar, es necesario destacar que el informador religioso necesita la ayuda de la institución, de sus jerarcas, fieles, portavoces, afiliados o simpatizantes. Con su ayuda y colaboración podrá realizar mejor su tarea. Si la única respuesta que recibe el informador religioso es una no-respuesta, buscará otras fuentes menos fiables. La institución tiene una responsabilidad enorme en la tarea de mejorar la información religiosa, y no puede eximirse de ella achacando las deficiencias exclusivamente a la hostilidad o incompetencia del periodista religioso, por muy real que esta pudiera ser.

6. Conclusión: la religión importa

La religión importa (*Religion clearly matters,* asevera Haynes), y no sólo en Estados Unidos, donde la discusión sobre el lugar que ocupa la religión en el espacio público es siempre controvertida. La religión importa y el periodismo religioso está dejando de ser marginal para empezar, todavía a tientas, a ocupar el lugar que le pertoca. Hasta hace poco tiempo existía una desproporción abismal entre la vida religiosa de la gente y su visibilidad y análisis en los medios, no sólo en Estados Unidos (Oertel, 2002: 54). Para paliarla empezaron a crearse centros de comunicación y religión para formar a periodistas que fueran capaces de cubrir la religión. El proceso sigue y crece. Hoy, la objeción según la cual la religión es un asunto privado no tiene ya fundamentos: que las religiones se expresan en la vida pública es un hecho. Aunque a inicios de la Edad Moderna se quisiera limitar el discurso de la esfera pública al significado pragmático de los objetos, para evitar conflictos y persecuciones religiosas, hoy esta desviación hacia el privado no tiene salida (White, 2001: 167). White continua afirmando la innegable capacidad simbólica de lo religioso, que no por ser simbólica es intrascendente o marginal. Esta capacidad simbólica es parte de la naturaleza humana, y es una realidad que el deseo de la Ilustración de imponer la razón como única explicación plausible del ser humano más allá de su capacidad simbólica no se ha realizado nunca. El periodismo religioso debe hacer frente a esta realidad difícil, delicada, ardua, de la religión, que se mueve entre lo simbólico y lo trascendente. Casi todos los temas tienen alguna dimensión religiosa. Los temas morales, como la guerra, las drogas, el aborto, la clonación, la pena de muerte, etc., tienen aspectos religiosos bien en su raíz, bien en sus repercusiones sociales y religiosas (González Gaitano, 2001: 56). La información religiosa, si entiende bien su naturaleza, no se agotará nunca. Su campo no se extingue pues abarca la práctica totalidad de la realidad. Y persistirá porqué la religión, cada vez más, importa.

Referencias bibliográficas

BIERNATZKI, W. E. (1995), "The Reporting of Religion", *Communication Research Trends* 15/2, 13-15.

BOSQUE ORERO, F. J. (1997), "La información religiosa y su tratamiento periodístico: interés, enfoque y tratamiento de las noticias religiosas", en D. BOROBIO – J. RAMOS, ed., *Evangelización y Medios de Comunicación,* Salamanca: Publicaciones UPSA, 181-184.

CONTRERAS, D. (2001), "La religión como noticia en la prensa internacional: cualidades y deficiencias", en *Iglesia y Medios de Comunicación. Razones de un desencuentro histórico*, Buenos Aires: Pontificia Universidad Católica de Buenos Aires, 83-115.

CONTRERAS, D. (2005), "La información religiosa, información especializada". Ponencia presentada en la Asamblea de Delegados Diocesanos de la CEMCS sobre "Estatuto y tratamiento de la información religiosa", Madrid, 14 febrero 2005, 5.
DONAIRE MARTÍN, F. (2004), "Elementos nucleares de la información religiosa", en J. CANTAVELLA – J. F. SERRANO, ed., *Católicos en la prensa*, Madrid: Libros Libres, 289-305.
DULLES, A. (1996), "Religion and the News Media: A Theologian Reflects", *Media Report* 3, 3-4.
GALDÓN LÓPEZ, G. (2001), "Concepto, método y aspectos de la información religiosa", en *Iglesia y Medios de Comunicación. Razones de un desencuentro histórico*, Buenos Aires: Pontificia Universidad Católica de Buenos Aires, 131-148.
GONZÁLEZ GAITANO, N. (2001), "Información religiosa y evangelización. Equívocos, sospechas, recelos, malicias... y clarificaciones conceptuales", en *Iglesia y Medios de Comunicación. Razones de un desencuentro histórico,* Buenos Aires: Pontificia Universidad Católica de Buenos Aires, 35-67.
GRAF, F. W. (2004), *Die Wiederkehr der Göttes. Religion in der Modernen Kultur,* München: C.H. Beck.
HAYNES, CH. H. (2000), "Faith, Fairness and the American Press. Why the news media should take religion more seriously", *Media Studies Journal* 14/3, 82-87.
HOOVER, S. M. – AL. (1994), *Religion in Public Discourse: The Role of the Media – Final Report*, Boulder: University of Colorado.
MARTÍN DESCALZO, J.L. (1990), "Tipología eclesial del informador religioso", en AA.VV., *La Iglesia, dato informativo. Ponencia de las primeras jornadas nacionales de informadores católicos*, Madrid: Paulinas.
MARTINI, C. M. (1991), "La singolarità dell'informazione religiosa", en *Comunicare nella Chiesa e nella società*, Bologna: EDB, 105-108.
OERTEL, F. (2002), "USA: Kirche kein Medienthema mehr?", *Communicatio Socialis* 1, 53-57.
PIRARD, A. (1987), "L'information religieuse: à quel prix?", *Lumen Vitae* 3, 329-333.
RANDALL, D. (2000), *The Universal Journalist*, London: Pluto Press.
RÖHRICH, W. (2004), *Die Macht der Religiones. Glaubenskonflikte in der Weltpolitik*, München: C.H. Beck.
UCIP (1998), *La religión en los Medios: un Desafío Profesional*, Luxemburgo.
WHITE, R. A. (2001), "La comunicazione pastorale", en T. STENICO, *Era mediatica e nuova evangelizzazione,* Roma: Libreria Editrice Vaticana, 163-181.

La radio come comunicatore
Paolo Prato

In Western countries, radio has for some time now changed its role and function: from the main medium for the formation of public opinion, it has become a medium which accompanies our free time and even our working hours. In the indistinct flow of words, music, news and commercials, simply being connected is more important than any contents. And it is precisely for this that radio saw the opportunity to encourage the participation of members of its audience who, because of the socio-economic status, are normally excluded from the spectacles of the media. The Catholic world has always favoured the medium of radio and, more recently, even the bishops of Italy have joined in, launching many initiatives aimed at giving more significance to the many radio stations spread out in their jurisdictions.

"*Half of what I say is meaningless / but I say it just to reach you, Julia*": sono le parole di una canzone di Lennon e McCartney che riassumono in modo efficace il senso della radio oggi, nei paesi occidentali ma non solo[1]. Una radio nella quale non è così importante quel che viene detto, ma il fatto che venga detto. Anche se non ha un gran significato, anche se mi sfugge qualcosa del discorso esso tuttavia ha senso per me in quanto ascoltatore. E anche se chi parla è perfettamente consapevole che sta dicendo cose "per metà" prive di senso... lui/lei sa che il suo scopo non è comunicare contenuti, ma "raggiungere" qualcuno, stabilire un contatto.

Nella comunicazione radiofonica la funzione fàtica oscura quella referenziale, circoscritta a pochi momenti in cui l'ascolto è focalizzato e fortemente motivato a comprendere (i giornali radio, le previsioni del tempo, le notizie sul traffico). La parola detta (in radio) ha molte risorse in più rispetto a quella scritta: anzitutto è personalizzata, dunque "suona" diversa se detta da un uomo o una donna, da una persona giovane o da una anziana, da un personaggio pubblico o da uno sconosciuto, da un italiano o da uno straniero, da uno affetto da raffreddore oppure no, e così via[2]. Dietro quelle parole, quelle frasi, quei dialoghi – il più delle volte chiacchiericcio fine a se stesso e dunque finalizzato a mantenere il contatto con una platea che si può solo immaginare – ci sono esseri umani in carne ed ossa, corpi che a quelle parole danno vita. Ed è la fisicità di questa comunicazione che produce senso. Poi, la parola detta ha a disposizione infiniti registri paralinguistici, che possono corroborare il messaggio oppure alludere a un significato opposto: i toni della voce (l'altezza dei suoni, il tipo di emissione più o meno gutturale, ad esempio, la pesantezza o leggerezza del respiro), gli artifici emotivi che colorano il messaggio (es. un colpo di tosse, gli "uhm" di commento, i rumori della lingua o delle labbra, le nasalizzazioni, le ispirazioni… cf. Eco, 1968: 392-394). Quindi ci sono i diversi stili con cui una parola viene detta e la radio privilegia da tempo quelli colloquiali, che creano un'atmosfera di complicità (ancora una volta l'importante è ottenere il coinvolgimento, l'assenso del pubblico indipendentemente dall'argomento trattato). Infine c'è la risorsa della musica, che trasforma la parola radiofonica in un *rap* infinito, data la presenza costante di una base ritmica che fa da sottofondo a ogni (o quasi) intervento parlato, giornale radio compreso. È la necessità di rispettare i tempi radiofonici che finisce per trasformare il parlato in un esercizio spesso fine a se stesso, in cui solo "la metà di quel che viene detto ha un senso": quando si hanno ancora trenta secondi per parlare prima che parta lo spot pubblicitario o quando "prendere l'intro"[3] obbliga a giri di parole, ripetizioni, riferimenti all'ora, alla frequenza, ai numeri di telefono per chiamare, pur di riempire quei secondi… ecco che la voce esegue una cantilena a tempo con la musica e diventa strumento essa stessa. Se ne apprezza la qualità timbrica, la destrezza nel compiere acrobazie verbali senza sbavature, ma non si presta alcuna attenzione al contenuto perché non è quello che tiene sintonizzati gli ascoltatori.

In sintesi, la comunicazione radiofonica dei giorni nostri promuove un'oralità di tipo nuovo che non solo tiene conto della scrittura (come potrebbe fare altrimenti?) – e qui siamo alla cosiddetta "oralità secondaria" (cf. Ong, 1986) – ma va oltre nell'appropriarsi di ritmi musicali, nel riciclare formule prese dalla pubblicità o dai teatrini della comicità televisiva, nell'interagire con la tecnologia per accelerare o decelerare l'enunciazione come un funambolo in bilico tra "effetto" e sua "messa in scena". Menduni la chiama "terza oralità", che si afferma contemporaneamente ad altri due macro-fenomeni di fine secolo responsabili di una rivincita della comunicazione orale: il *rap* e i telefonini (Menduni, 2001)[4].

1. Radio di flusso, radio di programmi

Fra gli svariati modelli di radio a disposizione, la scelta del pubblico si va orientando sempre di più sulla cosiddetta "radio di flusso", nella quale si susseguono in diretta (o falsa diretta)[5] parole, musica, news, jingles e spot pubblicitari all'interno di un clock predefinito che identifica i caratteri di quella o quell'altra emittente. È un modello di radio fondato su un ascolto casuale, che si adegua al tempo dell'ascoltatore inserendosi negli interstizi del suo tempo, accarezzandolo senza impegnarlo troppo. L'altro modello – in declino da tempo – è quello della radio di palinsesto, nel quale spicca l'individualità dei programmi, delle voci, dei contenuti. Un modello che propone un suo tempo radiofonico a cui l'ascoltatore deve adeguarsi, scegliendo ciò che più gli interessa a quell'orario preciso. Da un lato abbiamo un modello circolare, dall'altro uno lineare: la ritualità (ripetitività) vs l'unicità (l'evento). Ovviamente abbiamo bisogno di entrambi: di sicurezza, di riconoscibilità e di shock, di sorprese. Ma il primato del flusso è ormai una realtà ineludibile: quello è il linguaggio che parla la radio oggi. L'importante è stabilire il contatto e restare connessi con "altri" immaginati, al di là di quel che si dice o della musica che va in onda, che peraltro è sempre lo stesso omogeneizzante *pop* globale, anche quando parla la lingua locale.

A questo fenomeno, anche i vescovi italiani hanno dedicato qualche pagina nel Direttorio sulle Comunicazioni Sociali, laddove si parla della "musica leggera nella cultura odierna"[6]:

> Più che un medium, è un messaggio veicolato da altri media, primo tra tutti la radio. Attirando soprattutto tanti giovani, non può restare estranea all'attenzione pastorale della Chiesa. Occorre saper distinguere tra prodotto puramente commerciale, privo di creatività e spessore, e ciò che invece è destinato a durare, perché espressione creativa dotata di originalità (Conferenza Episcopale Italiana, 2004: 119).

È proprio questo prodotto commerciale a monopolizzare l'etere e non solo quello nazionale. In Italia il 75% della programmazione delle radio è fatta di musica – con una punta del 90% nelle private. Ma i 36 milioni di ascoltatori che mediamente si sintonizzano si trovano di fronte a un'offerta limitatissima. Ciò che "è destinato a durare" in quanto "espressione creativa originale" spesso è proprio ciò che la gente non è in grado di cogliere, per un generale appiattimento verso il basso che accomuna la radio alla ben più influente televisione. E tuttavia la sfida non si combatte tanto sul piano estetico quanto sul piano sociale: sul piano cioè della ricezione del messaggio radiofonico. Per far passare un messaggio (o meglio una sensibilità, una visione del mondo) – diciamo quello cristiano – occorre saper gestire anche una musica "puramente commerciale" che faccia da collante a contenuti spesso in antitesi con essa. È una regola alla quale nemmeno il mondo cattolico ha saputo derogare, pena il dirottamento di quella parte più fluttuante del pubblico verso altre emittenti. L'adesione a un modello radiofonico in larga misura simile a quello dominante ha caratterizzato le iniziative della Chiesa italiana negli ultimi anni[7].

2. Lo spazio della radio

Lontana dall'esposizione mediatica che tritura volti, esperienze e idee, ma purtuttavia stabilmente al centro dei meccanismi di formazione dell'identità, la radio ha da poco festeggiato i suoi 80 anni di vita in Italia (2004) e si avvia a passare splendidamente il suo primo secolo di vita accanto al cinema che l'ha preceduta di poco e che con essa si è spartito a lungo il dominio dell'immaginario novecentesco. Al cinema la seduzione dello sguardo, alla radio il piacere dell'ascolto. Rispetto ai "radio days", in cui dominava l'opinione pubblica, è forse declinato il ruolo della radio nella formazione del consenso, demandato alla televisione più ancora che ai giornali. Ma alla radio competono altre importanti sfere della vita privata e pubblica: quegli ambiti che storici, educatori, antropologi mettono sempre più in primo piano nella costruzione dell'identità personale e collettiva. Sulla radio si attiva anzitutto l'emisfero cerebrale destro, responsabile delle emozioni, della fantasia, dell'irrazionale[8]. Lo stesso nel quale dimora il pensiero musicale, da sempre stretto alleato della radio. Ma in molti paesi in cui lo sviluppo dei media è ancora incompleto, alla radio si affida anche l'emisfero sinistro del cervello, in cerca di quel sapere razionale che altrove è per lo più appannaggio di altri media.

Nella riflessione che i vescovi italiani hanno riservato alle comunicazioni sociali, si parla di "nuova primavera della radio" come uno dei fenomeni caratterizzanti la pervasiva diffusione dei media nella società contemporanea. È significativo che quella "rivoluzione culturale" che anche i vescovi attribuiscono alla centralità assunta dai mezzi di comunicazione di massa assuma per la radio valenze qualitative laddove per altri mezzi come la televisione o Internet, sia anzitutto l'aspetto quantitativo a impressionare[9]. Non che i numeri non parlino comunque a favore, anche in questo caso. Da tempo gli ascoltatori della radio in Italia sono oltre 36 milioni e il loro numero è inferiore solo a quello dei telespettatori[10]. Sul piano della raccolta pubblicitaria poi, la radio – con i suoi bassi costi e la sua capacità di raggiungere target di mercato molto circoscritti – si distingue per un trend positivo che sembra andare controcorrente rispetto ai media più quotati. Non a caso in questi ultimi anni l'economia del settore ha fatto segnare un incremento nelle acquisizioni da parte di gruppi editoriali e industriali di assoluta rilevanza, il che dimostra come il mezzo sia strategico in qualsiasi politica che coinvolga i media.

3. Perché studiarla, perché insegnarla

Negli ultimi anni è avvenuto un profondo cambiamento di paradigma nello studio dei media: dall'attenzione per l'offerta, cioè i contenuti che essi veicolano e i modi in cui questo avviene, si è passati a guardare i media in quanto interfacce comunicative, quindi si è prestato attenzione alle modalità di interazione che essi rendono possibili: identità, crescita (individuale e collettiva), interpretazione, decodifica e ricodifica dei significati... Ma la radio non è semplicemente un medium, né solo un linguaggio o un apparato produttivo: è essenzialmente un processo o, nel linguaggio della tradizione sociologica, un "fatto sociale" (Sorice, 2002: 161). La dimensione privilegiata della radio è la suggestione, più che l'affermazione: la sua messa in scena si limita "al suggerimento di una prospettiva di senso, costruita più per mezzo di sintomi che non di segni: una messa in scena che necessita di una partecipazione integrativa da parte dell'ascoltatore e che, nello stesso tempo, non si impone al suo mondo" (Bettetini, 1984: 44).

Nei paesi in via di sviluppo la radio è spesso l'unico medium di massa, economico, presente laddove manca l'elettricità. Un mezzo che si può rivelare indispensabile per realizzare quel processo di alfabetizzazione che in Italia è stato compiuto dalla televisione. Ancora oggi, a oltre vent'anni dal rapporto McBride che riferiva la presenza di un miliardo di "radioriceventi" nel mondo, la radio si conferma il primo medium nel pianeta per diffusione. Le emittenti radiofoniche sono oltre 40.000 di cui 11.000 negli USA, 9.000 in Europa, alcune migliaia in America Latina, Asia, Africa e Australia (Hendy, 2002: 14). Su tutte spicca il "caso italiano" con oltre 1.500 radio, un numero che pone il nostro paese al secondo posto dopo gli Stati Uniti. Per gli utenti occidentali la radio è soprattutto una compagna, che manda musica registrata. E già questa semplice constatazione colloca la radio in una posizione diversa rispetto non solo al sistema dei media, ma ai fondamenti antropologici stessi del vivere contemporaneo. Adorno scriveva che "l'udire, se paragonato con il vedere, è 'arcaico', non in linea con la tecnica". Vi è nella percezione acustica "un momento di arcaica collettività" che rimanda a "una moltitudine secondo il modello delle comunità religiose di una volta come al suo solo soggetto possibile"[11].

Nel 1964 McLuhan scriveva che la radio si reinventava come medium dei giovani, grazie al quale essi potevano ascoltare e trasportarsi dietro la musica preferita e isolarsi dalla famiglia (McLuhan, 1964: 268). Alla generazione cresciuta negli anni '60 la radio offriva mobilità (una caratteristica oggi presidiata dai telefoni cellulari) e isolamento (ribellione, identità, consumi diversi dai genitori). C'è sempre una radio fatta su misura per me e questi sono i bisogni che essa sembra soddisfare:

a) compagnia – diversivo da routine (sconfiggere il silenzio, la solitudine);
b) coscienza di sé, identità sociale (condividere l'esperienza con altri immaginari, sentirsi parte di...);
c) informazione (una finestra sul mondo).

La radio favorisce la partecipazione di chi ascolta, lo mette in interconnessione col mondo in ogni momento e luogo, lascia libertà di interpretazione, consente elasticità nella fruizione, rispetta l'autonomia del soggetto in ascolto (che è in grado di rispettare altre priorità) ma al tempo stesso lo gratifica enormemente perché lo coinvolge attraverso una trasmissione orale che ha la parola e il suono al centro del processo comunicativo. Basterebbero queste poche ragioni per fare della radio un oggetto meritevole di studio. E fin qui ho solo sfiorato alcuni risvolti antropologici della comunicazione. C'è ben altro. La radio può significare impegno attivo sul territorio, strumento democratico per contribuire alla coesione di una comunità, delineare percorsi dell'identità individuale e collettiva, servire – più semplicemente – a districarsi meglio nel mondo.

C'è qualcosa di più dei motivi pratici – ad es. il fatto che siamo impegnati in faccende domestiche o alla guida dell'auto – che ci induce ad accendere la radio anziché la televisione: c'è la libertà di pensiero e movimento che la radio favorisce, grazie all'evanescenza e onnipresenza del suono e della voce. Il suono non ci costringe a orientare lo sguardo su chicchessia, escludendoci dal resto. Si può ascoltare a occhi chiusi mentre non possiamo chiudere le orecchie.

Menduni parla dell'ascolto radiofonico come di una "ginnastica mentale ricostruttiva", un'opportunità che ci fa bene, ci garantisce un'oasi in cui non ci sottoponiamo alla dittatura dell'immagine o della parola scritta. E attribuisce alla radio il potere di rafforzare "l'idea dell'oralità come bricolage comunicativo" (Menduni, 2002: 9). "Il suono non ha il vincolo di dover rappresentare la realtà, ma di accompagnarla; la parola descrive o commenta la realtà, non è tenuta a sostituirla" (Menduni, 2002: 11).

Infine c'è l'insopprimibile voglia di essere connessi al mondo, che la radio soddisfa meglio di altri media, il desiderio di non essere isolati, ma al contrario di essere accompagnati e informati di tutto ciò che avviene altrove, anzitutto per un'esigenza di rassicurazione: news, bollettini meteo, dati sul traffico "segnalano implicitamente che non sono accadute cose più importanti". Le notizie che ci giungono in forma sintetica e veloce dalla radio "ribadiscono la presenza costante di un'arena pubblica, collettiva, che esiste anche se non si identifica in nessun luogo fisico esclusivo e anche se la frequentiamo solo episodicamente" (Menduni, 2002: 20).

Se nel 1800 Flaubert non sopportava l'idea di leggere in treno, per far passare più presto il tempo, oggi al contrario la radio favorisce quella simultaneità dei comportamenti esaltata a suo tempo da Marinetti e diventata un tratto irrinunciabile dell'individuo moderno: "nel comunicare mentre si cammina o nell'ascoltare mentre si lavora si reagisce all'ansia di un tempo che sembra non bastare mai, si ha l'impressione di mettere a profitto tempi obbligati" (Menduni, 2002: 18).

Quando arrivò la radio, non se ne sentiva affatto il bisogno, disse Bertolt Brecht. Ma una volta arrivata, la gente si rivolgeva ad essa per avere le notizie e dunque l'ascolto radiofonico aveva i caratteri della necessità, in un'epoca in cui la comunicazione audiovisiva era scarsa e l'informazione un bene raro e prezioso. Oggi, quando la comunicazione è ridondante e dobbiamo difenderci dalla quantità di informazioni che ci arrivano da ogni parte anche in forma audiovisiva, la radio non richiede più un ascolto per necessità ma un "ascolto elettivo" (Menduni, 2002: 8).

Se la TV resta un'esperienza da consumare in famiglia, la radio è in luoghi e circostanze diverse. La TV è una fuga consapevole, si guarda per scelta, mettendo da parte la realtà del momento ed entrando in quella (a volte persino più reale) del piccolo schermo. La radio non ti chiede di staccare la spina, convive con la tua realtà. La vista è centrifuga: separa dal mondo. L'ascolto è centripeto: spinge dentro il mondo. E se Internet è diventato il luogo deputato all'analisi e all'approfondimento, la radio diventa sempre più rapida nell'enunciazione, offrendo la vetrina di quelle notizie che poi si approfondiranno altrove.

4. La radio e il mondo cattolico: l'esperienza italiana

"L'impegno della Chiesa nel mondo dei media non si esaurisce nel discernimento e nella formazione", si legge nel Direttorio sulle Comunicazioni Sociali.

Oggi "i media, che danno accesso all'informazione in diretta, sopprimono la distanza di spazio e di tempo, ma soprattutto trasformano la maniera di percepire le cose: la realtà cede il passo a ciò che di essa viene mostrato. Perciò, la ripetizione continua di informazioni scelte diventa un fattore determinante per creare un'opinione considerata pubblica". Dinanzi al loro potere nel modellare l'opinione pubblica, la Chiesa avverte da una parte l'urgenza di dotarsi di propri media, dall'altra la necessità di rafforzare e precisare le modalità di intervento all'interno dei media stessi (Conferenza Episcopale Italiana, 2004: 85).

Il mondo cattolico ha visto nella radio, fin dal suo avvento, uno strumento prezioso per la propria presenza, mai come oggi tanto multiforme (*Ibid.*: 162). E il 26 gennaio 1998 nasce Blu Sat 2000, l'agenzia radiofonica voluta dalla Fondazione Comunicazione e Cultura che opera attraverso il satellite. Nasce per aiutare la radiofonia cattolica, molto forte e diffusa nel Paese, ma priva di riferimenti comuni. In Italia sono oltre duecento le radio cattoliche tra diocesane, devozionali e commerciali. Ma il solo tratto comune è la ricerca di identità da realizzare mediante una programmazione ispirata ai principi del cattolicesimo[12].

Blu Sat fornisce un palinsesto di 24 ore in cui si alternano informazione (news, approfondimenti, dibattiti), programmi religiosi ed ecclesiali (alcuni dei quali presi da Radio Vaticana), cultura, musica e rubriche di servizio. Elemento caratterizzante della strategia editoriale è la collaborazione fra centro e periferia, cioè fra le due sedi di Roma e Milano e le radio che aderiscono al circuito. Nell'estate del 2002 viene lanciato il marchio InBlu, che accomuna quelle emittenti che ritrasmettono fino a un massimo di sei ore giornaliere di programmi in contemporanea. All'interno di questo esperimento si viene a delineare un profilo di radio che non ha precedenti in Italia, frutto della straordinaria dedizione di operatori laici (molti dei quali volontari) e responsabili diocesani. Un modello unico, per quanto imperfetto, di radio nazionale e locale al tempo stesso, grazie a una rete di corrispondenti e centri di produzione capillare che nemmeno la radio pubblica è in grado di realizzare. Una radio che suona moderna e parla la lingua dei giovani, partecipa alle iniziative della Chiesa e le promuove, ma è presente in tutti i luoghi deputati dello spettacolo e della cultura. Una radio che si è anche riproposta di incoraggiare la creatività e la ricerca e nel 2003 ha lanciato "RadioFormat", il primo concorso nazionale per autori radiofonici.

La partecipazione sembra dunque essere la dimensione più affascinante della radio ed è a questo richiamo che il mondo cattolico risponde con grande intensità dai tempi delle prime radio libere (1975) e da qualche tempo lo fa con la consapevolezza e la professionalità di chi è protagonista, forte della capacità di orientare circa un sesto di tutte le emittenti della Penisola. È una partecipazione che avviene anzitutto al telefono, con gli SMS o con le e-mail, per ragioni le più diverse, comprese quelle decisamente futili, ma che futili sono spesso solo in apparenza. Perché nella telefonata del ragazzo timido e introverso che si apre solo perché non deve mostrare il volto, o dell'anziana signora che dialoga con il conduttore conosciuto da lungo tempo e lo fa in dialetto o comunque accentuando la propria origine di quartiere, c'è molto di più di un passaggio di informazione. C'è uno scambio fra esseri umani, un dialogo fra persone, qualcosa che parrebbe sempre più difficile da realizzare all'interno di un'esistenza che per altri versi tende a sfuggirci.

NOTE

[1] John Lennon-Paul McCartney, *Julia*, inciso dai Beatles in "The White Album", Appel-EMI, 1968.

[2] Il parlato radiofonico è stato catalogato nella categoria del "trasmesso" collocandosi a metà fra comunicazione scritta e parlata. Ma sempre più esso si va affrancando dai vincoli dello scritto per aderire in tutto e per tutto agli stili dell'oralità. Cf. Atzori, 2003.

[3] Espressione in uso tra gli operatori che indica il parlare sull'introduzione strumentale di un brano musicale smettendo in concomitanza con l'inizio della parte cantata o comunque della strofa o del riff.

[4] Sul tema cf. anche Prato, 1997.

[5] Per "falsa diretta" si intende un programma realizzato come se fosse una diretta (stesso ritmo, stessa sequenza tra parole e musica, stesso tono di voce...) ma registrato e mandato in onda in differita.

[6] Va precisato che il termine "musica leggera" è in disuso da tempo nella stampa specializzata e comunità degli studiosi, in quanto contiene in sé un giudizio di valore negativo. Al suo posto si preferisce usare "musica popolare", in quanto traduzione del più pertinente termine anglosassone "popular music".

[7] Sull'esempio di alcune realtà europee, prima fra tutte Radio Cope della Conferenza Episcopale Spagnola, anche la Conferenza Episcopale Italiana ha varato un proprio progetto radiofonico a partire dal 1998. Se ne parla più avanti.

[8] La comunicazione radiofonica "ha superato la soglia del dato e delle notizia, il livello di una scrittura neutrale e strumentale, per coinvolgere emotivamente ed esteticamente l'ascoltatore" (Bettetini, 1984: 43).

[9] Centinaia di canali televisivi, Internet in un numero sempre maggiore di famiglie, il satellite, una nuova primavera della radio, la stampa che soffre forse la concorrenza dei nuovi media, ma reagisce trasformandosi. Il nostro tempo è caratterizzato da una diffusione degli strumenti della comunicazione sociale sempre più rapida e pervasiva (Conferenza Episcopale Italiana, 2004: 1).

[10] I dati sull'ascolto radiofonico in Italia vengono da anni raccolti da Audiradio, una società che ha elaborato un proprio sistema di rilevazione tramite interviste a un campione della popolazione scelto sulla base del censimento ISTAT. Una sintesi di questa indagine, pubblicata ogni tre mesi, è consultabile sul sito *www.audiradio.it.*

[11] Adorno parla della musica classica, in particolare della polifonia armonico-contrappuntistica e della sua articolazione ritmica, ma il ragionamento funziona, anche meglio, per esperienze più moderne come il *pop* o la musica etnica (Adorno – Eisler, 1975: 35).

[12] Rifacendosi alla classificazione di Martínez de Toda, i programmi religiosi in Italia rientrano per lo più nella categoria "istituzionale", riservata alle emittenti diocesane e parrocchiali, con qualche residua partecipazione per la categoria "spiritualista", in cui agiscono emittenti devozionali come Radio Maria, e una piccola quota appartenente alla radio pubblica. Cf. Martínez de Toda, 2001: 35-38.

Riferimenti bibliografici

ADORNO, T. W. – EISLER, H. (1975, ed. or. 1949), *La musica per film*, Roma: Newton Compton.

BETTETINI, G. (1984), "La radio come mezzo di comunicazione", in *La radio: storia di sessant'anni 1924/1984*, Eri/Edizioni Rai, Torino, 43-44.

CONFERENZA EPISCOPALE ITALIANA (2004), *Comunicazione e missione. Direttorio sulle comunicazioni sociali nella missione della Chiesa*, Roma: Libreria Editrice Vaticana.

ECO, U. (1968), *La struttura assente*, Milano: Bompiani.

HENDY, D. (2002), *La radio nell'era globale*, Roma: Editori Riuniti.

MARTÍNEZ DE TODA, J. (2001), *Come realizzare programmi religiosi ed educativi alla radio, alla televisione ed in Internet*, Roma: PUG/CICS.

MCLUHAN, M. (1964), *Understanding Media: the Extension of Man*, New York: Signet.

MENDUNI, E. (2001), *Il mondo della radio*, Bologna: Il Mulino.

MENDUNI, E. (2002), "Introduzione: percorsi di un medium mobile e interattivo", in ID., *La radio*, Bologna: Baskerville, 5-22.
ONG, W. (1986), *Oralità e scrittura. La tecnologia della parola*, Bologna: Il Mulino.
PRATO, P. (1997), "Voglia di parole: dai salotti borghesi alle piazze telematiche", in *Riflessi* 1, 68-72.
SORICE, M. (2002), "La radio nell'industria culturale italiana", in Menduni, 2002: 161-178.

Gli studi sulla televisione
Michele Sorice

In this contribution, the author provides a series of critical reflections on aspects of contemporary television studies, also comparing them with the main perspectives in audience studies and in communication theory. By bringing together the work of the most important scholars and researchers, the author is also emphasizing the value of the new wave of cultural studies approaches and their methodological perspectives to television studies.

1. Introduzione

La storia dei *television studies* si intreccia e spesso si sovrappone con quella della sociologia dei mass media. Se i primi vent'anni della *communication research* sono essenzialmente il tempo della radio e degli studi che sul medium vennero realizzati dai padri della sociologia funzionalista dei media, dall'inizio degli anni Cinquanta in poi sarà la televisione a diventare oggetto di studio e luogo di confronto scientifico.

La radio, in effetti, era stato il terreno privilegiato della ricerca di personaggi come Lasswell, Lazarsfeld, Katz, nonché di gran parte delle origini di quegli approcci che altrove abbiamo già avuto modo di definire "teorie della trasmissione" (Sorice, 2005b); nell'alveo delle nascenti "teorie del dialogo", invece, è la stampa a rappresentare uno degli oggetti privilegiati di studio, come era avvenuto con Park e la Scuola di Chicago. Ma è la televisione a diventare molto presto il medium più studiato e analizzato, sia nei suoi testi, sia nel suo rapporto col pubblico, sia nella sua sempre più evidente funzione sociale.

Gli studi sulla televisione rappresentano oggi una parte consistente della sociologia dei mass media e spesso l'area dei *television studies* si sovrappone quasi integralmente a quella dell'intero settore dei *media studies*. Anche per questo motivo non è possibile, in questa sede, passare in rassegna tutti gli studi sulla televisione, i cui ambiti di applicazione peraltro attraversano diverse discipline scientifiche, dalla sociologia alla psicologia, dalla filosofia alla statistica, dalla semiotica all'antropologia. Ci limitiamo, allora, a discutere alcuni dei passaggi più importanti e significativi, operando una scelta da una parte discrezionale e dunque discutibile, dall'altra parte fondata sugli esiti più avanzati della ricerca sociale sui media.

2. Due filoni di ricerca

Se proviamo ad analizzare lo sviluppo storico della sociologia dei mass media possiamo facilmente individuare due grandi prospettive di analisi, generalmente corrispondenti ai due grandi filoni di ricerca rappresentati dal paradigma funzionalista da una parte e da quell'insieme di studi e teorie che trova negli approcci semiotici e nei *cultural studies* il suo sbocco, dall'altra parte. Questi due filoni di ricerca possono essere anche definiti – da una prospettiva teorica – come *teorie della trasmissione* e *teorie del dialogo*.

Il paradigma dominante nel periodo fra gli anni Quaranta e Sessanta – quello della cosiddetta "sociologia funzionalista dei media"[1] – si fondava su una prospettiva che Guido Gili (1998) ha opportunamente definito "realistica". In tale prospettiva, i cui massimi rappresentanti sono sicuramente Paul Lazarsfeld e i suoi colleghi del *Bureau of Applied Social Research*, il modello dominante è quello dei cosiddetti *effetti limitati dei media* che lo stesso Gili (1998: 127) propone, significativamente, di denominare *modello dei fattori intermediari*[2]. In questa temperie culturale, uno dei più significativi elementi di rottura rispetto al paradigma dominante funzionalista, fu rappresentato da Marshall McLuhan. Per lo studioso canadese, infatti, i media non si limitano a essere strumenti che ci portano *verso* il mondo, ma costituiscono essi stessi il *mondo reale*. Nello stesso periodo si aprono nuovi scenari di ricerca grazie alla semiotica (e in particolare alla svolta enunciazionale che avrà un suo grande interprete in Algirdas Julien Greimas) e all'affermazione dei *cultural studies*. Ma un'altra – e fondamentale – rottura si verifica nella teoria sociologica generale.

> I paradigmi struttural-funzionalista e conflittuale, che hanno dominato il campo fino a tutti gli anni Sessanta, condividevano una visione realistica: esiste un *ordine sociale* che va scoperto e analizzato. Differivano poi profondamente nella definizione delle caratteristiche di tale ordine: per il primo si trattava di un ordine immanente alimentato dall'adesione degli individui ai valori centrali della società; per il secondo era un ordine "dialettico", non realizzato e da realizzarsi superando l'imperfetta situazione presente. In questo orizzonte sostanzialmente *normativo* che accomunava i due grandi paradigmi sociologici rivali, i *mass media* apparivano come *veicoli* o *ostacoli*, a seconda che favorissero o impedissero l'adesione degli

individui a questo ordine "ideale". A partire dalla fine degli anni Sessanta si sono invece progressivamente affermati nuovi paradigmi sociologici – quali l'interazionismo simbolico, la fenomenologia, l'etnometodologia, la teoria della costruzione sociale della realtà, una concezione più cinica e relativistica del funzionalismo (rappresentata in particolare da Luhmann) – accomunati dall'idea che *la realtà sociale è costituita da e attraverso i processi comunicativi*. La comunicazione a tutti i livelli, dall'interazione faccia a faccia fino alla comunicazione di massa, non è solo un aspetto o una dimensione del sociale, ma il suo stesso fondamento e "sostanza" (Gili, 1998: 128).

In altre parole, i media rappresentano le cornici entro cui si attua la conoscenza sociale, come veri e propri *definers of social reality* (Bennet, 1982). Un'importante conseguenza della prospettiva *idealistica* (come ancora la definisce Gili) della ricerca sulla comunicazione si presenta proprio negli *studi sulla televisione*, ovvero del medium che contribuisce in maniera evidente al processo di costruzione dei significati sociali. Proprio all'interno dei movimenti di rinnovamento concettuale e metodologico si possono peraltro collocare le prospettive che considerano i media (e la televisione in particolare) come *forme culturali*, ovvero come appunto "cornici" entro cui si attua il processo interpretativo della realtà[3]. All'interno di tale idea si situano, almeno in parte, molti degli studi più interessanti e recenti sulla televisione come, per esempio, quello sui *target generazionali* della TV italiana, realizzato dall'OssCom dell'Università Cattolica del Sacro Cuore di Milano e diretta da Fausto Colombo (Aroldi – Colombo, 2003). In tale area può ancora collocarsi una ricerca sulla fruizione della fiction in Italia (De Blasio – Sorice, 2004) e ancora la recente ricerca sui media non-mainstream realizzata congiuntamente dall'OssCom di Milano e dal Crisc dell'Università di Roma "La Sapienza" (Pasquali – Sorice, 2005).

3. Il modello *encoding/decoding* e le ricerche sulla televisione

Proprio all'interno di questo ambito di studi si situano anche tutte le ricerche più specifiche dei *television studies*, in qualche modo riconducibili (almeno in origine) al concetto di *funzione bardica* della TV elaborato da John Fiske[4], senza peraltro dimenticare gli studi sulla televisione come agente di socializzazione. Dagli studi di Berger e Kellner (1973) sulla pluralizzazione dei mondi di vita, discendono conseguenze importanti sul ruolo dei media come particolari agenzie di socializzazione: i media, infatti, e la TV in particolare si pongono come "forme" della conoscenza e "ambienti" culturali, spesso capaci di entrare in competizione con la famiglia nella costruzione del "primo mondo" dell'individuo in cui si formano le caratteristiche della personalità di base. Fra i primi a occuparsi in Italia di tali problematiche, vanno sicuramente citati Cesareo (1982) e Besozzi (1993).

Ma sono i *cultural studies* – in particolare quelli che si sviluppano a partire dalla Scuola di Birmingham – che meglio di altri possono collocarsi all'interno di questa prospettiva *idealista*, come è peraltro evidente già negli assunti di base che Stuart Hall pone a fondamento della costruzione concettuale del *Centre for Contemporary Cultural Studies*.

Per gli scopi di questo saggio non possiamo non citare la pubblicazione – avvenuta nel 1980 – del saggio di Stuart Hall, *Encoding and Decoding in Television Discourse*[5] in cui lo studioso realizzava una duplice rottura: con la tradizione culturalista statunitense e con quegli studi che ritenevano i processi di produzione e ricezione come entità separate e distinte. Stuart Hall, infatti,

> riteneva che compito della ricerca fosse quello di porre la massima attenzione sul complesso delle relazioni che interconnettono produzione e ricezione generando senso. Allo stesso tempo non è possibile non considerare che l'attività di lettura riflette le condizioni materiali e sociali dei lettori, determinando pertanto – almeno in parte – una sostanziale limitazione della libertà del processo di decodifica (Sorice, 2005b: 141).

Proprio studiando le modalità di codifica e rappresentazione dei prodotti della cultura di massa, e in particolare concentrando la sua attenzione sui testi televisivi, Hall giunse a definire l'attività di codifica come un processo attraverso il quale vengono posti limiti e meccanismi di standardizzazione al testo stesso.

> L'attività di decodifica, allora, è funzione di una molteplicità di variabili che limitano la teorica illimitatezza delle possibilità di interpretazione. In altri termini Hall individua nel contesto un elemento estremamente importante nell'attività di decodifica: la comunicazione, cioè, si costituisce come una *relazione* fra i due momenti del processo comunicativo stesso (la codifica e la decodifica, intese quindi come processo unitario e continuativo e non come momenti disgiunti, anche se essi mantengono una loro autonomia connessa a variabili di carattere storico e ambientale). In tale accezione il pubblico percepisce i "messaggi" come *discorsi dotati di significato*: quando questi discorsi si inseriscono nelle pratiche sociali allora è possibile, per Stuart Hall, parlare di comunicazione in senso proprio (*Ibid.*).

Nel modello *encoding/decoding* di Stuart Hall, le diverse strutture di significato rendono di fatto possibile l'esistenza di una "disparità di codici" fra emittenti e destinatari[6]. Stuart Hall, in particolare, individua tre diverse modalità di decodifica.

1. La *lettura preferita*, in cui il processo di codifica avviene attraverso un *codice egemonico* [7], capace di definire in maniera univoca l'universo dei significati di una cultura. Tale codice, essendo percepito come "naturale", non ha bisogno di alcuna legittimazione sociale. "La definizione di un punto di vista egemonico è: a) che definisca, entro i propri termini, l'orizzonte mentale o l'universo dei significati possibili, di un intero settore di relazioni in una società o cultura e b) che abbia il crisma della legittimità, che sembri in sintonia con ciò che è 'naturale', 'inevitabile' e 'scontato' sull'ordine sociale" (Hall, 1980; ora anche in Marinelli – Fatelli, 2000: 83). La lettura preferita presume un'audience sostanzialmente passiva.
2. La *lettura negoziata*, in cui il destinatario procede a forme di "negoziazione" dei significati televisivi: in questo caso è evidente l'asimmetria dei soggetti attivi nel circuito comunicativo massmediatico, tuttavia l'audience appare dotata di una buona capacità critica e di un alto livello di "attività".
3. La *lettura oppositiva*, in cui i fenomeni di distorsione incidono in maniera significativa fra attività di codifica e processi di decodifica, determinando una frattura netta fra produttori e consumatori. In questo caso abbiamo un'audience non solo attiva, ma anche capace di produrre proprie forme di "antagonismo" o, almeno, di "resistenza".

Stuart Hall teorizza il processo di codifica (*encoding*) televisiva come un'articolazione dei momenti – connessi ma distinti – della produzione, circolazione, distribuzione e riproduzione, ognuno dei quali attiva meccanismi specifici senza tuttavia automaticamente garantire l'esistenza del momento successivo. Questo significa, in altri termini, che i *testi televisivi producono significati multipli che possono essere interpretati in modi diversi*. Si tratta di un punto importantissimo che ha come immediata conseguenza l'esistenza di un'audience concepita come individualità socialmente situata, la cui "lettura" è resa possibile dall'operazione di filtraggio attraverso significati e pratiche sociali condivise. La televisione, cioè, si pone come snodo socialmente rilevante, la cui fruizione è essa stessa una pratica sociale.

Non è un caso che proprio il modello *encoding/decoding* sia stato utilizzato da David Morley in un'altra celebre ricerca sulla televisione[8]: lo studio degli stili di fruizione del "news magazine" *Nationwide*. La ricerca di Morley sui diversi stili di consumo (spesso inattesi) di individui appartenenti a gruppi sociali differenti rappresenta uno dei contributi più importanti nella definizione del concetto di *active audience*. Con accenti simili a quelli di Morley si dipanano anche le ricerche di Mary Ellen Brown (1994) sulle modalità di fruizione delle *soap-opera* da parte delle donne e, in particolare, il suo concetto di *reactive pleasure*, in sostanza una forma di lettura oppositiva che si realizza all'interno delle forme "tradizionali" di fruizione estetica anche di tipo emozionale.

Un altro aspetto di grande importanza derivante dalle prospettive di ricerca inaugurate dalla Scuola di Birmingham è quello relativo all'analisi del rapporto fra significati del testo e formazione della soggettività. In effetti, questo tema (che è alla base anche degli studi di David Morley) rappresenta un fondamentale *asset* concettuale nelle ricerche di Dorothy Hobson (1982) sul *gender* come variabile centrale nelle modalità di decodifica e fruizione dei testi televisivi. Proprio lo studio di una *soap-opera* britannica come *Crossroads* (accuratamente studiata da Dorothy Hobson anche nei suoi aspetti testuali) pose in rilievo il rapporto strettissimo esistente fra stili di fruizione e ruoli familiari. La Hobson concentrò la sua attenzione sulle specificità del *female spectator* che si mostrava protagonista di forme di uso del testo televisivo in situazioni di subordinazione o, almeno, attraverso forme di fruizione che includevano anche la cura domestica[9]. L'analisi del *gender*, inteso non come mera variabile fisica, ma come principio che definisce processi d'identità e stili di fruizione, è di assoluta rilevanza nella prospettiva dei *cultural studies* e ha avuto il merito di emancipare la ricerca sui media – e in particolare proprio quella sulla televisione – da quelle ricerche, ormai inadeguate e insufficienti, ancora concentrate esclusivamente sui contenuti e sui canali[10].

4. Televisione e *audience studies*

Un altro elemento di svolta nei *television studies* è rappresentato dall'adozione di metodologie di ricerca che pongono al centro dell'analisi il punto di vista del telespettatore, soprattutto se considerato come soggetto attivo. Ci si riferisce in particolare alle metodologie etnografiche. D'accordo con Alasuutari (1999) potremmo individuare nello sviluppo della ricerca etnografica tre direttrici principali: la prima è costituita dal crescente interesse per i *gender studies*, grazie anche allo sviluppo degli studi "femministi" sulla fruizione delle soap e della fiction; la seconda coincide con la diminuzione di interesse per i contenuti della programmazione televisiva a favore di un'analisi più attenta delle funzioni esercitate dal medium nei diversi ambiti sociali (e domestici in particolare); la terza linea guida infine è rappresentata dall'adozione del "punto di vista dell'audience" nella ricezione dei programmi mediali. Nell'alveo di quest'ultima direttrice si situano le prime ricerche sulle "comunità interpretative" e, più in generale, delle relazioni esistenti fra media e vita quotidiana.

La svolta etnografica (Schrøder – Drotner – Kline – Murray, 2003), l'importanza via via crescente assunta dall'impostazione teorica della Scuola di Birmingham, l'efficacia applicativa delle teorie della ricezione, una nuova consapevolezza circa il ruolo del pubblico nei processi di costruzione di senso: sono alcuni degli elementi che hanno contraddistinto lo sviluppo degli *audience studies*[11].

Proprio all'interno dello sviluppo della ricerca etnografica si collocano gli studi di James Lull sugli usi della televisione. Lull ha prodotto un'efficace distinzione tra *usi strutturali* e *usi relazionali*. Gli usi strutturali sono di due tipi: *ambientale*, quando la televisione è utilizzata come "rumore di fondo"; *regolativo*, quando il mezzo scandisce i diversi momenti della giornata e può funzionare anche come meccanismo di regolazione dei momenti della giornata. Gli usi relazionali possono servire a: 1) facilitare la comunicazione: è il caso dello scambio di contenuti e valori a partire dai contenuti veicolati dalla TV; 2) determinare dinamiche di appartenenza e/o di esclusione sociale; 3) permettere l'apprendimento sociale, sia nel senso della crescita delle competenze culturali (è il caso della cosiddetta televisione pedagogica) sia nel senso dell'attivazione di processi di socializzazione; 4) favorire la competenza mediatica e, di fatto, incrementare le capacità di dominio sociale di alcuni individui e gruppi sociali. L'elaborazione di Lull è di straordinaria importanza concettuale: da una parte, infatti, lo studioso statunitense invera e supera l'approccio degli *uses and gratifications*, dall'altra, studiando la fruizione televisiva nel suo ambito naturale di fruizione[12], apre la strada per gli studi sui processi di *domestication* delle tecnologie.

Non stupisce che proprio utilizzando in maniera critica e originale il vasto apparato metodologico proposto da James Lull, si siano sviluppate in America Latina importantissime ricerche sull'uso della televisione (cf. per esempio Fuenzalida – Hermosilla, 1989).

Non è possibile in questa sede procedere a un'analisi puntuale dell'importanza dei metodi etnografici per i *television studies*. Da un punto di vista generale, tuttavia, è necessario sottolineare come la caratteristica più significativa di tutta l'area degli *audience studies* qui sinteticamente presentata, risieda in un'impostazione sostanzialmente *olistica* allo studio dei processi comunicativi.

Un'interessante schematizzazione di tale prospettiva è quella offerta da Norman Fairclough (1995), in cui una prima prospettiva è rappresentata dal prodotto comunicativo (sia esso definito "testo" o "messaggio" o anche "media" in un'accezione ampia); la seconda dimensione – correlata alla precedente – è rappresentata dalle *pratiche discorsive* che di fatto connettono produttori/emittenti e audiences[13]; la terza dimensione – che a sua volta "include" le precedenti – è quella che considera il processo comunicativo come un vero e proprio processo socio-culturale: le strutture sociali, in questo caso, costituiscono i luoghi che permettono e costringono al tempo stesso l'attività dell'audience.

5. La fruizione televisiva come *performance*

Il superamento e perfezionamento – negli studi sull'audience – della fase che viene definita *incorporation/resistance* è reso evidente dall'elaborazione da parte di Nicholas Abercrombie e Brian Longhurst del paradigma *spectacle/performance*[14]. L'attenzione ai rapporti fra *performer* e audience consente ad Abercrombie e Longhurst di individuare tre tipi di audience:

1. *simple audience:* i pubblici che vivono l'esperienza della simultaneità in spazi limitati e, comunque, condivisi come nel caso di chi partecipa a una rappresentazione: questo tipo di pubblico si inserisce in una cornice di elevata ritualizzazione della fruizione e la sua stessa partecipazione è spesso limitata a elementi rituali codificati;
2. *mass audience:* è il pubblico che sperimenta una forma di fruizione despazializzata, come avviene per esempio nella partecipazione domestica a qualunque tipo di *spettacolo*;
3. *diffused audience:* si tratta della forma più comune e più usuale della fruizione mediale contemporanea: l'individuo è costantemente parte di un pubblico a prescindere dalla compresenza di una qualche forma di *performance* e a prescindere anche dalle peculiarità del prodotto mediale (evento eccezionale o programmazione televisiva quotidiana).

Il concetto di *diffused audience* è di grande interesse culturale: esso, infatti, si fonda su un'idea ampia e sostanzialmente ibrida di comunicazione, in cui coesistono forme di connessione diretta con forme di connessione mediata. La dimensione contestuale, pur essendo universale, si pone comunque come *glocal* e la commistione di pubblico e privato nonché la sempre minore distanza fra *performer* e audience stessa favoriscono anche un ulteriore abbassamento della dimensione cerimoniale[15]. Non è un caso che in questa definizione si trovino anche tutte quelle modalità di "rottura delle cornici" (Sorice, 2002; Taggi, 2003; De Blasio – Sorice, 2004) tipiche del *reality*, ma anche, più genericamente, delle forme avanzate dell'esperienza post-televisiva, comprese quelle che potremmo definire *non-mainstream* (Pasquali – Sorice, 2005)[16]. La sovrapponibilità fra *performer* e audience, peraltro, favorisce la trasformazione della stessa "performance mediale" in esperienza collettiva condivisa. Tema questo assai importante per lo studio degli intrecci fra media e costruzione dell'identità.

Diventano molto importanti, allora, gli studi sulle forme di costruzione dei meccanismi interpretativi e di uso dei contenuti televisivi. La fruizione mediale, infatti, si connota sempre più come attività complessa e articolata;

> e se John Fiske aveva individuato la categoria instabile della "gente" (*people*) per individuare le forme di resistenza sociale e di riallocazione dei significati dei prodotti mediali, nel paradigma *spectacle/performance* è possibile fare riferimento al concetto di *comunità interpretative,* cioè di segmenti di audience capaci di attivare meccanismi di significazione sociale attraverso svariate modalità (Sorice 2005b: 189)[17].

Le *interpretive communities* sono state studiate in maniera efficace, fra gli altri, da Kim Christian Schrøder (1994) e costituiscono un altro degli snodi concettuali nei *television studies* contemporanei.

Ma il merito principale degli approcci più recenti alla ricerca sulla televisione (e in particolare sul pubblico della televisione) risiede nell'adozione del punto di vista dei soggetti sociali, delle persone reali che attraversano il nostro tempo. E, al tempo stesso, nella consapevolezza, da parte dei ricercatori, che compito della ricerca sui media è anche, come ha insegnato Luc Boltanski, fare emergere, nei comportamenti concreti delle persone, la loro capacità di resistenza e la loro competenza morale.

NOTE

[1] Bisogna tuttavia notare che, come sempre, tutte le definizioni così restrittive sono troppo semplicistiche per inquadrare correttamente un fenomeno in realtà ampio e assai articolato.

[2] Gli effetti dei media sono, infatti, "limitati" a causa di fattori di "intermediazione", dal contesto sociale al ruolo degli *opinion leaders,* come nel caso, per esempio, del *two-steps-flow-of-communication*, il modello elaborato nel 1955 dal Elihu Katz e Paul Lazarsfeld.

[3] All'interno di tale prospettiva *idealistica* possono collocarsi anche diversi approcci negli studi sui media come per esempio la teoria situazionale derivante dagli studi di Goffman.

[4] John Fiske individua nella fruizione televisiva quattro funzioni così schematizzabili: a) *Funzione Affabulatoria* (soddisfazione del bisogno di evasione); b) *Funzione Bardica* (la TV si pone come mediatrice di linguaggi); c) *Funzione Ritualizzante* (la TV scandisce i tempi sociali); *d) Funzione Modellizzante* (la TV costruisce rappresentazioni semplificate della realtà).

[5] Una traduzione in Marinelli – Fatelli, 2000.

[6] Così come già era stato teorizzato nel modello semiotico-informazionale elaborato da Umberto Eco e Paolo Fabbri. Per una schematizzazione del modello mi permetto di rimandare a Sorice, 2005b.

[7] Il codice egemonico è, per Hall, un *ordine del discorso*, che tende "a circoscrivere l'intero universo di valori e significati che la società classista può esprimere ed ammettere, apparendo però al tempo stesso come perfettamente 'naturale' e dato-per-scontato" (Gili, 1998: 131). Il codice egemonico è, di fatto, il punto di vista delle *élites* dominanti.

[8] Ricerca sulla televisione significa, a questo livello, ricerca sulla "fruizione" televisiva.

[9] Per esempio, fruizione delle *soap* frammentata dalla preparazione del cibo o dalla cura per i figli; questo implicava, fra l'altro, una diversa concezione dello spazio domestico, luogo di svago per gli uomini e luogo di lavoro per le donne, e conseguentemente una diversa percezione dei media.

[10] Proprio sulla televisione si sono concentrate anche le ricerche delle aree di studio che vanno sotto l'etichetta di *Feminist Cultural Television Criticism* nonché quelle provenienti dagli studiosi aggregati intorno alla rivista *Screen (Screen Theory)*. Proprio contro quest'ultimo approccio – accusato di avere una prospettiva troppo "deterministica" – si sono mosse le critiche di Morley e dello stesso Stuart Hall.

[11] Pertti Alasuutari (1999) individua tre fasi di sviluppo storico degli *audience studies*. Una *prima fase* è quella che lo studioso finlandese definisce "ricerca sulla ricezione". In questa fase si collocano principalmente gli studi che fanno riferimento da una parte al modello *Encoding/Decoding* di Stuart Hall e dall'altra alle teorie della ricezione. La *seconda fase* è quello che lo studioso finlandese fa corrispondere alla "seconda generazione" di ricercatori, ovvero quella che ha privilegiato l'*etnografia dei media* come proprio metodo principale di ricerca. Quella dell'etnografia dei media rappresenta, secondo Alasuutari, qualcosa di più di una metodologia: si tratta di un vero e proprio paradigma di ricerca che ha avuto notevoli implicazioni su tutti gli

studi sulla comunicazione. La *terza fase* è quella che Alasuutari identifica con una terza generazione di studiosi, quelli che hanno adottato un approccio che potremmo definire "costruzionista". Questa fase, che inizia alla fine degli anni Ottanta e giunge fino ad oggi, contiene al suo interno diverse prospettive di ricerca: dallo studio sull'autorappresentazione sociale dei soggetti attraverso i media fino all'analisi sul ruolo dei mezzi di comunicazione di massa nella costruzione dell'identità. In quest'ultima area la ricerca sull'audience (e in particolare proprio quella sulla televisione) torna a privilegiare strumenti sociologici ma, al tempo stesso, adotta metodologie ibride e approcci teorici provenienti da diversi ambiti disciplinari.

[12] L'ambiente domestico e familiare. *Family*, appunto, ma anche e molto opportunamente *household*. Per completezza, bisogna tuttavia notare che il cambiamento negli stili di fruizione televisiva nonché nella struttura delle famiglie e dei loro tempi di vita, ha reso inadeguata la classificazione di Lull. Le nuove modalità di "uso" della televisione, peraltro, impongono una revisione profonda della stessa metodologia di ricerca.

[13] In quest'ambito la ricerca sull'audience non può trascurare gli aspetti economici, politici e socio-culturali che funzionano da filtri fra audience e media.

[14] Il paradigma *spectacle/performance* (al cui interno si situano gran parte degli studi e delle ricerche sulla televisione dalla metà degli anni Novanta ad oggi) si rivolge allo studio dell'identità e dello statuto delle *audiences* contemporanee. In altre parole, le ricerche qui collocabili si fondano sui meccanismi di ricostruzione sociale delle audiences nel grande mondo possibile rappresentato dal *mediascape*. Il paradigma, cioè, tende a studiare anche i processi di formazione delle identità all'interno di un approccio che, dal punto di vista metodologico, dovremmo definire "autoriflessivo" in quanto parte dalla percezione che i membri del pubblico hanno di sé stessi come audience.

[15] Guardare ed essere guardati e forse, meglio, guardare come si viene guardati è, non a caso, divenuta una delle caratteristiche dell'esperienza televisiva degli ultimi anni.

[16] Comprese quindi le forme di TV comunitarie, quelle "dal basso" che utilizzano le tecnologie digitali, e le esperienze di "TV di strada".

[17] Mi permetto di rimandare ancora una volta a questo testo per una trattazione più ampia dello *spectacle/performance paradigm*, nonché ovviamente a Abercrombie – Longhurst, 1998.

Riferimenti bibliografici

ABERCROMBIE, N. – LONGHURST, B. (1998), *Audiences,* London: Sage.
ALASUUTARI, P. (1999), *Rethinking the Media Audience,* London: Sage.
AROLDI, P. – COLOMBO, F. (2003), *Le età della tv. Indagine su quattro generazioni di spettatori italiani,* Milano: Vita e Pensiero.
BOLTANSKI, L. (1993), *La souffrance à distance,* Paris: Editions Métailié (trad. it. 2000, *Lo spettacolo del dolore. Morale umanitaria, media e politica,* Milano: Raffaello Cortina Editore).

BOLTANSKI, L. (2000), *Le nouvel esprit du capitalisme,* Paris: Editions Métailié.
BOLTANSKI, L. (2005), *Stati di pace. Una sociologia dell'amore,* Milano: Vita e Pensiero (ed. orig. 1990, *L'Amour e la Justice comme compétences,* Paris: Editions Métailié).
BROWN, M. E. (1994), *Soap Opera and Women's Talk. The Pleasure of Resistance,* London: Sage.
DE BLASIO, E. – SORICE, M. (2004), *Cantastorie mediali. La fiction come story teller della società italiana,* Roma: Dino Audino Editore.
FAIRCLOUGH, N. (1995), *Media Discourse,* London: Edward Arnold.
FISKE, J. (1982), *Introduction to Communication Studies,* London: Methuen.
FISKE, J. (1987), *Television Culture,* London: Methuen.
FISKE, J. (1989), *Understanding popular culture,* Boston: Unwin Hyman.
FUENZALIDA, V. – HERMOSILLA, M. E. (1989), *Visiones y ambiciones del televidente,* Santiago (Chile): Ceneca.
GILI, G. (1998), "Il fantasma della realtà: prospettive realiste e idealiste nell'analisi dei mass media", *Studi di Sociologia* 36, 121-145.
HALL, S. (1980a), "Encoding/decoding in television discourse", in Hall – Hobson – Lowe – Willis, 1981.
HALL, S. (1980b), "Cultural Studies: two paradigms", *Media, Culture & Society* 2, 57-72.
HALL, S. – HOBSON, D. – LOWE, A. – WILLIS, P. (1981), *Culture, Media, Language: Working Papers in Cultural Studies, 1972-1979,* London: Hutchinson.
HOBSON, D. (1982), *Crossroads: The Drama of a Soap Opera,* London: Methuen.
LASSWELL, H. (1927), *Propaganda Technique in the World War,* New York: Harper.
LAZARSFELD, P. F. – BERELSON, B. – GAUDET, H. (1948), *The people's choice: How the Voter Makes up his Mind in A Presidential campaign,* New York: Columbia University Press.
MARINELLI, A. – FATELLI, G., ed., (2000), *Tele-visioni,* Roma: Meltemi.
MORLEY, D. (1980), *The "Nationwide" audience: structure and decoding,* London: British Film Institute.
MORLEY, D. (1981), "The Nationwide Audience – A Critical Postscript", *Screen Education,* n. 39.
MORLEY, D. (1986), *Family Television: Cultural Power and Domestic Leisure,* London: Comedia.

MORLEY, D. (1991), "Communication and context. Ethnographic perspectives on the media audience", in K. B. JENSEN – N. W. JANKOWSKI, ed. (1991), *A handbook of qualitative methodologies for mass communication research*, London: Routledge.
PASQUALI, F. – SORICE, M., ed. (2005), *Gli "altri" media. Ricerca nazionale sui media non mainstream*, Milano: Vita e Pensiero.
SCHRØDER, K. C. (1994), "Audience Semiotics, Interpretative Communities an the 'Ethnographic' Turn in Media Research", *Media Culture and Society* 16, 337-347.
SCHRØDER, K. C. – DROTNER, K. – KLINE, S. – MURRAY, C., (2003), *Researching Audiences*, London: Arnold.
SORICE, M. (2002), *Lo specchio magico. Linguaggi, formati, generi, pubblici della televisione italiana*, Roma: Editori Riuniti.
SORICE, M., ed. (2005a), *Programmi in scatola. Il format nella tv globale*, Torino: Effatà.
SORICE, M. (2005b), *I media. La prospettiva sociologica*, Roma: Carocci.

L'insegnamento di Internet in una Università Pontificia

Xavier Debanne

The aim of this paper is to offer an Internet teaching proposal for the Pontifical Universities. The paper begins with a positive answer to the question: given the challenges of the new evangelization, is the Internet essential for the Church? This is followed by an analysis of the religious presence within the "Net". The paper provides a representation of this presence based on different categories of people involved: the producers, for example of websites, and the pastoral operators who are using the Internet for creating meeting opportunities, etc. The last part of the paper is focused on the description of an Internet teaching proposal.

1. Introduzione

Il mondo nel quale viviamo, dominato dalla tecnologia che prevede sempre più l'utilizzo di componenti elettronici digitali, si è a poco a poco riempito di oggetti digitali: il telefonino, sempre più prodotto con fotocamera digitale incorporata, l'orologio digitale, il Personal Computer (PC), spesso collegato ad Internet, il lettore di CD e di DVD, la televisione satellitare, i videogiochi, ecc. Il fenomeno della digitalizzazione della società ha cambiato, in modo sostanziale, ma quasi impercettibile, la cultura occidentale: i giovani comunicano tramite il linguaggio SMS del telefonino, scattano fotografie digitali e scaricano la musica da Internet, senza curarsi dei diritti di autore. In particolare Internet è diventato uno straordinario mezzo di comunicazione e di progresso culturale della società. Il Pontificio Consiglio delle Comunicazioni Sociali rileva che "fra i mezzi di comunicazione, quali il telegrafo, il telefono, la radio, la televisione, che durante lo scorso secolo e mezzo hanno progressivamente eliminato il tempo e lo spazio come ostacoli alla comunicazione fra un gran numero di persone, Internet è il più recente e per molti aspetti il più potente" (2002a). Ma Internet è spesso percepito più come una minaccia che come un'opportunità; ad esempio, nell'era digitale, tutto cambia continuamente: un documento digitale è sempre "work in progress", una fotografia è sempre ritoccabile, nel giornalismo online il testo di un articolo può essere aggiornato tante volte (non esiste più un momento "di chiusura" della pagina, come nei giornali tradizionali, perché di fatto una notizia si considera "definitiva" solo quando non richiede ulteriori aggiornamenti). Questo significa che l'era digitale ha eliminato il concetto di "versione finale", e ciò accresce il relativismo e favorisce il "culto" della provvisorietà. Internet quindi porta con sé opportunità e pericoli e pertanto "la Chiesa ha bisogno di comprendere Internet. Ciò è necessario al fine di comunicare efficacemente con le persone, in particolare quelle giovani, immerse nell'esperienza di questa nuova tecnologia, ma anche per utilizzarlo al meglio" (Pontificio Consiglio delle Comunicazioni Sociali, 2002b). In questo contributo abbiamo deciso di analizzare il concetto di Internet come possibile spazio per la nuova evangelizzazione, tralasciando l'analisi dei rischi[1]. In particolare il testo cerca di chiarire perché gli studi su Internet siano importanti in una Università Pontificia e di concludere con una proposta di insegnamento.

2. Internet, Web e ciberspazio

La rete digitale Internet, nata nel 1969, è un "macrocircuito telematico formato da reti di computer interconnesse distribuite in tutto il mondo"[2]. All'inizio i servizi utilizzati erano la posta elettronica (nata nel 1972), le mailing list con il loro concetto di registrazione, i newsgroup[3] e le chat[4] nate nel 1988. Internet era quindi usato da pochi specialisti, quasi esclusivamente appartenenti al mondo universitario, per comunicare e per scambiare messaggi e documenti. L'avvento del Web[5] all'inizio degli anni Novanta e la veloce diffusione del "browser" Web[6], che diventano prodotto di massa, hanno contribuito a trasformare radicalmente l'utilizzo di Internet, rendendolo facilmente accessibile da chiunque possieda un Personal Computer e un modem. Il Web viene subito percepito come un nuovo mezzo di comunicazione di massa, alternativo ai mezzi di comunicazione tradizionali, capace di distribuire informazioni e documenti multimediali a livello planetario; perciò è stato velocemente adottato dal mondo commerciale. Il Web è diventato un immenso ipertesto multimediale distribuito; costituisce infatti il più grande archivio, mai realizzato dall'uomo, di informazioni memorizzate nei server di tutto il mondo.

Ma, per cogliere pienamente il significato di Internet, bisogna andare oltre i termini "Internet" e "Web" e utilizzare il termine "ciberspazio", che indica un luogo virtuale. Suor Angela Zukowski, durante il Convegno di Assisi nel 2000 organizzato dalla Conferenza Episcopale Italiana, parlava di Internet come di "un luogo o spazio 'reale'. Ci sono milioni di persone che vi trascorrono una parte significativa della loro giornata, per lavoro, educazione, e-commerce, comunicazione o divertimento. Sappiamo anche che la maggior parte di queste persone sono giovani" (Zukowski, 2000: 49). Infatti i giovani rappresentano la fascia della popolazione che maggiormente usa Internet per navigare, "chattare", scambiarsi file musicali, film, fotografie digitali, ecc. Anche Giovanni Paolo II (2002) riconosceva l'importanza del ciberspazio quando affermava che "per la Chiesa il nuovo mondo del ciberspazio esorta alla grande avventura di utilizzare il suo potenziale per annunciare il messaggio evangelico".

3. Perché Internet è importante per la Chiesa

Già nel 1988 Giovanni Paolo II sosteneva nella *Christifideles laici* (n. 34) che l'ora è venuta per intraprendere una nuova evangelizzazione. Lo stesso Pontefice, nella *Veritatis splendor*, affermava che "l'evangelizzazione è la sfida più forte ed esaltante che la Chiesa è chiamata ad affrontare sin dalla sua origine" (n. 106). A questo proposito Giuseppe De Rosa, riferendosi all'Italia, si pone la domanda:

> come annunciare il Vangelo in una società largamente scristianizzata e religiosamente indifferente, che chiede alla Chiesa un forte impegno nel campo sociale e nella cura delle più gravi piaghe che affliggono il nostro Paese (prostituzione, droga, devianze giovanili, accoglienza degli immigrati), ma mostra scarso interesse nei confronti di un annuncio religioso e morale, poiché i suoi interessi sono di ordine materiale e mondano, limitati alla ricerca del benessere fisico e psichico in questa vita, e quindi alla buona salute, alla riuscita nella carriera, al maggior godimento dei piaceri che offre la vita, all'evitare la sofferenza in tutte le sue forme? (De Rosa, 2003: 112).

Un inizio di soluzione potrebbe essere proprio Internet, perché si tratta di un luogo visitato da milioni di persone ogni giorno, che nessuno possiede, che invita alla collaborazione e che incita ad innovare perché chiunque abbia l'idea di una nuova applicazione, ad esempio per l'evangelizzazione, la può realizzare con mezzi modesti. D'altronde il Magistero della Chiesa, dal 1999, non ha cessato di promuovere lo sviluppo della presenza religiosa in rete per contribuire alla nuova evangelizzazione: "l'innovazione più sorprendente nel campo della tecnologia della comunicazione è probabilmente la rete Internet. [...] Senza dubbio, le immense potenzialità di Internet possono fornire un aiuto notevole alla diffusione della Buona Novella, come dimostrano alcune iniziative ecclesiali promettenti" (Pontificio Consiglio della Cultura, 1999: n. 33); "Internet può offrire magnifiche opportunità di evangelizzazione se utilizzato con competenza e con una chiara consapevolezza della sua forza e delle sue debolezze" (Giovanni Paolo II, *Messaggio per la XXXVI Giornata mondiale delle comunicazioni sociali*, 12 maggio 2002, n. 3); "il fatto che mediante Internet le persone moltiplichino i loro contatti in modi finora impensabili offre meravigliose possibilità alla diffusione del Vangelo" (*Ibid.*: n. 5); "siamo invitati a non esitare a utilizzare la 'rete delle reti' in riferimento all'evangelizzazione. [...] Il Vangelo merita di essere annunciato ed innestato anche in questo nuovo spazio comunicativo e di relazione. Per molti navigatori della rete informatica potrebbe non esserci altro modo di essere raggiunti dall'unica parola che salva" (Conferenza Episcopale Italiana, 2004: n. 173); "molti cristiani stanno già utilizzando in modo creativo questo nuovo strumento, esplorandone le potenzialità nell'evangelizzazione, nell'educazione, nella comunicazione interna, nell'amministrazione e nel governo" (Giovanni Paolo II, Lettera apostolica *Il rapido sviluppo*, n. 9). Inoltre il Pontificio Consiglio delle Comunicazioni Sociali, nel 2002, ha affermato che Internet permette oggi "l'accesso immediato e diretto a importanti fonti religiose e spirituali, a grandi biblioteche, a musei e luoghi di culto, a documenti magisteriali, a scritti dei Padri e Dottori della Chiesa e alla saggezza religiosa di secoli" e favorisce "molte attività e numerosi programmi ecclesiali quali l'evangelizzazione, la ri-evangelizzazione, la nuova evangelizzazione e la tradizionale opera missionaria *ad gentes*, la catechesi e altri tipi di educazione, notizie e informazioni, l'apologetica, governo, amministrazione e alcune forme di direzione spirituale e pastorale" (Pontificio Consiglio delle Comunicazioni Sociali, 2002b: n. 5).

Analizzeremo di seguito la presenza religiosa in rete e le relative sfide (Soukup, 2003) per costruire uno schema che ci aiuterà a scoprire dove si svolga la nuova evangelizzazione in rete e ad elaborare poi una proposta di insegnamento.

4. La presenza religiosa in rete

Per capire meglio le caratteristiche della presenza religiosa in rete, proponiamo di fare una distinzione tra i soggetti che creano nuove "cose" nel ciberspazio e quelli che le usano. Nella prima categoria rientrano i soggetti che sono portati verso la progettazione, promozione e realizzazione di un'opera in rete: può essere una semplice mailing list, una newsletter, un sito Web religioso oppure un blog[7]. Una parte preponderante di questi progetti consiste nella diffusione di notizie e contenuti. Quello che caratterizza questi soggetti è la loro progettualità e, pertanto, li chiamiamo "produttori". Nella seconda categoria rientrano i soggetti che utilizzano la rete per incontrare, dialogare ed ascoltare, perché Internet è un mezzo immediato, interattivo e partecipativo (Pontificio Consiglio delle Comunicazioni Sociali, 2002b: n. 6). Per esempio rispondono alle e-mail, incentivano la partecipazione degli utenti alla gestione di un sito, dedicano ogni sera un periodo del loro tempo a dialogare nelle chat oppure partecipano a progetti cooperativi[8]. Questi soggetti svolgono principalmente un'attività di servizio e, pertanto, li chiamiamo "operatori pastorali in rete".

I produttori hanno tendenza a realizzare siti composti da numerose pagine che offrono principalmente notizie, contenuti multimediali, documenti, ecc. perché la rete è concepita come strumento di comunicazione di tipo "broadcasting". Lo scopo di questi siti – chiamati "vetrina" – è di rendere più visibile l'istituzione religiosa promotrice del sito, le sue attività, le sue proposte, la sua storia e i suoi documenti. Un sito vetrina per antonomasia è quello del Vaticano[9], la cui finalità è rendere disponibili autorevolmente i documenti della Chiesa. Un altro sito vetrina è il sito della Congregazione per il Clero[10], la cui parte più ricca si trova nella sezione "biblioteca". Si tratta di un'enorme raccolta multimediale di testi cattolici suddivisa in ventisei discipline sotto le quali sono raggruppati i documenti disponibili nel sito. Per ogni testo è presente una breve scheda che ne riepiloga il contenuto, l'autore e la data di pubblicazione. Accanto alla scheda si può accedere al testo integrale oppure scaricare il file. Anche il sito parrocchiale è spesso un sito vetrina che contiene informazioni sulla parrocchia, sulla sua storia e sul presbiterio parrocchiale; si possono trovare anche alcuni cenni sulla vita del santo della parrocchia, la presentazione delle attività, dei gruppi e dei movimenti ecclesiali; infine c'è la possibilità di accedere a documenti e materiale per la pastorale, a fotografie degli eventi parrocchiali, ecc.

Un'evoluzione del sito vetrina è il "sito transazionale", che permette all'utente di accedere a varie risorse informatiche. In questo caso la rete viene utilizzata come un canale di accesso alle applicazioni informatiche delle istituzioni. Per esempio gli utenti possono consultare via Internet i cataloghi delle biblioteche (Ridi, 1996: capitolo 3) oppure accedere a banche dati come quella del progetto Beweb[11] della Conferenza Episcopale Italiana, che contiene gli inventari dei beni culturali ecclesiastici. Il sito transazionale favorisce la ricerca di contenuti (tramite motore di ricerca) oppure può proporre servizi informatici più complessi come, ad esempio, aste online per favorire l'incontro tra richiesta e domanda; in definitiva esso gioca sempre un ruolo di interfaccia più o meno evoluta tra l'utente e il sistema informativo. Il sito transazionale dispone quasi sempre di una sezione vetrina per "presentarsi". Per esempio il sito di una biblioteca fornisce, oltre all'accesso al catalogo elettronico, informazioni sull'orario di apertura e sulle condizioni di accesso nella sezione vetrina.

Ma la nuova evangelizzazione in rete richiede di andare decisamente oltre la dimensione del sito vetrina/transazionale. A questo proposito Stefano Martelli scrive che "non si deve confondere l'informazione religiosa – anche se offerta tramite i new media – con l'evangelizzazione. La prima è una presenza relativamente facile e certo opportuna, mentre l'e-vangelizzazione – se vuol divenire annuncio ad una o più persone anche se tramite un computer connesso telematicamente – non può limitarsi ad avvisi o informazioni, ma deve divenire annuncio-in-situazione, anche se virtuale" (Martelli, 2002: 71). Ciò significa che i produttori, nella realizzazione di un sito Web religioso per la nuova evangelizzazione, non possono prescindere da alcuni temi fondamentali della comunicazione pastorale (cf. White, 2001: 163) quali il simbolismo religioso e la narrazione. Infatti i siti orientati alla nuova evangelizzazione hanno una sezione nella quale vengono narrate testimonianze con il linguaggio proprio di Internet, facendo ampio ricorso ad immagini simboliche per ottenere una comunicazione intesa mediante il senso che ad essa attribuisce Robert White, ossia quello di "creazione di un significato condiviso attraverso un processo di interazione comune, sia essa di natura consensuale o conflittuale" (White, 2001: 166).

Gli operatori pastorali invece usano Internet per generare opportunità di incontro e di annuncio, soprattutto con i giovani, perché è proprio dal mondo giovanile che emerge a chiare lettere il desiderio di comunicare. Anche se Internet è un'ottima maschera dietro la quale nascondersi, anche se il dialogo spirituale in rete non è immune da pericoli, la rete offre alla Chiesa la possibilità di ascoltare tante persone che, per diversi motivi, non passano più per i canali istituzionali: parrocchia, oratorio, ecc. Gli operatori pastorali possono costituire un "Web Team" per la creazione di un sito Web interattivo, fatto anche di pochissime pagine, dal momento che esse non sono più basate sul concetto di "contenuto", ma su quello di "servizio" svolto dai membri del Team[12]. La missione di un sito interattivo è favorire sia l'interazione, tra gli utenti e il Web Team e tra gli utenti stessi, sia la partecipazione al sito. I servizi interattivi e partecipativi che il Team di un sito Web religioso può proporre sono tanti; si possono citare i servizi interattivi anonimi che permettono all'utente di interagire in rete con, ad esempio, sondaggi, giochi, quiz, concorsi, ecc. Il sito della parrocchia della Resurrezione di Nostro Signore Gesù Cristo a Roma[13] propone una serie di quiz biblici "online" basati su alcuni quesiti a risposta multipla. I servizi interattivi personali sono basati su "moduli" che permettono all'utente, da una pagina Web, di inviare commenti, suggerimenti, richieste, ecc. al Web Team che risponderà normalmente via posta elettronica. I servizi partecipativi personali sono concepiti per favorire la partecipazione mediante l'invio di materiale da parte dell'utente al Web Team. Il materiale può consistere, ad esempio, in fotografie, brani musicali in formato mp3, preghiere, notizie, ecc. Sarà cura del Web Team pubblicare sul sito una parte o tutto il materiale ricevuto. Un esempio di questo genere di servizio è Qumran[14], basato sulla condivisione di contenuti circa la pastorale giovanile, in modo che l'utente possa partecipare al sito inviando i propri contributi. Infine il Web Team può erogare servizi partecipativi personalizzati con lo scopo di svolgere attività formativa a distanza oppure attività di accompagnamento spirituale in rete. Un esempio di sito con servizi partecipativi personalizzati è il sito "Ti ascolto"[15]. Si tratta di un sito interattivo particolarmente efficace anche se costituito da un'unica pagina Web. In pratica "Padre Net" e "don Server" si rendono disponibili per ascoltare e rispondere a domande formulate dagli utenti tramite un semplice "modulo" che rappresenta il centro della pagina Web. Il dialogo spirituale avviene semplicemente con lo scambio di messaggi di posta elettronica. Un altro esempio è il sito Pretionline[16], concepito da don Giovanni Benvenuto per favorire l'accompagnamento spirituale online. La comunità è composta da più di ottocento sacerdoti pronti a rispondere agli utenti via posta elettronica. Molti operatori pastorali hanno deciso di essere presenti anche nelle chat cattoliche e non, dal momento che le chat, come strumenti di comunicazione in tempo reale, rappresentano un fenomeno di proporzioni incredibili[17]. Esistono tuttavia numerose perplessità sulla possibilità di svolgere un dialogo spirituale in rete. Il primo rischio che gli utenti corrono è la superficialità, molto frequente in rete e conseguenza della cultura postmoderna, che valuta positivamente l'episodico e spinge a vivere il dialogo in rete un po' come un videogioco dove viene negata la complessità dei problemi e dove tutto è semplice ed accettabile. Difficilmente il dialogo in rete va oltre uno schema basato su risposte facili a problemi complessi, oppure su soluzioni semplicistiche e immediate ai problemi. Un altro rischio è legato all'anonimato. Infatti ciascuno può far credere di essere ciò che non è a livello di età, sesso e professione e può dialogare per quello che si sente di essere o di voler essere (Spadaro, 2001: 24). Ciò nonostante, esistono presenze religiose sane nella rete: con esse la condivisione può essere anche molto positiva, nel caso in cui – ad esempio – l'anonimato consenta ad una persona di dire di sé cose che difficilmente direbbe in un rapporto "faccia a faccia"; allora il dialogo può diventare molto aperto, vero e confidenziale. Un esempio per tutti è il caso di "Punto Giovane"[18], i cui operatori pastorali sono attivi in chat dal 1999.

Dall'analisi fatta della presenza religiosa in rete, abbiamo scoperto che la nuova evangelizzazione in rete non viene svolta dappertutto, ma avviene secondo due principali modalità di attuazione. La prima è legata al tema della progettualità e riguarda la creazione, promozione e gestione di un progetto religioso nel ciberspazio, incentrato sulla narrazione di testimonianze e di esperienze religiose con l'utilizzo di immagini simboliche. La seconda è legata al tema del servizio e si basa sullo svolgimento di attività pastorale in rete, sia con siti Web interattivi, sia con una presenza effettiva nelle chat.

Possiamo concludere che Internet è importante per la Chiesa perché la presenza religiosa in rete costituisce una reale opportunità di incontro e di annuncio, dal momento che "rende possibile un primo incontro con il messaggio cristiano, in particolare ai giovani che sempre più ricorrono al ciberspazio quale finestra sul mondo" (Giovanni Paolo II, 2002: n. 3). A questo proposito Antonio Spadaro ricorda che oggi "l'uomo alla ricerca di Dio si pone anche di fronte ad uno schermo e avvia una navigazione" (Spadaro, 2001: 21). Di conseguenza gli studi su Internet sono indispensabili per costruire una presenza religiosa in rete sempre più capace di raccogliere questa sfida.

5. Cosa si dovrebbe insegnare

A questo punto possiamo tentare di delineare una proposta di insegnamento su Internet per le Università Pontificie. Anzitutto la formazione dovrebbe essere rivolta a chi sarà – o è già – responsabile di una presenza religiosa in rete. Si tratta di studenti che vengono chiamati "animatori della comunicazione e della cultura" nel Direttorio sulle Comunicazioni Sociali (Conferenza Episcopale Italiana, 2004: nn. 95-105), il quale dedica il sesto capitolo a descrivere il profilo di questo nuovo protagonista per la missione della Chiesa. Questi studenti vogliono saper utilizzare Internet per comunicare in modo autorevole, per ideare e sperimentare nuovi percorsi di evangelizzazione e per testimoniare la propria fede (cf. Marchessault, 2005).

Nel Centro Interdisciplinare sulla Comunicazione Sociale (CICS), l'insegnamento di Internet iniziò nel 2002 con un semplice corso[19]. Nell'anno accademico 2005-2006 l'insegnamento di Internet è risultato composto di quattro corsi: "Informatica", "Informatica per l'Internet", "Il sito Web religioso: progettazione e realizzazione" e "La presenza religiosa in Internet"; questo insegnamento è inquadrato nella dimensione pratico-pastorale del programma del CICS.

Sulla base dell'analisi condotta circa la presenza religiosa in rete, sarebbe consigliabile organizzare l'insegnamento su Internet in tre aree[20]: la prima riguarda il linguaggio Internet, i servizi base[21] e la loro evoluzione, quali i *social network* e gli ambienti cooperativi; la seconda riguarda temi generali quali l'educazione all'uso critico dei media (Rivoltella, 2001; Conferenza Episcopale Italiana, 2004: n. 73), i pericoli del ciberspazio e l'etica in Internet (Fabris, 2002: 105) e temi specifici, divisi in due specializzazioni distinte ma complementari: una per i produttori e una per gli operatori pastorali in rete; la terza riguarda la dimensione informatica. La proposta dovrebbe anche essere completata con una riflessione sulle modalità di erogazione dell'insegnamento, in presenza o mediata dalla tecnologia, come nel caso dell'*e-learning*.

Poiché i contenuti dell'area relativa al linguaggio Internet sono ben noti, vorrei soffermarmi sulle due specializzazioni e concludere con una riflessione sull'area informatica. La specializzazione per i produttori è finalizzata ad aiutare gli studenti ad acquisire la capacità di valutare le potenzialità di un progetto religioso in rete e successivamente a guidarne lo sviluppo. I temi potrebbero essere il ciclo di vita di un sito Web religioso (progetto editoriale, realizzazione, promozione, motori di ricerca) e i processi inerenti al Web Team. Verranno così approfonditi i modi per scrivere pagine per il Web capaci di generare un processo di interazione da cui trae origine un significato, perché "uno dei motivi principali della crisi della comunicazione pastorale della Chiesa è stato il graduale allontanamento dalla forma narrativa a favore di una comunicazione più analitica e astratta" (Fabris, 2002: 177). L'insegnamento tratterà quindi sia della narrazione di testimonianze tramite tecniche di "Web writing" (ma non nell'accezione di marketing del termine, bensì nel contesto della comunicazione pastorale) che dell'utilizzo delle immagini digitali simboliche tramite la grafica computerizzata. La formazione contemplerà una riflessione su temi inerenti la dimensione etica della produzione in Internet, quali ad esempio il rischio di realizzare siti Web "autistici"[22], a causa del fatto che spesso il Web Team è composto da una sola persona (il produttore), e la possibilità di trascurare l'integrità e l'accuratezza delle notizie pubblicate (cf. Pontificio Consiglio delle Comunicazioni Sociali, 2002a: n. 14). Infine il progetto di formazione si occuperà anche degli standard qualitativi paragonabili a quelli del settore privato e cercherà di sviluppare la capacità progettuale dello studente e la sua capacità a lavorare in team.

La specializzazione per gli operatori pastorali dovrebbe studiare la fenomenologia dell'incontro e fornire indicazioni sulle tecniche del discorso scritto interattivo mediato dal computer, in particolare la posta elettronica e le chat: quello che conta, infatti, non è cosa dire in rete, ma come dirlo. La specializzazione insegnerà a gestire un sito Web interattivo, ad ascoltare e a rispondere a sollecitazioni provenienti dagli utenti (dialogo utente-sito), a proporre spunti di riflessioni (dialogo sito-utente) o a promuovere le comunità virtuali (dialogo utente-utente). La formazione si baserà su esempi concreti di alcune presenze religiose in rete "di successo", in particolare attraverso l'analisi di come siano state realizzate la dimensione dell'ascolto e la dimensione del dialogo, sia con i credenti, sia con le persone e gli ambiti spesso periferici, se non estranei, alla vita della Chiesa.

Oggi è ancora necessario insegnare temi informatici perché essere in Internet richiede numerose conoscenze e competenze; si spera che in un prossimo futuro non sia più necessario farlo. Cercherò di spiegarmi con un esempio preso dalla telefonia. Oggi possiamo affermare che il fatto di telefonare non necessita di alcuna conoscenza tecnica relativa alla telefonia. Ma all'inizio del secolo scorso non era così, visto che telefonare era arduo per tanti motivi: il processo era complesso, i numeri non erano disponibili, lo strumento era manuale, ossia il telefono era dotato di una manovella per chiamare l'operatrice, ecc. La complessità della tecnologia digitale soggiacente ad Internet è oggi dello stesso ordine – se non di ordine superiore – rispetto a quella della telefonia all'inizio del secolo scorso. Finché la tecnologia digitale non saprà farsi dimenticare, l'animatore della comunicazione avrà sempre bisogno di conoscenze informatiche[23] e telematiche[24] e di competenze multimediali[25] per operare efficacemente in rete.

6. Conclusione

Internet è una rete digitale che sta portando profonde modifiche economiche e sociali grazie alla sua natura pervasiva, capace cioè di trovare applicazioni in ogni settore della società. Internet è in costante evoluzione, è diventato un ambiente culturale ed educativo ed è un luogo interattivo e partecipativo frequentato da milioni di persone, credenti e non. Il ciberspazio rappresenta per la Chiesa una formidabile opportunità per la comunicazione di massa, per esempio tramite la pubblicazione di contenuti all'interno di un sito Web, di un newsgroup, di un blog, ecc. e per l'incontro "face-to-face" mediato dalla tecnologia, tramite ad esempio l'utilizzo della posta elettronica e delle chat. La Chiesa è già attivamente presente nel ciberspazio in forme variegate: ci sono siti istituzionali autorevoli e siti provenienti dall'iniziativa personale; siti per informare e divulgare contenuti e siti per la nuova evangelizzazione in rete.

Il Pontificio Consiglio delle Comunicazioni Sociali sottolinea che "la Chiesa riceverebbe un servizio migliore se quanti detengono cariche e svolgono funzioni a suo nome venissero formati nella comunicazione" (Pontificio Consiglio delle Comunicazioni Sociali, 2000: n. 26). Per quanto riguarda Internet, il suo insegnamento in una Università Pontificia dovrebbe focalizzarsi sui temi quali la costruzione di una presenza religiosa in rete, la comunicazione secondo il linguaggio proprio di Internet stesso e la gestione degli incontri in rete, tenendo conto delle caratteristiche specifiche dello strumento: Internet è un mezzo immediato, interattivo e partecipativo (Pontificio Consiglio delle Comunicazioni Sociali, 2002b: n. 6). L'insegnamento relativo alla nuova evangelizzazione in rete sarà aiutato dai temi della comunicazione pastorale, in particolare dal simbolismo religioso e dalla narrazione. Più in generale l'insegnamento di Internet in una Università Pontificia dovrebbe essere completato da corsi provenienti dalle materie fondanti della Comunicazione Sociale, ad esempio la teologia fondamentale per una riflessione sulle condizioni e sugli aspetti che caratterizzano l'evento della comunicazione della rivelazione divina nella storia, la missiologia e la teologia pastorale per una verifica delle opportunità e dei rischi di una comunicazione pastorale in rete. A questo proposito, Giuseppe Lorizio sottolinea che "la comunicazione del credere avverrà solo nella misura in cui anche nella rete ci sarà una comunicazione testimoniale della fede, perché la vera apologia si coniuga felicemente soltanto con la *martyria*, cioè con la testimonianza" (Lorizio, 2000: 44). Possiamo concludere con il famoso detto di Paolo VI: "l'uomo contemporaneo ascolta più volentieri i testimoni che i maestri [...] o se ascolta i maestri lo fa perché sono dei testimoni" (*Evangelii Nuntiandi*, n. 41), assolutamente valido in Internet.

Note

[1] Una posizione molto critica sull'utilizzo di Internet si trova in Breton, 2001.
[2] Cf. la voce "Internet" nell'*Enciclopedia Universale Garzanti*.
[3] Le mailing list e i newsgroup utilizzano la posta elettronica per comunicare. Un esempio di newsgroup cattolico molto attivo in Italia è it.cultura.cattolica (ultima visita ottobre 2005).
[4] Le chat permettono a due o più persone di "chiacchierare" online mediante l'uso della tastiera del PC. Le chat rappresentano un fenomeno di proporzioni incredibili e il motivo di questo enorme successo risiede nell'immediatezza con cui questo fenomeno è capace di raggiungere lo scopo per cui è nato: mettere in contatto le persone.
[5] Il Web è la contrazione della formula World Wide Web, il cui acronimo è "www". Si tratta del sistema ipertestuale di distribuzione dell'informazione sviluppato dal CERN nel 1993. Un sito Web è una collezione di pagine riconducibili ad una medesima responsabilità autoriale o editoriale, e talvolta, ma non necessariamente, caratterizzate da coerenza semantica, strutturale o grafica.
[6] Il browser è il software residente sul Personal Computer che permette di navigare in rete. Il browser più usato è il programma Microsoft Internet Explorer.
[7] Blog è la contrazione di due parole: "web" e "log". Per "log" s'intende un registro, un diario, ecc. I blog sono quindi diari accessibili dal Web. Normalmente i blog sono scritti da una sola persona e sono più o meno incentrati sulla vita personale di chi li scrive; contengono notizie visualizzate in ordine cronologico, dalla più recente alla più vecchia. Per approfondire questo tema, si può consultare l'articolo: Spadaro, 2005a.
[8] I progetti cooperativi sono applicazioni Web disegnate per far collaborare migliaia (a volte milioni) di utenti. L'enciclopedia online Wikipedia *www.wikipedia.org* è un esempio di ambiente cooperativo. Il principio di base è semplice: sfruttare la motivazione individuale per produrre valore per il gruppo. Per un approfondimento di questo tema, si può consultare l'articolo: Spadaro, 2005b.
[9] Cf. *www.vatican.va* (ultima visita: ottobre 2005).
[10] Cf. *www.clerus.org* (ultima visita: ottobre 2005).
[11] Cf. *www.chiesacattolica.it/beweb/* (ultima visita: ottobre 2005).
[12] Gli operatori possono realizzare non soltanto siti Web interattivi, ma anche mailing list, blog, ecc.
[13] Cf. *www.resurrezione.net* (ultima visita: 30/10/2005).
[14] Qumran *www.qumran2.net* (ultima visita: ottobre 2005) è una banca dati di materiale per la pastorale, la più ricca disponibile oggi nella rete cattolica italiana, progettata da don Giovanni Benvenuto e Andrea Ros (ultima visita: ottobre 2005); si può anche consultare "Qumran.net", 2000, 175-177.
[15] Cf. *www.0721.net/ascolto/* (ultima visita: ottobre 2005). Il sito viene descritto in Ruggeri, 2002: 37-43.
[16] Pretionline (*www.pretionline.it*).
[17] Non esistono soltanto le chat, ma anche l'instant messaging; cf. *Teenage Life*, 2001.
[18] Punto Giovane è un progetto di Pastorale Giovanile della Diocesi di Rimini. Nato nel 1998, la pastorale si svolge sia nel mondo reale che in quello virtuale. Accor-

gendosi che tantissimi giovani erano su Internet, nel 1999, Punto Giovane decide di entrare come educatore nel mondo di Internet, di andare nei luoghi dove i giovani sono, utilizzando le chat. Oltre al sito *www.puntogiovane.org* (ultima visita: ottobre 2005) che contiene numerose informazioni sul progetto, si può consultare Mastrolonardo, 2002.

[19] Cf. la pagina "La storia del CICS alla PUG" del sito Web del CICS, all'indirizzo *www.unigre.it/pug/cics/C_B1.htm* (ultima visita: ottobre 2005).

[20] L'autore ha definito un insegnamento secondo questi criteri e ha predisposto un ambiente di prova online disponibile all'indirizzo *www.ananiainrete.it/corsi/*.

[21] I servizi sono: la posta elettronica, le mailing list, le newsletter, i newsgroup, le chat e il Web.

[22] Il termine "autistico" viene usato da Merlini (1999: 30), per caratterizzare i siti Web autoreferenziali, privi di link.

[23] L'uso di Internet richiede oggi la conoscenza del Personal Computer e del suo ambiente software, ad esempio Microsoft Windows. Nozioni di file, di applicazioni, ecc. sono anche indispensabili.

[24] Accedere ad Internet richiede competenze in connettività: reti di computer, modem, collegamento ADSL, Digitale Terrestre, VoIP, ecc.

[25] Competenze sulla musica digitale, sulla fotografia digitale, sulla riproduzione multimediale in rete, ecc.

Riferimenti bibliografici

BRETON, P. (2001), "Internet. La communication contre la parole?", *Revue Etudes*, 394/6, 775-784.

CONFERENZA EPISCOPALE ITALIANA (2001), *Comunicare il Vangelo in un mondo che cambia*, Orientamenti pastorali dell'Episcopato italiano per il primo decennio del 2000, Casale Monferrato: Piemme.

CONFERENZA EPISCOPALE ITALIANA (2004), *Direttorio sulle comunicazioni sociali nella missione della Chiesa*, Città del Vaticano: Libreria Editrice Vaticana.

DEBANNE, X. (2004), "La domanda religiosa in Internet", in G. ZAMBON, ed., *Formazione teologica e comunicazione. Internet: nuova frontiera*, Padova: Federazione Scuole di Formazione Teologica del Triveneto, 43-55.

DE ROSA, G. (2003), "Il clero italiano di fronte alle sfide della modernità", *La Civiltà Cattolica*, n. 3674, III, 105-116.

FABRIS A. (2002), "Etica e comunicazione in rete", in P. AROLDI – B. SCIFO, ed., *Internet e l'esperienza religiosa in rete*, Milano: Vita e Pensiero, 105-116.

GIOVANNI PAOLO II (2002), *Internet: un nuovo Forum per proclamare il Vangelo*, Messaggio per la XXXVI Giornata mondiale delle

comunicazioni sociali, accessibile all'indirizzo *http://www.vatican. va/holy_father/john_paul_ii/messages/communications/documents/ hf_jp-ii_mes_20020122_world-communications-day_it.html*.
LORIZIO, G. (2000), "La Rivelazione: un Dio che comunica", in UCS-SI CEI, ed., *Convegno wwwchiesainrete – Nuove tecnologie e pastorale*, Atti del seminario di Assisi, 9-11 marzo 2000, 42-46.
MARCHESSAULT, G., ed. (2005), *Témoigner de sa foi, dans les médias, aujourd'hui*, Ottawa: Les Presses de l'Université d'Ottawa.
MARTELLI, S. (2002), "Comunicare glocalmente", in P. AROLDI – B. SCIFO, ed., *Internet e l'esperienza religiosa in rete*, Milano: Vita e Pensiero, 47-76.
MASTROLONARDO, F. (2002), "L'esperienza di www.puntogiovane.org", in P. AROLDI – B. SCIFO, ed., *Internet e l'esperienza religiosa in rete*, Milano: Vita e Pensiero, 167-172.
MERLINI, M. (1999), *Pescatori di anime*, Avverbi: Roma.
PONTIFICIO CONSIGLIO DELLE COMUNICAZIONI SOCIALI (2000), *Etica nelle Comunicazioni Sociali*, accessibile all'indirizzo *http://www.vatican. va/roman_curia/pontifical_councils/pccs/documents/rc_pc_pccs_doc _20000530_ethics-communications_it.html*.
PONTIFICIO CONSIGLIO DELLE COMUNICAZIONI SOCIALI (2002a), *Etica in Internet*, accessibile all'indirizzo *http://www.vatican.va/roman_ curia/pontifical_councils/pccs/documents/rc_pc_pccs_doc_20020228 _ethics-internet_it.html*.
PONTIFICIO CONSIGLIO DELLE COMUNICAZIONI SOCIALI (2002b), *La Chiesa e Internet*, accessibile all'indirizzo *http://www.vatican.va/roman_ curia/pontifical_councils/pccs/documents/rc_pc_pccs_doc_20020228 _church-internet_it.html*.
PONTIFICIO CONSIGLIO DELLA CULTURA (1999), *Per una pastorale della cultura*, accessibile all'indirizzo *http://www.vatican.va/roman_curia/ pontifical_councils/cultr/documents/rc_pc_pc-cultr_doc_03061999_ pastoral_it.html*.
"Qumran.net e preti on line", in UCS-SI CEI, ed., *Convegno wwwchiesainrete – Nuove tecnologie e pastorale*, Atti del seminario di Assisi, 9-11 marzo 2000, 175-177.
RIDI, R. (1996), *Internet in biblioteca*, Milano: Editrice Bibliografica.
RIVOLTELLA, P. C. (2001), *Media Education. Modelli, esperienze, profilo disciplinare*, Roma: Carocci.

RUGGERI, G. (2002), *Sussidio Pastorale alle 36a Giornata Mondiale delle Comunicazioni Sociali*, Cinisello Balsamo: Paoline.

SPADARO, A. (2001), "Dio nella 'rete'. Forme del religioso in Internet", *La Civiltà Cattolica*, n. 3625, III, 15-27.

SPADARO, A. (2005a), "Il fenomeno 'Blog'", *La Civiltà Cattolica*, n. 3711, I, 234-247.

SPADARO, A. (2005b), "Wiki. Utopie e limiti di una forma di 'intelligenza collettiva'", *La Civiltà Cattolica*, n. 3722, III, 130-138.

SOUKUP, P. (2003), *Challenges for Evangelization in the Digital Age*, Relazione tenuta il 3 aprile 2003 al Congresso continentale "Iglesia y Informatica", Monterrey, Messico, 2003; accessibile in rete dall'indirizzo *www.iglesiaeinformatica.org/documentos_preguntas.html*

Teenage Life Online: The rise of the instant-message generation and the Internet's impact on friendship and family relationships, Pew Internet & American Online, June 2001. Disponibile sul sito *www.pewinternet.org* (ultima visita: ottobre 2005).

ZUKOWSKI, A. A. (2000), "Un nuovo senso del luogo per l'evangelizzazione: l'era virtuale e il Vangelo", in UCS-SI CEI, ed., *Convegno wwwchiesainrete – Nuove tecnologie e pastorale*, Atti del seminario di Assisi, 9-11 marzo 2000, 49-59.

WHITE, R. A. (2001), "La comunicazione pastorale", in T. STENICO, ed., *Era mediatica e nuova evangelizzazione*, Roma: Libreria Editrice Vaticana, 163-181.

THE THEOLOGICAL-PASTORAL DIMENSION

Recent work in communication and theology: a guide for the CICS*

Paul A. Soukup, SJ

La ricerca recente nei settori di studio su teologia e comunicazione si divide in sette categorie: la teologia pastorale, che si occupa della comunicazione del messaggio cristiano; la teologia applicata, che usa strumenti della teologia per rispondere alle domande sulla comunicazione; l'applicazione di categorie della teologia (Trinità, incarnazione) alla comunicazione per meglio comprenderla; l'uso di strumenti della comunicazione per analizzare testi religiosi; lo studio della comunicazione come contesto per la teologia; l'uso dei contenuti di "testi" della comunicazione (film, televisione, musica) per promuovere la riflessione teologica; e l'uso di strutture della comunicazione per modulare la riflessione teologica. Facendo una rapida panoramica delle sette categorie – attraverso gli autori e le principali tematiche – l'articolo sottolinea i temi comuni, ma anche le debolezze della ricerca in questo campo interdisciplinare.

Theology occupies a small but fairly distinct corner within the larger world of communication. Theology, as the systematic reflection on belief or faith practices, seeks understanding of both individual commitments and corporate actions. And so, theological investigations often begin from materials within the faith tradition, such as the Scriptures, or from cultural practices, such as worship. At other times, theology seeks to understand faith through a dialogue with culture or learning, something apparent in the long association of theology with philosophy.

In these places we also find theological interest in communication, an interest which grows up in two distinct, but related ways. On the one hand, theology follows the path made familiar by philosophy and locates in communication study a lens through which it can view and understand contemporary life and culture. In so doing, it hopes to better understand faith, personal commitment, and ecclesial life. On the other

---

* This essay is based on a paper presented to the 4th International Conference on Media, Religion, and Culture, Louisville, KY, September 2004.

hand, churches look to theology to make sense of the communication culture and, particularly with an applied area like communication, to guide church action. The last century raised churches' awareness of communication and technology as groups produced films, set up radio stations, and developed television ministries. That growth in audiovisual technologies, much more than any expansion of printed resources, led to repeated calls for theological reflection on communication.

Perhaps the most prominent of these calls for theological reflection on communication media came from the Pontifical Council for Social Communications in *Communio et Progressio*: "The whole question of social communications deserves attention from theologians particularly in the areas of moral and pastoral theology. [...] This will be more readily achieved when theologians have studied the suggestions in the First Part of this Instruction [on theological principles] and enriched them with their research and insight" (1971, n. 108). It is in these words that we find the background and justification for the Interdisciplinary Centre for Social Communications (CICS).

Over the years, many other requests for theological evaluation stemmed from a perceived need for guidance in the face of a media culture and of growing religious involvement with mass communication. The rise of the (mostly evangelical) televangelists on cable television in the United States prompted a good deal of concern among the non-evangelical denominations (Horsfield, 1984), which, in turn, led to calls for more theological work.

Early theological interest in communication, then, followed several courses. Jorgenson (n.d.) classifies World Council of Churches' statements into the broad theological themes of evangelization, education (especially for peace), and ethics. Soukup (1983) proposed four dimensions: religious self-understanding, Christian attitudes towards communication, pastoral uses of communication, and ethics and society (p. 21). Many of the earlier theological writings about communication, however, tended to take a purely instrumental view of communication, one criticized by Hamelink (1975) among others as insufficient to understand either communication or culture. Some historical studies highlight a kind of corrective: they note that concerns for what we would today classify as communication media (images, texts, church decor) did elicit nuanced theological responses and rationales in the fifth, ninth, and sixteenth centuries, from Christian theologians such as Augustine, John of Damascus, Gregory the Great, Martin Luther, and Ullrich Zwingli.

Churches or theologians reflecting on communication media, practices, or products tell only part of the story. As a consciousness of communication grew in the later twentieth century, theologians began to use the tools and ideas developed in understanding human communication as part of their own repertoire to seek a better understanding of God and of God's action in creation.

When theologians and communication scholars address one another's concerns in the later twentieth century, they fall into seven general categories: pastoral theology, which communicates the Christian message or supporting communication among believers; applied theology, which answers questions about communication using theological categories (for example, should churches use television?); applying theological categories (Trinity, Incarnation) to communication in an effort to understand communication; using communication tools to analyze religious texts; examining communication as a context for theology; using communication content (film, television, music) to prompt religious reflection; and using communication constructs to inform theological reflection.

This ordering of the general categories is somewhat arbitrary. I have also tried to organize this report from the more typical or more predictable to the more original. Without attempting comprehensiveness, this chapter reviews each of the areas and introduces some of the more recent work at those intersections of communication and theology.

1. Pastoral theology: communicating the Christian message

Among other things, pastoral theology addresses questions of applied communication: how should churches or individuals proclaim the Christian message? What communicative forms best suit religious education? How do people talk about spiritual matters? Where communication study and theology meet here, the typical encounter has theology borrowing the practical advice offered by communication.

Not surprisingly, many writers examine evangelization. Rose, Sander, and Kayser (1998) emphasize the proclamation of the gospel as giving voice to the oppressed. They choose the sender-message-receiver model of communication but insist that theological analysis and priorities (for example, liberation) must precede any actual choice of communication media (p. 267). Using a similar sending and receiving information model, Puloka (1998) emphasizes the need for contextualization in support of evangelization. Dalton (1999) and Flemming (2002) develop similar arguments for contextualization, and both use the example of Paul's preaching in Athens to anchor their analyses. Dalton compares Paul's "communication principles" – critically engage the content of the culture, use the language and discourse of the culture, and know and proclaim the˙ Gospel message (pp. 18-21) – with the practice of G. Ernest Thomas, a well-known Methodist preacher. Flemming cites Paul's Areopagus address as a model of both contextualization and awareness of one's audience. Writing like Puloka from the context of the South Pacific, Teinaore (2001) stresses not only preaching but also witnessing for effective evangelization.

Raja (2000, 2001) presents a carefully developed theology of proclamation for India, basing his thinking on the World Council of Churches' Uppsala statement and on Kierkegaard's model of indirect communication. He notes, "Christian communication is not primarily information about doctrines or about the churches' activities or about Christian faith. It is the process of sharing the experience of God's involvement in people's lives and interpreting the gospel through all forms of communication" (2000: 100). With this in mind, he suggests a contextualization that makes "use [of] the communicative forms that are shared by the audience" (p. 103), in this instance, Hindu forms and musical instruments. These can take their place alongside the more traditional Christian forms of worship and service. Beginning with the parables of Jesus, Raja (2001) develops the argument in more detail, citing not only Kierkegaard (on indirect communication) but also James Carey (on communication as ritual) and Paolo Freire (on the pedagogy of the oppressed).

Sorenson (2000) looks more explicitly at religious ritual as a means of communication. Calling ritual a "universal mode for communicating about the meaning of life and the nature of divine and human powers" (pp. 119-120), he asks: "Is theology involved when Latter-Day Saints participate in these rituals? Virtually every principle and concept of the gospel are brought to attention, either explicitly or by reflection, by the repertoire of rites" (p. 123). Ultimately he argues for the *lex orandi, lex credendi* and notes that increased use of rituals has replaced theologizing in the Latter-Day Saints church as it has expanded and encompasses increasing cultural diversity. Schwier (1998) also stresses ritual, but takes a "ritual as language" approach within worship. He argues for the progression from perception to context to the theological concept.

Communication practice also plays its role in religious education. Steinmann (1997) reports a survey of the understandings of theological terminology in adult Bible study classes, noting that simplicity of language leads to greater effectiveness. Wimberly (1996) develops a theoretical model for the use of narrative and storytelling in African-American religious education. Building on the strong oral traditions in the culture, she argues, "the narrative paradigm involves both remembering the personal and cultural story and *re-membering* a faithful and hope-filled community that is guided by God's Story. [...] Narrative is to be shared" (p. 318). Such pastoral use of stories is another kind of contextualization, as it builds on the existing resources and practices of the community. Jordan (2001), in contrast, stresses not narrative but nonverbal communication as an integral part of theological education.

Knippenberg (1998) publishes a series of essays from a conference on spiritual counseling and spiritual direction. Drawing heavily on the psychological side of communication research, the contributors wrestle with what happens when people communicate, how people communicate, what those communication patterns means for religious/spiritual/theological understanding. Rossi and Soukup (1994) offer a series of essays that address moral theology from a communication perspective. While contributors approach the subject in different ways, the unifying theme is the "moral imagination", particularly as that imagination is formed by and through the mass media.

In each of these areas of pastoral concern (evangelization, ritual, education, counseling, moral theology), communication plays a central role and pastoral theologians have not hesitated to look to communication studies to form a theological approach.

2. Pastoral theology: using communications media

Pastoral theology also addresses what we might term policy questions for the churches: should they or how should they use the mass media? How might Christians evaluate media productions? What theological principles guide these choices?

The most detailed analysis by far comes from Hoover (1993). Writing as part of a symposium for the Mennonite *Conrad Grebel Review*, Hoover, with degrees in both theology and communication studies, provides an overview of communication as well as a careful consideration of the church's position. He sketches the various ways that Christian churches use the media before he turns to options for the Anabaptists. In offering these options, he grounds the discussion in the theological values of the church.

Admittedly, there are many barriers to Anabaptists coming to adapt to the style and approach of the televangelists. First, technology and particularly media technology, has long been problematic for Anabaptist groups. Coming to accept and adopt these devices carries with it today the same sort of dangers and challenges it always has. Second, Anabaptist groups tend to be deliberative and communitarian in discipline and organization. Surrendering to one-man (and media figures tend to be men – another critical issue) power and control to "tell our story" would be a major break with tradition and practice. Third, while Anabaptists do believe in personal transformation, they believe that this must take place in the context of community to be authentic. Fourth, the Anabaptists have not traditionally sought cultural or social acceptance, much less ascendence and power. The fact that the media are largely used for promotion of symbols of power and control, for the Anabaptists makes the media environment one that seems basically at odds with who we are. Fifth, the kind of almost mercenary pragmatism demonstrated by those are the most successful in the media seems also to run counter to some basic Anabaptist social and spiritual precepts. They want to be open to all, to many positions and perspectives and so to eliminate any position or approach simply it does not "work" in the media seems the them to be a confusion of priorities. Finally, they would be unlikely to adapt to a mythology of the media that would put seemingly "mechanistic" approaches to community and discourse ahead of "authentic" (p. 105).

The same issue of the *Conrad Grebel Review* publishes a talk by Roman Catholic theologian Gregory Baum (1993), who notes that Christian attitudes toward the world divide between "liberal" and "radical", with the former being optimistic of inculcating Gospel values in the world while the latter see the Gospel only as a judgment on the world. These attitudes characterize the different approaches of Christian churches to the media as well.

Papathanasiou (1999) addresses the question of church use of the media from the perspective of Christian Orthodoxy. Within a larger context of language and the vernaculars, he concludes that media use is consistent with Christianity; of particular interest is the grounding of his argument in the example of the saints, who did not hesitate to translate the Scriptures and theology into the languages of the various nations.

Peterson (1997) suggests that "public theology" should take a critical perspective on the media and media ownership. This places him more along Baum's radical axis as he asks: "As the Church attempts to be faithful to such traditional values as equality, justice, and human dignity, what should the Church say in criticism of the dominant value of commercial mass media, which is possessive individualism?" (p. 16).

Finally, a report from the World Evangelical Fellowship theological commission consultation (Adeney – al., 1997), raises theological concerns about media use, even within a group that has typically led the way for involvement with the mass media. The commission stresses the need for community, understanding God, clarity in language, and a relationship with God. All derive from the theological analysis of how God communicates with us.

These five essays illustrate the general approach within pastoral theology to questions of media use. A parallel question deals with how the churches should evaluate the media: is television, for example, harmful to Christian living? Having dealt with television in *Communio et Progressio*, the Pontifical Council turned to other media. More recently, it has issued a series of very carefully reasoned statements on ethics in advertising (1997), ethics in communication (2000), and ethics in the Internet (2002). Each statement follows a similar pattern of highlighting the good of the communication media, sketching theological principles (such as community, solidarity, primacy of the human person, 2002, nn. 3-4), and identifying the ethical challenges posed by the media.

3. Theological categories applied to communication

A number of writers apply theological categories to communication, in the attempt to develop a theological model for communication. One highly developed, and quite typical, example of this approach appears in *Communio et Progressio*, which includes references to the Trinity, the Incarnation, and human community as bases for a theology of communication.

More recent writers follow this lead. Peterson (2000) proposes a Trinitarian model for communication when he notes that the Trinity is active in creating and advancing communication (p. 17). He illustrates this for each Person of the Trinity:

> "God said, let there be light" [...] Such a basic interpersonal act of communication, simple speech, can have very creative results. [...] God also created the possibility for mass communication and long-distance communication when he created light.
> The Word becoming flesh is also an act of communication, an act of sharing. It was not possible for God to share our experience as human beings until the Word became flesh. [...] "They were all filled with the Holy Spirit

and began to speak foreign languages, as the Spirit gave them the gift of speech" (Acts 2,4ff). The gift of the Holy Spirit on Pentecost was speech. There are other gifts of the Spirit, but the first gift was the gift of speech in foreign languages (pp. 18-19).

From this, Peterson argues that all human communication should make reference to such biblical models.

Medhurst (2004) seeks to develop a Christian rhetoric, again with reference to biblical values and models. While not ignoring the traditional rhetorical concerns with audience and context, he looks to the teachings of Jesus for central concepts (love of God and neighbor, service, repentance, faithfulness, peacemaking, reconciliation); to biblical metaphors for figurative language; to the witness of the Church Fathers and twentieth century sources like C. S. Lewis, for rhetorical sources.

Kim (1995) also chooses biblical themes to develop a theological understanding of Christian communication. The notion of the People of God or of community flows from such New Testament themes as participation, solidarity, and reconciliation, and stands in contrast to the Old Testament loss of linguistic unity at Babel. Such biblically-informed communication also works to correct the dangers of Western models and globalization. Kaufmann (1994) chooses a starting point grounded in later theology: that of the *sensus fidelium*. This concept refers to the collective belief of the Christian community, and he uses it to examine the social role of communication.

A less typical example of the use of theological categories to illuminate communication practices comes from Boureux (1995) who re-reads Michel Serres in the light of angelology. Serres (1993) likens the role of the mass media to that of the angels in traditional theology. Boureux explores the origins of the concept and proposes that a stronger theological reading of the concept of angels (as divine communication, in the line of Karl Rahner's theology) develops Serres' ideas with more coherence.

Poole (2003), in contrast, reports an historical investigation of how seventeenth century linguists/theologians wrestled with questions of the origins and universality of language. Here the theological presuppositions of the interlocutors influenced their reading of the empirical data before them. While Poole does not develop the theological implications of the debate, he does show how scholars of an earlier era used theological concepts in their concerns about language.

Each of these writers either proposes or summarizes ways that theologians can understand communication on theological grounds. Others turn the tables and explore how communication studies can lead to a better grasp of theology.

4. Communication tools: analyzing religious texts

A number of communication scholars use the methods of study appropriate to their own disciplines to better understand theology. The first group encompasses primarily rhetoricians who choose to analyze religious discourse. Apple and Messner (2001) study the rhetoric of the Christian Identity Movement, a racist group in North America. By applying concepts from apocalyptic and paranoid discourse, they reveal the underlying theological structures in the group's belief system. Gring (1998) approaches the texts of the reflections of the people on revolution in Nicaragua in a similar rhetorical fashion; he, too, makes manifest the theological presuppositions that structured the revolutionary discourse. Litfin (1994) takes on a more ambitious project in his extended study of ancient rhetoric as the background for Pauline discourse. Beginning with 1 Corinthians 1–4, he separates the Pauline theology from the classical and intertestamental period rhetoric, noting how Paul challenges and changes the tradition.

Chase (2003) explores ways "to generate Christian discourses of peace" through an analysis of the rhetorical situation of Christian teaching and the development of two theological principles from the New Testament (the sufficiency of Christ's death, and the ultimate justice of God's judgment). He submits each principle to a rhetorical analysis (following Kenneth Burke and René Girard) to craft an argument that carefully integrates communication tools with theology.

Though not in the direct ambit of Christian theology, studies of Jewish rhetoric also shed light on the theology that developed out of Judaism. Katz (2003), for example, explicates the rabbinical practice of interpretation, one based on the Hebrew alphabet. These practices come to function as a kind of hidden foundation to later Christian practice.

Rather than rhetoric, Hughes (2001) draws on aesthetics as he contrasts theological exegesis and aesthetic exegesis in his examination of the theology illustrated in medieval art. He acknowledges that medieval artists and viewers knew that "artworks can enhance theological ideas and take them in startlingly original directions or create new ones – all by their own visual devices" (p. 185). Focusing on typology, he shows how the artistic use of this Pauline concept sheds light on medieval theology.

Written in a much earlier period but only published in 1999, Marshall McLuhan's reflections on religion offer his typical probing, aphoristic analyses, but in these instances devoted to religious communication and practices. McLuhan is certainly one of the most cited authors by theologians interested in communication. Here, we read his own words as he teases out the deeper communication and cultural consequences of religious texts and rituals.

5. Communication: a context for theology

McLuhan's work provides a bridge to a different approach that communication scholars take towards theology. Following his lead in examining the ecology of the media – that is, the environment that the media create for human living – they argue that this larger media context has an indirect, but nonetheless, indelible effect on theology as communication media make their imprint on human thought and action. A key phrase, "global village", the interaction created by instantaneous communication, stands among McLuhan's enduring ideas. Schüssler-Fiorenza and Corsani (1993) integrate this concept together with feminism to create a larger context for reading the Bible.

Several others look not so much to the global village as to the impact of the forms of media. Boomershine (1995) argues that Christian theology must adjust to the reality of contemporary thought patterns.

> Instead of continuing to invest our energy, our money and our thought in reinvigorating the forms that have made the gospel boring in electronic culture we could reinvestigate our tradition to discover the forms of the religion that will be meaningful in the communication system of electronic culture and invest our energy in them. [...] The tradition of the Church has many forms – story, sacrament, liturgy, song, prayer, icon, poem, proverb, diatribe – that are directly relevant to this culture and that will work in its communication system (p. 97).

Boomershine goes on to encourage churches, pastors, and theologians to develop new forms for theology since the context of contemporary human life has changed so. Weber (1993) similarly argues for a homiletic style matched to the electronic culture in which people live. Following the work on oral cultures of Walter Ong, Green (1999) sees the contemporary world as moving towards a return to oral forms; on this basis we must replace "the bourgeois hegemony of religion", the "'let-me-explain-the-answers-to-you' type of religion" (p. 334) with a theological style that better fits oral patterns: experience, analysis, theological reflection, and action.

Soukup (2002) proposes a more sweeping connection between the context of the media and theology, suggesting that communication forms and affects the approach, the context, and the content of theology. Communication also affects theological method and reception; it has the possibility of offering fresh insights into traditional theological questions. In a later article (Soukup, 2003), he investigates how media forms allow people to substitute one thing for another: the book (Bible) for the temple, information for experience, graphical spaces for ritual places. Soukup, Buckley, and Robinson (2001) argue that similar changes enter into the teaching of theology due to digital media. Berger (1996) makes the point more dramatically, following the reflections of Lanham and Birkerts on the digital world to their logical conclusion. The impact of these media will be profound:

> If, as Lanham and Birkerts so convincingly argue, the electronic media and related rhetorical devices radically alter the way we communicate, even think, how do they affect the way theology is done? The way catechesis is carried out? The way worship is structured and planned? More fundamentally, how do they modify the authoritative status granted to carefully crafted creeds and confessions? (p. 195).

In fact, Berger maintains, such new media will change the nature of the church. They will give the laity a greater prominence in the church, will decentralize church polity, will change religious education, and will even affect pastoral counseling (p. 198). Each of these changes, of course, reflects substantial theological differences from the tradition.

Walhout (1994) presents a carefully crafted explanation of how such changes occur by placing Ong's thought into dialogue with that of Jacques Derrida. After reviewing the challenges posed by Derrida's thinking, Walhout argues that Ong's positions, built on his understanding of orality and literacy and on the impact of communicative forms, may help to resolve some of the theological issues:

> Two lines of argument are implicit in Ong's work, I believe, even though he does not himself develop them. First, his emphasis on the historicity of thoughts and the history of logic itself, supports the view that metaphysics cannot be built on the foundation of reason alone. Logic and theoretical thought have their own histories and are meaningful in the final analysis in relationship to those histories. This view seems to coincide with Derrida's. However, Derrida's claim about the limits of language and thought seems

to be a claim about the limits of understanding generally; the limits of language and of logical uses of language determine the limits of all theorizing. [...] Ong, in contrast, develops a different line of argumentation, namely, that historical interpretation is heuristically more useful and ultimately more basic to human understanding than the internal coherence of logical systems (pp. 448-449).

This larger, partly rhetorical and partly interpretive, context allows theology to develop its themes more freely and with greater historical grounding. Communication, both as media and as content, forms the cultural matrix for such theology.

6. Communication: a source for religious reflection

Another general intersection between theology and communication has the theologian look to the popular culture created by the communication industries. Here, the culture provides sources of theological reflection as well as the locus of inculturation for faith and religious practice. Schultze, Anker, Bratt, Romanowski, Worst, and Zuidervaart (1991) offer a survey of one particular group: youth culture in the electronic media. While they do not specifically address theology, the motivating force for the book is a religious one and they acknowledge as a bias the Reformed Church commitment that they bring: "For us this means, among other things, that the world belongs to God, that God created humankind, that humankind's purpose in life is to magnify the Creator, and that Christians should not only save souls but also transform society and culture for the good of all people" (p. x). The book itself provides a history of popular culture and the ongoing presence of religion and popular religious movements, a review of the entertainment industry, and examinations of popular music, music television, teen films, popular art, and leisure culture. Schultze (2002) continues this kind of work with a detailed consideration of the information society as the cultural matrix for religious understanding and practice. Hess (1993) endorses such approaches, terming them a "hermeneutic of popular culture" and seeing them as a condition for the possibility of theology. Beaudoin (1998) raises theological questions more explicitly as he examines the faith of Generation X. He, too, provides a reading of popular culture and suggests that it forms the theological sensibility of contemporary young people in the United States.

Film studies represents one area that holds continuing interest for theologians. Many regard film as an ideal medium that implicitly engages in theological debate; others take film to be theological in their very nature. May's (1997) collection presents essays that articulate a variety of theoretical positions on the religious and theological dimensions of film, some situated in aesthetics, some in narrative, and some in the specific kinds of consciousness induced by the film going experience. May (2001) takes a different approach, this time using the Apostles' Creed as a theological lens through which to experience film. In this work he suggests particular films to view in conjunction with the various parts of the Creed. Malone and Pacatte (2001, 2002, 2003) similarly tie films to specific faith statements; in their books they propose films for each of the sets of readings in the church's three lectionary cycles.

Marsh and Ortiz (1998) combine these approaches. Their collection includes both theoretical pieces and case studies of individual films that pose theological questions. Marsh's (1998) introductory essay situates the film and theology intersection within the tradition of Niebuhr's *Christ and Culture* and Tillich's method of correlation. After offering correctives to each approach, Marsh suggests the value of film for theology. First, using film in theology is a key way in which Christian theology can work out what it is going to be possible to say in our contemporary climate about any of theology's major themes. Second, using film in theology reminds us of the importance of the public dimension of any Christian theology. In the same way as Tillich's theology can be viewed as apologetics, so also a theology of culture unavoidably enters the realm of missiology. Third, films enable Christian theology to be reminded that it is a discipline which seeks to do justice to the emotional and esthetic aspects of human life, as it deals with life's issues. Fourth, films are vulgar in the sense of being "of/for the people", i.e. they constitute arguably one of the most influential cultural media at the moment in the West today (television alone being perhaps more influential). Fifth, and finally, theology comes much closer to journalism than it may ever care to admit. Theology which takes film seriously reminds itself of its own ephemeral character (pp. 32-33).

Other essays in the book develop these approaches. For example, Graham (1998) takes film as a medium for theology, in which people can experience the religious through the media. In their summary essay, Marsh and Ortiz bring the discussion back to the meaning of incarnation for theology and for contemporary living. A truly incarnational theology takes flight from these considerations of film.

Blake, a film critic, takes a similar approach. He restricts his study (2000) to only six film directors (Scorsese, Hitchcock, Capra, Ford,

Coppola, and DePalma) for his case studies, but introduces them with a careful theoretical statement of how very specific theological themes come through their films. The introductory chapter on Catholic imaging provides an excellent introduction to this kind of theology-in-film approach.

Both Malits (1998) and Hess (1999) incorporate the habit of using popular culture products into their teaching of religious educators and seminarians. Malits recounts how students learn to do theology in dialogue with their (often, youth) culture. Hess, both here and in other, unpublished work, argues that media "texts" form the raw materials out of which people shape their identities and theological understanding. Writing from India, Carr (1995) also raises the issue of identity and explores the role of the media in shaping people's identity. For him, the theological challenge lies in finding a way for the biblical word to inform actions and identities within the media content.

7. Communication: constructs in theology

The final intersection between communication and theology occurs when theologians adopt concepts and ideas from communication study to enrich or resolve issues within theology. The last 10 to 15 years has seen more and more theologians conversant enough with communication to adopt its tools.

A. *Language*

Communication scholars and linguistic philosophers have long examined how language works, particularly in specialized or restrictive settings like religious discourse. Both Austin (1975) and Searle (1979) single out liturgical and theological language as they develop the theory of speech acts – the theory that language goes beyond description to action. De Jong (2001) follows Searle's distinction between illocutionary and perlocutionary acts to analyze theological language and theological practice about talking about God, especially in catechesis and daily talk. In this project, De Jong attempts to restate theological understandings of meaningful expression in the light of speech act theory, recovering as he does so the classical theological concept of participation. In his study, he provides a different grounding for theological hermeneutics.

De Jong and his colleagues turn also to the insights from social constructionism to illuminate religious language. Hermans (2002) explains:

Therefore, the focus of this chapter will be on the anthropologic side of religious communication instead of the "theistic side" [...] [C]ommunication is challenged not so much by the otherness of God [...] but by the separateness of other people, each expressing different religious viewpoints. Here social constructionism is useful because it stresses the transformative power of dialogue. [...] [T]he main topic of this chapter concerns the idea that truth in religious communication is relative to meaning within a certain tradition, place and time and form of life (pp. 113-114).

Since the social construction model within communication challenges individualism, Hermans sets up a contrast between two models of God. Borrowing terminology from Bakhtin, he calls them the author hero-God and the polyphonic author-God. In the former, "God gives form to the life of the hero" (p. 135) and encounters humans in a kind of personal dialogue, a situation Hermans judges more fitting for a premodern context. The latter model allows for many voices and for the larger human community to play a role, along with greater levels of uncertainty in God-talk.

Rather than examining the social context of religious communication, Parmentier (2001) examines the form of that communication. She takes the inspiration for her theology from studies of narrative. In so doing, she wishes to reclaim narrative, especially biblical narratives, for theology in the light of contemporary research. "During the last 30 years, research on narratives in different areas of human sciences has led theology to reconsider the story, not only as an educational tool, but as a basic structure of the theology itself" (p. 29).

B. *Communicative action*

Moving beyond these questions of religious discourse, a group of primarily German theologians has fairly systematically explored communication as the conditions for theology itself. Building on the communicative action theory of Jürgen Habermas and largely following the lead of Helmut Peukert (1984) in fundamental theology, they examine the theological implications of communicative action.

A number of papers and essays appear in works edited by Edmund Arens (1995, 1997). Lamb (1995) follows Peukert to examine the church (the kingdom of God): communicative action gives an approach to truth to balance power. He sees connections with nature, history, and culture (and in this way opens the theological dialogue to include Benjamin and Adorno). For him, the communicative emphasis on action leads to an emphasis on community. In the same volume, Schreiter

(1995) builds a bridge from communicative action to intercultural communication. In his view, this combination calls for a rethinking of theology from an intercultural hermeneutic and praxis, with more attention paid to reception, the need to bring practical theology together with systematic theology, the consideration of identity, and the rethinking of evangelization. The 1997 book more explicitly sets out points of dialogue with the thought of Habermas, with contributors addressing questions of faith, theological aesthetics, eschatology, inspiration, consensus, and church structure.

Pieterse (1998) provides a comprehensive English-language introduction to the theological theory of communicative action, albeit from the perspective of South African theology. Because of the importance of reconciliation in South Africa, a theology that stresses dialogue and domination-free communication acquires a vital interest. He writes:

> The concept of communicative actions is built on Habermas's idea of the ideal speech situation. [...] From the perspective of Jesus' communicative actions religious communication in all its facets ought to be domination free. It should be conducted on an equal footing with the freedom of every participant to bring her/his own perspectives, interpretations and ideas to the communication on and of, our faith (p. 185).

In this kind of dialogue, the partners must include not only believers, but also the Scriptures, their history of interpretation, and the contemporary understanding of the tradition.

Hawkins (2000) also uses concepts from the ideal speech situation, but draws more on Apel's ethical readings. Because of his interest in Christian millennialism, his essay suggests the "reign of Christ with the martyrs" from Revelation 20, 4-6 can function as the ideal communication community. In so doing, he situates the variants found in the millennial movements in theology.

Fresacher (2001) takes up the theme of participation, particularly participation within the church and theology. He criticizes fundamental theology for not adequately incorporating the "turn to society" (in the theory of communicative action). In his view, fundamental theology depends too much on "its two dominant trends of theory formation, to subject-oriented reasoning ('anthropological theology') and to consensus-oriented theory ('communio-theology'). Communication, however, differs both from subjective consciousness and from collective community" (p. 283). He proposes a more comprehensive model of both communication and social reality that can work as a new ground for theory formation in theology.

Afrasiabi (1998) remains skeptical of the whole project. He feels that theologians have uncritically accepted Habermas's approach, including his secular orientation. He summarizes his argument in this way:

> Contrary to what has become an article of faith in recent theological forays into social theory, I contend: (a) that Habermasian theory has little to contribute to theological thought and is more valuable as an indirect aid in critiquing various deficient theological discourses, and (b) that the current Habermas-sympathetic attempts at a communicative theology are, by and large, open to criticism for the same shortcomings and problems found in Habermas's own works: and (c) that the need to address these problems necessarily points us toward an alternative post-communication theology (p. 75).

In this very thorough article he attempts to situate each of the theologians in the communicative action movement. But even acknowledging their contributions, they still fall short.

> Despite its usefulness as a critique of deficient theologies illustrated above, one of the problem with communicative theology, as formulated by Peukert and others, is that it is limited in its freedom to reconstruct the theoretical framework within which its theology works itself out. It is exposed to the syndrome of a methodological atheism that forms a specific barrier to the stated objective of a transcendental hermeneutics. To elaborate, communicative theology is wedded to Habermas's pragmatic theory of meaning, in which meaning is assimilated to intersubjectivity. This is, however, precisely what makes communicative theory a theology-nullifying endeavor; the theological leanings nullified are those that belong to the elements of "God-consciousness". This corresponds to the dissolution of any sense of foundational "transcendental grounding" (p. 81).

Afrasiabi then offers a corrective in the proposal of a "post-communicative" theology, in other words a theology that offers a self-conscious critique of communication and the role of communication in society and in religious discourse.

C. Church

While the communicative action approach touches in some ways on the nature of the church, other communication approaches are possible. Granfield (1994) presents a collection of essays that root the understanding of the church in communication concepts ranging from symbol formation, dialogue, personal witness, and interaction technologies. Granfield himself suggests a cybernetic model. Cornelius (1995) applies a model involving acceptance theory to the local parish.

D. Self-communication

Although Karl Rahner's term to describe God's activity, "self-communication", has resonance with communication, he did not derive the term from communication study. However, a number of theologians have turned more explicitly to communication in order to develop this key idea. The most creative and detailed project appears in Beeck (1991), which seeks to resolve several issues in the theology of revelation. After a critique of the impact that Enlightenment models of knowledge have had on theology, Beeck attempts to recover Patristic insights about the relation of the immanence of God and revelation. To do this, he turns to communication studies and the distinction between the content and relational components of any interpersonal communication. In constructing his argument, he demonstrates first the anthropological infrastructure for revelation: that communication is both process and content; that interpersonal self-communication presumes the other and implies the possibility of transcendence; that interpersonal communication implies both responsibility and freedom; that communication requires the role of tradition; and that interpersonal communication has transcendent preconditions. Then he applies this by analogy to divine revelation, which occurs, he says, not from the outside, but in relationship.

Molnar (1997) uses the concept of "self-communication" to contrast the theologies of Rahner (Roman Catholic) and Thomas F. Torrance (Reformed). For Rahner, "self-communication" describes the human person as well as God.

> Thus, creatures have a positive affinity, given by grace, to the Christian mysteries of faith which he [Rahner] conceptualizes as our obediential potency and supernatural existential. The former refers to our openness to being (as spirit in the world) and as such it refers to our openness to God's self-communication, at least as a possibility. This potency is [...] our human nature as such. If the divine self-communication did not occur, our openness toward being would still be meaningful [...], we are by nature possible recipients of God's self-communication, listeners for a possible divine word (p. 306).

Self-communication, then, both establishes and describes revelation and the human participation in the divine mystery, a mystery which includes "the self-communication of God in the depths of existence, called grace, and in history, called Jesus Christ, and this already includes the mystery of the Trinity in the economy of salvation and of the immanent Trinity" (p. 307). Torrance, too, explores the relationship between theology and science (particularly human knowing). He considers both natural theology and the resurrection and holds that the resurrection, as a unique event, is the point of scientific access to God's self-communication. In examining the two theological traditions, Molnar finds keys differences, especially in doctrine of immanent Trinity, but acknowledges the similarities in the desire to unite fundamental and dogmatic theology. While both theologians use the concept of "self-communication", they understand it differently; neither draws directly on communication study.

The consideration of "self-communication", especially by Beeck, includes some sense of interpersonal communication. Several other theologians use this construct in developing their thinking. Gorsuch (1999) incorporates an interpersonal model in her understanding of revelation.

> Three understandings of revelation have been discussed in relation to their meaning and role in pastoral theology: a cooperative view of sensing and laboring with God's presence in creation, the notion of collision between Christian and personal narratives, and the analogy of interpersonal communication which reclaims mutual relationship and its ongoing development as the content of revelation (p. 45).

Muers (2001) also looks to interpersonal communication as a model for revelation; however, her focus is more on listening and speaking, contact and silence. Finally, Hedahl (2000) puts interpersonal listening at the heart of Lutheran theology, but in this case, listening in multiple contexts, ranging from revelation to homiletics to pastoral counseling.

8. Conclusion

While communication remains a minor part of contemporary theology, it also retains its place as a contact between theology and culture, between theology and the human person. This review of more recent writings on theology and communication reveals a number of important things. First, some theologians do take communication seriously as a dialogue partner, as something which says something significant about being human. Second, these theologians have an increasingly sophisticated understanding of communication; they have moved beyond the simple sender-message-receiver model to models that include culture, structures, and audiences. Third, theologians with an interest in communication work together more and more to develop their ideas. Fourth, the Christian churches and theologians show a greater understanding of the importance of popular culture in the identity of believers. Fifth, communication scholars also show a growing interest in theology.

On the other hand, this review reveals several weakness. First, those theologians showing the greatest interest in communication draw only indirectly on communication studies. For example, the group around Peukert and Arens, which considers communicative action, draws inspiration from Habermas, a philosopher. Their knowledge of communication seems filtered through his approach rather than directed by communication scholars. The same applies to the work of Beeck, whose ideas about interpersonal communication come more from philosophical analysis, and De Jong and his colleagues, who draw on the philosophy of language tradition. Second, a similar weakness applies to communication scholars interested in theology.

Third, an interpersonal communication model dominates theological reflection. Few people seem to develop their ideas from mass communication study. Here, much of the writing about communication and theology still regards communication only in an instrumental fashion. Some, while addressing important questions, content themselves with pointing out problems rather than resolving them. Few have undertaken historical studies of theology to see how "the story takes a different form if you structure it around communication" (Edwards, 1994: 171).

Comment on popular culture products always runs the risk of succumbing to the ephemeral. However, those with an interest in communication and theology should begin an investigation into those doing theology in forms other than the traditional printed statements or sermons of the churches, other than in theological journals. Christians throughout the centuries have expressed their theology in art, music, and ritual. In today's culture, we should expect to find theologians working in film, television, and graphic novels. One can only wonder whether those associated with a program like "Joan of Arcadia" regard themselves as theologians. The topics they explore (Does God exist? Does God communicate with us? How do we discern what is of God?) certainly sound like theological ones.

Bibliographical references

ADENEY, M. – AL. (1997), "Reflecting on the role of media in communication in the ministries of the church", *Evangelical Review of Theology* 21, 37-40.

AFRASIABI, K. L. (1998), "Communicative theory and theology: A reconsideration", *Harvard Theological Review* 91, 75-87.
APPLE, A. A. – MESSNER, B. A. (2001), "Paranoia and paradox: The apocalyptic rhetoric of Christian Identity", *Western Journal of Communication* 65, 206-227.
ARENS, E., ed. (1995), *Anerkennung der Anderen: Eine theologische Grunddimension interkultureller Kommunikation*, Freiburg im Breisgrau: Herder.
ARENS, E., ed. (1997), *Kommunikatives Handeln und christlicher Glaube: Ein theologisches Diskurs mit Jürgen Habermas*, Paderborn: Ferdinand Schöringh.
AUSTIN, J. L. (1975), *How to do things with words* (2nd ed., ed. J. O. Urmson – M. Sbisà), Cambridge, MA: Harvard University Press.
BAUM, G. (1993), "Christians in the communications media", *Conrad Grebel Review* 11, 137-144.
BEAUDOIN, T. (1998), *Virtual faith: The irreverent spiritual quest of generation X.*, San Francisco: Jossey-Bass.
BEECK, F. J. van (1991), "Divine revelation: Intervention or self-communication?", *Theological Studies* 52, 199-226. Also (1997) in W. R. BARR, ed., *Constructive Christian theology in the worldwide church*, Grand Rapids: Eerdmans, 14-40.
BERGER, D. O. (1996), "Theology in the brave new world", *Concordia Journal* 22, 189-200.
BLAKE, R. A. (2000), *Afterimage: The indelible Catholic imagination of six American filmmakers*, Chicago: Loyola Press.
BOOMERSHINE, T. E (1995), "The Polish cavalry and Christianity in electronic culture", *Journal of Theology* (United Theological Seminary) 99, 90-102.
BOUREUX, C. (1995), "Une angelologie apollinienne: Convergences et divergences theologiques a propos de *La Legende des Anges* de M. Serres", *Revue des sciences philosophiques et theologiques* 79, 283-292.
CARR, D. (1995), "Communication, identity and the church: A theological reflection", in *Communication and human dignity*, Delhi: ISPCK, 86-95.
CHASE, K. R. (2003), "Christian discourse and the humility of peace", in K. R. CHASE – A. JACOBS, ed., *Must Christianity be violent? Reflections on history, practice, and theology*, Grand Rapids, MI: Brazos Press.

CORNELIUS-BUNDSCHUH, J. (1995), "Brucken bauen" – Kritische Anmerkungen zu einem Kommunikationsmodell fur evangelische Kirchenkreise", *Evangelische Theologie* 55/4, 373-391.

DALTON, R. W. (1999), "'Electronic Areopagus': Communicating the Gospel in multimedia culture", *Journal of Theology* (United Theological Seminary) 103, 17-33.

DE JONG, A.(2001), "God in our talk", in H.-G. ZIEBERTZ – F. SCHWEITZER – H. HÄRING – D. BROWNING, ed., *The human image of God*, Leiden, Boston, Köln: Brill, 193-214.

EDWARDS, M. U. (1994), *Printing, propaganda, and Martin Luther*, Berkeley: University of California Press.

FLEMMING, D. (2002), "Contextualizing the Gospel in Athens: Paul's Areopagus address as a paradigm for missionary communication", *Missiology* 30/2, 199-214.

FRESACHER, B. (2001), "Kommunikation: Leitbegriff theologischer Theoriebildung: fundamentaltheologische Anstosse", *Zeitschrift für katholische Theologie* 123 (2-3), 269-283.

GORSUCH, N. J. (1999), "Revelation and pastoral theology: Cooperation, collision, and communication", *Journal of Pastoral Theology* 9, 35-48.

GRAHAM, D. J. (1998), "The uses of film in theology", in C. MARSH – G. ORTIZ, ed., *Explorations in theology and film: Movies and meaning*, Oxford: Blackwell, 35-43

GRANFIELD, P., ed. (1994), *The church and communication*, Kansas City, MO: Sheed & Ward.

GREEN, L. (1999), "Oral culture and the world of words", *Theology* 102, 328-335.

GRING, M. A. (1998), "Attention, power, and need: The rhetoric of religion and revolution in Nicaragua", *World Communication* 27/4, 27-37.

HAMELINK, C. (1975), *Perspectives for public communication: A study of the churches' participation in public communication*, Baarn, Holland: Ten Have.

HAWKINS, C. S. (2000), "The millennium and the ideal speech community", *Review and Expositor* 97/3, 355-365.

HEDAHL, S. K. (2000), "Installation address – Gettysburg Lutheran Theological Seminary", *Seminary Ridge Review* 2/2, 53-61.

HERMANS, C. A. M. (2002), "Ultimate meaning as silence: The monologic and polyphonic author-God in religious communication", in C. A. M. HERMANS – G. IMMINK – A. DEJONG – J. VAN DER LANS, ed., *Social Constructionism and Theology*, Leiden, Boston, Köln: Brill, 113-145.

HESS, J. D. (1993), "Toward a hermeneutic of popular culture", *Conrad Grebel Review* 11.
HESS, M. E. (1999), "From trucks carrying messages to ritualized identities: Implications for religious educators of the postmodern paradigm shift in media studies", *Religious Education* 94, 273-288.
HOOVER, S. M. (1993), "What do we do about the media?", *Conrad Grebel Review* 11, 97-107.
HORSFIELD, P. G. (1984), *Religious television: The American experience*, New York: Longman.
HUGHES, C. (2001), "Visual typology: An Ottonian example", *Word and Image* 17/3, 185-198.
JORDAN, S. (2001), "Embodied pedagogy: The body and teaching theology", *Teaching Theology and Religion* 4/2, 98-101.
JORGENSON, L. (n.d.), "The WCC and communication: A survey of the discussion so far. Geneva: World Council of Churches" [Although not dated, this report seems to have been written in 1982, in preparation for the WCC Vancouver Assembly in 1983].
KATZ, S. B. (2003), "Letter as essence: The rhetorical (im)pulse of the Hebrew alefbet", *Journal of communication and religion* 26, 126-162.
KAUFMANN, F. X. (1994), "Glaube und Kommunikation: eine soziologische Perspektive", in D. WIEDERKEHR, ed., *Glaubenssinn des Gottesvolkes – Konkurrent oder Partner des Lehramts*, Freiburg im Breisgrau: Herder, 132-160.
KIM, Y.-B. (1995), "The Church in Asia and people's struggles: Towards a Gospel for life", in *Communication and human dignity*, Delhi: ISPCK, 67-85.
KNIPPENBERG, T. van, ed. (1998), *Between two languages: Spiritual guidance and communication of Christian faith*, Tilburg: Tilburg University Press.
LAMB, M. L. (1995), "Kommunikative Praxis, die Offenheit der Geschichte und die Dialektik von Gemeinschaft und Herrschaft", in E. ARENS, ed., *Anerkennung der Anderen: Eine theologische Grunddimension interkultureller Kommunikation*, Freiburg im Breisgrau: Herder, 167-192.
LITFIN, D. (1994), *St. Paul's theology of proclamation: 1 Corinthians 1–4 and Greco-Roman rhetoric*, Cambridge, UK: Cambridge University Press.
MALITS, E. (1998), "Teaching theology by exploring the ordinary", in E. O. SPRINGFIELD, ed., *Spirituality and theology*, Louisville, KY: Westminster/John Knox Press, 124-132.

MALONE, P. – PACATTE, R. (2001), *Lights, camera... faith!: A movie lover's guide to Scripture (A movie lectionary – cycle A)*, Boston: Pauline Books and Media.

MALONE, P. – PACATTE, R. (2002), *Lights, camera... faith!: A movie lover's guide to Scripture (A movie lectionary – cycle B)*, Boston: Pauline Books and Media.

MALONE, P. – PACATTE, R. (2003), *Lights, camera... faith!: A movie lover's guide to Scripture (A movie lectionary – cycle C)*, Boston: Pauline Books and Media.

MARSH, C. – ORTIZ, G. (1998), *Explorations in theology and film: Movies and meaning*, Oxford: Blackwell.

MAY, J. R., ed. (1997), *New image of religious film*, Kansas City: Sheed & Ward.

MAY, J. R. (2001), *Nourishing faith through fiction: Reflections of the Apostles' Creed though literature and film*, Franklin, WI: Sheed & Ward.

MCLUHAN, M. (1999), *The medium and the light: Reflections on religion*, ed. E. McLuhan – J. Szklarek, Toronto: Stoddart.

MEDHURST, M. J. (2004), "Religious belief and scholarship: A complex relationship", *Journal of Communication and Religion* 27, 40-47.

MOLNAR, P. D. (1997), "God's self-communication in Christ: A comparison of Thomas F. Torrance and Karl Rahner", *Scottish Journal of Theology* 50/3, 288-320.

MUERS, R. (2001), "Silence and the patience of God", *Modern Theology* 17/1, 85-98.

PAPATHANASIOU, A. N. (1999), "The language of Church and world: An adventure of communication or conflict?", *Ecumenical Review* 51, 40-45.

PARMENTIER, E. (2001), "Le récit comme théologie: Statut, sens et portée du récit biblique", *Revue d'histoire et de philosophie religieuses* 81/1, 29-44.

PETERSON, C. (1997), "Theology and mass media from a critical perspective", *Covenant Quarterly* 55/1, 14-22.

PETERSON, C. (2000), "Communication, media, and the Christian life", *Covenant Quarterly* 58/2, 17-26.

PEUKERT, H. (1984), *Science, action, and fundamental theology: Toward a theology of communicative action* (trans. J. Bohman), Cambridge, MA: MIT Press.

PIETERSE, H. J. C. (1998), "A theological theory of communicative actions", *Religion and Theology/Religie and teologie* 5/2, 176-194.

PONTIFICAL COUNCIL FOR SOCIAL COMMUNICATIONS (1971), *Communio et Progressio*. Retrieved July 5, 2004 from *http://www.vatican.va/ roman_curia/pontifical_councils/pccs/documents/rc_pc_pccs_doc_ 23051971_communio_en.html*
PONTIFICAL COUNCIL FOR SOCIAL COMMUNICATIONS (1997), *Ethics in Advertising*. Retrieved July 5, 2004 from *http://www.vatican.va/ roman_curia/pontifical_councils/pccs/documents/rc_pc_pccs_doc_2 2021997_ethics-in-ad_en.html*
PONTIFICAL COUNCIL FOR SOCIAL COMMUNICATIONS (2000), *Ethics in communications*. Retrieved July 5, 2004 from *http://www.vatican.va/ roman_curia/pontifical_councils/pccs/documents/rc_pc_pccs_doc_ 20000530_ethics-communications_en.html*
PONTIFICAL COUNCIL FOR SOCIAL COMMUNICATIONS (2002), *Ethics in Internet*. Retrieved July 5, 2004 from *http://www.vatican.va/ roman_curia/pontifical_councils/pccs/documents/rc_pc_pccs_doc_2 0020228_ethics-internet_en.html*
POOLE, W. (2003), "The divine and the grammarian: Theological disputes in the seventeenth century universal language movement", *Historiographia Linguistica* 30/3, 273-300.
PULOKA, T. T. M. (1998), "Evangelization: Culture and communication", *Pacific Journal of Theology*, ns 19, 42-54.
RAJA, J. (2000), "Church and sign of contradiction: Relevance of Kierkegaard's concept of indirect communication to Indian churches", *Bangalore Theological Forum* 32/2, 94-107.
RAJA, J. (2001), *Facing the reality of communication: Cultures, church and communication*, Delhi: ISPCK.
ROSE, M. – SANDER, L. M. – KAYSER, I. (1998), "Comunicação", *Estudos teologicos* 38, 252-272.
ROSSI, P. J. – SOUKUP, P. A. (1994), *Mass media and the moral imagination*, Kansas City, MO: Sheed & Ward.
SCHREITER, R. J. (1995), "Theories und Praxis interkultureller Kommunikationskompetenz inder Theologie", in E. ARENS, ed., *Anerkennung der Anderen: Eine theologische Grunddimension interkultureller Kommunikation*, Freiburg im Breslau: Herder, 9-30.
SCHULTZE, Q. J. (2002), *Habits of the high-tech heart: Living virtuously in the information age*, Grand Rapids: Baker Academic.
SCHULTZE, Q. J. – ANKER, R. M. – BRAAT, J. D. – ROMANOWSKI, W. D. – WORST, J. W. – ZUIDERVAART, L. (1991), *Dancing in the dark: Youth, popular culture and the electronic media*, Grand Rapids, MI: William B. Eerdmans Publishing Company.

SCHÜSSLER-FIORENZA, E. – CORSANI, M. (1993), "Leggere la Bibbia nel 'villaggio globale': Riflessioni teologiche femministe", *Protestantesimo* 48/2, 80-93.
SCHWIER, H. (1998), "Blickrichtungen im Gottesdienst: Pladoyer fur ein elementares Modell", *Jahrbuch für Liturgik und Hymnologie* 37, 87-97.
SEARLE, J. R. (1979), *Expression and meaning: Studies in the theory of speech act*, Cambridge, UK: Cambridge University Press.
SERRES, M. (1993), *La legende des Anges*, Paris: Flammion.
SOUKUP, P. A. (1983), *Communication and theology: Introduction and review of the literature*, London: World Association for Christian Communication.
SOUKUP, P. A. (2002), "The context, structure, and content of theology from a communication perspective", *Gregorianum* 83/1, 131-143.
SOUKUP, P. A. (2003), "The structure of communication as a challenge for theology", *Teologia y Vida* 44/1, 102-122. [Facultad de teologìa, Universidad Catolica de Chile, Santiago].
SOUKUP, P. A. – BUCKLEY, F. J. – ROBINSON, D. C. (2001), "The influence of information technologies on theology", *Theological Studies* 62, 366-377.
STEINMANN, A. E. (1997), "Communicating the Gospel without theological jargon", *Concordia Theological Quarterly* 61, 201-214.
TEINAORE, R. (2001), "From communication to communion", *Pacific Journal of Theology*, ns 26, 55-68.
WALHOUT, C. (1994), "Christianity, history, and literary criticism: Walter Ong's global vision", *Journal of the American Academy of Religion* 62, 435-459.
WEBER, D. C. (1993), *Preaching to be heard in a television age: A study of the homiletical response to the modern media context*. Unpublished Thesis (PhD), Edinburgh: University of Edinburgh.
WIMBERLY, A. S. (1996), "An African-American pathway to hope: Belief formation through uses of narrative in Christian education", *Religious Education* 91, 316-333.
WORLD COUNCIL OF CHURCHES (1968), "The Church and the media of mass communication", in *The Uppsala report 1968*, Geneva: World Council of Churches, 389-401.

Verso una teologia pastorale della comunicazione nell'era globale

Giuseppe Mazza

This article begins with a critical terminological explanation and tries to explore the inner structure of pastoral communication from the point of view of fundamental theology. The author outlines the resources and difficulties of a modern concept of pastoral theology of communication in the face of today's challenges, including its basic foundations. Further clarification reveals the analogical principle that balances and synchronizes both pastoral communicative action and the globality of God's self-communication, as the main concept for understanding and stimulating every operative pastoral dimension.

Il presente contributo, partendo da un excursus terminologico ragionato, si preoccuperà di inquadrare la struttura epistemica della comunicazione pastorale da un punto di vista teologico-fondamentale capace di coglierne gli aspetti di attinenza e di problematicità per rapporto alle sfide dell'età contemporanea, le radici fondanti e il principio analogico che, unendo vitalmente l'azione pastorale alla globalità dell'autocomunicazione divina, diviene anche criterio e stimolo per le sue concrezioni operative.

1. Terminologia e collocazione epistemica

L'esistenza di una dimensione comunicativa nell'azione pastorale della Chiesa è oggi praticamente indiscussa. A qualificarla intercorre una ricca e complessa terminologia, la cui varietà e mutevolezza non ha avvantaggiato una pur necessaria chiarificazione del campo, già azzardata, in verità, sin dalla metà del secolo scorso in ambito tanto cattolico quanto protestante. Le prime avanguardie teologiche che mostrarono interesse verso le dinamiche comunicazionali preferirono assommare sotto l'unica dizione di "teologia della comunicazione del vangelo" le già complesse problematiche legate ai risvolti comunicativi dell'azione pastorale (così, ad esempio, nell'impostazione protestante del *pastoral counseling* in S. Hiltner, 1958). In pratica, il discorso teologico non smise mai di riferirsi all'intreccio relazionale tra comunicazioni e pastorale, anche se finì per dissimulare dietro una coltre di termini e significati differenti il naturale imbarazzo derivante dal non poter mettere ordine in un campo di ricerca fin troppo fluido e variabile. Nacquero le espressioni più varie: comunicazione pastorale, prassi comunicativa, comunicazione religiosa. Ciascuna di esse compendiava, con maggiore o minore enfasi, il riferimento alla *comunicazione del vangelo* e, fatte le dovute eccezioni per qualche caso, una forte influenza derivante dai *modelli lineari* della comunicazione sociale.

La riflessione degli ultimi anni, com'è noto, ha integrato la semplice acquisizione (a tratti ingenua) dell'interazione operativa tra pastorale e comunicazioni attraverso un'analisi più rigorosa di alcuni degli elementi che la qualificano, come il contesto/ambiente dell'annuncio e della ricezione del messaggio, la tipologia e l'entità delle eventuali distorsioni, il valore del *frame reference*, l'attenzione alla bidirezionalità o multidirezionalità dei vettori comunicativi.

Il guadagno che si prospettava – tanto per la pastorale e la riflessione teologica su di essa, quanto per una comprensione più equilibrata delle comunicazioni stesse – era ovviamente legato ad altri fattori che disponevano ad una riflessione più matura. Parliamo evidentemente delle intuizioni sviluppate nel campo della teologia della rivelazione soprattutto dopo il Vaticano II, ed alla peculiare considerazione riservata al carattere *globale* della comunicazione divina, al suo *aspetto dinamico* (processuale, relazionale, ecc.) prima che al suo *contenuto oggettivo*.

Il legame tra teologia e comunicazione si rivelò, com'è facile prevedere, più complesso di quanto potesse sembrare a prima vista. Da un lato divenne chiara la necessità, ancora oggi molto sentita, di "sviluppare lo studio di una teologia della comunicazione che non si annoveri tra le ormai codificate teologie del genitivo, ma *all'interno della teologia pastorale*". Ad essere interpellata non è, in termini generici, semplicemente una delle tante possibili coniugazioni del discorso teologico e, con esso, dell'ecclesiologia: si tratta piuttosto di "riflettere su una ermeneutica della storia per un discernimento che sappia cogliere la *possibilità*, oltre che l'attualità, *della prassi credente*", al fine di ripensare creativamente nuove forme dell'essere Chiesa e nuovi stili di attestazione per le dinamiche dell'annunzio cristiano (Viganò, 2004: 216; i corsivi sono nostri). Il taglio necessariamente ecclesiologico di tutta la riflessione sull'azione pastorale non può prescindere dal *carattere globalmente comunicativo* dell'*essere* e del *fare* Chiesa. Devono considerarsi definitivamente superati i tempi in cui comunicazione e azione pastorale si trovavano congiunti sono nell'esplicitazione di alcuni esercizi di funzionalità comunicativa da parte delle comunità (evangelizzazione, attività missionaria, processi di inculturazione, dialogo culturale ad intra e ad extra, predicazione, catechesi, accompagnamento spirituale, celebrazioni liturgiche) o nell'approfondimento di alcuni sotto-temi di interesse ristretto (opinione pubblica nella Chiesa, rapporto gerarchia-laicato, autorità e dissenso, rapporto magistero-teologia, collegialità, ermeneutica degli enunciati dogmatici, ecc.). *Tutta la Chiesa è e fa comunicazione*: la dimensione comunicativa appartiene alla struttura epistemologica (fondamentale) di ogni modello ecclesiologico, qualunque esso sia[1].

Non si tratta, come è stato osservato, di "scrivere una teologia della comunicazione o una pastorale della comunicazione, ma di ripensare la teologia e la pastorale partendo dalla constatazione che *la salvezza si realizza fondamentalmente in un atto di comunicazione*": si tratta di partire, quindi, da un punto di vista fondamentale (Lever, 2002: 96; il corsivo è nostro). Ci sembra quindi importante insistere sul fatto che una teologia dell'azione pastorale, *prima che teologia pastorale, debba innanzitutto essere teologia fondamentale* e, in considerazione di questo, debba gradualmente inquadrasi non più (solo) come *teologia della comunicazione pastorale*, quanto piuttosto come *teologia pastorale della comunicazione*[2]. Tale impostazione fondamentale permetterà, in seguito, una riflessione più ponderata tanto sull'assunto per cui la Chiesa sia comunicazione, quanto sulle modalità concrete di *come* possa esserlo, in un dialogo efficace con le istanze del postmoderno. È precisamente in questi termini e con questo ordine di priorità che vogliamo sviluppare la nostra riflessione: crediamo infatti che un'efficace pastorale delle/nelle comunicazioni potrà aver luogo solo a partire da un contesto teologico-fondamentale, che sappia scoprire le sue radici multidimensionali ed il costante, imprescindibile legame con la globalità della comunicazione divina.

2. Risorse e sfide nell'età della dimenticanza di Dio

Quali nuove sfide e quali nuove risorse si prospettano per la comunicazione pastorale, all'inizio del Terzo Millennio? Le istanze fondamentali a partire dalle quali dovranno imporsi un nuovo stile ed un nuovo ordine di maturità pastorale richiedono anzitutto la disincantata consapevolezza di un contesto socio-culturale che sperimenta (o costruisce?) l'assenza di Dio. La contemporaneità è chiamata insistentemente a registrare che "una percezione religiosa della realtà non fa parte della nostra cultura", tanto da lasciar avvertire con urgenza la necessità di una "restaurazione del significato religioso simbolico di oggetti ed eventi nel linguaggio della sfera pubblica": opera tutt'altro che agevole (White, 2001: 188). Nuova creatività pastorale viene richiesta in relazione a un vissuto frammentato, in cui scompare il senso del gruppo-comunità (familiare, affettiva) e prevale quello dell'individualità, e nel quale non esistono più comunità omogenee, ma solo segmenti sociali diversamente connotati (giovani, anziani, lavoratori, ecc.). La dislocazione effettivamente prodotta dalla grande mobilità geografica e sociale e la pluralità dei sistemi valoriali oggi recepiti stimolano inoltre il dovere di ripensare la nostra concreta capacità di comunicare come "narratori" significativi e qualificati al cospetto di una contemporaneità distratta e spesso disinteressata (cf. *Ibid.*).

È stato suggerito, in passato, che buona parte delle difficoltà che giungono alla comunicazione pastorale derivino sostanzialmente dall'intreccio dei complessi fattori che relazionano emittenti, recettori e codici in uso per la diffusione del messaggio cristiano. Dalla prospettiva dell'emittente, svolgono un ruolo critico l'immagine e la coerenza della comunità cristiana, mentre giocano nettamente a sfavore la frequente carenza di modelli di identificazione proponibili al mondo, la mancanza di professionalità e la carenza di contenuti di qualità e di metodologie discorsive. Dal punto di vista del recettore, condizionano negativamente l'incapacità di cogliere il messaggio come proposta di pienezza di vita (prima che come imperativo e/o proibizione), l'assenza di una formazione critica all'uso dei media, di un confronto dialogale e comunitario. Dalla prospettiva del codice, infine, ciò che scoraggia è un linguaggio a volte troppo "tecnico", istituzionale, distante o, in molti casi, troppo "interno" e autoreferenziale (cf. Ramos, 1997).

Dal un punto di vista specificamente teologico, però, riteniamo che siano anche altri i fattori che influenzino oggi le applicazioni e l'efficacia della comunicazione pastorale. Intanto, è certamente da annoverare tra le sfide e i nodi problematici aperti il forte senso di de-verticalizzazione della proposta di senso delle micro-culture brulicanti sullo scacchiere planetario: lo smarrimento di una trascendenza intesa in senso cristiano (Dio personale e/o tripersonale) diventa la più immediata chiave per l'interpretazione del crollo di interesse per le metanarrazioni e per la nozione stessa di verità (assoluta). La "paralisi" operativa che consegue a molti relativismi della contemporaneità produce di fatto un "esilio" dalla realtà, dalla sua fruizione più immediata e dal carattere vincolante del regime normativo in essa vigente. Ne nasce la tipica e ben nota "anomia selvaggia" del virtuale, popolato da presenze che dissimulano la propria identità, negoziandola e sfumandola continuamente. A questi nodi problematici corrispondono, però, almeno altrettante risorse: alla de-verticalizzazione corrisponde, quasi paradossalmente, un continuo desiderio di progresso e di emancipazione. Si tratta di un'ansia di (auto)superamento che articola le sue spinte prometeiche non più verso cieli troppo alti, ma verso la finitezza e la compassione nei riguardi di ciò che termina e decade. È la fedeltà al finito, al presente, che costituisce la vera attenzione postmoderna: a partire da qui, al crollo delle epistemologie e alla liquidazione del concetto di verità assoluta si sostituisce la cura della "verità" del finito stesso, da ricercarsi in ogni angolo di ciò che esiste, anche e soprattutto in quegli angoli più bui e dimenticati dalle epopee metafisiche della storia. Al già visto esilio dal reale si accompagna una sorta di mobilità "esodale" ed un nuovo concetto (dinamico) dell' "aver casa" in mezzo alle cose. Il reale stesso non viene dichiaratamente rifiutato, ma subisce una sorta di reinterpretazione che vi innesta le dinamiche del possibile, del virtuale, dell'immaginativo e dell'onirico. L'essere umano vi si installa mediante nuove, potenziate capacità relazionali ed una più consapevole sensibilità prospettica, simbolica e olistica (cf. Mazza, 2005: parte prima).

Proprio in questo senso, cioè a partire da questa ritrovata sensibilità nei riguardi del "tutto" e del nesso simbolico-associativo fra le sue parti, si può oggi ripensare una nuova coniugazione teologico-fondamentale dell'azione pastorale. Essa può offrirsi concretamente come rivisitata attenzione "religiosa" verso quella semiosi universale che la contemporaneità è già di per sé in grado di recepire come rete, sistema globale di riferimenti incrociati e inclusivi. La reintegrazione – proposta da R. White (2001) – di un simbolismo in grado di incidere nella sfera del linguaggio pubblico potrebbe assumere esattamente questa forma: quella, cioè, di una risposta teologica finalmente adeguata alle risorse/capacità percettive dell'età contemporanea, una risposta capace di articolare iniziative di azione e comunicazione pastorale *dal di dentro* di quella sfera di interesse in cui l'uomo di oggi realizza e interpreta se stesso.

3. Radici teologiche

Quali sono o potrebbero essere le radici teologiche di questa auspicata, nuova "corripondenza" tra la comunicazione pastorale e le istanze della contemporaneità? Certamente, esse non potranno discostarsi da alcune idee teologiche forti che hanno inteso normare la comunicazione della fede nell'ultimo secolo e particolarmente dopo il Concilio Vaticano II. Si tratta del riferimento imprescindibile alla centralità di Cristo, perfetto comunicatore e Parola stessa di Dio, e la qualificazione di questa centralità come pienezza di vita e salvezza per quanti credono. Ciò che però merita particolare approfondimento, all'interno e non al di fuori di questa stessa impostazione teologica, è il delicato rapporto di costante mediazione che essa stessa suppone. È possibile riconoscere un *carattere peculiarmente analogico della parola*, tanto divina quanto umana, in quello che potremmo considerare un processo di incessante scambio di idiomi: parliamo di una sorta di osmosi di "grammatiche" del dono che congiunge, non senza scarti problematici dovuti alle impurità della traduzione/riduzione storica, la parola di Dio alla parola in/di Cristo, questa alla parola sacramentale e quest'ultima, a sua volta, alla parola del mondo, nella sua ampiezza e varietà di orizzonti e nella sua plurivoca declinazione culturale.

Alle sorgenti di tutto, questa radicale analogia – che potremmo definire *strutturale*, costituendo l'intelaiatura stessa dell'essere comunicativo tanto di Dio quanto dell'uomo – ci richiama al carattere *kenotico* di quel dono che è di per sé la rivelazione. Nel suo dirsi all'uomo, Dio con-discende donandosi: si dona in un linguaggio che assume, integralmente e senza riserve. Prima di tutto, però, dev'essere chiaro che *Dio può comunicarsi "globalmente" perché, nell'Incarnazione, si è offerto come presenza "globale"*. Proprio facendosi uomo, Dio compie e universalizza il proprio dono all'uomo: sceglie di parlare da uomo, per l'uomo, con l'uomo. La comunicazione di Dio, con e attraverso la rivelazione della/nella carne del Figlio eterno, assume dimensioni globali, onniavvolgenti, onnicomprensive, dal momento che, accogliendo la "voce" della carne, assume di fatto diritto di asilo nel circuito del linguaggio e pregnanza nel gioco della semiosi universale, *habitat* umano per eccellenza in quanto dall'uomo continuamente popolato e (ri)strutturato.

È in questo senso che vogliamo anzitutto intendere la rivelazione nel suo essere fondamento della comunicazione pastorale: come *"esser-ci" interessato* di una Presenza che si dona (cf. Mazza, 2005: parte seconda, soprattutto cap. 3). Dio sceglie di mettersi in mezzo, di essere con e per le sue creature. L'essere trinitario di Dio si dona proprio come esserci, *inter-esse* originario che struttura la sua Presenza nel mondo attraverso la rivelazione (Mazza, 2005: 7; cf. anche 84-86, e tutta la parte terza sulla prospettiva trinitaria). Essa raggiunge l'uomo in ogni aspetto del suo essere e della sua storia: nel suo desiderio di farsi, di progredire, di crescere (meccanismi performativi) e nella sua capacità di sperimentare, nell'intimo, la radicalità di un appello che lo trascende (meccanismi osmotici). Dio dunque si comunica rispondendo all'uomo in tutto ciò che esso è e chiede per sé, senza riserve: lo incontra "in tempo reale", lo visita nella sua stessa umanità, che fa propria. La comunicazione Dio-uomo diventa orientamento per ogni protocollo di comunicazione che voglia abbracciare efficacemente e multidimensionalmente il suo oggetto. In questo senso possiamo dire che Dio (per la sua comunicazione all'uomo) norma la comunicazione umana (verso di Lui stesso, verso gli altri uomini e verso il mondo). Lungi dall'essere una restrizione, ciò appare felicemente consono a quanto esigono oggi le istanze della contemporaneità "globale", preoccupate del rispetto assoluto di tutte le dinamiche dell'essere umano: le stesse assunte – integralmente – dalla rivelazione divina.

4. Il principio analogico: una comunicazione globale per una rivelazione globale

Sicut in caelo et in terra: è dunque sulla rivelazione "globale" di Dio che può essere ricalcato un rinnovato paradigma di comunicazione pastorale "globale". Lo stesso riferimento ad una "pastoralità" della Chiesa non può prescindere da quello stato "incarnazionale", dinamico e sempre potenziale, mediante il quale la comunità dei credenti contestualizza in maniera "globale" la propria identità ed esercita la propria funzione salvante e liberante, proprio sulla base del modello divino. Come declinare, però, questo genere di interazione globale?

Dovrà trattarsi evidentemente di una comunicazione che testimoni una *chiara credibilità* e diventi *naturalmente rilevante* per il postmoderno. È definitivamente concluso il tempo delle comunicazioni unidirezionali ed incapaci di valutare la propria stessa ricezione, considerandola di importanza marginale. Il successo di una comunicazione pastorale all'altezza della nostra era sta invece in un'attenzione tutta speciale alla "connaturalità" comunicativa tra l'emittente, il messaggio ed i suoi possibili recettori: proprio sul modello, anche in questo caso, del Dio che ha preso carne per parlare ad ogni carne. Dovrà, in altri termini, offrirsi come *comunicazione "dimensionata"*, proporzionata cioè alle coordinate ed ai registri espressivi/recettivi dell'essere umano, capace di farsi capire e di capire, di accogliere e di farsi accogliere. In funzione di ciò, dovrà necessariamente essere *plurivoca e plurale*, *strutturata e strutturale*, senza per questo smettere di essere *kairologica*. Dovrà rendersi capace di rimandare alla *mediata immediatezza* di un *contatto asintotico* con il divino, sempre prossimo eppure mai del tutto raggiunto, gustato ma mai "posseduto", contro ciò che invece propongono le facili utopie delle nuove religiosità e le loro semplicistiche "isotropie" del sacro. Si tratterà piuttosto di una comunicazione capace di *accettare la totalità "infranta" del postmoderno*, e soprattutto il *finito* come dono e compito: insegnerà quindi ad "abitare" il mondo, a non fuggire da esso, a rileggere le tracce dell'Assenza-Presenza di Dio nei sentieri del tempo e della storia, anche in quelli più nascosti e dimenticati. Si tratterà, insomma, di una comunicazione capace di trovare *nell'umanità* la grammatica della rivelazione divina e, proprio per questo, capace di porsi sempre più in "religioso ascolto" della "parola" del proprio essere storico per comprendere ogni comunicazione (per queste osservazioni ed altre simili, cf. Mazza, 2005: conclusioni).

Le dimensioni operative dischiuse alla comunicazione pastorale saranno almeno tante quante sono le prospettive di un possibile approccio al reale dal punto di vista (variabile) dell'interazione che con esso hanno le creature umane. Un buon comunicatore sa che il suo compito non si esaurisce mai nella mera trasmissione verbale di un messaggio, ma deve sempre tener presente uno spettro molto ampio di spazi di risonanza. Essi si identificano con dimensioni che tradizionalmente non è sempre stato immediato riconoscere come luoghi di comunicazione: il cosmo, la sensibilità/sensorietà, la ritualità (Mazza, 2005: parte quarta). Circa il rapporto peculiare che esiste tra ciascuna di esse e la comunicazione sarebbe doveroso offrire una trattazione separata, cosa che purtroppo qui non ci è concessa. Possiamo però tracciare di seguito almeno alcune delle linee operative in cui potrebbe incarnarsi una comunicazione globale nell'era della globalità.

5. Le dinamiche operative: una proposta

Un'orientazione teologica correttamente modulata sugli schemi della globalità implica l'urgenza di applicare alla comunicazione pastorale linee operative conformi alla sua natura multidimensionale. La prima esigenza cui occorre far fronte riguarda senza dubbio un'opportuna *correzione dei modelli lineari di comunicazione*, in ordine ad una comunicazione-scambio veramente interattiva. Ciò comporta, sul fronte pastorale, il bilanciamento degli schemi relazionali sulla base di criteri di *reciprocità* ed *uguaglianza in dignità* comunicativa. Solo in questi termini è veramente pensabile la progettazione e l'interpretazione di un *sistema* di comunicazione nelle cui variabili non risultino occultati, bensì piuttosto messi in risalto i valori dell'interscambio simbolico, della libertà e creatività del consenso, del dialogo interattivo (Bartholomäus, 1978: 168).

Parlare di *consenso*, in merito alla comunicazione legata all'azione pastorale, è sempre stato considerato rischioso. In realtà, la "felice intesa" tra i soggetti – realizzata attraverso la costruzione condivisa del significato, negoziato ed articolato secondo codici comuni – è una condizione imprescindibile per evitare la "reificazione" costrittiva dei partners in relazione (Bartholomäus, 1978: 167). Dev'essere ben chiaro che il fatto di comunicare pastoralmente non può semplicemente consistere in un processo di trasmissione preoccupato anzitutto di inoculare proposizioni "vere". Entro limiti ragionevoli, tanto il linguaggio quanto il contenuto della comunicazione pastorale dovranno trovare nella situazione concreta (effettivo spazio comunicativo) dei due partners a confronto la "fonte teologica" della propria conoscenza e conoscibilità (Bartholomäus, 1978: 181).

Questa consapevolezza apre di fatto le porte alla rivalutazione della *complessità intrinseca* del fenomeno comunicativo, anche e soprattutto in ambito pastorale. È qui che infatti si fa tangibile l'esigenza di una *comunicazione a 360 gradi*, in cui l'individuo sia davvero capace di organizzare "tutte le forme della sua estrinsecazione vitale", sfruttando "le sue possibilità cognitive (percezione, pensiero), emozionali (sentimento) e normativo-pratiche (azione, etica, diritto)" (Bartholomäus, 1978: 169). La comunicazione pastorale, lungi dall'offrirsi come blanda sintesi del gioco delle grammatiche e dei linguaggi del sacro, diventa l'interfaccia attraverso cui l'intera esistenza creata viene posta in grado di interpretare la *parola di Dio sul mondo* e di trasformare se stessa, nella complessità di tutte le sue componenti, in *parola del mondo su Dio*. Si tratta di due dimensioni complementari. L'esigenza di parlare in modo nuovo, più "umano" o anche più comprensibile di Dio, deve sempre fare i conti con le esigenze di una teologia "comunicativa" che sappia incorporare l'interesse per l'esperienza creata nel quadro di investigazione del suo "oggetto" formale. D'altra parte, si fa sempre più presente il bisogno "di vedere in che modo – teologicamente giustificato – la stessa realtà d'esperienza possa diventar segno simbolico di una presenza liberata di Dio" (Bartholomäus, 1978: 182). Liberare la comunicazione umana perché impari a *dire tutto di Dio* significherà così darle una possibilità in più per *dire tutto dell'uomo*, sul modello di quella relazionalità libera e liberante che costituisce la comunicazione globale di Dio.

Non insisteremo mai abbastanza circa la necessità, per l'azione pastorale, di affacciarsi responsabilmente sulle sponde della comunicazione globale secondo un approccio definitivamente e genuinamente a misura d'uomo. Il punto di partenza potrà essere, in questo senso, ciò che abbiamo altrove identificato come una *fenomenologia-estetica della sensorietà* (cf. in questo senso Mazza, 2005: 549-600). Nell'era della "nuova oralità" riconosciuta e descritta da Ong e da McLuhan, l'azione pastorale della Chiesa ha il suo bel da fare nel garantire diritto d'asilo a quelle formule di predicazione del messaggio cristiano che per secoli sono state codificate quasi esclusivamente entro i protocolli della verbalità. Le nuove sfide comunicative richiedono un impegno più audace e un investimento più creativo in nuovi moduli relazionali che includano, accanto alla codifica auditiva, un'analoga presa in carico dei canali della visualità e della tattilità. Ciò comporta, in altri termini, un'assunzione senza riserve dell'espressività umana "globale", non circoscritta solo a quei canali relazionali più facilmente riconoscibili per la loro plasmabilità comunicativa. È un "dire" cui corrisponde un ascolto polisensoriale, avvolgente e totale: una parola "plurale" i cui centri di irradiazione si dislocano in maniera speculare rispetto agli equivalenti nodi nevralgici della costruzione di senso propria della sensibilità postmoderna. È, in ultima analisi, uno spazio di visibilità della parola incarnata che, comunicata all'uomo, dalla carne stessa – dalla carne del cosmo, dalla carne della storia, dalla carne della temporalità – vuole essere riverberata in tutta la ricchezza del suo spettro diffusivo. È questa *processualità incarnazionale*, a nostro avviso, la dinamica operativa più feconda per un'iscrizione dell'azione pastorale nei circuiti di fruizione dell'era globale.

6. Conclusioni

La comunicazione pastorale – ci sembra di poterlo dire – non può evitare oggi di avanzare una proposta di "domiciliarità" globale per il messaggio globale di Dio verso l'uomo. I campi di applicazione in questo senso non mancano: dalla ritualità alla simbolica dell'interiorità, dall'ermeneutica del complesso alle convergenze macrocosmiche della semiosi universale, molti sono gli stimoli in ordine all'esigenza di (ri)attivare uno specifico livello di attenzione verso la ricchezza multidimensionale di quel messaggio il cui annunzio è al cuore dell'azione pastorale. Totalizzante il messaggio ricevuto, totalizzante l'annunzio da offrire; globale sin dalla sua divina scaturigine la parola comunicata, globale nelle sue umanissime declinazioni la sua stessa riproposizione:

è solo equilibrando questa formula che la comunicazione pastorale onorerà il delicato compito di essere sinergia "incarnata" tra l'autocomunicazione divina e la sua stessa, lussureggiante risonanza nella "carne" del creato.

NOTE

[1] "La comunicazione non esprime soltanto un ambito della prassi ecclesiale: è una dimensione dell'essere e dell'agire della chiesa stessa. Non c'è niente nella chiesa che si possa precludere ad una elaborazione teoretico-teologica evoluta entro questa prospettiva" (Bartholomäus, 1978: 166). Ancor di più, "si potrà comprendere l'importanza del tema della comunicazione soltanto se sarà chiaro che la chiesa non intrattiene dei rapporti e non produce degli effetti soltanto quando a questo mirano le sue intenzioni. Il suo agire comunicativo viene definito mediante l'effetto comunicativo, il quale però va riconosciuto ad ogni comportamento umano. È dunque impossibile non comunicare" (*Ibid.*). La Chiesa, struttura comunicativa in sé e non solo nelle sue funzioni, partecipa di quel processo di (auto)comunicazione con cui Dio si è voluto e vuole rivelarsi all'umanità (cf. in questo senso Dulles, 1971).

[2] Si tratta di un punto di vista che ci sembra essere più completo ed aggiornato rispetto a quello presupposto dalla definizione di D. Felton, per cui "a pastoral theology of communication seeks to give expression within theology as a whole to the questions and issues raised by Communication practice, activities, and decisions; and reflects upon Scripture and tradition to formulate pastoral communication goals, and plans for communicators and their communication activities" (Felton, 1989: 20).

Riferimenti bibliografici

BARTHOLOMÄUS, W. (1978), "La comunicazione nella chiesa. Aspetti di un tema teologico", *Concilium* 14/1, 165-187.

DULLES, A. (1971), *The Church is Communication*, Roma: Multimedia International.

FELTON, D. A. (1989), "The Unavoidable Dialogue: Five Interfaces between Theology and Communication", *Media Development* 36, 17-23.

HILTNER, S. (1958), *Preface to Pastoral Theology. The Ministry and Theory of Shepherding*, Nashville, NY: Abingdon Press.

LEVER, F. (1992), "Mass media e catechesi", in B. SEVESO – L. PACOMIO, ed., *Enciclopedia di pastorale*, II, Casale Monferrato: Piemme.

MAZZA, G. (2005), *La liminalità come dinamica di passaggio. La rivelazione come struttura osmotico-performativa dell'inter-esse trinitario*, Roma: Editrice PUG.

RAMOS, J. (1997), "Pastoral de la comunicación", in D. BOROBIO – J. RAMOS, ed., *Evangelización y medios de comunicación*, Salamanca: Publicaciones Universidad Pontificia Salamanca, 129-150.

VIGANÒ, D. E. (2004), "La Chiesa nella società dei media. Per una pastorale della comunicazione", *La Rivista del Clero Italiano* 85, 209-221.

WHITE, R. A. (2001), "La comunicazione pastorale", in C. GIULIODORI – G. LORIZIO, ed., *Teologia e comunicazione*, Cinisello Balsamo: San Paolo, 187-210.

Comunicar a Palavra da Cruz

Nuno Brás Martins

Even if this is difficult, the dialogue between the culture of the media and Church culture is inevitable. In this dialogue, we discover communication as a reality that characterizes and structures both human experience and the Christian revelation. In effect, revelation defines itself as the self-communication of God in Jesus Christ: God communicates God's-own-Self to human beings in the person of Jesus. Jesus is much more that one who uses in an exemplary, perfect way the techniques of oral communication to speak directly to people living in an oral culture. Jesus and his communication remain active because of the "scandalous" event in which all communications appear to fail: the Cross. This is what St. Paul calls the "word of the Cross" or the "Gospel", and it is this word that must distinguish all of Christian communication.

1. Um diálogo inevitável

No final de decénios de mútua desconfiança – que poderemos classificar mesmo de "demonização" dos *media* por parte do magistério eclesiástico (em que, apesar de tudo, se foram dando alguns passos na mútua compreensão: cf. Soares, 1998) – com a época conciliar, e, em particular com os grandes gestos mediáticos do Papa João XXIII, bem como com a cobertura essencialmente positiva que a imprensa efectuou do Concílio Vaticano II, Igreja e comunicação social pareciam ter caído, definitivamente, nos braços uma da outra, numa aliança perpétua[1].

Contudo, depois de uma certa euforia, mesmo optimismo, que se estendeu aos anos imediatamente posteriores à publicação da Instrução Pastoral *Communio et progressio* (1971), as relações entre *Media* e Igreja voltaram de novo a esfriar[2]. Os *media* continuaram o seu percurso e a sua lógica globalizante, justificando com as audiências conseguidas os caminhos imparáveis que percorriam. Por seu lado, a Igreja continuou a ter dificuldade em se adaptar ao mundo mediático, cada vez mais determinante da cultura contemporânea. Durante estes últimos anos, existiram e existem figuras eclesiais que conseguiram, não sem dificuldades e incompreensões, "brilhar" simultaneamente no mundo eclesial e naquele mediático: é o caso exemplar da pessoa do Papa João Paulo II. Mas estas figuras constituíram e constituem uma excepção à regra, fazendo, por isso mesmo, ressaltar a dificuldade que a maioria dos homens de Igreja e a própria cultura eclesial têm em conviver com o mundo dos *media*.

Ao mesmo tempo, os *media*, conscientes do seu lugar de *condottieri* culturais ignoraram progressivamente a Igreja. No entanto, apesar desse esquecimento, a Igreja constitui uma realidade que, apesar de tudo, persiste em barrar o passo à lógica de erosão social que caracteriza a cultura mediática, pelo simples facto de fazer apelo a realidades centrais da existência e com as quais, mais tarde ou mais cedo, qualquer ser humano se confronta. O mundo dos *media* sente claras dificuldades em dominar essas realidades últimas, que estão para além dos seus limites, apesar das inúmeras tentativas de produções no domínio do "fantástico" e no campo da *New Age* que, obtendo sucesso num primeiro momento, mostram, finalmente, toda a sua fragilidade. Talvez aí encontre justificação o silêncio dos *media* (conscientes de que uma realidade que não aparece nos seus produtos deixa de existir) ou o sublinhar do lado ridículo (ultrapassado) ou incoerente das atitudes de muitos eclesiásticos (como no caso do escândalo de pedofilia dos sacerdotes americanos).

Esta lógica de confronto entre dois horizontes culturais diferentes foi reconhecida pelo Papa João Paulo II na sua mensagem para o Dia Mundial das Comunicações Sociais de 1999. Dizia então o Papa: "É verdade que a cultura da Igreja e a cultura mediática são diferentes; existe, com efeito, acerca de certos pontos, um contraste muito forte". Mas logo depois acrescentava: "Não há razão alguma para que as diferenças tornem impossível a amizade e o diálogo. Muitas das amizades mais profundas encontram precisamente nas suas diferenças o encorajamento da sua criatividade e os seus laços recíprocos" (João Paulo II, 1999). João Paulo II apontava, de seguida, três pontos de confronto mas também de possível diálogo entre estas duas culturas: a recordação eclesial frente às novidades transitórias, a sabedoria da Igreja em contraste com a informação e a alegria do Evangelho por oposição ao divertimento mediático.

Poderão estes dois modos de entender a vida humana conformar-se com uma mútua ignorância? O comportamento "esquizofrénico" é uma das características do homem mediático: ele assume perante os produtos dos *media* atitudes que depois não deixa de condenar quando procura realizar um discurso "razoável" e consciente. Pode parecer pois que uma certa esquizofrenia em termos religiosos seja apenas mais uma das muitas com as quais a cultura mediática tão bem convive. O facto, no entanto, é que a dimensão religiosa do homem não tem exclusivamente a ver com um apartado da sua existência mas com a sua totalidade. Mais tarde ou mais cedo, cada ser humano confrontar-se-á com o sentido da sua vida. Sobretudo, confrontar-se-á com a realidade da morte – daqueles que o rodeiam e da sua própria morte – e com a necessidade de encontrar o sentido para as questões últimas e fundamentais que ela coloca. Os *media* poderão, uma vez mais, procurar distrai-lo das questões últimas e fundamentais, mas essa distracção não poderá subsistir eternamente nem ser a última atitude perante a vida: a um dado momento a distracção torna-se mesmo insuportavelmente banal, a ponto de colocar em causa toda a construção mediática da existência.

Por outro lado, a Igreja não pode ignorar a cultura dos *media*. Ela é demasiado central para passar despercebida ou para ser olhada com o desprezo de quem tem o seu coração na eternidade[3]. Os *media* e a cultura que deles deriva constituem um sinal dos tempos no mundo contemporâneo – como todos os sinais dos tempos também este está ferido pela ambiguidade que caracteriza todas as realidades humanas; mas, como todos eles, também a centralidade dos *media* constitui um sinal da presença de Deus na história (cf. Fisichella, 1990; Policarpo, 2003).

2. A centralidade da comunicação

Os *media* e a sua cultura chamam a atenção para uma realidade central da vida humana: a comunicação. Esta constituía uma realidade tão essencial que raras vezes fora objecto de uma reflexão expressa por parte do pensamento, e muito particularmente do pensamento teológico (cf. Henrici, 1983). Ao amplificarem de uma forma exponencial a capacidade humana de comunicar, de tal modo que criaram um novo modo de viver, os *media* mostraram também toda a centralidade e todo o poder da comunicação humana. Obrigaram, por isso, a tomar a sério esta realidade – e não apenas na sua expressão mediática mas igualmente naquela outra sua dimensão mais fundamental, sem a qual toda a cultura mediática cai por terra: a comunicação humana. Com efeito, os *media* podem maltratar a comunicação humana; podem até pô-la em causa nas suas dimensões mais excelentes, manipulando e fingindo a comunicação sem que ela verdadeiramente exista (Breton, 2001). Mas não podem passar sem a comunicação.

Enquanto reflexão que pretende mostrar as razões da fé ao homem contemporâneo a partir do dinamismo da revelação, pode a teologia ignorar este "sinal dos tempos"? A resposta não pode deixar de ser negativa, tanto mais quanto a Constituição Dogmática *Dei Verbum* do Concílio Vaticano II apresenta a revelação cristã a partir da categoria do "diálogo salvífico" entre Deus e o homem (DV 2; cf. Paulo VI, *Ecclesiam Suam*, 1964: n. 41).

Assim, ao considerar a "comunicação" como objecto da sua reflexão, a teologia não está a usar de um mero oportunismo "pastoral" de quem deseja estar presente no desfile da moda do pensamento contemporâneo. Nem basta, para satisfazer a exigência desta reflexão, uma simples abordagem teológica aos "Instrumentos da Comunicação Social": esta será sempre insuficiente e secundária, porque aborda exclusivamente uma pequena e superficial parte da questão, ou seja, a perspectiva técnica da comunicação, passando-lhe ao lado toda a profundidade humana do "comunicar". Para uma abordagem deste tipo, é suficiente tudo o que já foi escrito acerca da técnica e de como, através dela, o homem colabora com a actividade criadora de Deus. E, muito menos, é suficiente uma teologia moral acerca dos conteúdos mediáticos e dos valores culturais que eles geram (ou destroem). Este tipo de reflexão tem o seu lugar (e de não pouca importância) mas não constitui a questão central, antes dela deriva[4].

No concerto do pensamento científico, a teologia deve assumir a sua responsabilidade não apenas contribuindo para ele com uma reflexão acerca de questões mais evidentes ou superficiais, ainda que, eventualmente, mais presentes na "agenda cultural", mas apresentando uma reflexão acerca da realidade mais fundamental do homem, aquela que diz respeito à vida eterna, ou seja, aquela que tem a ver com o modo como Deus e o homem podem e devem relacionar-se. O mesmo é dizer: como é que pode existir comunicação (comunhão) entre Deus e o homem. Por isso, diante do universo da comunicação, mesmo da comunicação mediática, a teologia não pode deixar de responder à questão fundamental sobre o que significa comunicar e que lugar tem a comunicação na nossa relação com Deus[5].

3. Que ponto de partida para uma reflexão teológica sobre a comunicação?

Onde podemos encontrar um ponto de ancoragem para uma reflexão teológica sobre a comunicação? Deus e o homem não estarão, à partida, tão distantes que entre eles não pode existir qualquer tipo de comunicação? Se assim fosse, restar-nos-ia o silêncio acerca de Deus – quando muito, ser-nos-ia possível apenas uma teologia negativa, que mostrasse como a realidade divina supera infinitamente aquilo que dela poderemos algum dia pensar e (o que é mais) dizer, comunicar.

Toda a revelação judaico-cristã constitui uma afirmação clara e constante de que isso não é assim. O ponto de partida do Antigo Testamento é precisamente o contrário: num determinado momento da história, Deus tomou a iniciativa de se aproximar, de se mostrar, de dirigir a sua palavra a homens concretos (Gn 12,1-2), de uma forma que o homem não pode deixar de considerar indevida e gratuita, e de mudar, com essa sua intervenção, não apenas o rumo de vidas individuais como sobretudo dos povos e do próprio mundo.

Esta intervenção divina não se realiza apenas a partir da realidade criada e das suas maravilhas que são surpreendentes e que desafiam o pensamento humano, mas no seio da própria história; e ela tem lugar como acontecimento e como palavra dirigida ao profeta, que interpreta o desenrolar da história, descobrindo-lhe o sentido último e mostrando-a como história de salvação. Deus dirige a palavra a homens que escolhe e, através destes, apresenta-se como actor da história humana.

A esta reivindicação – já por si surpreendente e solicitando uma reflexão teológica sobre a comunicação – junta-se aquela outra, própria do cristianismo, que afirma a presença de Deus no seio da história não já simplesmente através da pessoa do profeta mas em primeira pessoa, em Jesus Cristo, Palavra feita carne. Esta reivindicação, formulada teologicamente no dogma cristológico "verdadeiro Deus e verdadeiro homem", encontra a sua raiz naquela outra, realizada pelo próprio Jesus de Nazaré, de ele mesmo constituir alguém único, acima dos profetas e da própria Lei mosaica (Mt 5,21-48; 12,41-42): com efeito, perante a sua pessoa Jesus reivindica dos seus ouvintes a decisão de entrega total, unicamente devida a Deus, não numa atitude patológica de um soberbo complexo de superioridade mas no realismo de quem se percebe, numa constante atitude de obediência ao Pai, o ponto-chave do universo, momento decisivo e centro da história, perante o qual e no qual tudo se decide de uma vez por todas, e que, por isso, tem o dever de se propor à humanidade de todos os tempos, numa atitude de amor, como possibilidade de decisão por Deus e pelo homem (cf. Lambiasi, 1997).

Jesus de Nazaré mostra-se, pois, também para uma teologia da comunicação, como um caso único e sério, a ser tomado assim mesmo. Ao fazê-lo não nos podemos limitar ao estudo de algumas das suas técnicas comunicativas: essas mostram-se próprias do mundo comunicativo da Palestina do seu tempo, e pouco têm a dizer ao nosso mundo mediático ou a qualquer outro cuja cultura se distinga do Médio Oriente de há dois mil anos. Que Jesus tenha falado em parábolas; que a sua comunicação seja baseada num domínio genial da oralidade; que os seus gestos chocassem e atraíssem multidões é, por si mesmo, pouco significativo. São apenas técnicas de comunicação do mundo rural da Palestina do início da era cristã, em nada superiores ou inferiores àquelas outras que caracterizam a nossa cultura mediática (algumas delas são, aliás, espantosamente próximas destas): a sua análise pode apenas satisfazer a curiosidade humana, mas não responder à questão fundamental acerca da comunicação entre Deus e o homem. Sinal de que aqueles constituem modos humanos de comunicar é precisamente o facto de o próprio cristianismo não ter hesitado em colocá-los de lado logo depois de Jesus. E, assim, à oralidade do Mestre sucede-se a escrita das narrações evangélicas e das cartas paulinas, técnicas de comunicação completamente diferentes das primeiras, usadas com não menor saber e eficácia; e a estas suceder-se-ão ainda a pintura, a escultura, a música e, mais perto de nós, o cinema e todos os outros processos mediáticos. Sob o ponto de vista das "técnicas de comunicação", em Jesus nada encontramos de normativo. Jesus usou a oralidade mas nunca proibiu os seus discípulos de escreverem ou de usarem outras técnicas de comunicação, nem afirmou que para a missão cristã apenas a oralidade poderia ser utilizada (cf. Kocher, 1986).

Aliás, mesmo a perfeição do uso da oralidade por parte de Jesus pode ser colocada em causa, se usarmos os critérios actuais do sucesso na comunicação mediática, ou seja, a conquista de audiência e a capacidade da sua manutenção (cf. Owens, 1984: 35). Jesus foi capaz num primeiro momento de arrastar multidões, entusiasmadas pelas curas que realizava, pelo seu modo de falar com autoridade, pela radicalidade da sua existência. Mas, para sermos verdadeiros, temos igualmente que reconhecer a sua incapacidade de manter essas multidões e de as convencer, e mesmo de persuadir aquele grupo mais chegado, os Doze. Jesus morrerá na solidão, abandonado por todos, quando muito acompanhado por sua mãe, três mulheres e um discípulo (Jo 20,25-26). O Nazareno desbaratou, em pouco tempo, a muita audiência que conquistou nos momentos iniciais. Por este prisma, longe de constituir um sucesso, a sua comunicação foi um completo fracasso.

Mas esta é apenas uma perspectiva superficial. Porque, de facto, dois mil anos depois, Jesus continua ainda a ser tema, a estar presente, no mundo inteiro, como sujeito e objecto de conversa, de discussão, de opinião, de reflexão grupal, de pensamento e de oração, seja do místico mais excelente, do teólogo mais competente, do filósofo mais arguto, do pastor mais dedicado ou do simples homem e mulher, ignorante e analfabeto, crente ou descrente. Nunca ninguém como ele foi tão discutido, pensado, falado, comunicado: e, com ele, é discutido, falado, pensado e comunicado o próprio Deus. O fracasso de Jesus de Nazaré transformou-se num retumbante sucesso para si próprio e para Deus.

4. A Palavra da Cruz

Qual a razão do fracasso e qual a razão do sucesso? Existe na comunicação de Jesus, para além das "técnicas comunicativas" alguma realidade que seja normativa para a comunicação cristã?

O fracasso da reflexão habitual sobre a comunicação de Jesus é devido a uma razão muito simples: tomamos habitualmente como ponto de partida para a sua análise aquilo que os cânones das ciências da comunicação nos apresentam como "a comunicação bem sucedida". O mesmo é dizer: procuramos medir a eficácia da comunicação de Jesus com as técnicas que medem o sucesso da nossa comunicação humana. Esquecemos, precisamente, que, a ser verdade o dogma cristológico, Jesus é um caso único e sério e que, por isso, se encontra para além de toda e qualquer medida humana.

Parece, pois, que, esgotada esta derradeira possibilidade, nada podemos dizer sobre Deus e muito menos sobre a sua "comunicação". Mas não é verdade. E não o é se, humildemente, nos colocarmos em atitude de acolhimento e aprendizagem de Jesus. No campo da comunicação, como em qualquer outro que seja central para uma reflexão teológica, a pessoa de Jesus só nos é dada a partir dele próprio, sem outra medida a não ser a sua própria pessoa, uma vez que constitui um "caso único e sério", impossível pois de ser entendido a partir de outros critérios que não aqueles que ele próprio nos oferece.

O falhanço das categorias humanas para entender a pessoa de Jesus é assinalado nas próprias narrativas evangélicas, particularmente quando tem lugar o primeiro anúncio da Paixão: isso é claro em Mc 8,27-33, considerado "um corte" na narrativa que colocará em primeiro plano a "ideia de Paixão" (Gnilka, 1997: 37; Lentzen-Deis, 1997: 25), mas tal acontece também no quarto evangelho, no final do discurso do Pão da Vida (Jo 6,61-69). O anúncio da Paixão fará com que não poucos discípulos abandonem Jesus; a Cruz fará mesmo com que os Doze se dispersem. A Cruz constitui, em última análise, a razão do fracasso comunicativo de Jesus se analisado de acordo com os parâmetros habituais das ciências da comunicação. E, no entanto, é nela que a verdadeira identidade de Jesus pode ser conhecida: "Verdadeiramente, este homem era o Filho de Deus", exclama o centurião ao ver a morte de Jesus (Mc 15,39). A Cruz coincide com o fracasso de todas as tentativas humanas de perceber Jesus e, simultaneamente, coincide também com a única possibilidade de o conhecer verdadeiramente. Jesus permanecerá não por ser o contador de parábolas ou o comunicador exemplar na oralidade, mas por ser o Crucificado. É na Cruz, onde toda a comunicação humana parece fracassar, que a comunicação do homem com Deus se estabelece efectivamente e, ao mesmo tempo, que o cristianismo fundará toda a sua proposta de comunicação verdadeira entre os homens[6].

A este paradoxo, S. Paulo chamará a "linguagem da Cruz" (1Cor 1,18), aquela mesma que humanamente é "loucura" mas que, segundo Deus, é "sabedoria"[7]. Aquilo que Deus tem a dizer ao homem encontra-se compendiado na Cruz de Jesus Cristo, e, assim, aquilo que a Igreja tem a dizer ao homem de todos os tempos mais não é que a Cruz – e importa, como acontece com Paulo, que ela não seja "esvaziada" (1Cor 1,17). O anúncio paulino, a que o Apóstolo chama "Evangelho" (1Cor 1,17; Rm 1,1), coincide com o anúncio do Crucificado. Tudo o resto que Jesus disse e fez se torna verdadeiramente incompreensível ou mesmo banal se não for lido à luz do Crucificado e do amor de Deus que nele resplandece. E, pelo contrário, tudo se torna verdadeiramente significativo se for entendido como antecipação do Mistério Pascal.

Mas em que se concretiza a Cruz de Jesus para o discípulo e, de uma forma muito particular, na comunicação? A comunicação/revelação de Deus na Cruz é, em primeiro lugar, afirmação da centralidade de Deus na existência humana. A Cruz é o lugar onde ao homem é dado perceber a verdade do amor enquanto amor absoluto de Deus que amou tanto o mundo a ponto de lhe entregar o seu Filho único (Jo 3,16). Neste amor, o homem (cada homem) descobre a realidade central da sua existência (da existência concreta de cada indivíduo). Ali se percebe como o lugar do homem na criação, ele que é visto como a obra mais excelente de Deus e aquele a quem foi entregue todo o criado só faz sentido enquanto imagem de Deus. Na Cruz, morre, por isso, toda a comunicação que procure encontrar no homem a sua fonte: o homem que procura afirmar-se a si mesmo como origem do saber e da vida, em concorrência com Deus, de tal modo que o procura matar, descobre-se, ao confrontar-se com a Cruz, como pecado e como morte, o mesmo é dizer, como ilusão comunicativa, Torre de Babel (Gn 11,1-9).

Mas, na Cruz, aparece igualmente claro que a única palavra que merece ser pronunciada e que a única imagem que merece ser vista é a do Verbo feito carne, aquela onde o Homem é pronunciado e visto juntamente com Deus (Jo 19,5; Col 1,15). Porque, diante de Deus que morre na Cruz por de cada um de nós, o falar humano na multiplicidade e dispersão das palavras dá lugar à Palavra, como reconhece o Apóstolo: "não quis saber outra coisa entre vós a não ser Jesus Cristo, e Jesus Cristo crucificado" (1Cor 2,2)[8]; e as imagens, sempre humanamente narcísicas, onde o homem se procura admirar a si mesmo, dão lugar ao Ícone do Crucificado, onde resplandece o rosto do Pai (2Cor 4,6).

O convite – mesmo exigência – de renunciar a si mesmo e de tomar a Cruz para seguir o Senhor (Mc 8,34) continua pois a ressoar hoje não apenas como atitude de vida interior individual mas como a atitude requerida ao discípulo e à Igreja em todo e qualquer momento da sua existência. Só aquele que toma a Cruz de Jesus e a vive na sua vida é verdadeiramente seu discípulo. Afirma a este propósito D. Bonhoeffer: "A Cruz não é uma adversidade ou um duro destino, mas é aquele sofrer que nos chega apenas por causa do nosso vínculo com Jesus Cristo. Não é sofrimento casual, mas necessário. A Cruz não é sofrimento ligado à existência natural, mas ao ser cristão" (Bonhoeffer, 2004: 78).

As palavras, as imagens, a comunicação do cristão só podem ser aquelas que se possam igualmente encontrar no Crucificado. A Cruz constitui pois o critério – o único verdadeiro critério – para toda e qualquer comunicação realizada pelos cristãos, pela Igreja e mesmo, em última análise, pelo próprio homem. Tudo o que não possa ser pronunciado ou mostrado pelo Crucificado é apenas vaidade humana, mesmo que disfarçada com objectivos piedosos: pura perda de tempo. A presença do cristão no mundo e a transformação cultural que ela traz consigo só farão verdadeiro sentido, e só serão portadores de significado último para a existência humana, hoje como sempre, se forem a "Palavra da Cruz".

NOTAS

[1] Veja-se, por exemplo, o discurso de Paulo VI em 29 de Junho de 1963: "Este mesmo encontro nos possibilita uma outra ocasião propícia [...] para redescobrir e quase medir as relações, existentes ou possíveis, entre o nosso ministério apostólico e o

vosso ofício de jornalistas. O tema parece-nos tão belo e tão fecundo, que não o pensamos poder explorar adequadamente com estas brevíssimas palavras" (Baragli, 1973: 2308).
[2] Sobre o capítulo teológico da *Communio et progressio* cf. Martins, 2000.
[4] Cf. White, 1991, 7: "O diálogo entre os campos da teologia e da comunicação já está a ter lugar, simplesmente porque é inevitável".
[4] Sobre as diferentes abordagens teológicas da comunicação cf. Felton, 1989: 17-23.
[5] Sobre a noção de "teologia da comunicação" cf. Martins, 2003.
[6] Cf. von Balthasar, 1988, 88: "Assim como Deus amou tanto o mundo, no seu conjunto, que lhe entregou o seu Filho, assim o amado de Deus só deve pretender salvar-se juntamente com os seus semelhantes, e não deve pretender renunciar à parte de padecimento que lhe caiba sofrer em benefício de todos. Deve actuar no seio da esperança cristã no único modo em que esta é permitida ao cristão: como esperança na salvação de todos os homens".
[7] Cf. *Ibid.*, 64: "O que Deus realizou em favor do homem só se pode entender na medida em que não se pode compreender nem justificar com base no fragmentário, humano e mundano, uma vez que, calibrado nessa base, aparece como 'loucura' e 'ignorância'".
[8] Este é também o entender de S. Agostinho. Cf. Martins, 2005: 153-165.

Referências bibliográficas

BALTHASAR, H. U. von (1988), *Solo el amor es digno de fe*, Salamanca.
BARAGLI, E. (1973), *Comunicazione, Comunione, Chiesa*, Roma.
BONHOEFFER, D. (2004), *Sequela*, Brescia: Queriniana.
BRETON, P. (2001), *A palavra manipulada*, Lisboa: Editorial Caminho.
FELTON, D. (1989), "The Unavoidable Dialogue: Five Interfaces Between Theology and Communication", *Media Development* (Oct. 1989), 17-23.
FISICHELLA, R. (1990), "Segni dei tempi", in R. LATOURELLE – R. FISI-CHELLA, ed., *Dizionario di teologia fondamentale*, Assisi: Cittadella, 1107-1115.
GNILKA, J. (1986), *El evangelio según san Marcos*, I, Salamanca: Sígueme.
HENRICI, P. (1983), "Towards an Anthropological Philosophy of Communication", *Communication Resource* (March), 1-4.
JOÃO PAULO II (1999), "Les médias: un ami précieux près de ceux qui recherchent le Père". Message pour la 33ème. Journée mondiale des communications sociales (16 mai 1999), *La documentation catholique* 96/6, 251-252.

KOCHER, M. (1986) (1987), "Jésus communicateur: Essai sur la figure du communicateur chrétien", *Hokhma* 33, 63-80; 34, 21-36.
LAMBIASI, F. (1997), "Credo in Gesù Cristo", in F. LAMBIASI – G. TANGORRA, *Gesù Cristo comunicatore. Cristologia e comunicazione*, Milano: Paoline.
LENTZEN-DEIS, F. (1997), *Evangelho de Marcos*, Lisboa: Difosora Biblica.
MARTINS, N. (2000), *Cristo o comunicador perfeito. Delineamento de uma teologia da comunicação à luz da Instrução Pastoral Communio et progressio*, Lisboa.
MARTINS, N. (2003), "O estatuto teológico de uma teologia da comunicação", *Didaskalia* 33, 349-364.
MARTINS, N. (2005), "De las palabras a la Palabra: significatividad y comunicación en las *Confessiones* de San Agustín", in F. CONESA, ed., *El cristianismo, una propuesta con sentido*, Madrid, 153-165.
OWENS, V. (1984), "Was Christ the 'Perfect Communicator'?", *Media Development* (Jan. 1984).
POLICARPO, J. (2003), *Sinais dos tempos. Génese histórica e interpretação teológica*, Lisboa (doutorado).
SOARES, I. (1988), *Do Santo Ofício à libertação*, S. Paulo: Paulinas.
WHITE, R., "The Growing Dialogue between Theology and Communications", in P. SOUKUP, *Communication and Theology. Introduction and Review of the Literature*, London: WACC-CSCC.

Communication theology in priestly formation
Joseph Palakeel

La comunicazione è una dimensione costitutiva della teologia cristiana, sia come proclamazione che come praxis. Perciò un cambiamento radicale nei media e nella cultura della comunicazione esige un ripensamento della teologia e della praxis pastorale. Oggi la tecnologia digitale ha reso possibile l'integrazione dei precedenti media e delle precedenti forme di comunicazione, grazie alla comunicazione multimediale e multisensoriale (audiovisuale-testuale). I pastori dell'era digitale devono essere ben informati e ben formati ad essere consumatori critici dei media; devono usare in modo creativo gli strumenti e le tecniche tradizionali e contemporanee circa i media. Potranno così diventare evangelizzatori efficaci della cultura e comunicatori competenti della fede nella cultura digitale. E' per questo che i seminari devono farsi scuole di comunicazione.

The establishment of ecclesiastical seminaries could be considered as the most significant reform of the Council of Trent. Ever since Trent, seminaries have remained the primary form of clerical training in the Catholic Church. The Council Fathers are said to have congratulated each other on that day, saying that this one decision was worth all their labor in the council[1]. What started off as a discussion on the necessity of teaching grammar and Holy Scripture to Catholic clerics had ended up declaring that these clerics were to be given a liberal education alongside the "professional" knowledge and skills, because such was the need of well-trained clergy after the Reformation. However, a closer look at what went on reveals that, beyond their fear of the Reformation and the impulse towards the Counter-Reformation, the decision of the Council Fathers was a clever strategy to adapt priestly formation to the emerging print media and the consequent situation of major cultural shift. Previous major reforms in clerical training, such as the Cathedral schools of Augustine and the medieval universities of the twelfth century, also took place at similar moments of colossal cultural change[2].

Today we are faced with a similar challenge. As *Aetatis Novae* says, the "developments in the technology of communicating" have inaugurated a new era in human history, by "a fundamental reshaping of the elements by which people comprehend the world about them, verify and express what they comprehend" (*Aetatis Novae* = AN 1-4). The communication revolution has profound consequences for persons, societies and humanity as a whole and affects the "perception and transmission of values, worldviews, ideologies, and religious beliefs" (*Ibid.*). The new media has "new languages" and "new techniques" which have "given birth to new possibilities for the mission of the Church as well as to new pastoral problems" (*Redemptoris Missio* = RM 37; AN 2).

Naturally the Catholic Church must face the challenge and devise new models of priestly formation in order to form shepherds for the digital age. While most seminaries in the world have introduced a few communication courses into their curricula, that is not a sufficient response, when one considers the immensity and impact of the communication revolution. The failure and the inability to incorporate communications into different pastoral ministries of the Church can be directly linked to its absence in priestly formation. In the present article, I attempt to outline a theoretical framework for making communications a constitutive dimension of seminary formation.

1. Church and communication formation

Several Church documents have underlined the importance of communication in the life and activity of the Church and the formation of the pastoral personnel[3]. The Vatican II document *Inter Mirifica* (1965) states emphatically that "priests, religious and laity should be trained *at once*" for the critical use of media (*Inter Mirifica* = IM 15, 16). The Pastoral Instruction *Communio et Progressio* (1971) further clarifies that communication education "should be an *integral part of the ordinary priestly training*" and adds that "without this knowledge an effective apostolate is impossible in a society which is increasingly conditioned by the media". Further, it says that "if students for priesthood and religious in training are to be part of modern life and also to be effective at all in their apostolate, they should know how the media work upon the fabric of the society and the technique of their use" (*Communio et Progressio* = CP, 107, 111).

Two major documents of the Congregation for Catholic Education are of crucial importance in this regard. The *Ratio Fundamentalis* (1970) observes that the various forms of social communication have created a totally new condition of living (*Ratio Fundamentalis* = RF 4) and proposes that candidates for priesthood be trained to "use the media prudently and with reason [...] to educate the faithful and to make effective use of the media in their apostolate" (RF 68). Taking into consideration the importance of communication studies in pastoral formation, the same Congregation in fact has devoted an entire document to it, the *Guide to the training of future priests concerning the instruments of social communication* (1986). The *Guide* has laid down common principles and guidelines (*Guide* = G 9-13) and has proposed a communication education plan in three levels, that is, a basic level of training receivers (G 14-19), second level of pastoral training in philosophy and theology (G 20-26), and a specialized level for selected candidates (G 27-28).

The Encyclical *Redemptoris Missio* and the Pastoral Instruction *Aetatis Novae* present a new vision of the means of social communication and emphasize the importance of a pastoral plan for social communication in every activity of the Church. While *Redemptoris Missio* defines the impact of communication revolution on the apostolate (RM 37c), *Aetatis Novae* states unambiguously that "education and training in communications should be an integral part of the formation of pastoral workers and priests" (AN 18).

These and other Church documents reveal a clear awareness of the importance of the integration of communications in the pastoral ministry as well as priestly formation: "The priests today must not only receive solid and complete formation in the sacred sciences; they must know how to communicate Christian faith in 'effective and convincing ways' making use of all possibilities offered by modern means of Social Communication"[4].

2. Goals and levels of communication formation

The *Guide to the training of future priests concerning the instruments of social communication* speaks of *integral training* in communication, including theoretical knowledge of the cultural, political and religious functions and moral trends of media and practical formation in using the tools of social communication. The goals of such a communication formation are to educate the future priests to "impose self-discipline", "train the faithful to exercise discipline" and "use the media in their apostolate". For these goals, three levels of training are recommended: moral (the receiver of media messages), instrumental (the user of media) and specialized (the producer); the third level is intended primarily for those who will be engaging fully in communication ministry (G 9). *Redemptoris Missio* and *Aetatis Novae* recommend a wider and deeper concern of "evangelization of cultures" through these levels and goals.

This three-level approach of the Church to communication is not, in my opinion, the best response to the communication revolution and the resultant cultural change. To make communications "an integral part of their ordinary education", a fourth approach is needed which could be characterized as a constitutive approach, one which transcends the moral, instrumental and the inculturational perspectives.

3. For receivers: the moral approach

The Church proposes to train future priests "in the *correct* use of these instruments", "for the *protection* and benefit" of themselves and the faithful against the *evil effects* of the media. We can call this a moralist approach based on the strong conviction that Church is the guardian of faith and morals of its people and the concern is clearly legitimate considering "the cultural and moral ambivalence" and "the moral and pastoral problems created by the mass media. Priests, seminarians and faithful need to receive training to become critical and creative receivers of the media. However, such a cautious, perhaps negative approach risks becoming a predominantly defensive attitude which seeks to isolate the faithful from the influence of mediated communication. The Church's interest in promoting communication education and formation should go beyond this and move towards a more critical appreciation based on a positive valuation of the media.

4. For users: the instrumental approach

The document *Inter Mirifica* announces the Church's prerogative to own and use the communications media for the proclamation of the Gospel and *Evangelii Nuntiandi* adds that we "would feel guilty before the Lord if she did not utilize these powerful means" (EN 45). The *Guide* also states that Church sees "the instruments of social communication as providential means for the accomplishment of its mission to "preach from the housetops" (Lk 12,3), "to all nations" (Mk 16,15), even "to the end of the earth" (Acts 1,8) (G 1-8). Pope John Paul II sagely advocates that "it is inopportune to leave their use [of the media] completely up to the initiatives of individuals or small groups". The entire Church community needs to understand and appreciate the media and make sure that these new ways of communicating are "decisively inserted into pastoral programs" (RM 37; *Rapid Development* = RD 8).

It is beyond doubt that the potent means of communication are "a precious aid for spreading the Gospel [...] and to expand the boundaries of evangelization" (RD 7), amplifying and multiplying the voices and reaching them far and wide. The success of the Church in each epoch depended primarily on the appropriation and use of the predominant media of communication. The Gospel was initially transmitted orally and later put into writing by the early Christian thinkers; Church was the custodian of writing and manuscripts in the middle ages; Church used the full potential of printing and radio for evangelization and faith formation. Catholics and Protestants have invested significant amount of money and resources in order to tap the potential of the means of communication for religious information, for evangelization and catechesis, for the formation of pastoral workers. The immense influence and vast reach of the communications media makes it necessary to train all pastoral personnel in the use of all modern means of communication. This however, should go beyond the acquisition and utilization of the "instruments" (means) for efficient "transportation" of messages to effective communication through creative use of the media and constructive dialogue with the media culture.

5. For evangelizers: the inculturational approach

In the recent years we find a growing awareness that while "the use of the techniques and the technologies of contemporary communications is an integral part of its mission in the third millennium", it is *"not enough to use media* simply to spread the Christian message and the Church's authentic teaching. It is also necessary to *integrate* that message into the *new culture* created by modern communications" (RM 37c; RD 2). Speaking in the context of evangelization, the Pope is saying that the Gospel should *shed light* on the dark areas of media culture to purify them because "the means of communication have become so important as to be for many the chief means of information and education, of guidance and inspiration in their behavior as individuals, families and within society at large" (RM 37). Clearly the Gospel is to be the "salt" and "leaven" of the new culture, permeating it with Christian values.

Calling the media the "areopagus" and the "forum" of the modern world is definitely a step forward from the instrumental approach, because media are thus considered the market place or the public sphere where politics and business are transacted, where religious social duties are fulfilled, and where the best and the worst of human nature is on display. When St. Paul spoke on the Areopagus of Athens (Acts 17), he was not merely "using" public forum but making a clever move to shift the Christian discourse from simple narratives of an agrarian-pastoral culture of the synagogues, homes and villages of Palestine into the critical, rational and analytic urban culture. St. Paul's move is often interpreted as a new rhetoric, a new way of presenting Christianity, in fact, as inculturation. But it could also be interpreted better as a shift into another medium – a transmediation – of communication, rather than a mere innovation in rhetorical strategy. Today communication studies have made us more aware of the cultural and semantic implications of a shift in medium. Hence we can see the emerging digital communication revolution as a new culture, something beyond even a change in medium, and so necessitates a more integral and constitutive approach.

6. Communicators: constitutive approach

Recent communication researches point beyond the sender-message-impact (transportation) model of communication, partly because of the new interactive tools and technology and largely because of the cultural studies approach which places communication media at the core of the cultural process of the construction of meaning through ongoing negotiation or interaction among the Sender, Message, Medium and Receiver in the context of the Receiver. This has profound implications not only for the understanding of the media and process of communication but also for all cultural institutions such religion, politics and social life. Thus communications media are not mere tools for packaging and transporting ideas, concepts or meaning, but a constitutive dimension of being human. The statements of McLuhan that media are "extensions of man" and that "the medium is the message" have indicated this direction.

In this context we can say that *Redemptoris Missio* makes the best assessment of the communication revolution by speaking of a *"new culture"* which "originates not just from whatever content is eventually expressed", but "from the very existence of new ways to communicate with hitherto unknown techniques, and vocabulary" (RM 37c). Considering communication as the constituent dimension of culture and life serves as the best paradigm for integration of communications in priestly formation because only such a constitutive approach would be capable of seeing communication as an inherent and important dimension of the theological-pastoral process. The three approaches we have listed and analyzed consider communication as a tool or technique of transferring ideas, information or meaning from an expert sender to a quasi-ignorant receiver and, hence, can be reduced to the instrumental-moralistic approach. This becomes the most fitting model of communication in the Church because it rightly fulfills the role of the Church as the authentic and authoritative teacher of truth and the official herald of the Gospel and it serves the hierarchical and institutional structure (Horsfield, 2004: 24).

The current phenomenon of communications, however, impels the Church towards a sort of pastoral and cultural revision. We are faced with three fundamental options: *formation, participation* and *dialogue* (RD 11). It is in this wider cultural context that we must formulate ways to integrate communication formation in seminaries.

7. Communication in theology and seminary formation

McLuhan, Walter Ong and other communication scholars have established that culture is shaped by the dominant structure of communication media and all other systems adapt to it. From myths and stories of ancient times to the highly rational and abstract thinking of modernity, we find a connection between the available medium of communication – oral, written, print – and the predominant pattern of thinking and living, from mythical and cosmocentric to rational and anthropocentric. We find the height of rational conceptual thinking together with the printing technology and culture, which is also the most abstract form of human communication. If we take the fundamental correlatives of human thinking and expression such as head-heart, reason-emotion, conscious-unconscious, object-subject, text-context, sender-receiver, form-ground, abstract-concrete, we find that the print culture and the corresponding philosophy, progressively favored the former set of correlatives, whereas the oral cultures were more allied to the latter.

Digital communication has opened a new chapter in human thinking where the storage and retrieval of information and creation and expression of meaning are very different from the linear, conceptual and rational methods of print era. It is an integration of all previous media and cultures, making "orality, literacy and electricity meet" (Boomershine, 1991). Literacy today is not just the ability to read and write texts or to do pure impassioned and critical reasoning, but the capacity to make sense of the multi-media and multi-sensorial communication of audio-visual-textual stimuli, with multi-layered meaning. Written and printed texts and their interpretation were predominantly monosemic, because the sender produced the meaning and transported it to the receiver through static text and faithful textual interpretation. Whereas in the digital media of sights, sounds and hypertexts, the producer-sender has very little control over the text, because the images, sounds and texts are received and interpreted within the context and world view of the receiver, without the barrier of time and space. The simultaneity and interactivity of the digital communication makes possible a participatory construction of meanings through negotiation. This has enormous consequence for the faith formation through religious education, teaching and preaching.

8. Theologizing in the digital culture

The Church adapted well to the manuscript and the print, literate culture, by translating the oral-tribal Bible into the written and urban communication and later to print and rational culture by mastering the dominant medium of each succeeding age. Today's Church and its dominant theology still find themselves bound in a print-media space and culture, and remain rational and conceptual and far removed from the common language of the people. Can the Church and theology of another media culture effectively communicate without the dominant medium of communication of the present day?

Communication theologians argue that communications is a constitutive, and not simply functional factor in the process of theologizing: "Theologizing is a continuous and renewed process of interpretation, systematic reflection, articulation and praxis after encountering a God who communicates himself with humans and their world" (Parappally, 2003: 73). In this sense, theologizing can be considered as a communication process or a meaning-making exercise. In fact both theology and pastoral ministry are fundamentally about communication; even the decisions about the media to use in given circumstances are primarily theological rather than technical decisions because they reflect the pertinent model of the Church. Thus communication theology does not mean a theology of communication or a method for communicating theology, rather it is like doing a "theology of theology" (*Ibid.*). Communication theology is theologizing in the emerging digital language and literacy.

If theology is considered as a process of constructing meaning, we must ask certain questions to theology: is the dominant theology "sensitive to the questions and searches of the people? Do priests talk about God in a language people can understand?". Does it reflect local religious symbols and expressions, and speak in the "local religious language which expresses the religious sentiments of the people?". Does it give pastoral persons the capacity "to see, with the Christian community, what God is calling the community to do in a given context", to "see the action of God in a context" and "to *listen to and discern what God is saying in the hearts of all*" (White, 2003: 26)?

Digital culture is a more adept medium to communicate God's interventions in life through actions in history which are "experienced and celebrated in a multitude of media" like narratives, images and symbols. This adds a plural, global and contextual or experiential dimension to theology. But digital culture calls for an emphasis on the theological *method* along with the theological content, a shift from being a body of knowledge – formulas and dogma to stories and symbols and celebrations, from knowledge of the Scriptures and tradition to discerning the action of the Spirit in life. This offers a more appropriate and effective way to see the totality of Christian life, with sacraments, rituals, music and drama, largely integrated into the theological system.

9. The seminary as a school of communication

Like theology itself, the present seminary system is also a child of the print media and culture. In order to form pastors for ministry in the digital culture, seminaries should make some critical shifts, because the candidates for priesthood they must train are from the digital culture, and the people to whom they are going to minister are living in this new culture. Hence a constitutive communication theology calls for a revision and renewal of the entire program of seminary formation including the structures, curriculum, pedagogy and life. The human, intellectual and spiritual formation, as well as its philosophical-theological presuppositions, need to be reexamined and there should be a plan for each seminary and for each stage of formation, with fitting content, style and method of integration.

To give an integral formation in communication, theoretical knowledge and practical skills of communication should be imparted. This could – and should – be done without adding many new courses into an already heavy curriculum. The study of communication theory could be integrated into the existing courses in philosophy, sociology and theology. For example, communication theology could be integrated into introduction to theology; moral aspects of communication could be made part of the moral theology; other deeper theological issues related to communication could form part of the courses in revelation, Trinity, christology, anthropology and ecclesiology. Biblical story-telling and performance criticism of the Bible could be employed with other forms of criticism to recover the original meaning and context of the biblical narratives and as a more appropriate way to communicate faith in the era of digital literacy, which, in fact, is a new form of orality.

Communication is about connections and networking. The dominant theological formation today is too fragmented in the name of specialization and it often fails to give a comprehensive vision of faith, theology and life. The hypertext style of the digital culture challenges us to make a comprehensive vision of God, man and world in the life situation or context of the modern man through the study of Scripture and theology. The world-wide-web and other communication networks offer the possibility and the challenge of linking all the seminaries in a given region or country. Learning and teaching theology can be seen as establishing connections, between God and man, faith and life, text and context, sender and receiver.

The post-literate man is soaked in the universe of sights, sounds and hypertexts, and his consciousness is constituted by the mediated sounds and images of reality. Theological formation should address this phenomenon and make theological formation a multimedia and multisensorial experience. The electronic and digital images on TV-, computer- and projection-screens could serve as the modern day icons and sacred images. Together with images, sound bytes of all frequencies reign the atmosphere in the form of broadcasting and podcasting, audio books and music albums. To this could be added the technique of the hypertext which is an ingenious new way to read and write. Unfortunately, right now all these areas are dominated by the secular media which fills the field of communication with worldly images, sounds and texts.

Most young men who enter the seminary today have already been exposed to the modern technology of communication. If the seminaries can make communication facilities available and provide guidance for effective and mature use of them, students will master the skills by themselves. If the teaching methods could be changed from lecturing and note-taking to more interactive learning using participatory teaching methods and audio-visual presentations, these skills will be automatically picked up by the students. It is important that all seminaries have the necessary infrastructures for this shift. Today a library of textbooks is mandatory for all seminaries; likewise, appropriate multimedia resources and the possibility of access to Internet could become a basic tool in all seminaries.

Integration means a balanced use of all communication skills and styles, according to the demands of the ministry in a particular place, time and culture. It is important to maintain a balance between the technological and the traditional methods of communication. Group and personal media are still very relevant to pastoral ministry. Together with the introduction of the modern tools and techniques of communication, the existing and forgotten dimensions of Church communication such as story telling and parables, music and images, art and architecture, rituals and sacraments, liturgy and popular pieties should be encouraged and promoted. Above all, to respond to God and to his people, pastors today need competence in intrapersonal, interpersonal, group and communitarian communication. While silence, meditation and love for nature could be promoted as important countercultural values, training in "people skills", like counseling, conflict resolution, negotiation, personnel and resource management, public relation could be very valuable skills in ministry. In short, seminaries should innovate to become schools of communication, training shepherds for the digital age.

10. Shepherds for a digital age

The shepherds of the digital age should be master communicators with expertise in all forms of communication. The ministers should be well informed and well formed to be critical consumers, creative users, effective evangelizers and competent communicators. Media literacy and media education will enable them to safeguard themselves against the evils of the media and to train the faithful to be critical and discerning receivers. Exposure and expertise in the media tools and techniques will empower them to utilize the immense potential of the media for spreading the Gospel values. The original missionary mandate in Luke, to go and proclaim the Gospel to all *ethne* – nations, peoples or *cultures* – can be interpreted as an invitation to permeate the digital culture with the transforming power of the Gospel. For this the pastors should be skilled in understanding the cultural implications of the media and address these in their own terms.

The best way to counter the inevitable negative dimensions of the media is to highlight the positive elements and values; in the world today, it is impossible to isolate any one from the reach and power of media. Regarding interpretation, the process of cultural negotiation can be used to construct noble and worthy meanings out of the media events. For this the future pastoral personnel should also master the technical and cultural skills of digital communication, in addition to the theological pastoral knowledge. They should be able to discern the presence and action of God in history and culture and to articulate the faith experiences of the people. Faithful to the essential biblical and ecclesial expressions of Christian living, they have to become artisans rather than guardians of faith, awakeners of the spirit rather than educators of doctrines, seers who animate people than overseers who rule them and prophets of God to fight against all idolatry (Palakeel, 2003a: 53).

11. Conclusion

The Council of Trent introduced the institution of the seminary to form clergy for the new medium, the printed text, and its cultural, philosophical and theological impact. It served the well-defined purpose of training the Catholic clergy for the new culture they were facing. The shift to digital communication, which marks a much more complex change in media and culture, demands a similar visionary and prophetic renewal of the theological-pastoral formation to make the Church a faithful and fitting witness of the Gospel in the twenty-first century. Face to face with the new communication phenomena, the Church's reaction should shift from simply asking how to make use of the media of communications to spread the Good News to asking how to make theology and formation most fitting to the digital culture. For this we need to establish new pastoral priorities which better respond to the needs and context of each Christian community and which renew the theological presuppositions, processes as well as formation accordingly. The essentially moral, instrumental and even the inculturational understanding of communication media has its origin in a theology *of* communication which sees theology from the point of view of the fundamental communicability of theological content. The need of the time is a communication theology which sees communication as a theological category and theology as a communication process. Seminary has to be envisaged as a school of communication.

Today many speak of the antagonistic, isolationist and instrumentalist attitude of the Church to the media; but a glimpse through the history of theology and Church shows that it has always tried to be closely associated with the predominant communication media of each time. It was most successful in the early years of Christianity and during the

Reformation, but now seems to be lagging behind in the blooming digital culture. Church has to take courage and consider communication as an integral dimension of Christian theology, proclamation and praxis. The first step towards this is to integrate communications in the formation of the pastoral persons, because a well-trained and enlightened clergy will be able to reform and renew the Church.

NOTES

[1] See "Ecclesiastical Seminary" in *www.newadvent.org/cathen*.

[2] In the early centuries of Christianity individuals were chosen and trained in Christian schools of theology. St. Augustine established a *monasterium clericorum* near the cathedral (*in domo ecclesiæ*), in which his clergy lived together. The second Council of Toledo (531) exhorted parish priests to have young clerics in their houses and to instruct them with fatherly zeal so as to prepare worthy successors. Gradually, many of the cathedral and monastic schools declined, while some of them grew into medieval universities. A large proportion of the students in the universities were ecclesiastics or members of religious orders but the vast majority of these received little or no clerical training. Only about one per cent of the clergy were properly educated.

[3] A complete chronological listing of "Training of the Clergy for the mass media in official documents of the Church" is given in the Appendix 1 of *Guide to the training of future priests concerning the instruments of social communication*, issued by the Congregation for the Catholic Education in 1986.

[4] Message of the Holy Father through Cardinal Sodano to BISCOM 3, May 7-12, 2001 on the theme *Social Communication formation in priestly Ministry and Mission:* see Eilers, 2002: 7.

Bibliographical references

BOOMERSHINE, T. E. (1991), "Doing Theology in the Electronic Age: Meeting of Orality and Electricity", *Journal of Theology*, 4-14.

EILERS, F.J. (2002), *Social Communication Formation in Priestly Ministry*, Manila: Logos.

MCLUHAN, M. (1964), *Understanding Media: The Extensions of Man*, New York: McGraw Hill.

MCLUHAN, M. (1967), *The Medium is the Message*, New York: Bentham Books.

ONG, W. (1982), *Orality and Literacy*, New York: Methuen.

PALAKEEL, J. (2003), *Towards a Communication Theology*, Bangalore: ATC.

PALAKEEL, J. (2003a), "Theologizing with Insights from Communication", in Palakeel, 2003: 35-59.
PALAKEEL, J. (2005), "Interfaces between Theology and Communications", in Traber, 2005: 38-60.
PARAPPALLY, J. (2003), "Theologizing as Commuciation", in Palakeel, 2003: 72-82.
TRABER, M., ed. (2005), *Communication in Theological Education: New Directions*, New Delhi: ISPCK.
WHITE, R. (2003), "Theologizing to Communicate God's Love", in Palakeel, 2003: 19-32.

THE SPIRITUAL DIMENSION

The spirituality of the Christian communicator
Franz-Josef Eilers, SVD

La spiritualità del comunicatore cristiano dovrà essere fondata su prospettiva biblica, secondo il modello proposto dal Cardinal Martini, iniziatore del CICS. Dovrà essere basata su una solida teologia della comunicazione, in grado di comprendere l'intera teologia sotto la prospettiva della comunicazione stessa. Ciò significa che la comunicazione deve divenire un principio teologico a partire dal quale tutta la teologia possa essere compresa, con evidenti conseguenze per la stessa spiritualità del comunicatore, dal punto di vista delle sue personali disposizioni. Egli avrà infatti necessità di una spiritualità di apertura a Dio, a se stesso e agli altri. Avrà anche bisogno, come nel caso dei sacerdoti, di uno spirito di carità pastorale per mezzo del quale "imitare Cristo nella sua autodonazione e nel suo servizio" (Giovanni Paolo II). Il modello cristiano di comunicazione dovrebbe essere la prospettiva-guida per ogni comunicazione cristiana.

Pedro Arrupe, the Superior General of the Jesuits from 1965 to 1983, was particularly concerned about research and serious reflection concerning the role of social communication in the world and in the Church. In 1973 he tasked his communication secretary, Stephan Bamberger, SJ, with a study on the possibilities for an involvement of the Society of Jesus in the field of communication research. Bamberger created a task force which also included non-Jesuits like the writer of this paper. Out of their considerations which took place mainly in Rome but also in Milwaukee (USA), a "Research Facilitator Unit for Social Communication" was created on 8 June 1976 and established in London. From the beginning there was the conviction that such a project had to be interdisciplinary. The main tasks of the new office were described in the following way:

1. To establish contacts between researchers and the institutions which need research. 2. To formulate and draw attention to the as yet unanswered questions on which research has to be done. 3. To counsel and encourage the efforts of young research workers in the field of communications. 4. To offer direct assistance to research projects in places where local research personnel have in-adequate resources to carry through their work.

In 1979 the Unit was re-named "The Centre for the Study of Communication and Culture". Robert White was Research Director of this Centre when he later was called to Gregorian University.

Already during the considerations for the London Unit, the question was raised about the Gregorian University's taking on such an initiative but the structures and mentality of those days did not, at that point, allow for such a project. It was Carlo Maria Martini, SJ, who, as the Rector of the Gregorian – he later became Cardinal Archbishop of Milan – called for an initiative of this kind. From within the university, he was supported by Peter Henrici, SJ, the Dean of Philosophy – later he became Bishop of Chur, Switzerland – who was named the first Director of the nascent Centre. Henrici was supported by a study group from within the University and some outside consultants, which included the late Bishop Agnellus Andrew, OFM, then Vice-President of the Pontifical Council for Social Communications. This group developed a program which was open to all faculties of the university and which, more than being concerned with developing practical skills, would be a place of academic excellence, deeper insights and research into the operations and obligations of the Church in this field. The *Interdisciplinary Centre for Social Communications – Centro Interdisciplinare sulla Comunicazione Sociale*, or CICS – was established in February 1981. Its first director was Henrici, who was followed by Robert White, as proposed by the study group for the program.

1. The biblical considerations of Carlo Martini

Biblical scholar Carlo Martini maintained his interest in social communication from his time at the Gregorian through his years as Cardinal-Archbishop of Milan. Among the annual pastoral plans he developed for his archdiocese, twice the theme was social communications, in 1990 and 1991. He himself wrote the basic documents for these pastoral plans and his *Effatà, Apriti* of 1990 became the Magna Carta for a biblical communication spirituality. (Martini, 1990; 1994) In this document, Martini repeats his conviction that communication "is not a secondary or 'luxury' theme. It is a matter of our very condition of being man and woman and being Church" (n. 3). The spirituality of a Christian communicator must be grounded in Scripture, the source of all the basic considerations of Martini. The Scriptures not only consider God's ways and means of communication in revelation and incarnation but they also give directions for the life and the spiritual challenge of the Christian communicator. Martini divides his considerations into three chapters with the headings: Seeing, Listening and Contemplating, and Action. All of these are important elements for a spirituality of a Christian communicator.

In the chapter "Seeing", Martini points to the danger of interfering with or blocking authentic communication through "a will to possess, to dominate, to use, to identify all things with one's self", and he qualifies these blocks as "parodies of true communication" (n. 16). The spirituality of a Christian communicator calls for an opening up of the person: "Jesus, who made the deaf hear and the mute speak (Mk 7, 37) comes to us as the teacher of communication if we open ourselves to follow him on the way of hope which he proposes to us" (n. 17).

In the "Listening and Contemplating" chapter, Martini speaks of the experience of Pentecost, which he calls the "Gospel of Communication", and which he sees as sparking "an extraordinary ability to communicate" (n. 19). Like the covenant of the Old Testament (Ex 19, 1-7), Pentecost shows that "God wants to enter into communion with his people, wants to communicate with them in a spirit of reciprocity and mutual belonging". This communication is a "free and gratuitous initiative of the living God [...] [and it] calls for a free and grateful response of faith" (n. 20), which Martini sees as another important element in the spirituality of Christian communicators. They have a duty to listen and respond to God's word but unfortunately, they are always in the danger of refusing God's gift. As the first step towards this refusal of God's offer, Martini sees diffidence, "the fear that the other is not communicating gratuitously, but has some hidden interest or agenda". Clearly the basis of this diffidence is "the lack of trust in the gratuity and sincerity of the communicative act" which might begin, Martini suggests, with a doubt like that of Adam: "Did God really say...?" (Gn 3,1), a doubt that divides the person "from God, person from person, group from group, planting the suspicion that others want to promote themselves".

The spirituality of a Christian communicator must be based on the fact that "all human relationships need to be imbued with the selflessness that comes in abundance from on high, from the mystery of the gracious love of God, from the mystery of Jesus' death for us, suffered for pure love and for no other motive, from the gift of the Holy Spirit" (n. 22).

Martini then considers "Action" for Christian communicators in the light of these considerations by developing a sort of an examination of conscience for communicators. They have to clarify their fundamental dispositions and interiorize the reality of the experience of individual redemption. As the basis for this self-evaluation, Martini proposes the following seven questions:

> What signs do I find *in myself* of blocks in my communicating [...]? What "grade" would I give to communication in my family [...]? From my point of view, how would I describe the difficulties in communications between the different *social strata* with which I have direct contact, especially in my workplace [...]? How would I rate my relationships within the Christian community [...]? Do I sometimes experience regrets that come from not knowing how to communicate or irritation that comes from not succeeding in communication [...]? Do I *pray* that the Lord will communicate himself to me, and heal my human relationships [...]? Do I keep before my eyes this axiom: that we are made to love and to communicate [...]? (nn. 41-47).

Martini then proposes to the communicators to re-read the texts about Pentecost and the covenant-experience, to prepare for the sacrament of reconciliation and adoration before the Eucharist. He proposes to communicators to entrust themselves to the Holy Trinity and trust in God's time, to love and read the Bible as the book of God's communication, to feel the evangelical passion of Jesus and entrust themselves to Mary (nn. 48-56).

2. A spirituality based on communication theology

The spirituality of a Christian communicator is not simply a personalized and individual spirituality or a pious exercise of some few virtues. Rather, such a spirituality is based on solid theological structures which consider the whole of theology under the perspective of communication (Dulles, 1992: 22; Plude, 2001; Eilers, 2002: 41; 2004: 17-29; Soukup, 2001; Palakeel, 2003) and which see the communicator as living out such communication. Communication, in this perspective, becomes a "theological principle" and Trinity, revelation, incarnation and the Church are seen under the perspective of communication. The Trinitarian God, Father and Son communicate in the Holy Spirit, and human beings are created in this "image and likeness". Thus the vocation of communicator is part of our created being and structures. The whole of biblical theology is concerned with the ways and means by which a communicating God "speaks" in many and various ways to his people (Heb 1,1). The high point of this development is the incarnation of Jesus Christ, a transcendent "event" in which God communicates to us through his Son as the "perfect communicator" (*Communio et Progressio*, n. 11).

For Christian communicators, spirituality reflects *in revelation* on the ways and means by which God communicates with the Israelites, and challenges these communicators to consider how their own communicating reflects that of God. In the Old Testament, when God speaks to Adam and Eve and others like Cain, he makes the communication direct and personal: Where are you? Where is your brother Abel? (Gn 3,9). God uses human dialogue as in Jeremiah's complaint (Jer 20,7-9): "You have seduced me and I was deceived, you overpowered me and prevailed". God calls the prophets and the kings in a very human way and he sends them confirmed with symbols like anointing. God talks to Moses "face to face" in such a way that the prophet's face becomes shining and cannot be looked at with "normal" eyes (Dt 34,10). God appears to the prophet Elijah on the mountain of Horeb not in the mighty wind, nor in the earthquake or the fire, but in the gentle breeze of silence (1 Kings 19,11-13). God expresses his anger: "I will wipe out humankind whom I have created from the face of the earth" (Gn 6,7). God appears in thunder and lightning, with a thick cloud over the mountain and a loud trumpet blast (Ex 19,16). In summary: God uses all ways and means of human communication embedded in the culture of the people he is addressing.

In the Incarnation, Jesus Christ is the "perfect communicator" and his ways and means of communication offers examples according to which Christian communicators are called to pattern their lives and actions. Jesus communicates already through the circumstances of his life, like his birth in the manger, the silence in his upbringing in Nazareth and the forty days in the desert and finally in his death on the cross. He communicates everywhere he goes, on the roads, on the sea, on mountains and in the temple, and he communicates through word and deed. Jesus communicates through storytelling and parables and his narratives always reflect the life experiences of the people around him: the sower, the fishermen, the housewife, the king and his servants, but also the widow and the mother mourning for her child.

Further, Jesus adopts different models and forms of communication. He talks in intimate personal communication with Nicodemus, with the Samaritan and Martha and Mary; he shares in group communication with his apostles but also in other closed groups such as wedding guests or participants in a meal. Jesus also teaches larger crowds of people, on the mountain, at the seashore and even from a boat.

Jesus is not afraid to offend people if they do not do God's will, like the Pharisees and Scribes; he even challenges his own disciples. In the end, Jesus communicates in a very special and unique way through his passion and death on the cross. The spirituality of the Christian communicator must be based on the reflection, contemplation and internalization of these facts, a program which calls for a prayerful and contemplative life where all exterior activities flow from an interior, spiritual experience.

Communication theology also demonstrates that it is the essence of the Church and her mission to carry the communication of the Trinity, revelation and especially the incarnation into the lives and experiences of people in the complex and ambiguous world of today. Thus the concern of communicators today should not be, first and foremost, the modern techniques and possibilities offered in the communications field, but rather the experience and knowledge of faith, the foundation of any Christian communication. For example, a convincing spiritual person like Mother Teresa of Calcutta is a better and more effective communicator, because the Holy Spirit shines through everything she does and says: she has no need of the most recent, digital technology. Without a strong interior life of faith and prayer, and a message coming out of this experience, Christian communicators cannot really transmit the experience of the Good News of redemption into the lives of the people who today sorely need that Good News.

3. Communication spirituality as openness

Communication spirituality begins with the experience and the fire of the Holy Spirit who wants to express and share His fullness with others. Any Christian communication, but especially pastoral and evangelizing communication, offers in a special way this Spirit of Jesus Christ to those who much need it. Such a spirituality of Christian communication has as its essential structure a triple openness: the openness to God, to self and to others.

The openness to God and God's Spirit begins with the personal experience of the Lord and His word in prayer and meditation but also through liturgical celebration and community life. Such a total openness to the Spirit is the foundational condition for any communication spirituality as Pope John Paul II confirmed in his message for World Communication Day 1998:

> Christian communicators need to be men and women of Spirit filled prayer, entering even more deeply into communication with God in order to grow in their ability to foster communication among their fellow human beings.

THE SPIRITUALITY OF THE CHRISTIAN COMMUNICATOR 193

They must be schooled in hope by the Holy Spirit, the principal agent of evangelization.

Marked by this openness, communication spirituality is like missionary spirituality as outlined by John Paul II in *Redemptoris Missio* (= RM), his encyclical letter on mission (1990). Communication spirituality is first and foremost expressed, the Pope says,

> by a life of *complete docility to the Spirit*. It commits us to be molded from within by the Spirit, so that we may become ever more like Christ. It is not possible to bear witness to Christ without reflecting His image, which is made alive in us by grace and the power of the Spirit. This docility then commits us to receive the gifts of fortitude and discernment, which are essential elements of missionary spirituality (n. 87)...

... and clearly of a communication spirituality. The apostles of the Lord can be an example to us here, because

> despite their love for Him and their generous response to His call, they proved to be incapable of understanding His words and reluctant to follow him along the path of suffering and humiliation. The Spirit transformed them into courageous witnesses to Christ and enlightened heralds of His word. It was the Spirit himself who guided them along the difficult and new paths of mission (n. 87).

Like mission, also Christian communication today "is difficult and complex and demands courage and the light of the Spirit" (n. 87).

Communication Spirituality lives out of an experience of "intimate communion with Christ. We can not understand or carry out the mission unless we refer it to Christ as the one who was sent to evangelize", which, of course, means to communicate. Christ's incarnation and his redemptive offering of self are described by the apostle Paul (Phil 2,5-8) "as a total self-emptying which leads Christ to experience fully the human condition and accept totally the Father's plan. This is an emptying of self which is permeated by love and expresses love" (n. 88). A Christian communicator must be deeply united in communion with this self-emptying Christ to realize communication as "giving of Self in Love", to quote the Pastoral Instruction on communication, *Communio et Progressio* (1971, n. 11; cf. Eph 5,25). The ideal Christian communicator therefore is finally, like the missionary required to "renounce himself and everything that up to this point he considered as his own, and make himself everything to everyone", as the mission document *Ad Gentes* of the Second Vatican Council puts it (n. 24). This means that

Christian communicators are totally available to the people with whom and for whom they communicate.

Further, an authentic communication spirituality is marked by *apostolic charity* which is the "charity of Christ who came 'to gather into one the children of God who are scattered abroad' (Jn 11,52), the charity of the Good Shepherd who knows his sheep, who searches them out and offers his life for them" (Jn 10). Like the missionary, the Christian communicator is

> urged by "zeal for souls", a zeal inspired by Christ's own charity, which takes the form of concern, tenderness, compassion, openness, availability and interest in people's problems. Jesus' love is very deep: he who "knew what is man" (Jn 2,25) loved everyone by offering them redemption and suffered when it was rejected (n. 89).

Similarly, the Christian communicator is called to be "a person of charity. In order to proclaim to all his brothers and sisters that they are loved by God and are capable of loving, he must show love towards all, giving his life for his neighbor" (n. 89). He is

> the "universal brother", bearing himself the Church's spirit, her openness to and interest in all peoples and individuals, especially the least and poorest of his brethren. As such he overcomes barriers and divisions of race, caste or ideology. He is the sign of God's love in the world – a love without exclusion or partiality (*Ibid.*).

The spirituality of a Christian communicator is also a *call to personal holiness*. He is an authentic Christian communicator only if he commits himself to this challenge and if all his communicating flows out from this commitment. "Holiness must be called the fundamental presupposition and irreplaceable condition for everyone in fulfilling the mission of salvation in the Church" (*Christifideles Laici,* 1988: n. 17). This universal call to holiness is also a special calling for Christian communicators, who must strive to renew themselves in the Spirit, to grow in their appreciation of the Scriptures and to "strive to also update their doctrinal and pastoral formation" (RM 91).

Contemplata tradere – to pass on what one has contemplated – is the mission and motto of the Order of Preachers, the Dominicans. This profound and provocative statement could serve well as a focus for the Christian communicator. In a similar expression, Ignatius of Loyola was called a "contemplative in action", something his sons, the Jesuits today, are called to be.

What John Paul II requires of a missionary – it should be also the mark of the Christian communicator – is to

> find answers to problems in the light of God's word and in personal and community prayer. My contact with representatives of the non-Christian spiritual traditions, particularly those of Asia, has confirmed me in the view that the future of mission depends to a great extent on contemplation. Unless the missionary is a contemplative he cannot proclaim Christ in a credible way. He is a witness to the experience of God, and must be able to say with the apostles: "that which we have looked upon...concerning the word of life...we also proclaim to you" (1 Jn 1,1-3) (RM 91).

What the Pope says to missionaries also holds true for the Christian communicator: "The characteristic of every authentic missionary life is the inner joy that comes from faith. In a world tormented and oppressed by so many problems, a world tempted by pessimism, the one who proclaims the 'Good News' must be a person who has found true hope in Christ" (RM 91).

The openness of Christian communicators to God is also reflected in their openness to themselves and to their own personal needs. Only when they face their own personal reality can they be genuine communication partners with God and with others. People have the right to communicate with a concrete, balanced, mature and spirit-filled responsible person and not with puppets who are inauthentic or persons who are not able themselves to face reality and who are preoccupied with themselves and their own agendas instead of being free for objective reporting and sharing. Thus Christian communicators must be concerned with their own spiritual lives and authentic human development. They need to appreciate and experience the value of good spiritual direction, which should also be part of their lives. Regular spiritual sharing helps to discern and encourage a deeper human and spiritual growth from which communication should flow. In fact such spiritual exchanges are the deepest and most personal way of interpersonal communication which ideally goes beyond the strictly spiritual to include other experiences and challenges of life. This experience helps to deepen one's personal communication with God. A discerning and deeply-grounded Christian communicator will gratefully acknowledge and accept the value of Christian community. It is in the openness to all this that real spirituality shines through everything we do; a spiritual communicator will be easily recognized and thus contribute to "building communities through love, sharing, communion, relationship and equality" (FABC-OSC Bishops' Meet 1999, Final Statement).

Openness to God and to one's self leads to openness to others; it encourages the communicator to listen to their stories and experiences, to recognize their needs and aspirations, to share their faith experiences and to creating and supporting communities of believers and communicators. The Christian community is an essential source of the spiritual life of Christian communicators. They cannot stand alone, isolated but they need the community for nourishment and support. Not without reason have the two words "*comm*unity" and "*comm*unication" the same Latin root word "*communis*" which means common. Probing into the original meaning of these words, Gisbert Greshake sees two dimensions in the root of this word: it comes from the stem "*mum*" which means something like bulwark or surrounding wall. People who are in communion, communicating "are together behind the same wall" and depend on each other. The second meaning of "*mum*", as reflected in the Latin word "*munus*", is that of gift, service and commitment.

These etymologies suggest that communicators are in the service of the other, sharing themselves and their lives and work in such a way that community, and division, evolves. Communication spirituality therefore is not only individual but also communal spirituality. The experience of community in prayer, in the Eucharist and in the sacraments, Bible sharing and common life experiences nourish and give strength to the communicator. It is from this that the Christian communicator develops and grows in commitment to the needs of others and can thus become the "voice of the voiceless". Such an experience of community also helps to develop creativity and new ideas for further communication developments. It helps to go beyond the actual and to develop visions for the future but always in the light of faith and Christian community.

Like the priest, also the Christian Communicator is called to "Pastoral charity" which John Paul II defines as "the virtue by which we imitate Christ in his self-giving and service. It is not just what we do, but our gift of self, which manifests Christ love for his flock. 'Pastoral charity' determines our way of thinking and acting, our way of relating to people. It makes special demands on us". This "pastoral charity" is a dynamic principle which, the Pope goes on to say, "is capable of unifying the many different activities" and is an essential and permanent demand for unity between the interior life and the external activities and obligations of a modern communicator (cf. apostolic exhortation *Pastores dabo Vobis*, n. 24). This is especially urgent in a time where our sociocultural context "is strongly marked by complexity, fragmentation and dispersion".

4. Christian Communication Model as challenge

In the history of communication research there have been many attempts to develop communication models. They are to clarify the flow, dynamics and efficiency of the communication process. Most of them are especially concerned about the sender and his/her attempt to reach the recipient in an effective way. These "linear" communication models with Sender, Message, and Receiver as the main elements have been around for a long time. Other models like the "convergence model" of Everett Rogers and Kincaid or the ritual model of James Carey are especially concerned about the partnership in the communication process to develop a common ground of understanding and experience. Different from all these is the *Christian Communication Model* which was developed at the University of Santo Tomas in Manila. This model is based on St. Augustine's teachings and puts the message in the centre of the communication process. For the Christian communicator the message stays central which is the Word of God or Jesus Christ as the incarnate Word of God himself. The Christian communicator is only the messenger of the *Word*, he is like the ambassador who represents his country. The more s/he not only communicates but also lives and reflects in his/her life this *Word* the more convincing s/he will be as a communicator. This does not depend on techniques but rather on the spirituality of the communicator. The more s/he is filled with the Spirit of the Lord, the more s/he is the person who in a convincing way transmits and reflects that message. This means in practical terms: the more the messenger reflects and meditates the word of God in Scripture, the more he listens to the promptings of the Holy Spirit the more he becomes a real *Christian* communicator. The Christian Communication Model: Message-Messenger-Recipient reminds us of the real centre for any spirituality of a Christian Communicator. It reflects the Christian reality of revelation, incarnation and the real role of the communicator as a servant and the one who stays and lives fully in the service of the message. It is not him/her who "calls the shots" but rather the Lord himself who is the message and His Spirit.

5. Conclusion

Carlo Maria Martini's biblically-based spirituality is a most valuable legacy of the *Interdisciplinary Centre for Social Communications* at the Gregorian University. In its first years the program of the *Centre* was closely related to the faculties of Missiology, Philosophy and later to Social Sciences. Perhaps after 25 years it would be good also to align with the Gregorian's Institute of Spirituality. A Catholic and Ecclesiastical university like the Gregorian should be concerned in a particular way with the spirituality of communications and of the communicator at a time when consumerism, relativism and materialism seem to dominate the communication scene.

Bibliographical references

DULLES, A. (1992), *The Craft of Theology. From Symbol to System*, Dublin: Gill and Macmillan.

EILERS, F.-J. (2002), *Communicating in Community. Introduction to Social Communication*, Third enlarged edition, Manila: Logos.

EILERS, F.-J. (2004), *Communicating in Ministry and Mission. An Introduction to Pastoral and Evangelizing Communication*, 2nd Edition, Manila: Logos.

MARTINI, C. M. (1990), *Effatà, Apriti*, Milano: Centro Ambrosiano. English Edition (1994): *Communicating Christ to the World*, Kansas City: Sheed and Ward; Philippine Edition (1996): Manila: Claretians.

PALAKEEL, J., ed. (2003), *Towards a Communication Theology,* Bangalore: Asian Trading.

PLUDE, F. F., ed. (2001), "Communication Theology", in *Catholic International*, 12/4.

SOUKUP, P. (2001), "Communication Theology as a basis for Social Communication Formation", in F.-J. EILERS, ed., *Social Communication Formation in Priestly Ministry,* FABC-OSC Books, Vol. 2, Manila: Logos.

Maybe angels: glimpses of spirituality in popular culture
Jim McDonnell

L'articolo esamina la sempre crescente popolarità delle tematiche "soprannaturali" e religiose ricorrenti nella serie televisiva Star Trek ed in altri programmi simili degli anni '90 e fino ad oggi. I campi della fantasy o della fantascienza attraggono sempre di più il pubblico, perché sembrano offrire sia una via d'uscita dalla routine e dalle preoccupazioni della vita quotidiana che un valido commento di esse. Il grande successo popolare della serie X-Files e di altra programmazione del genere lascia intuire che le strutture religiose tradizionali non rispondano in modo adeguato alle domande religiose e spirituali della gente. Questi media di intrattenimento nutrono ciò che in molte persone si potrebbe chiamare una spiritualità di "apertura alle possibilità". Il successo di tali programmi popolari avanza per tutte le tradizioni religiose stabili la sfida di prendere più sul serio simili narrazioni come punto di incontro e di connessione con la sensibilità e la spiritualità postmoderna.

1. Introduction: a host of angels

The cinema has long had a preoccupation with angels. A spate of movies appeared just after the ending of the Second World War, including *It's a Wonderful Life* (1946) and *Stairway to Heaven* (1946), perhaps tapping into so many people's experience of loss of loved ones and offering a kind of consolation. Recently the approach of the Millennium saw the production of increasing number of movies in the late 1990s (e.g. *Michael* [1997], *City of Angels* [1998] and *Dogma* [1999]) and television series (*Touched by an Angel* [1994-2003]), featuring angels as protagonists.

In the United States today nearly three quarters of the population (72%) profess a belief in angels. The appeal may be that:

> Angels are not demanding. They ask for nothing in return. They do not demand that you go to church on Sunday [...] Americans like the fact that angels don't demand any specific code of behaviour, especially sexual behaviour [...] Angels of the 1990's aren't churchy or preachy. They have their peccadilloes and, perhaps, anyone of us can get our wings (Dawson, 1998).

The film *City of Angels*, a remake of Wim Wenders' *Wings of Desire* (1987), with the location moved from a divided Berlin to a modern Los Angeles, exemplifies this current interest in angels and their role in human affairs. Unlike traditional Christian angelic figures like Gabriel or Raphael, for example, these angels bring no messages from a personal God. They announce no good tidings nor demand any moral or spiritual response. The angels stand on the rooftops of Los Angeles and watch over the city and its inhabitants. They can be seen by innocent children but not by adults. In *City of Angels,* angels are messengers of comfort and consolation, guardian angels who avert disasters (only some disasters, however) and are companions of the dying. The power they serve is symbolised by the sunrise, but its intervention in human affairs seems capricious and inconsistent.

In its unfocused sense of the spiritual in the face of death and its longing for emotional reassurance, the mood of *City of Angels* reminds one strongly of the sense of the spiritual dimension to the outpouring of grief which followed the tragic death of Diana, Princess of Wales, and which brought to the surface the usually hidden sense of the sacred, which, according to Professor David Hay (1996: 292), is shared by the majority of people in Britain.

This "sense of the sacred", is a kind of generalised consciousness of the holy, the *"numinous"*, something at once fascinating, awe inspiring and perhaps even frightening. This spiritual sense belongs to no coherent system of doctrine but is a kind of intuitive consciousness that all aspects of life are related in a meaningful whole. Spirituality has become divorced from religion. Nearly twice as many people claim to have had a spiritual experience than go to church regularly. Adherence to organised religion continues to fall, but interest in matters spiritual seems to be on the increase. Every large bookstore has more and more space given over to "mind, body, spirit", New Age and fantasy literature while websites of a religious, spiritual or transcendental nature proliferate on the Internet. The religiously deracinated angelic host in *City of Angels* in this context stands as an apt symbol for a spiritual consciousness that floats free of any specific religious tradition.

The appeal of the spirituality exemplified by a film like *City of Angels* is summed up well by Gillian Anderson, who played FBI agent Dana Scully in the television series *The X-Files*. In an interview in 1995 she spoke of her own spiritual journey: "When I was in high school... I was in a very atheist crowd and it was the consensus that religion was a crutch; but over the past few years I have grown to appreciate that feeling of safety or trust, that there is a light at the end of the tunnel and that there is a reason for us to be here" (Billen, 1995).

It seems appropriate, if paradoxical (Scully, after all, was the *The X-Files'* arch sceptic), that such sentiments should come from the mouth of one of the stars of a television series that in recent years has propelled spiritual and supernatural issues into mainstream popular entertainment. *The X-Files* mixture of conspiracy thriller, paranormal speculation and spiritual quest suggests that at a personal level people are deeply unsatisfied with the ability of science and technology to answer questions of meaning.

The theme of *The X-Files* (1993-2002) was that "the truth is out there" but truth in the X-Files-universe is a slippery entity. Throughout the decade-long series, in the ongoing dramatic interaction between two FBI agents, the sceptic Scully and the believer Mulder, the audience was invited to balance the competing claims of faith and reason. In a radio interview in 1995, the series creator, Chris Carter, remarked that "people who see the show oftentimes they feel the show is actually a very religious show, which is funny because when I've thought about this, I think of myself as a non-religious person looking for religious experience, so I think that's what the characters are sort of doing too"[1]. Chris Carter's vision seemed to tap directly into the mixture of confusion, fears, hopes, credulity and scepticism that is modern (or postmodern) spirituality for so many people.

2. Amazing worlds: the appeal of speculative fiction

The X-Files belongs to what has come to be called speculative fiction. A multi-faceted literature that "includes utopian fiction, hard science fiction, near future thrillers and disaster scenarios, supernatural fiction, heroic fantasy, magic realism, and various other sub-genres". (Runté, 2000). In broad terms the two dominant trends are science fiction and fantasy (including horror). These genres, the boundaries of which are increasingly blurred, are both concerned with pushing back the boundaries of the everyday and asking "what if?". The attraction of such genres is that, in the famous opening words of *Star Trek*, they can "boldly go" into a "space" (inner and outer) which is "the final frontier". Both science fiction and fantasies operate according to their own logic and sense of reality. In this dramatic context characters can more easily interact with persons and forces, including supernatural ones, that have theoretically been banished from our everyday world.

The realm of fantasy or science fiction provides both an escape from and a commentary on the routines and concerns of everyday life. Filmmakers like George Lucas and Steven Spielberg, best selling authors like J.R.R. Tolkien, Isaac Asimov, Frank Herbert, Robert Jordan, Dan Simmons, Katherine Kerr, Raymond Feist, Anne McCaffrey, or to comic effect, Terry Pratchett, and more recently, children's authors J.K. Rowlings and Philip Pullman, build imaginary alternative or future worlds.

The fantasy or speculative worlds created by both science fiction and fantasy authors have their own physical laws, cultures and social structures – and theologies. Elements from Arthurian, Norse and Graeco-Roman legends are combined with biblical stories and myths from Eastern or other religions as well as from science (quantum physics, artificial intelligence, robotics, cloning, genetic manipulation) to create new interpretations of the world and its ultimate meaning. Particularly under the influence of the writings of Joseph Campbell, authors and film-makers have plundered the myths of the world to create new heroic myths suitable for today. Campbell's analysis of the mythic journey and the hero's quest have now become standard templates for Hollywood script-writer.

The result of this fascination with mythic structures is a typically post-modern (or New Age) proliferation of stories that throw together elements from science and fantasy together with borrowings from a multitude of religious and spiritual cultures. In films, television series, videos, DVDs, books, comics, computer games and the Internet, the world of the imagination is peopled with gods and demons, angels, ghosts, vampires (*Buffy the Vampire Slayer, Angel*), wizards and witches (*Charmed, Sabrina the Teenage Witch, Bewitched, Harry Potter*), heroes and heroines (*Star Wars, Batman, The Adventures of Hercules, Xenia Warrior Princess, Dark Angel, Mutant X, AI*), saviors and messiahs (*ET, Superman, Mad Max, Dune, Terminator, The Matrix, Lord of the Rings*).

One explanation for the popular success of these stories is fundamentally due to the fact that they are just that, "stories". The children's author, Philip Pullman, whose fantasy novel trilogy, *His Dark Materials*, are now the subject of much attention, said in 1996 that "Stories never fail us. In adult literary fiction, stories are there on sufferance. Other things are felt to be more important: technique, style, literary knowingness. But stories are vital. There's more wisdom in a story than in volumes of poetry" (Ferguson, 2001: 24).

Another element in their success may be that these expressions of popular culture all speak, in however attenuated a form, of the quest for personal authenticity and transcendent meanings in a fragmented, mysterious and chaotic world. Mythic structures, whether of the New Age or the commercial Hollywood variety, are frameworks for interpreting and exploring messy, confusing reality. Chris Carter, for example, talks about the underlying "mythology" of *The X-Files*.

3. Star Trek: from outer to inner space

Perhaps the single most successful attempt made to create a modern myth in television and film terms is *Star Trek*, a television series that has now endured for over thirty years and has become a truly global phenomenon. The reason for the immense popularity of *Star Trek* and the intense loyalty it evokes in its devotees has prompted much speculation. A good attempt at beginning to explain its appeal is made by Jeff Greenwald:

> *Star Trek* invokes an almost primeval wanderlust – a hardwired compulsion to break away from the familiar, and plumb the depths of outer and inner space. It inspires a desire to build society where technology is partnered with conscience. It evokes a yearning for family and friendship, which is played out in a thousand different fan clubs and Web sites around the world. And it fulfils a deep and eternal need for something to believe in: something vast and powerful, yet rational and contemporary. Something that makes sense (Greenwald, 1998: 2).

The originator of *Star Trek*, Gene Rodenberry, had an optimistic liberal-humanist view of a future in which the world would be united as part of a wider Federation of planets, in which advances in science and technology would have conquered most diseases, abolished hunger and poverty, and where racism, sexual inequality, wars and organised religion would have faded away.

The *Star Trek* of the 1960's, 1970's and early 1980's embodied the values of Rodenberry's technological future. In this future, religion was a throwback to earlier eras of superstition and when religion appeared it did so as a feature of more primitive alien societies. In the four series and in the Star Trek movies, "not a single human crew member of any Federation ship professes any form of religious belief. Formal religious belief is something reserved for aliens and is usually a sign of cultural weakness" (Richards, 1997: 140). Religious delusions had to be unmasked and confronted by a more rational humanism.

Star Trek: The Next Generation began in 1987. However, though religious and spiritual themes appear throughout the series, the underlying presuppositions of the Rodenberry view are not fundamentally challenged. The most "religious" character in the whole series is an alien, the Klingon, Worf, and though his "spiritual quest" is seen as important to him, the edifice of Klingon religion and ritual is seen more in terms of psychological needs and cultural identity than as revealing truths about the universe. However, there is a greater respect shown towards personal beliefs and a growing sense that religious myths and some ritual practices have value, at least for their practitioners.

Then in 1993, the same year that *The X-Files* first aired, the series *Deep Space Nine* was introduced. *Deep Space Nine* was a political drama, which takes place in the vicinity of a "wormhole" (a distortion in space-time that allows access to another normally far off region of the galaxy) near a planet called Bajor. The complications of the plot concern the battle between different alien races and the Federation for control of the wormhole. Even more surprisingly for Star Trek "the spiritual traditions and prophecies of Bajor form a constant backdrop to the action and a continual challenge to the scientific humanism of the Federation" (Gregory, 2000: 69).

Throughout this series religious or spiritual interpretations of reality are accorded more respect than hitherto in the *Star Trek* universe. Reality is seen to be more complex than a strictly scientific explanation would allow. In contrast to the journeyings into outer space of the *Star Trek*'s captains Kirk and Picard, the central character, Benjamin Sisko embarks upon an inward journey in which he gradually begins to accept and value his spiritual role as an Emissary, a kind of Messiah figure. In an extraordinary episode called "Rapture", for example, Sisko has a series of spiritual visions that reveal the future. However, this episode, which first aired in 1997, marks a huge shift, as "for the first time Star Trek acknowledges the 'reality' of spirituality and makes no attempt to explain it away 'scientifically' or relegate it to the status of 'primitive' belief" (Gregory, 2000: 112).

The climax to the series, the episode "What You Leave Behind" (1999), is even more extraordinary. The series enters the realm of "fantasy". Sisko fights an apocalyptic battle, vanquishes the "demon" enemy by sacrificing himself and is translated to a state of being described as "non-linear". In other words he becomes eternal, outside the bounds of time and space. He leaves only a promise that he will return. His fate can be interpreted in religious or spiritual terms as an "apotheosis", an ascension to a state of quasi-divinity, or in more secular terms as a transition to another physical state.

The opening up of the spiritual dimension within the *Star Trek* universe is continued in the parallel series *Voyager* (1995-2001). Like *Deep Space Nine*, *Voyager* is interested in the inner voyage. However, the "spiritual" is still the preserve of those who can be classed in one way or another as "exotic" or outside the dominant religious or social power structures. Religion in *Deep Space Nine* is still a religion of aliens and the religious hierarchy is seen as essentially compromised, Benjamin Sisko is a senior officer and a man, but he is a black man, while those who take religion seriously in *Voyager* are the Native American Chakotay, the half Klingon female Belanna Torres and the female Captain Janeway.

The last series of *Star Trek*, simply called *Enterprise*, which began in September 2001, returned to the era before the first series began and charted the voyages of the first Enterprise. It moved away from the *Voyager* style to a less thoughtful, more action adventure approach and ignored questions of myth and spirituality. Indeed, in one episode it exposed a spiritual centre, supposedly dedicated to meditation and learning, as simply a cover for spying. It is perhaps indicative that the "bad guys" in the first series were called the Suliban, a name explicitly based on the Taliban. In so far as there were spiritual battles to be fought the enemy was largely externalised, the inner life and its struggles is less evident. This new approach seemed to reflect both a shift in American culture, particularly the growing fear of terrorism, especially after September 11th, and an attempt to re-vamp the series in order to win ratings; an attempt that proved ultimately unsuccessful when the producers announced in 2005 that no more *Star Trek* episodes would be made[2]. The demise of *Star Trek* seemed to indicate that the ability of the series to reinvent itself successfully for another generation and to capture the spirit of the age had finally ended.

Because of its longevity, *Star Trek* provides us with a helpful way into understanding some of the changes in the ways popular culture has treated religious and spiritual themes over the past three decades. In the scope of this one continually unfolding mythic drama we can see how religious and spiritual questions and possibilities were taken increasingly seriously through the 1990's. *Star Trek*'s handling of these themes, and its final turning away from them, also reveals the deep ambivalences in our Western culture to the status of the supernatural and the relationship it might have to our largely taken-for-granted scientific and technological world view.

Until its final series *Star Trek* had successfully embodied the essentially opened ended character of speculative fiction. It could be argued that in its final seasons it tended to lose that imaginative scope and so failed to satisfy one of the basic strengths of the genre. Certainly, the popular entertainment industry continues to show no lack of continuing interest in supernatural themes. During roughly the same period as *Enterprise*, for example, global film goers were treated to the *Matrix* trilogy (1999, 2003), the *Star Wars* prequels (1999, 2002, 2005), the *Lord of the Rings* (2001, 2002, 2003) and the ongoing *Harry Potter* series (2001- ...).

4. A spirituality of possibilities

At the end of her stimulating study of U.S. teenagers and their involvement with fantasy TV and films that deal with the supernatural, Lynn Scholfield Clark concludes that "many young audience members do seem to embrace one belief that may best be described as an openness to possibility" (Clark, 2003: 228).

That openness is well expressed by the lyrics of the Sheryl Crow song, "Maybe Angels" (1996). At one point she sings: "My sister, she says she knows Elvis/ She knows Jesus, John Lennon and Cobain personally/ Well, I'm too wise to believe my eyes". Sheryl Crow expresses the ambivalence that is so often at the heart of the popular feeling about religious experiences of whatever kind. So for Sheryl Crow, there are "maybe angels" but she is "too wise" to believe her eyes. It is the possibilities of belief and the possibility that beliefs might be true, and the concomitant fear that it is all a hoax, that both expresses the spiritual experience of many people and helps explain why contemporary popular media have a role in helping to shape religious identity and belief.

Moreover, as Clark notes, the stories told by the entertainment media "compete or co-exist with other stories, such as those from the religious traditions, that may be viewed as equally possible and plausible – or equally fictional" (Clark, 2003: 228). In the world of multi-media and the Internet the searcher for understanding is confronted with a huge variety of competing visions and claims with little sense of how to choose between them.

The popular success of *The X-Files* and other such programmes also suggests that traditional religious frameworks seem inadequate to the task of answering the religious and spiritual questions that trouble people. As Clark puts it :

> These fictional programs raise a question that resonates particularly well in the context of our times, an age in which the certainties of Modernism – science, theology, reality itself – have come into question: there are happenings and events in this world and beyond that remain unexplained. These are profoundly religious considerations, of course. Unfortunately, religion is not handling them well (Clark, 1999).

The inadequacy of traditional religious frameworks is also raised by the American fantasy writer, Robert Jordan, author of the monumental *Wheel of Time* series, who comments:

> In the beginning, religion and fantasy were linked, and I really believe humanity has a need for that. In modernizing, we've put all that aside – the fantastical part of religion. And that leaves a void, something that people want [...] Good fantasy fills a part of that need, because there is discussion of right and wrong, the necessary complications, the struggle to identify what is good, what is evil, right, wrong. These are all inherent in good fantasy just as they were once inherent in religion[3].

This emphasis on the questions that people raise, is also noted by the creator of the TV science fiction series *Babylon 5* (1994-1998), J. Michael Straczynski. According to Straczynski, science fiction is not a genre to be lightly dismissed. For him, "the questions that science fiction asks, at its best, are not ephemeral; they are questions of moment, of importance, that take the mirror of reality and turn it this way, that much, to see the problems in a different light" (Straczynski, 1998a). In a debate at the Massachusetts Institute of Technology, he commented:

> I mean, I'm an atheist myself but [...] I also like to look at the dynamic that takes place between religion and science because, in a way, both are asking the same questions: Who are we? Where do we come from? Why are we here? Where are we going? The methodologies are diametrically opposed, but their motivation is the same; the wellspring is the same in both cases. And they are often more complementary than they are contradictory (Straczynski, 1998b).

Straczynski's statement is of some significance. It is commonplace for theologians to claim that science and religion are complementary. It is not so common for that claim to be made by a writer of television science fiction. The comment is an indicator of how some of the old antagonism between popular views of science and religion may be quietly dissolving.

Like other popular television series, *Babylon 5* has a number of Web sites devoted to it. On the official Web site there are a number of discussion groups, and on one of these a contributor had noticed that in one episode a character asks the hero, Captain Sheridan, "What do you live for?". That question posted to the Web site then stimulated a range of other people to attempt to answer it. The fact that films and television shows can generate such questions and that many different kinds of people can then be stimulated to try and respond shows how unwise it is to dismiss such shows as mere escapist entertainment.

In *The Matrix* (1999), the character who first awakens the hero Neo to a realisation of his own destiny is called "Morpheus". Morpheus in Greco-Roman mythology is the God of dreams. The world of dreams, like the cinema experience itself, is a fragile one, full of confusing images needing careful interpretation. Above all, it is a world in which contradictory images and ideas can co-exist. It is a world which is comfortable with inconsistency and paradox.

The dream world is one of possibilities, options, explorations, even probabilities, but answers, if there are any at all, can only be provisional, temporary, limited and open-ended. There is, and can be, no definitive satisfactory answers to the problem of free will or whether there is life after death, for example. This attitude does not sit comfortably with adherence to a system of beliefs, like Christianity, in which answers are deemed available even if hard to come by. It challenges the notion of truth itself and seems to presage a descent into chaos. No wonder then that some people are drawn to less fluid and more determinate, even fundamentalist, religious belief systems

However in modern secularised western societies the abiding characteristic of what we might call a postmodern sensibility is the conviction that there are questions for which there are no answers. As fraught with philosophical and theological difficulties as it is, this conviction seems to be the place where increasing numbers of people find themselves. As Clark observes, media "stories that tie the supernatural to a specific religious tradition are out of favour". The stories which "explicitly embrace religious language and traditions" are often rejected by those outside those traditions. Readers and viewers that are "not greatly interested in religion are not interested in stories where the possibilities are limited to religion" (Clark, 2003: 228). The challenge for those who belong to more established religious traditions is to enter that place with humility and confidence ready to accompany people along the diverse and often shifting paths that their explorations lead them. There may be angels, but whether there are or not, they should surely boldly go where no one has gone before.

NOTES

[1] *The Gabereau show,* CBC, Friday, May 5, 1995, *http://www.mjq.net/xfiles/ccarter.htm.*
[2] *Star Trek: Enterprise Cancelled,* in *http://www.startrek.com/startrek/view/news/article/9469.html* (03/02/05).
[3] Interview with Robert Jordan. *Locus Magazine,* March 2000.

Bibliographical references

BILLEN, A. (1995), intervista *Observer Life,* 25 giugno.
CLARK, L. S. (1999), "Popular Culture: Replacing Religion for Today's Teens?", *The Bible in TransMission,* December.
CLARK, L. S. (2003), *From Angels to Aliens: Teenagers, the Media, and the Supernatural,* New York: OUP.
DAWSON, J. (1998), "How to make a film take off: just add wings", *The Independent,* 11 June.
FERGUSON, E. (2001), "Battle of the Wizards", *The Observer,* 4 November.
GREENWALD, J. (1998), *Future Perfect: How Star Trek Conquered Planet Earth,* Harmondsworth: Penguin Books.
GREGORY, C. (2000), *Star Trek: Parallel Narratives,* London: Macmillan.
HAY, D. (1996), "Religion Lacking Spirit", *The Tablet,* 2 March.
RICHARDS, T. (1997), *Star Trek in Myth and Legend,* London: Millennium.
RUNTÉ, R. (2000), *The NCF Guide to Canadian Science Fiction,* in *http://www.uleth.ca/edu/runte/ncfguide/sfdef.htm*
STRACZYNSKI, J. M. (1998a), *What the Networks Don't Know About Science Fiction,* May 4th, in *http:/web.mit.edu/comm-forum/papers/straczynski.html*
STRACZYNSKI, J. M. (1998b), Discussion at MIT, May 4th, in *http://web.mit.edu/science_fiction/transcripts/jms_jablokov_index.html*

La lettura come realtà virtuale
Tra letteratura, spiritualità e *media* elettronici
Antonio Spadaro, SJ

Every spirituality has an effect not only on one's way of praying and living, but also on the way one reads a literary text. The article examines how the Spiritual Exercises of Ignatius of Loyola can develop in the exercitant a particular way of reading literary works, beginning with the reading of Sacred Scripture. The instructions that Ignatius offers for the interaction of the exercitant with the biblical text correspond to three basic elements of the grammar of a narrative: setting, character, plot. The present article, developing also a formal analogy between the virtual reality of the videogame and the experience of reading the Spiritual Exercises, reaches three conclusions: a text exists when it is read, just as a piece of music exists when it is performed; a text has a "virtual" character; and reading a text is not a process of simply interiorizing its content but a process of dynamic interaction between the text and its reader; those who live the spirituality of the Exercises develop a real predilection for narrative texts, because they have become accustomed to contemplate God through stories, in a historical context and with vivid images.

Ogni spiritualità cristiana è anche un modo di vedere la realtà e di stare al mondo: essa dà "forma" a una vita umana e le conferisce una particolare sensibilità. In concreto, chi si riconosce in una via spirituale (francescana, carmelitana, ignaziana...) non solo vive la propria fede, ma anche tutta la propria esperienza alla luce di un carisma particolare, che coinvolge anche molti aspetti dell'esistenza ordinaria. Alla luce di questa semplice considerazione è possibile chiedersi: esistono spiritualità cristiane capaci di avere una ricaduta specifica anche a livello della lettura di un testo letterario? Semplificando: una persona formata alla spiritualità del *Castello interiore* di Teresa d'Avila o della *Salita al Monte Carmelo* di Giovanni della Croce, quando si pone davanti a un'opera letteraria, la legge in modo differente rispetto a una persona formata alla *lectio* benedettina o alla spiritualità degli Esercizi di Ignazio di Loyola? Cercheremo in queste pagine di riassumere brevemente il rapporto tra spiritualità e poesia, così come è stato posto dagli inizi del Novecento, per poi proseguire scegliendo, a titolo esemplificativo, un modello spirituale preciso, quello degli *Esercizi* ignaziani, per indagare come esso possa indicare un modo peculiare di leggere un testo letterario[1].

1. "Tocca al mistico di spiegarci il poeta"?

Possiamo far risalire idealmente la questione al 1913, quando L. de Grandmaison (1913: 289-302) accennò all'affinità tra sentimento religioso e ispirazione poetica, chiedendo a quest'ultima un contributo per meglio comprendere la dinamica spirituale. Nel 1926 Henri Bremond nel suo *Preghiera e poesia* sviluppò lo spunto di Grandmaison, provocando un intenso dibattito (Bremond, 1983; Savignano, 2000): egli ipotizzava, sulla base del riconoscimento di alcuni gesti profondi comuni tra esperienza spirituale ed esperienza poetica (raccoglimento, semplificazione, ritmo di attività e passività, di iniziativa e di accoglienza della gratuità di una "visita"), un'analogia e una continuità. Bremond propone un paragone:

> *Possiamo imparare – quel che s'intende precisamente per imparare – a nuotare? Pare di no. Nuotare, è in fin dei conti non toccare il fondo, e quest'atto di fiducia non si insegna né si impone. È l'acqua stessa che, sostenendoci, giustifica la fiducia che abbiamo avuto in essa. Non si impara a nuotare, ma un giorno, nel mezzo della prima lezione o, alla fine della ventesima, constatiamo che, pur avendo perduto piede, non andiamo a fondo, e che senza camminare ci spostiamo. La medesima cosa si produce nell'esperienza poetica*[2] (Bremond, 1983: 27).

In particolare nella sua argomentazione egli cita Shelley, per il quale

> la poesia è una creazione, indubbiamente, ma prima di tutto una rivelazione. L'ispirazione sovrasta tutto. Un'influenza che viene dal di fuori si impadronisce del poeta, il quale non può né capirla né controllarla: una potenza divina penetra in lui, lo costringe a creare certe immagini perfette, attraverso le quali egli cerca di contendere al nulla queste visite di Dio all'uomo (Bremond, 1983: 83).

Bremond tuttavia compie un rovesciamento di ottica: invece di chiarire l'esperienza mistica attraverso l'esperienza poetica, è alla prima che chiede di rivelargli la vera natura della seconda. Non è l'esperienza di Shelley che aiuta a penetrare meglio l'esperienza di Giovanni della Croce, ma, al contrario, è questa a rendere un po' meno oscuro il mistero di quella. Da dove provengono le somiglianze tra queste due realtà così diverse? Il carattere soprannaturale della vita interiore, afferma Bremond, non modifica necessariamente il disegno psicologico di una persona ed è proprio in virtù della propria esperienza psicologica che il poeta può essere paragonato al mistico. Sono stati i mistici come Giovanni della Croce o Teresa d'Avila a descrivere questa linea psicologica, che raramente si trova nelle confessioni dei poeti. Ecco allora l'assioma bremondiano: "Tocca al mistico di spiegarci il poeta" (Bremond, 1983: 100). La poesia non è la preghiera, ma per Bremond la poesia tende di sua natura a raggiungere la preghiera. Ciò significa che nell'esperienza poetica viene messa in moto la stessa dinamica psicologica di cui la Grazia si serve per elevare alla preghiera. La poesia è insomma il segno di una facoltà elevata che ci appartiene, in grado di ricevere Dio e incapace da sé di comprenderlo[3].

Un simile approccio alla poesia evidentemente pone in questione non solo lo statuto della poesia, ma anche la lettura di un testo poetico. Se la poesia è – passi il termine bremondiano – "spiegata" dalla mistica, la lettura della poesia deve avere qualche relazione con gli atteggiamenti interiori tipici della preghiera. La letteratura mondiale ha prodotto pagine splendide a questo proposito. Non si fa fatica, ad esempio, a riconoscere nelle pagine che Proust dedica alla "sapiente bellezza" della lettura[4] i gesti che dispongono all'apertura di un luogo interiore che sono molto simili proprio a quelli dell'orazione. Bremond definisce questa lettura intensa e creativa come "leggere in modo poetico" (Bremond, 1983: 29).

È possibile proseguire nell'analisi dal punto in cui l'ha lasciata Bremond, ma occorre scegliere un binario più preciso per comprendere come un'esperienza spirituale possa contribuire a comprendere la lettura poetica dei poeti. Ci si potrebbe fermare qui e scavare nella relazione tra i due termini (spiritualità e poesia), diciamo così, "in generale", come ha fatto Bremond. Si può essere tentati di far riferimento a un tipo di esperienza che si chiama esperienza religiosa o spirituale in genere. In realtà, non esiste l'esperienza "spirituale" in genere, ma sempre una sua forma concreta. Occorre dunque scegliere un'esperienza spirituale precisa che ci faccia comprendere meglio, dal proprio punto di vista, l'esperienza della lettura che essa può generare.

2. Un modello: gli "Esercizi" di Ignazio di Loyola

Seguendo le intuizioni di un semiologo quale Roland Barthes (1977) e di una studiosa di narratologia come Marie-Laure Ryan (2003)[5], proseguiamo la riflessione scegliendo l'esperienza spirituale legata al libretto degli *Esercizi Spirituali* di Ignazio di Loyola[6]. Essi non sono un testo da leggere di seguito, perché, in realtà, costituiscono un insieme di indicazioni per la preghiera offerte a chi dà gli Esercizi spirituali perché possa aiutare chi li riceve. Essi dunque non presentano meditazioni e preghiere, ma modi di meditare e di pregare che coinvolgono chi li applica nel contemplare il mistero scelto, anche con l'immaginazione e i sensi spirituali. L'esercitante viene invitato a immergersi nel testo biblico in almeno tre modi: proiettando con l'immaginazione il proprio corpo nella scena rappresentata; partecipando alle emozioni dei personaggi; rivivendo passo passo le vicende del mistero contemplato. Si nota così come ogni esperienza spirituale sia associata a un elemento costitutivo della grammatica di una narrazione: ambientazione, personaggio e intreccio[7].

Come esempio paradigmatico si può leggere il secondo "preambolo" alla contemplazione sulla Natività:

> Qui sarà da vedere con gli occhi dell'immaginazione la via da Nazareth a Betlemme, considerandone la lunghezza e la larghezza, se tale via è pianeggiante o se attraversa valli o alture. Nello stesso modo, guardando il luogo o grotta della Natività, vedere quanto sia grande o piccolo, basso o alto e come sia addobbato [...] vedere le persone; vale a dire vedere la Madonna, Giuseppe e l'ancella e il bambino Gesù, appena nato. Mi farò simile a un povero e indegno schiavo, guardandoli, contemplandoli e servendoli nei loro bisogni, *come se fossi lì presente*, con tutto il rispetto e la riverenza possibili; [...] guardare, notare e contemplare ciò che dicono, [...] guardare e considerare ciò che fanno, per esempio, camminare e lavorare..." (ES 112-116, corsivo nostro).

L'esercizio spirituale implica un pieno coinvolgimento dell'esercitante, anche affettivo, il quale sperimenta "varie mozioni (*mociones*) che si causano nell'anima": egli è chiamato "in qualche maniera [a] sentire e conoscere" (ES 313). I due verbi *sentir* e *conocer* costituiscono un binomio inscindibile, indicando una forma peculiare di conoscenza per la quale sono necessarie vere e proprie "regole" (ES 313-336). Ignazio presuppone infatti che esistano "tre tipi di pensieri, cioè uno mio proprio, che deriva unicamente dalla mia libertà e dalla mia volontà, e gli altri due che provengono dall'esterno, uno dallo spirito buono e l'altro dallo spirito cattivo" (ES 32) e dunque occorre "discernere" tra gli "spiriti" e i loro effetti, cioè pensieri e mozioni interiori (affetti e sentimenti quali pace, agitazione, confusione, gioia...) da essi generati. In tal modo, infatti, è possibile riconoscere l'azione di Dio nella propria vita, come anche le forze che spingono l'esercitante ad allontanarsi da lui.

Come possiamo concludere? Che per fare gli Esercizi non bisogna leggere il libro ignaziano, ma occorre eseguire le indicazioni che esso offre: guardare, sentire, ma anche fare, "toccare con il tatto"[8] e discernere tra le reazioni affettive. L'esercitante dunque è chiamato a entrare in un vero e proprio ambiente virtuale, che è la cosiddetta *composición viendo el lugar*, composizione vedendo il luogo (ES 47)[9], una vera e propria visione stereoscopica totale. Facciamo un paragone esplicativo oggi possibile perché l'attuale tecnologia ci ha resi familiari alle simulazioni virtuali, entrate in molte case grazie ai *videogame*. Giocare a un *videogame* generalmente significa muovere un protagonista attraverso tutti gli ambienti, i livelli del gioco, mediante la pressione di pulsanti e di un cursore o manopola: esiste sì un'interazione, ma la distanza tra reale e virtuale rimane netta. Negli Esercizi, al contrario, non è prevista una separazione tra lo spettatore-attore (il giocatore) e lo spazio virtuale visualizzato nello schermo (cf. Ryan, 2003: 118): l'esercitante è chiamato a immergersi nella realtà contemplata e a interagire pienamente con essa senza filtri. Ha ragione dunque la Ryan quando afferma che gli *Esercizi* rappresentano "una prefigurazione di molti dei temi sviluppati dalla tecnologia VR [cioè della "Realtà Virtuale]" (Ryan, 2003: 115). Ovviamente si tratta di un'analogia logico-formale[10]: negli Esercizi è l'azione della Grazia a ispirare e accompagnare tutto il processo, che dunque, se veramente "spirituale", non è mai frutto della semplice volontà dell'esercitante o di una combinazione di tecniche.

3. La letteralità infranta degli "Esercizi"

Gli *Esercizi* dunque per essere "letti" devono essere "fatti": soltanto così si sperimenta la loro forza potente ed efficace[11]: la destinazione più autentica del testo di Ignazio non è la semplice lettura ma, appunto, l'esercizio spirituale che incide nella vita e nell'azione. Leggere gli *Esercizi* equivarrebbe al consultare un orario ferroviario: è utile per chi viaggia, ma è noioso e inutile per chi resta fermo. Si sarebbe tentati di dire che il testo è "altrove" o rimanda ad "altrove" rispetto al testo stampato. Spesso intendiamo per testo la "semplice comunicazione" tra un autore e un lettore. Questo schema è assolutamente falso per gli *Esercizi*.

La letteralità del testo scritto richiede di essere infranta. La "verità" dell'esperienza spirituale dell'esercitante si trova non nella pagina scritta, ma nel vivo effetto che essa produce. L'esercitante dunque appare in una posizione di vero "autore" degli Esercizi che fa. Semplificando: il vero "lettore" del testo ignaziano è un vero "autore". La dinamica che si sviluppa negli *Esercizi* può essere descritta come un "giocarsi": l'esercitante "si mette in gioco". All'essere proprio del gioco non è pertinente che il giocatore si atteggi nei suoi confronti come verso un "oggetto". Infatti, ad esempio, giocare a calcio non significa soltanto tirare una palla, ma anche correrle dietro, "essere giocati" dalle situazioni che si verificano in campo: *"ogni giocare è un esser-giocato"* (Gadamer, 1983: 137). Proprio su questa base H.G. Gadamer si occupa dell'opera d'arte, negando nei confronti di essa un rapporto di soggetto a oggetto e affermando anzi che il soggetto dell'esperienza artistica non è colui che fa esperienza dell'opera d'arte, ma l'opera stessa. Infatti "il gioco raggiunge il proprio scopo solo se il giocatore si immerge totalmente in esso" (Gadamer, 1983: 133). Il soggetto del gioco dunque non è il giocatore, ma il gioco stesso, che si produce attraverso i giocatori. Così chi contempla negli *Esercizi* non è "soggetto" nel senso che è colui che guida l'azione. Il soggetto degli *Esercizi* è il mistero stesso nel quale l'esercitante viene coinvolto attivamente. Così l'esercitante è vero "autore" in modo formalmente simile a un giocatore sul campo: egli fa il gioco, ma nello stesso tempo il gioco si fa attraverso di lui, nel senso che egli è totalmente preso dalla situazione che vive[12].

Fin qui abbiamo descritto l'esperienza di lettura proposta dagli *Esercizi*. Ecco allora la domanda: una persona che si è formata alla luce di questo metodo di preghiera e che ha interiorizzato la pratica spirituale ignaziana viene anche abilitata a un modo peculiare di affrontare la lettura di un testo narrativo (ma, in modo simile, potremmo dire anche di vedere un film)? Gli *Esercizi Spirituali* possono costituire un modello di lettura?

4. La lettura come "esecuzione" di un'opera "virtuale"

Alla luce della presentazione degli *Esercizi* fin qui fatta, a noi sembra di poter rispondere affermativamente: come la spiritualità non è astratta dalla vita, così la pratica di una particolare lettura spirituale non può non avere una ricaduta nel modo di leggere un testo particolarmente significativo come un testo letterario (von Balthasar, 1969: 463).

La prima conclusione è che la prospettiva ignaziana è vicina a un'idea di lettura secondo la quale essa non sopraggiunge al testo come un avvenimento estrinseco e contingente: se un testo non è letto, è *come se* non ci fosse. In questa prospettiva leggere un libro non può che voler dire leggersi *in* esso, cioè nell'esperienza che di esso si fa. Lettura, come aveva scritto il filosofo Luigi Pareyson, è sinonimo di "esecuzione", proprio nel senso che questa parola ha nel campo musicale: l'esecuzione dell'opera musicale "non è quella inerte e muta dello spartito, ma quella viva e sonora dell'esecuzione" (Pareyson, 1982: 68s.). Eseguire significa non "abbandonarsi all'effetto dell'opera subendolo passivamente, ma impadronirsi dell'opera stessa rendendola presente e viva, cioè *facendone* operare l'effetto" (Pareyson, 1996: 222s.). L'esecuzione non è un qualcosa di secondario e opzionale, ma è co-originaria all'opera. In questa esecuzione si trovano insieme l'identità immutabile dell'opera e la sempre diversa personalità dell'interprete che la esegue. I due aspetti sono inseparabili. Così la verità delle esecuzioni ha il suo fondamento nella natura complessa della persona dell'interprete e nell'opera da eseguire. C'è interpretazione soltanto se l'intento dell'interprete è di "voler *lui stesso* eseguire l'*opera in sé*, sì che la sua esecuzione sia l'opera stessa, da lui resa presente e viva, e insieme la sua interpretazione dell'opera" (Pareyson, 1996: 229).

L'opera vive nelle proprie esecuzioni, pur non riducendosi alla sua esecuzione. L'opera dell'esecutore non coincide con quella dell'autore, ma, all'interno di ogni esecuzione, interpretazione e opera fanno tutt'uno e sono due cose distinte solamente in vista di una nuova esecuzione differente. L'esecutore non "completa" l'opera nel senso che la finisce, perché l'opera consegnata è già finita e determinata. Ma proprio grazie alla sua definitezza e compiutezza l'opera è in grado di offrire l'avvio a infinite letture ed esecuzioni, tutte coinvolgenti personalmente e responsabilmente il lettore. Il fatto che la possibilità di letture sia infinita significa che tutti possono essere esecutori. L'interpretazione è sempre personalizzata: ciò comporta che il significato dell'opera possa "nascondersi" a chi non sa integrarla. La comprensione presuppone una congenialità, una sintonizzazione, un'affinità.

In tale prospettiva la personalità dell'interprete non è ostacolo all'esecuzione perché impegnata a volersi esprimere, ma anzi ne è l'unica condizione di possibilità. Così la "fedeltà è allora *personale* "esercizio" di fedeltà diretto a rendere l'opera com'essa vuole, e la libertà è il carattere personale, e quindi l'irripetibile singolarità, del modo con cui si cerca di far vivere l'opera nella *sua* realtà" (Pareyson, 1996: 231). Le raccomandazioni di Pareyson alla fedeltà allora non possono che assumere questi toni: fa' "di te stesso, della tua intera personalità e spiritualità, del tuo modo di pensare, vivere, sentire, un organo di penetrazione, una condizione di accesso, uno strumento di rivelazione dell'opera d'arte; rammenta che il tuo assunto non è né di *dover* rinunciare a te stesso né di *voler* esprimere te stesso [...]; ricordati invece che *tu* in persona devi interpretare l'*opera*, cioè è ben quell'opera che tu devi interpretare, e insieme sei ben tu quello che deve interpretarla" (Pareyson, 1996).

5. La lettura come immersione interattiva

La seconda conclusione, strettamente legata alla prima, è che la prospettiva ignaziana genera un'idea di lettura secondo la quale la relazione tra testo e lettore è molto diversa da quella che intercorre fra un oggetto e un osservatore: l'opera possiede un carattere "virtuale", perché non può essere ridotta né alla realtà del testo né alla soggettività del lettore. Essa può essere affrontata soltanto in un modo insieme obbediente e libero: obbediente all'oggettività ineliminabile della pagina scritta e libero nel modo di affrontarla e farla propria. Da questa virtualità deriva il dinamismo di ogni opera letteraria; "poiché il lettore passa attraverso le varie prospettive aperte dal testo e riferisce i diversi punti di vista e modelli l'uno all'altro, egli mette in azione l'opera e anche se stesso" (Iser, 1987: 56). Sartre aggiunge anzi che "l'atto creatore non è che un momento incompleto e astratto della produzione di un'opera; se esistesse solo l'autore, egli potrebbe scrivere finché vuole, ma mai l'opera come oggetto vedrebbe la luce, e bisognerebbe che lo scrittore posasse la penna o disperasse. Ma l'operazione dello scrivere implica quella di leggere come proprio correlativo dialettico, e questi due atti distinti comportano due agenti distinti. È lo sforzo congiunto dell'autore e del lettore che farà nascere quell'oggetto concreto e immaginario che è l'opera dello spirito. Non vi è arte che per e attraverso gli altri" (Sartre, 1995: 146); dunque "un testo letterario può produrre una risposta soltanto quando è letto" (Iser, 1987: 25). Il suo significato è un avvenimento dinamico, è qualcosa di potenziale che "accade", al di là di ogni oggettivismo e soggettivismo[13]. Invece di una relazione tra un soggetto e un oggetto, si dà un punto di vista mobile che viaggia lungo l'interno di ciò che si deve cogliere.

Nel suo *Narrative as Virtual Reality*, Marie-Laure Ryan, sviluppando l'idea della Realtà Virtuale come metafora globale dell'arte, distingue una poetica dell'immersione e una poetica dell'interattività: la prima intende il testo come un mondo all'interno del quale il lettore è chiamato a immergersi; la seconda lo intende come un gioco nel quale il lettore si coinvolge interattivamente. La Ryan assume proprio gli *Esercizi* ignaziani come modello di immersione, in questo caso nel testo biblico. Tuttavia sembra non dare altrettanta importanza al significato dell'interattività così come l'abbiamo descritta. In effetti gli *Esercizi* ignaziani immergono colui che li fa nel mistero biblico-cristiano e lo abilitano a interagire attivamente con personaggi, eventi, discorsi, anche grazie agli "occhi dell'immaginazione" (cf. Spadaro, 1994a: 687-712). Gli *Esercizi* dunque possono costituire il modello per un paradigma di lettura che consideri il testo e la lettura come i due poli nell'atto di comunicazione, il cui successo dipenderà dal grado in cui il testo si pone come un correlativo nella coscienza del lettore. La lettura non è una diretta interiorizzazione, perché non è un processo a senso unico, ma un processo di interazione dinamica fra testo e lettore. Il coinvolgimento del lettore, alla luce degli *Esercizi*, è una situazione nella quale il soggetto entra con tutto se stesso (memoria, intelletto, volontà, direbbe Ignazio, e cioè con le sue aspettative, i suoi ricordi, la sua comprensione del reale) e lì riesce a compiere un'operazione di lettura di sé attraverso e nel testo. Nella prospettiva degli *Esercizi* comprendiamo dunque come il testo letterario possa rivelarsi non tanto un "oggetto", un fatto, quanto una "energia", una guida che articola un linguaggio e un testo che nasce nel suo significato dall'interazione con il lettore. Il testo è guida a un'esperienza che è ulteriore rispetto al testo e che chiamiamo "lettura".

6. La lettura può diventare esperienza spirituale

Una terza conclusione riguarda la rilevanza di una storia narrata per la vita di fede. Chi è formato alla spiritualità degli Esercizi sa che il suo coinvolgimento nel mistero contemplato non è mai asettico, distaccato o tale da distaccarlo dalla storia. Negli *Esercizi* Dio non è contemplato in se stesso o tramite il superamento della storia, del mondo e delle immagini sensibili, ma va cercato e trovato proprio in esse: non è Dio l'oggetto primo della contemplazione ignaziana, ma il mondo storico e le vicende salvifiche che in esso sono accadute e nel quale egli si è manifestato (cf. Perniola, 2001: 117). Potremmo dire che la spiritualità degli *Esercizi* è più "narrativa" che "lirica": al di fuori di un contesto narrativo sarebbe impossibile. Chi è formato a questa via spirituale allora avrà familiarità con le storie narrate e sarà in grado di leggerle, così come abbiamo descritto fino a questo punto, attento all'esperienza del "sentire e conoscere le mozioni che si causano nell'anima". Gli "spiriti" di cui parla Ignazio sono all'opera in noi anche quando leggiamo un libro o vediamo un film. Non è raro che alcune immagini o alcune espressioni agiscano in noi in maniera profonda e siano fonte di consolazione o di desolazione spirituale, le quali spesso sono "sentite" ma non "conosciute". Perché avvenga questo riconoscimento è necessario il metodo ermeneutico del discernimento spirituale.

M.P. Gallagher, teologo e studioso di letteratura, ha offerto due intuizioni frutto dell'applicazione delle "regole" ignaziane: la prima è che "la consolazione può sembrare autentica, ma può non esserlo nella realtà"; un racconto infatti "può indurre un certo appagamento, persino un senso di allargamento del cuore, ma questo non rappresenta di per sé un valido criterio di autenticità. Il secondo contributo ignaziano è rappresentato dalla sua insistenza sul prestare attenzione all'intero processo dei movimenti spirituali di una persona: non solo agli effetti consolatori che lo stato d'animo riflette, ma all'orientamento d'insieme di esso. Questo significa mettere alla prova la durata dei sentimenti suscitati" dalla lettura della narrazione e quindi "domandarsi dove essi conducano la persona"[14]. Facciamo un esempio: se un romanzo rappresenta la vita umana come assurda, ovviamente afferma un contenuto oggettivamente non cristiano. Tuttavia la sua radicalità nel porre il problema e nel mettere tutto in dubbio per ciò che riguarda l'uomo, potrebbe servire a scuotere una vita appiattita e soltanto apparentemente soddisfatta (Rahner, 1968: 502). La "letteratura dell'assurdo", che potrebbe condurre alcuni allo scoraggiamento e alla desolazione, potrebbe d'altra parte scuotere chi non si pone domande, chi non ascolta e non fa silenzio perché già sazio, l'uomo chiuso in se stesso, incapace di ascoltare la chiamata della Grazia. La letteratura o il cinema dell'assurdo possono lavorare spiritualmente su questo genere di uomo attraverso una suggestione di inquietudine che può rivelarsi alla lunga anche salvifica, scuotendo l'uomo dalle sue false certezze, facendo cadere la maschera delle apparenze[15].

Così per il lettore formato alla spiritualità degli *Esercizi* non sarà insolito interrogare se stesso o discutere nel dialogo con una guida spirituale sulle mozioni che egli ha provato leggendo un romanzo o un racconto o anche guardando un film, notando – come chiede più volte Ignazio negli *Esercizi* – i "punti" o le "parti più importanti", dove si sia sentita "qualche conoscenza, consolazione o desolazione" o dove siano state avvertite "maggiori mozioni e gusti spirituali" (ES 62, 118 e 227)[16].

Il lettore, così come emerge dalle riflessioni che abbiamo proposto, è un viaggiatore: egli compie il suo itinerario attraverso il romanzo dal suo punto di vista mobile, combina tutto ciò che vede nella sua memoria, mescolando ricordi della propria vita reale, immagini, ricordi delle pagine precedenti che ha letto e, in tal modo, crea un modello di lettura che ha una sua coerenza (Iser, 1987: 50). In nessun momento, tuttavia, egli può avere una visione totale di questo itinerario. Ogni momento articolato di lettura costituisce un'inseparabile combinazione di prospettive differenziate, ricordi, affetti, conoscenze presenti, tensioni interiori e aspettative future. A tal punto che durante la lettura ciò che è avvenuto nelle pagine precedenti può cambiare di significato nelle pagine successive o un evento negativo della vita passata può essere improvvisamente ricompreso nelle sue valenze positive. Chi legge è spinto a inserire se stesso e cioè le proprie idee, le proprie esperienze, le proprie attese nel processo di lettura (Iser, 1987: 116) che si modifica in continuazione, coinvolgendo il lettore anche in una dinamica di valore spirituale. La lettura è sperimentata come un vero e proprio viaggio: è forse proprio questa l'immagine che meglio descrive la forma di lettura di un testo letterario che la pratica degli Esercizi di Ignazio di Loyola è in grado di suscitare.

NOTE

[1] Riprendiamo e approfondiamo qui alcune riflessioni espresse in Spadaro, 2002.
[2] In corsivo nel testo.
[3] Notiamo che, se male intese, queste posizioni non renderebbero ragione della distinzione tra ordine naturale e ordine soprannaturale: esse, cioè, falsificherebbero il religioso, trasformandolo in emozione estetica e falsificherebbero anche l'estetico, trasformandolo in esperienza religiosa diminuita; cf. Daniélou, 1964: 53. Tuttavia occorre ricordare che l'interesse di Bremond non è di ordine teologico, ma di psicologia religiosa, e questo dovrebbe bastare, da una parte, a evitare la confusione dei piani tra mistica e poesia e, dall'altra, a cogliere le linee di tensione tra l'una e l'altra, come successivamente è stato messo in luce anche da K. Rahner: cf. Rahner, 1965; Spadaro, 2000.
[4] Cf. Proust, 1997: 33s. Si tratta di un noto testo apparso per la prima volta su *La Renaissance latine* nel 1905 e l'anno seguente pubblicato come prefazione alla traduzione di Sesamo e i gigli di John Ruskin. Cf. Spadaro, 1998.
[5] In particolare cf. "The Discipline of Immersion. Ignatius of Loyola" alle pp. 115-119.
[6] Gli *Esercizi Spirituali* sono un libretto scritto per "colui che dà" gli Esercizi, cioè una guida (o "direttore", come spesso lo si è definito nel passato), affinché conduca l'"esercitante" per un cammino spirituale. Esso si compie in quattro tempi, detti "settimane". La giornata è scandita da tempi di "esercizio" e di "esame" di coscienza: sono previsti cinque tempi di preghiera e tre tempi di esame (cf. ES 24-26). Durante gli Esercizi l'esercitante si confronta con i misteri della fede e, in particolare, con i misteri della vita di Cristo, raccolti in fondo al libro (ES 261-312), che sono un preciso richiamo al testo biblico. Qui, per chiarezza, indicheremo con *Esercizi* (cioè in

corsivo) il testo ignaziano e con Esercizi (cioè in tondo) l'esperienza spirituale. Abbrevieremo le citazioni dei paragrafi del testo ignaziano con la sigla ES.

[7] Cf. Ryan, 2003: 119. Come sarà chiaro anche dallo sviluppo della nostra riflessione, ci riferiamo innanzitutto alla possibilità di una lettura "ignaziana" di un testo narrativo (sia esso un racconto, una poesia o un film). Per la poesia lirica o altre forme artistico-espressive comunque non narrative il discorso dovrebbe subire qualche precisazione ulteriore. Per un'applicazione a livello didattico cf. Spadaro, 1994b.

[8] Ad esempio ES 125: "Toccare col tatto, per esempio abbracciare e baciare i luoghi dove tali persone camminano e siedono".

[9] Ovviamente qui per "virtuale" non intendiamo affatto fittizio o illusorio o comunque opposto a "reale", ma, d'accordo con la definizione di Pierre Lévy, "potenziale": Lévy, 1997.

[10] Logicamente il problema è riconducibile al teorema dell'incompletezza di Gödel, secondo il quale, semplificando, nessun sistema formale può essere simultaneamente completo perché contiene almeno una proposizione indecidibile all'interno dello stesso sistema. Nel nostro caso ciò significa che, quando il testo è vissuto, è insieme vero e non contraddittorio che l'esercitante sia "dentro" e, allo stesso tempo, "fuori" della scena contemplata. Cf. anche le intuizioni circa il quadro Gallerie di stampe di Escher, in Hofstadter, 1984: 773-777.

[11] Cf. "Directorium", 1919: 883.

[12] Ogni gioco ha le sue regole e così, legate alle prime due settimane degli Esercizi, vi sono "regole" dette comunemente "per il discernimento": ES, nn. 313-327 e 328-336.

[13] In tal modo trovano una conciliazione due differenti atteggiamenti di fronte al testo, eredi uno della lezione di Origene e l'altro di quella di Agostino. Cf. von Balthazar, 1969: 458.

[14] Gallagher, 1995: 391s. La riflessione dell'Autore è di per sé sul cinema, ma si adatta perfettamente anche alla letteratura. Cf. anche Gallagher, 1999: 155-172.

[15] Questa sarebbe l'applicazione letterale della prima regola ignaziana del discernimento degli spiriti riservata a coloro che "vanno di peccato mortale in peccato mortale" e cioè che in tali persone lo spirito buono si comporta "pungendole e rimordendo la loro coscienza con la sinderesi della ragione" (ES 314). La "sinderesi" è per san Tommaso uno speciale abito naturale che "spinge al bene e mormora del male" (*Summa Th.*, I, q. 79, a. 12).

[16] Il primo a fare questo genere di esperienza fu proprio Ignazio di Loyola, lettore nella sua convalescenza dopo il ferimento durante la presa di Pamplona da parte dei francesi nel 1521. Fu proprio da una lettura di questo tipo che prese avvio la sua esperienza di discernimento spirituale, come afferma egli stesso nella sua *Autobiografia*, nn. 6-9.

Riferimenti bibliografici

VON BALTHASAR, H. U. (1969), "Vedere, ascoltare, leggere nell'ambito della Chiesa", in ID., *Sponsa Verbi. Saggi teologici*, II, Brescia: Morcelliana, 455-471.

BARTHES, R. (1977), *Sade, Fourier, Loyola. La scrittura come eccesso*, Torino: Einaudi.

BREMOND, H. (1983), *Preghiera e poesia*, Milano: Rusconi.
DANIÉLOU, J. (1964), "Poesia e verità", in *Lo scandalo della verità*, Torino: Marietti.
"Directorium anonymum BI", in *Exercitia spiritualia S. Ignatii de Loyola et eorum directoria*, vol. II, Matriti: MHSI - Monumenta Ignatiana, 1919.
GADAMER, H. G. (1983), *Verità e Metodo*, Milano: Bompiani.
GALLAGHER, M. P. (1995), "Teologia, arte, discernimento e cinema", *La Civiltà Cattolica* II, 388-398.
GALLAGHER, M. P. (1999), *Fede e cultura. Un rapporto cruciale e conflittuale*, Cinisello Balsamo: San Paolo.
DE GRANDMAISON, L. (1913), "La religion personelle", *Études* 134.
HOFSTADTER, D. R. (1984), *Gödel, Escher, Bach: un'Eterna Ghirlanda Brillante. Una fuga metaforica su menti e macchine nello spirito di Lewis Carroll*, Milano: Adelphi.
ISER, W. (1987), *L'atto della lettura. Una teoria della risposta estetica*, Bologna: Il Mulino.
LÉVY, P. (1997), *Il virtuale*, Milano: Raffaello Cortina.
PAREYSON, L. (1982), *Verità e interpretazione*, Milano: Mursia.
PAREYSON, L. (1996), *Estetica. Teoria della formatività*, Milano: Bompiani.
PERNIOLA, M. (2001), *Del sentire cattolico. La forma culturale di una religione universale*, Bologna: Il Mulino.
PROUST, M. (1997), *Del piacere di leggere*, Scandicci (FI): Passigli.
RAHNER, K. (1965), "La parola della poesia e il cristiano", in ID., *Saggi di spiritualità*, Roma: Ed. Paoline, 231-251.
RAHNER, K. (1968), "La missione del letterato e l'esistenza cristiana", in ID., *Nuovi saggi*, II, Roma: Ed. Paoline, 489-507.
RYAN, M.-L. (2003), *Narrative as Virtual Reality. Immersion and Interactivity in Literature and Electronic Media*, Baltimore – London: The Johns Hopkins University Press.
SARTRE, J.-P. (1995), *Che cos'è la letteratura?*, Milano: Il Saggiatore.
SAVIGNANO, A. (2000), *Preghiera e poesia. L'esperienza religiosa di H. Bremond*, Padova: Messaggero.
SPADARO, A. (1994), "Gli 'occhi dell'immaginazione' negli Esercizi di Ignazio di Loyola", *Rassegna di Teologia* 35.
SPADARO, A. (1994b), "Didattica creativa e educazione letteraria. Un approccio comparatistico", *La Civiltà Cattolica* III, 391-404.
SPADARO, A. (1998), "Marcel Proust e la sapiente bellezza della lettura", *La Civiltà Cattolica* II, 480-485.

SPADARO, A. (2000), "Il contributo di Karl Rahner per una teologia delle letteratura", *Rassegna di Teologia* 41, 661-676.
SPADARO, A. (2002), *A che cosa "serve" la letteratura?*, Torino, Leumann – Roma: Elledici – La Civiltà Cattolica.

THE ETHICAL-PHILOSOPHICAL DIMENSION AND OTHER HUMAN SCIENCES

Wieso braucht Kommunikation Philosophie?

Johannes Ehrat

Some tacit philosophical assumptions of communication research are exemplified in order to prove the necessity to pose, as a philosophical problem, the question of communication. This cannot be a what-question, because this presupposes already the answer which is object of the question. So, it can only become the question, how communication as a problem originates. Various loci philosophici, classical and contemporary, are briefly examined, and then the main thrust of the argument converges on Pragmatism, in a critical debate with Systems theory. The problem of knowing Generality, without ever knowing it experientially, is not solved as the autopoiesis of ultimate systems, but in a logic of relations as the triadic sign relation, which is the concrete form of meaning, which controls human behaviour, and from there societal rules take their origin. Communication, then, is exactly this pragmatic meaning, which we encounter both as sign users, i.e. interpretants, and when acting in mundane, objective reality.

Heutige Kommunikationswissenschaft ist immer noch sehr jung und hat wenig eigene Theorie vorzuweisen. Theoreme und Theoriversatzstücke haben sich folglich mit dem Gewißheits-Grad des Selbstverständlichen eingebürgert[1]. Dies ist zu einem Ausmaß der Fall, daß empirische Forscher sie bereitwillig als "Theorie" für ihre "Forschungshypothese" einsetzen. Ihnen ist dabei aber in der Regel nicht bewußt, daß es sich bei diesen "Theorien" um rein philosophisches Denken handelt.

Eine dieser "Anleihen", beispielsweise, ist "Hegemonie". Lassen wir einmal die Konnotation militärischer Kriegsführung bei diesem Begriff beiseite; Dann führt er uns direkt zu G.W.F. Hegel, dann müssen wir plötzlich "Dialektik" denken – egal ob Dialektik des Geistes oder materialistische Dialektik. Dies funktioniert aber nur dann, wenn wir von der Zwangsläufigkeit im dialektischen Fortschritt des Denkens überzeugt sind, also daß sich das Denken entäußert in sein Anderes und dann wieder zu sich zurückkehrt durch die Aufhebung dieses Widerspruchs. Wenn die Hegelsche Linke, Karl Marx et al., diese Zwangsläufigkeit in den materiellen Produktionsbedingungen ausmacht, folgen sie immer noch demselben Denkmuster.

Dieses Gespenst aus dem weitläufigen Schloß der Philosophiegeschichte feiert neuerdings wieder Urstände in Gramsci-esker Kommunikationswissenschaft. Und plötzlich geben neue empirische Daten den alten Hegel wieder. Dies muß aber philosophisch nicht verwundern, denn Hegel ist grundsätzlich durch Daten nie falsifizierbar.

Die Beispiele ließen sich vermehren: Kritische Theorie, Postmodernismus, Strukturalismus, etc.; all dies ist endemisch geworden als Theorievorgabe in der Kommunikationswissenschaft. Tatsächlich sind es fast immer reine, ungeprüfte, unkritische Anleihen aus der Philosophie. Angesichts dieser Pandemie – und der Theoriearmut der Kommunikationswissenschaft selbst – ist es vielleicht sinnvoller umgekehrt zu fragen, ob dies nicht so sein muß vom Gegenstand der Kommunikationswissenschaften her. Versuche einer die Frage zu stellen, was denn Kommunikation sei, so wird er in der Wissenschaft davon erschlagen mit mindestens 160 verschiedenen und teilweise widersprüchlichen Definitionen (Merten, 1977). Wenn Kommunikation selbst schon nicht mehr eindeutig zu definieren ist, ist sie auch nicht mehr leicht zu reflektieren: denn wir tun dies immer schon mittels Kommunikation.

Der Gegenstand von Kommunikationswissenschaften ist also kein physisches Objekt, nicht einmal ein Sachverhalt, den man feststellen kann. Negativ formuliert bedeutet dies, daß man auf nichts hinweisen kann, was nicht Kommunikation ist. Alles ist Kommunikation, auch die Gegenstände, die uns umgeben, und die sozial definiert sind in ihrem Zweck, ihrer Bedeutung, ihrer Qualität. Damit kann sich auch kein Beobachter mehr auf einen neutralen dritten Standpunkt versetzen und Kommunikation so beobachten wie sie in sich selbst ist. Er ist immer schon involviert und somit Teil des Objekts. In der Philosophie nach Kant hätte man vielleicht dazu gesagt, daß Kommunikation "transzendental" sei (wie dies heute noch K.O. Apel tut); aber dieser Begriff präjudiziert schon zu viel von der Weise, wie dieser Umstand zu reflektieren ist. Für welchen philosophischen Ansatz man sich auch immer entscheidet: die Aufgabe, Kommunikation (und "Gesellschaft" und "Sprache" usw.) zu denken, ist delikat und verlangt irgendeine Methode, sich über (oder vor, oder hinter) das Erkennen zu stellen.

Philosophie der Kommunikation ist also nicht eine weitere der "Genetiv-Philosophien". Es gibt in den verschiedenen philosophischen Disziplinen genügend Berührungspunkte mit ähnlichen Problemen, wo

sich eine Philosophie der Kommunikation inspirieren kann und sich auch unterscheiden muß.
- Sprachphilosophie, insbesondere Wittgensteins Sprachspiele als Lebensformen (d.h. kein Verifikationismus), Speech Act Philosophy (Lokutionäre Kräfte = kommunikative Klassen), Ordinary language philosophy, Bühlers Organontheorie.
- Kulturphilosophie (= Relativität von Bedeutungen auf eine geschichtliche Kommunikationsgemeinschaft hin)
- Semiotik oder Philosophie der Zeichen
- Philosophie der Technologie (McLuhan, Ong)
- Argumentationstheorie (Rhetorik)
- Wissenschaftstheorie (Verifikations- bzw. Falsifikationskriterium)

Sicher jedenfalls ist das "Objektivitätsideal", mit dem sich die Kommunikationstheorie ihren Wissenschaftsstatus erkaufen will, eine gefährliche Illusion und stellt eine disziplinäre Blindheit dar. Daraus resultieren nicht zuletzt unvermeidliche "Artefakte" der Forschung. Ihren Gegenstand konstituiert sie aus mindestens drei Akteuren: (Gesellschaft) – Kommunikator – Kommunikat – Rezipient. Darin kommt aber typischerweise der Forscher selber nicht mehr vor. Dies hat übrigens Mary Hesse zum Anlaß einer sehr nüchternen wissenschaftstheoretischen Bestandsaufnahme für alle Sozialwissenschaften genommen (s. Hesse, 1978).

Dabei setzt Kommunikationstheorie als unhinterfragbare Voraussetzung voraus, daß es überhaupt schon Sinn gibt. Sie kann mit ihren Mitteln nicht mehr thematisieren, daß es sich bei der Kommunikation wie auch bei der Massen-Kommunikation um Sinnereignisse handelt. Sie weiß weder um die Natur des Sinns, noch kann sie sich sinnvoll fragen, wie Sinn zustande kommt. Im Rahmen ihrer Disziplin muß diese Frage als abwegig erscheinen. Genau dies aber ist die Thematik der Philosophie der Kommunikation.

Nehmen wir als Illustration dieser philosophieblinden Forschungshaltung den Klassiker McQuail (1983); Der beantwortet die Frage *"What is Mass Communication?"* (17) mit drei Theorien: die "common-sense" Theorie der Fernsehzuschauer, die "working" Theorie der Medien-macher, und die "social-scientific" Theorie. Die letzte ist die der Disziplin, die *"tries to generalize from evidence and observation about the nature and consequences of mass media"* (18) Der letzte Sinngrund auch der dritten Theorie ist ausdrücklich *"What people think it is"* (18) und wird auch beantwortet mit einer Geschichte (!) der Medien. Thema ist also nicht die Natur der Massenmedien als spezifische Sinnereignisse.

1. Die Konstitution von Kommunikation als philosophisches Thema

Für die philosophische Behandlung von Kommunikation gilt also, daß es sich nicht um einen Gegenstand handelt. Vielmehr ist – im Rahmen der philosophischen Disziplinen – die Angabe Kommunikation zu verstehen als die Art der Lösung desselben Problems, das die Sprachphilosophie als Problem der Sprache definiert, und das Wissenschaftstheorie als Problem der Wahrheitsfeststellung aufzieht. Es handelt sich immer um dasselbe: Sinn. In einem Fall wird er verstanden als etwas, was sich aus der wahren Erkenntnis von Sachverhalten einstellt. In einem anderen Fall ist Sinn, was sich aus dem richtigen Gebrauch von Sprache ergibt. In unserem Fall ist Sinn das Ergebnis von Kommunikation.

Diese Vorentscheidung wird dann zu begründen sein: Kommunikationsphilosophie beantwortet also die Frage nach Sinn mit Kommunikation. (Hier liegt schon ein wichtiger Unterschied zur Systemtheorie Luhmanns, der das Problem der Kommunikation mit Sinn beantwortet.) Die Antwort auf die Sinnfrage kann allerdings dann auf durchaus verschiedene Weise passieren. Sinn ist ein "transzendentaler" Begriff, d.h. es gibt nichts was nicht Sinn ist. M.a.W. es handelt sich um einen nicht mehr diskriminierenden Begriff: er hat kein Gegenüber mehr. Zu erklären, wie es zu Sinn kommt, ist dennoch nicht überflüssig, sondern Die zentrale Aufgabe der Philosophie schlechthin.

In der Antike war es auf philosophischer Seite ein Konsens, daß Sinn immer mit Sein zu tun habe. Aber auf einer verläßlich ontologischen Basis gibt es kein Problem Kommunikation. Was an Restunklarheiten bleibt, kann über die Kategorien der Rede geklärt werden. Nicht als ob es einen ontologischen Glauben in die Sprache gäbe, "Ordinary Language Philosophy" ante litteram! Aber immerhin läßt sich Sprache soweit klären, daß sie wahre Erkenntnis nicht verhindern muß. Dies sind die beiden separaten Ideen des Aristelischen Organon + Rhetorica, mit den beiden Logiken, die damit postuliert sind, die des Syllogismus einerseits und ganz anders Enthymemata. Letztere sind dann nicht mehr den Kategorien unterworfen, sondern zielen nur noch auf Wirkung.

Rhetorica 1355a.6-14:

Der rhetorische Beweis ist ein Enthymem (ἔστι δ'ἀπόδειξις ῥητορικὴ ἐνθύμημα), was im allgemeinen die wirksamste Art des Überzeugens ist (καὶ ἔστι τοῦτο ὡς εἰπεῖν ἁπλῶς κυριώτατον τῶν πίστεων). Das Enthymem ist eine Art Syllogismus τὸ δ'ἐντθύμημα συλλογισμός τις), aber es gehört zur Dialektik, Syllogismen aller Art unterschiedslos zu uneruchen (περὶ δὲ συλλογισμοῦ ὁμοίως ἅπαντος τῆς διαλεδτικῆς ἐστιν ἰδεῖν), sei es dialektische insgesamt oder ein Zweig davon (ἢ αὐτῆς ὅλης ἢ μέρους τινός). Offensichtlich ist wer die beste Einsicht hat wie und woraus der Syllogismus entsteht, (δῆλον ὅτι ὁ μάλιστα τοῦτο δυμάνεος θεωρεῖν, ἐκ τίνων καὶ πῶς γίνεται συλλογισμός) auch am fähigsten ist in Enthymemen (οὗτος καὶ ἐνθυμηματικὸς ἂν εἴη μάλιστα), wenn er ihr Wesen versteht und was sie unterscheidet von den streng logischen Syllogismen (προσλαβὼν περὶ ποῖά τέ ἐστι τὸ ἐνθύμημα καὶ τίνας ἔχει διαφορὰς πρὸς τοὺς λογικοὺς σιλλογισμούς)... Man muß als Übereugungsmittel und Schlußfolgern die Begriffe einsetzen, die alle haben, wie wir in der Topik sagten als es darum ging, die Masse zu beandeln[2].

Es ist interessant, daß die Rhetorik für das nicht-Sein-basierte Schließen nur das Wahrscheinliche (ἐξ εἰκότων), das gewöhnlich sich ereignet, und Zeichen (ἐκ σημείων) zuläßt, nicht aber was allgemein und notwendig wahr ist (vgl. Rhetorica 1357a.29-b.10).

Erst in der "Rhetorischen Krise" könnte man einen Vorläufer der modernen Kommunikationsproblematik erkennen. Kommunikation war deshalb auf der anderen Seite, der Rhetorik und den Sophisten. Deren Argumentation war nicht die von Syllogismen, sondern in Enthymemata. Der Unterschied war genau der in der Seinsverwurzelung. Letztlich war diese Wurzel aber nicht mehr argumentativ zu erweisen, sondern nur noch in einem bios philosophicos, dem Lebenszeugnis des Philosophen.

(a) Solange man die Frage nach dem Sinn beantwortete mit wahrer Erkenntnis, hieß die Disziplin Epistemologie. Es ist also dann Geistestätigkeit, geistige Erfahrung von nicht-geistigem Materiellen, die Sinn als Produkt hervorbringt. Alles was ist, ist nur weil es erkannt ist und somit Sinn geworden ist. Es gab dann Gründe, die Verankerung im Bewußtsein aufzugeben.

(b) Eine neue Leitidee, Sinn zu denken, ist der Begriff des Handelns. Erkennen ist tatsächlich ein Erkennungshandeln, also ein menschlicher Akt, der sich nicht nur mit dem Bewußtsein auf sein anderes, die Welt, bezieht. Die Welt ist das Gegenüber des handelnden Veränderns. Der

Vorteil ist zweifach: 1. Kommt die Objektivität der Welt notwendig in den Blickpunkt. 2. (für uns wichtiger) ist Handeln immer schon kooperativ. Man kann gar nicht alleine handeln (auch bei Heidegger: Mitsein). Beides Muß mitgedacht werden, wenn man vom Sinn beim Handeln spricht. Beim Menschen ist alles Handeln sinnhaft, auch wenn der Sinn recht einfach oder "instinktiv" ist. Eine Philosophie muß imstande sein, die unterschiedlichen Arten des Sinns zu behandeln, wie sie sich aus dem konkreten Handeln-können ergeben.

(c) Erst durch die Handlungskoordination kommt plötzlich eine Entität ins Spiel, die es bei bewußtseinsphilosophischen Ansätzen noch gar nicht gab: Gesellschaft. Es ist klar, daß sich Sinn in irgendeiner Weise auf die Gesellschaft als das Allgemeinere beziehen muß. Aber Koordination geschieht durch Kommunikation zwischen Handlungssubjekten, im Hinblick auf ein sie verbindendes, ihnen vorausliegendes Allgemeines.

Gesellschaft führt schon über Sinn (verstanden als Geistigkeit, also irgendwie vor der Kommunikation) hinaus, wenn sie als Letztes und als Totum behandelt wird. Soll man Luhmann glauben, dann ist dies eine Überwindung des "alteuropäischen Denkens".

Es wäre aber zu einfach, die Philosophie der Kommunikation als Spezialfall der Philosophie der Gesellschaft zu behandeln. Das Problem wie sich explanans und explanandum verhält ist nicht einfach. Zunächst war Gesellschaft logisch notwendig, um etwas Bestimmtes an der Handlung zu erklären. Wenn die Handlung zur Kommunikationshandlung wird, kommt eigentlich nichts Neues zur Handlung hinzu, weil jede Handlung immer schon kommuniziert. Es wäre m.a.W. eine Abstraktion Handlung auf Manipulation mundaner Objekte zu reduzieren, weil das allein noch nicht sinnvoll ist.

2. Die Idee des Pragmatizismus

a) Wenn wir das Problem von unten angehen, dann müssen wir feststellen, daß es nahezu sinnlos ist, von "Sinn" als solchem zu reden. Diesen gibt es gar nicht, sondern immer nur als den jeweils "nächsten Gedanken".

b) Sinn als Gesamtheit zu behandeln ist ebenso sinnlos, weil es irgendwie eine Erkennbarkeit allen Sinns, aktuellen, potentiellen, und möglichen, voraussetzt. Dieser Versuchung unterliegt die Sozialphilosophie nicht ungern, allerdings in wenig offensichtlicher Form. (So haben wir auch bei Habermas' Theorie des kommunikativen Handelns noch einen Sinn-Rahmen "Lebenswelt" als Horizont. Obwohl er ausdrücklich als nicht thematisierbar gekennzeichnet wird, wird er dann doch reifiziert und thematisiert als ob es ihn als Objekt der Erkenntnis gäbe.) Die Konsequenz für uns ist, daß wir konkreten Sinn nur als sich entwickelnden behandeln können, wenn wir nicht in eine falsche Ontologisierung des Sinns als solchen verfallen wollen.

c) Deshalb können wir auch den medialen Sinn behandeln: ohne Blick auf ein metaphysisches Totum.

d) Es kommt jetzt auf zwei Dinge an: Wie entwickelt sich dieser Sinn als "nächster Gedanke"? Gibt es eine Möglichkeit, ihn zu begreifen im Rahmen einer formalen Bestimmung des möglichen Sinns (d.h. nicht "allen Sinns" als konkrete Gesamtheit)? Dies ist bei Ch. S. Peirce die Grundidee der Kategorien.

Auf unseren kommunikationswissenschaftlichen Problemhorizont abgestellt, gilt jedoch schon eine Besonderheit für den massenmedialen Sinn. Dessen zeichendeterminierte Einschränkung besteht darin, daß er keine Theorie-Erkenntnis sein will. Dies ist dann schon eine bestimmte Art des nächsten Gedankens, d.h. Denken als pro-gressus. Medialer Sinn ist überwiegend zeitlich organisiert, nicht als allgemeine Erkenntnis. Dies bedeutet zwar nicht, daß er Narration im Sinne eines genre littéraire ist, aber daß de facto Narration das Modell ist: Textualität.

Angesichts einer nicht-abstrakten Auffassung des Handlungsbegriffs bietet sich eine thematische Unterteilung an zwischen Philosophie der Gesellschaft und Philosophie der Kommunikation. Wie soll man beide Thematiken auseinanderhalten (auch wenn feststeht, daß sie nicht zu trennen sind)? Dann würde für die speziell zwischenmenschlichen Beziehungshandlungen (Koordinationsaspekt von Handlung) die Thematik Kommunikation gelten. Und die ganz großen Zusammenhänge (also für den Sinnaspekt von Handlung), das gemeinsame Handeln aller, würde der Begriff Gesellschaft abdecken. Doch die Relation von Kommunikation und Gesellschaft entspricht nicht der Relation von Speziellem und Allgemeinem. Denn – erstens – ist sowieso "Handlung" das theorie-begründende Paradigma der meisten Gesellschaftstheorien. Gesellschaft wird dadurch zu einem quasi-handelnden Quasi-Subjekt. Seine Elemente sind Kommunikationen. Zweitens – meint man mit Kommunikation sowieso i.d.R. mediale Massen-Kommunikation. Es geht also von der Thematik eher spezieller darum zu reflektieren, was sich an Sinn durch die Medien ereignet.

Dies ist nicht unmittelbar einsichtig. Man darf nicht ceteris-paribus annehmen, daß mediale Kommunikation interaktive Kommunikation sei, nur etwas spezieller (so wird sie allerdings oft noch behandelt). Damit ist auch noch nicht gesagt, daß dies ein sektorialer Sinn sein muß. Denn medialer Sinn kann unter den heutigen Kommunikationsbedingungen auch unschwer als totalisierend aufgefaßt werden. Nach die These Luhmanns ereignet sich jeglicher menschliche Sinn heute unter der Herrschaft medial hervorgebrachten Sinns. Wenn Sinn das Universalste ist, dann ist medial produzierter Sinn sehr eingeengt. Es ist nicht einfach das jeder Handlung eigene Allgemeine (Habermas würde sage: seine Legitimation). Medien produzieren ein formal sehr spezifisches Allgemeines, das sich dann aber auch jeglicher Handlung als Sinn anbietet und sie so leiten kann. Es geht uns also der Sache nach um zwei verschiedene Problematiken: 1. um den Sinnaspekt am Handeln, 2. um die speziell medialen Zwänge, die auf diesen Sinn einwirken.

Es geht bei der praxisnahen Thematik medialer Kommunikation also der Sache nach um den Bezug des Sinns auf etwas Globales, Überindividuelles. Also Gesellschaft konkret. Dies ist ein Aspekt, der auch bei der Betrachtung zwischenmenschlicher Kommunikation notwendigerweise in den Blick kommt. Anstatt das abstrakte Produkt/Ergebnis, Gesellschaft, zu reflektieren, geht es in der Philosophie der Kommunikation darum, den Prozeß zu erfassen.

Was erklärt was? Diese Frage stellt sich grundsätzlich bei allen "transzendentalen" Erklärungen. Hier hat Kommunikationsphilosophie zusammen mit der Philosophie der Gesellschaft ein schweres philosophiegeschichtliches Erbe angetreten (s.u.). In unserer grundlegenden Problematik geht es darum, Handlung als sinnbestimmt zu erklären. Was ist hier das *explanans*, das ja Sinn erklären muß? Es kann sicher über den Sinn hinaus kein noch Allgemeineres geben! Man kann nicht Gesellschaft mit Handlung, und Handlung mit Gesellschaftlichkeit erklären. Wenn man beides als Sinnereignis versteht, dann erklärt Sinn Handlung und Gesellschaft; aber was erklärt Sinn, und zwar so, daß nicht schon Sinn in Anspruch genommen wird? Die an Descartes erinnernde Suche nach einem ganz sicheren unbezweifelbaren Ersten führt aber auch in seine Sackgasse, die Alternative zwischen Fideismus und Methodischem Zweifel. Also kommen nur Methoden in Frage, die entweder phänomenologisch vorgehen, oder aber formal.

In der speziellen Problematik, Philosophie der Kommunikation, reflektiert also, wie es zu medialem Sinn kommt. Damit ist zwar das *explanandum* einigermaßen umrissen, aber womit erklären wir mediale

Kommunikation, was ist das *explanans* dieses Sinns? Man wird es nicht mehr mit etwas unterhalb (weniger allgemein) von Sinn erklären können.

Was den auf Sinn basierenden Ansatz einer Kommunikationsphilosophie angeht: Ich will mich hier nicht mit der Leitidee System auseinandersetzen, sondern eine grundsätzlich andere Art, die Grundaufgabe der Gesellschaftlichkeit oder Vergesellschaftung zu lösen, angehen. Wir machen uns dabei den Umstand zunutze, daß öffentlicher, kommunizierbarer Sinn überhaupt, und massenmedialer Sinn besonders, fast immer in Form von Text vorliegt. Mit anderen Worten, im Sinne der erwähnten Alternative der Sinnerklärung geht es hier um eine formale Antwort. Dies ist wichtig für Methode und Zugang allgemein. Beispielsweise in der narrativen Text-Form scheint eine Sinn-Form vorzuliegen, die es ermöglicht, öffentlich so zu kommunizieren, daß die Handlungen aller koordiniert werden (soweit sie interaktiv sind und nicht gänzlich individuell). Wenn wir der revolutionären Einsicht von Charles S. Peirce folgen, der den Sinnprozeß, jede Form von Kognition, als Spekulative Grammatik oder Semiotik aufgefaßt hat, erfolgt Erkennen über Zeichen; und Narrativität ist nichts anderes, als eine spezielle, zeitliche Form von Zeichen.

Das Revolutionäre an dieser philosophischen Antwort ist nicht gerade offenkundig. Dies wird aber deutlicher aus dem Kontext der Philosophiegeschichte mit ihren z.T. nicht sehr glücklichen Antworten auf das Problem der Gesellschaft.

Noch einmal ist gegen die kommunikationswissenschaftliche Praxis festzuhalten, daß es entgegen landläufiger Ansicht Kommunikation als natürlichen Gegenstand gar nicht gibt (s.o.). Dies ist lediglich eine semantische Täuschung. Um Kommunikation zu verstehen, müssen wir vielmehr an einem Prozeß partizipieren. Dieser Prozeß ist immer Sinngesteuert, aber der Umkehrschluß ist noch nicht erbracht, daß alles was Sinn ist auch schon in der Kommunikation vorkommen kann.

Daher kann man auch in der Kommunikationswissenschaft nicht so tun, als ob man einen Naturgegenstand untersuche. Es gibt wie in der Sozialwissenschaft zwei grundsätzlich verschiedene Methoden: Innenperspektive und Aussenperspektive. Wer innen ist, versteht, wer außen ist, erklärt (d.h. kausal). Bei der Kausalerklärung (übrigens ein Standardthema der analytischen Sozialphilosophie) werden die Gründe nicht im kommunikativen Sinn gesucht (obschon durch kommunikative Weise), sondern in Abhängigkeiten. Bei der Interpretation solcher (nur numerisch feststellbarer) Abhängigkeiten aber, muß man wieder einen sozialen Sinn, der allgemein zugänglich ist, in Anspruch nehmen. Es ist irreführend, den Unterschied der beiden Methoden qualitativ und quantitativ zu nennen, denn die Kausalität wird auch im zweiten Fall nicht durch die zahlenmäßige Beschreibung erreicht.

Philosophiegeschichtlich kann für die Aufarbeitung des Kommunikationsproblems der Abschied von der Bewußtseinsphilosophie nur von Vorteil sein, weil dort in der Regel unüberwindbare Dualismen von Gedanke-Welt, Wille-Welt vorherrschen. Dies begann mit Descartes Problem des falschen methodischen Zweifels. Kants scheinbare Lösung dieses Dualismus stellte der Transzendentalismus dar, der aber als hohen Preis zu entrichten hatte die (nominalistische) Verdoppelung des Subjekts i.S. der Kritik Foucaults.

Erst mit Hegels Geschichtsphilosophie gelang eine Versöhnung des Praktischen mit der Idee. Dies überwindet somit im Prinzip die Kantsche Trennung von Pragmatik und Erkenntnis. Andererseits wird die Gefahr der Geschichtsphilosophie recht konkret, wie sie dann auch prompt von Simmel kritisiert wurde mit seinem Beispiel des insignifikanten Todes eines insignifikanten schlesischen Soldaten irgendeiner Schlacht. Ist aber die Alternative von Geschichtsphilosophie unbedingt die explizite Rückkehr zum Nominalismus wie bei Simmel und Weber? Die historische Konfiguration, Narration, reduziert sich zum bloßen Formalismus, entweder um den reinen Tausch-Wert herum wie bei Simmel, oder um sprachliche Quasi-Universalien wie in der Semiologie und dann vor allem dem Strukturalismus Lévy-Strauss'.

Erst mit dem Pragmatismus kommt eine radikal anti-nominalistische Wende, wie das Problem von Sinn überhaupt angegangen werden kann. Allgemein bekannt ist Meads Generalisierung des anderen, das trotz des psychologischen Anscheins ins koordinierte Handeln die Realität als Korrektiv einsetzt. Dadurch ist mit unserem Ansatz beim Sinn, in seiner besonderen Form als Text, ist es auch möglich, die weitere Frage nach dem Wesen der Gesellschaft zu beantworten. Allerdings nicht in der Art, wie dieses Objekt in den Anfängen der Soziologie als Disziplin definiert wurde.

Zunächst ist "Gesellschaft" eine neu entdeckte Realität, die es nicht "schon immer" gegeben hat (man könnte sie in Anlehnung an Foucaults Archäologie des Wissens auch als Episteme bezeichnen). Erst als sie "erfunden" war, konnte Simmels berühmte Frage "Wie ist Gesellschaft möglich?" (Simmel, 1968: s. 42ff) formuliert werden. Nicht zufällig ist die Formulierung an Kant angelehnt, und sie soll auch zu einer transzendentalistischen Antwort einer apriori Bedingung des gesellschaftlichen Zusammenlebens führen. Ohne diese Episteme gibt es keine Gesellschaft, weder mittelalterliche, römische oder indische. So aber entsteht semantisch ein uniformes Objekt, das sich aber ausschließlich dem Bewußtsein der europäischen Moderne verdankt. Es besteht nur in einer spezifischen Differenz (was außerhalb dieses Kontexts sinnlos ist): Individuum ⇔ Gesellschaft. Nur im Ausgang vom Individuum kann man so eine Frage stellen: wie ist Gesellschaft möglich? In ständischen (Kasten) Stratifikationen ist schon die Frage sinnlos; es gibt keine Individuen, man wird in einen Stand hineingeboren und bleibt davon vollständig zeitlebens definiert. Die gesellschaftliche Moderne mit ihrer Entdeckung des Individuums ist aber wohl eher die Ausnahme als die Regel menschlichen Zusammenlebens.

Schon die soziologische Fragestellung verdankt sich also dem Zerfall eines einheitlichen Weltbildes religiöser, physischer, legitimierender und gemeinschaftlicher Art. Gesellschaft und Individuum retrospektiv auf vormoderne anzuwenden (auf postmoderne weiß man noch nicht) ist ein methodologischer Anachronismus; Für die moderne Gesellschaft aber stellt sich die Frage zwangsläufig: Was hält Individuen als Gesellschaft zusammen? Es ist nicht die animal sociale Menschennatur, nicht die kompakte (ontologische, religiöse Stammes-) Welt.

Ganz grob lassen sich einige wenige zeitgenössische Gesellschaftsbegriffe unterscheiden:

(1a) Latente Normativität in der Gesellschaftsordnung durch eine Art "Zivilreligion" in der Manier Durkheims und Webers.
(1b) Latente Normativität aber auf der Basis eines "shared symbolic system" in T. Parsons.
(2a) Kantianismus der Sozialen Form und der Vergesellschaftung in G. Simmel.
(2b) Generativismus der Semionarratologie Greimas'.
(3a) Diskursivität der Verständigung auf Gültigkeitsansprüche auf Grundlage einer prä-existenten Lebenswelt (Alfred Schütz, Luckmann, Berger), Apel e Habermas.
(3b) Generalisierung des individuellen Sinns (Pragmatismus).
(4a) Existenziell-hermeneutisches Ganz-Sein in der sozialen Zeitlichkeit vermittelt durch die Mimesis des Handelns in P. Ricoeur.
(4b) Ganz-Sein vermittelt durch die Machtrelation in Foucault.

Das Wesen der gesellschaftlichen Kommunikation läßt sich am besten pragmatisch erfassen. Dies ist dann keine Normativität im Sinne einer positiven Gültigkeit mehr, die dann zum Objekt eines wissenschaftlichen Erkenntnishandelns wird. Gesellschaft wird jetzt im pragmatizistischen Sinn aufgefaßt als eine formale Leitidee eines "consensus catholicus" einer zeitlich und räumlich ungegrenzten "community of researchers". Dies ist auch der Unterschied zum "generalized other" des Meadschen Pragmatismus. Dort bleibt nur noch die Vorstellung der Verallgemeinerung einer Subjektivität in eine allgemeine Subjektivität hinein. Im Pragmatizismus hingegen ist Gesellschaft nur noch eine metaphysische Annahme, die sich nur noch formal aus der Analyse des Handelns "beschreiben" läßt. Sie "ist" damit eine Sinn-Form, kein objektiver Gegenstand. Wenn man sie als Konstruktion bezeichnen will, dann im Sinne einer "Fiktion", als ein bestimmtes Resultat eines Aspekts eines Zeichenprozesses. (Damit wird aber noch kein transzendentales gesellschaftliches Apriori postuliert wie bei Apel.)

Die grundlegende Frage nach der Kommunikation (der Sinnbestimmung des Handelns) hat demnach mehrere Vorbedingungen, damit sie sinnvoll gestellt werden kann. Negative – Die Frage nach der Kommunikation kommt also gar nicht vor wenn die relevante philosophische Frage das Bewußtsein und sein fragliches Welt-Gegenüber ist (Descartes). Aber auch in einer transzendentalen Lösung braucht es keine Kommunikation, weil die a priori Formen der Synthese der Erfahrung schon feststehen. Die davon vollkommen separate Moralität mit ihrem eigenen kategorischen Imperativ ist ebenfalls a priori und nicht erst kommunikativ erzeugt.

Positiv bestimmt wird sie (ausgehend von Peirces Argumenterweiterung der Pragmatischen Maxime) wenn sie als echter Zweifel faktisch vorkommt. Von Kommunikation "weiß" man erst, wenn sie problematisch erscheint. Nach dem reinen Denken ist die realistischere Grundannahme, daß Menschen in-der-Welt-Handelnde sind. Wenn sie aber handeln, dann kann es nicht einfach um eine Objektmanipulation gehen (d.h. nur Veränderung eines Weltzustandes). Vielmehr ist immer schon eine Adäquatheit impliziert. Dadurch stellt sich die Frage nach den Normen von Handlungen. Normen sind aber niemals existent, sondern immer ideal.

Grundsätzlich muß jeder Diskurs über Kommunikation als Frage der Normenbestimmung anfangen[3].

(1) Einige bestimmen die Gerichtetheit der Handlungen aus anthropologischer Wesensbestimmung (Gehlen).
(2) Andere bestimmen sie als Handlungskoordination über gemeinsame Objekte (Mead).

(3) Wieder andere bestimmen sie als unhinterfragbaren lebensweltlichen Horizont, wie Schütz, nicht aber Husserl, der sich transzendentalphilosophischer Reduktion bedient, und dies an der Unhinterfragbarkeit der intentionalen Subjektivität festmacht (vgl. Luhmann, 1996).
(4) Die pragmatische Grundoption Heideggers (dazu Joas, 1999[2]) determiniert die Gerichtetheit des Handelns "anthropologisch" vom Tod her, als Dasein. Die Ganzheit des Handelns, und damit das Ziel, ist die Ganzheit des Lebens. Damit aber kommt eine fundamental Vereinsamung in den Handlungsbegriff, der nur noch repariert werden kann in abgeleiteter Existenz. Dort ist dann wieder Kommunikation möglich, aber im Modus der Uneigentlichkeit. Es geht dann im Prinzip darum, zwei Ganzheiten zu vereinigen. Ricoeur dient dazu die Narration als öffentliche, abgeleitete Zeitlichkeit.

Der zentrale Handlungsbegriff ist allen gemeinsam. Kommunikation geht über eine gewisse Gemeinsamkeit des Handelns. Diese "gibt" es aber nicht. Sie muß erst hergestellt werden. Dazu muß Handeln öffentlich werden, d.h. eine Handlung, die auf reine Intentionalität (Modell: Innerlichkeit des Willens) beschränkt bleibt, führt nicht zum anderen.

ANMERKUNGEN

[1] Elihu Katz versuchte, die wissenschaftliche Jugend abzuschließen mit dreizehn kanonischen Texten, die seiner Meinung nach klassische Modelle für heutige Wissenschaftspraxis sind (Katz – al., 2002). Unter diesen Klassikern (aus den Schulen Columbia, Frankfurt, Chicago, Toronto und "British Cultural Studies") finden sich nicht wenige Philosophen. So wird unter der "Frankfurter Schule" (die ja insgesamt eine starke philosophische Position darstellt) Walter Benjamin behandelt; Paul Lazarsfeld gehörte wiederum zum Wiener Kreis. Nach den Klassikern kamen weitere jüngere Anleihen aus der Philosophie dazu, so daß sich die Frage eher umgekehrt stellt: Welche Theoriebildung in Kommunikationswissenschaft ist nicht irgendeiner philosophischen Option tributpflichtig?
[2] Rhet 1355a.26-b.4: διδασκαλίας γάρ ἐστι ὁ κατὰ τὴν ἐπιστήμην λόγος, τοῦτο δὲ ἀδύνατον, ἀλλ'ἀνάγκη διὰ τῶν κοινῶν ποιεῖσθαι τὰς πίστεις καὶ τοὺς λόγους, ὥσπερ καὶ ἐν τοῖς Τοπικοῖς ἐλέγομεν περὶ τῆς πρὸς τοὺς πολλοὺς ἐντεύξεως ἔτι δὲ τἀναντία δεῖ δύνασθαι πείθειν, καθάπερ καὶ ἐν τοῖς συλλογισμοῖς, οὐχ ὅπως ἀμφότερα πράττωμεν οὐ γὰρ δεῖ τὰ φαῦλα πείθειν, ἀλλ' ἵνα μὴ λανθάνῃ πῶς ἔχει, καὶ ὅπως ἄλλου χρωμένου τοῖς λόγοις. Vgl Rhet 1355a.14-18

[3] Auch in der Systemtheorie, wo es sich um die sinngesteuerte gegenseitige Beobachtung handelt und darum, wie sich Handlungssysteme koordinieren. Hier aber enden auch schon die Gemeinsamkeiten unter den Theorien.

Bibliographisce Hinweise

HESSE, M. (1978), "Theory and Value in the Social Sciences", in *Action and Interpretation: Studies in the Philosophy of the Social Sciences*, Cambridge: Cambridge University Press.

JOAS, H. (1999), *Pragmatismus und Gesellschaftstheorie*, 2. Aufl., Frankfurt: Suhrkamp.

KATZ, E. – PETERS, J. D. – LIEBES, T. – ORLOFF, A., ed. (2002), *Canonic texts in media research: are there any? Should there be any? How about these?* Cambridge – Oxford: Polity.

LUHMANN, N. (1996), "Die Lebenswelt nach Rücksprache mit Phänomenologen", in *Protosoziologie im Kontext: "Lebenswelt" und "System" in Philosophie und Soziologie*, ed. G. Preyer – G. Peter – A. Ulfig, Würzburg: Königshausen und Neumann.

McQUAIL, D. (1983), *Mass communication theory: an introduction*, London: Sage.

MERTEN, K. (1977), *Kommunikation. Eine Begriffs- und Prozeßanalyse*, Opladen: Westdeutscher Verlag.

SIMMEL, G. (1968), *Soziologie. Untersuchungen über die Formen der Vergesellschaftung*, 5. Aufl., Berlin: Duncker & Humblot.

Semiotica ai media
Sante Babolin

The article recalls how the Interdisciplinary Centre for Social Communications was established in order to reclaim its purpose, as it was conceived by Pedro Arrupe, the General Superior of the Jesuits and so it underlines the contribution to be made by the faculty of Philosophy. The idea is to give communicators the means necessary to carry to completion the discernment in the use of the media that was so close to the heart of Arrupe. The author deems it important to propose several notions regarding culture, semiotics and aesthetics. Concerning culture, it is important to develop a vision that justifies, as a positive fact, the plurality of cultures. Concerning semiotics, several basic ideas should be proposed that allow one to discover the connection between semiotics and culture, and thus, the derivation of the sign from the symbol and the symbol from the archetype. Concerning aesthetics, it would be useful to discover how aesthetics can determine a consensus to mediumistic proposals.

Mi piace dare al mio contributo l'ultimo titolo del corso di semiotica al CICS, perché vorrei inserire le mie riflessioni nel supporto di una memoria: quello che vale per una cultura, vale anche per una istituzione. Tante volte ho detto agli studenti che una cultura, se perde la propria memoria, è destinata a scomparire in breve tempo; così è di un'istituzione. Però una simile scomparsa non sarebbe evidente, come lo sarebbe per una persona fisica, in quanto ordinariamente si mimetizza trasformandosi in qualcosa di simile ma di altro significato, come accade per la celebrazione dei sacramenti (si veda, ad esempio, come il battesimo o il matrimonio, perso il loro valore di sacramento, si trasformano in semplici riti di identificazione sociale).

Ho iniziato la mia collaborazione con il CICS nel 1983, anno in cui il padre Henrici mi invitò a partecipare con lui ad un incontro con i padri René Latourelle (decano della facoltà di teologia) e Johann Schasching (decano di Scienze Sociali): fui presentato come nuovo docente di semiotica, quindi si parlò su come impostare l'insegnamento, richiamando l'idea del padre generale Pedro Arrupe, che aveva voluto il

Centro Interdisciplinare sulla Comunicazione Sociale, chiedendo la collaborazione delle tre facoltà di Teologia, Filosofia e Scienze Sociali.

Il piano di studi, che si elaborò allora e che fu poi ripreso negli anni successivi, ha sempre avuto come obiettivo la formazione di comunicatori, soprattutto sacerdoti e religiosi, con lo scopo di renderli capaci di realizzare un sicuro discernimento nella valutazione e nell'uso dei mezzi di comunicazione. Per questo il Centro si impegnava ad offrire sia un contenuto, su cui discernere, sia dei criteri di discernimento; l'intervento delle tre facoltà era orientato soprattutto alla elaborazione dei criteri, che dovevano essere teologici, filosofici e sociologici. Questo incontro, con gli altri che si sono succeduti a villa Cavalletti, rimase fisso nella mia memoria, tanto che questa idea della interdisciplinarietà mi guidò sempre come criterio normativo.

I miei corsi si presentavano con la sigla di corsi opzionali di filosofia (ed era importante che fossero tali, perché dovevano essere il contributo della filosofia per la valutazione dei media) e presero titoli diversi negli anni: "L'azione comunicativa: segni e simboli" (1983-1984); "Simbologia: la funzione comunicativa del simbolo" (1985-1991); "Semiotica e simbologia" (1992-1994); "Semiotica" (1995-1996); e quindi "Semiotica ai media", dal 1996, con la sigla dei corsi prescritti di comunicazione, cui si aggiunse, per tre anni, anche un seminario di esercitazioni. Da questo riepilogo emerge chiaramente l'aggancio della comunicazione e della semiotica con i simboli; a questo aggancio mi stimolava padre Henrici, allora direttore del CICS; così nacque la dispensa (primo testo stampato con i colori del CICS) del 1985: "Sulla funzione comunicativa del simbolo".

Approfondendo la relazione tra simbolo e comunicazione, giunsi alla posizione che divenne definitiva: la comunicazione prende forma sociale inserendosi nella cultura (tema che divenne emergente, quando arrivò come direttore il padre Robert White) e servendosi di segni e simboli. Con ciò è detto che i media hanno bisogno della semiotica, ma non di una semiotica qualsiasi, poiché si devono scoprire anche il contesto culturale e le motivazioni che stanno all'origine dei processi comunicativi. Due quindi i temi da trattare: semiotica e cultura; e il punto di convergenza delle due aree, subito, si rivelò essere il simbolo, inteso come origine dei processi di significazione e della cultura. Un terzo tema, costante e parallelo, fu l'estetica, il cui corso, siglato come opzionale di filosofia, fu sempre offerto ai comunicatori; e la nozione cardine che sembra unificare tutto è ancora quella del simbolo, poiché l'opera d'arte, in genere, assume una chiara connotazione simbolica.

Ora il simbolo si presenta incorporato nel campo più vasto della cultura e, di conseguenza, interviene con una sua connotazione specifica nella produzione di senso, nel linguaggio e nel comportamento. Per questo il simbolo risulta operante anche nel segno (linguaggio) e nel segnale (comportamento), al punto che, negli studi e nelle teorie di semiotica, non sempre si riesce a individuarlo distintamente.

D'altra parte la comunicazione è delimitata da due soglie, quella inferiore dell'informazione e quella superiore della comunità. Però un discorso sulla comunità ci obbliga a porre il problema dell'identità culturale e a raggiungere, anche per quest'altra via, il campo simbolico, come attività, tipicamente umana, generatrice di simboli. Alla fine, simbolo e comunicazione diventano un campo unico, dove il simbolo produce cultura, e la cultura produce comunicazione. Per tutto questo la mia attenzione si orientò, di preferenza, sempre sull'attività simbolizzatrice della mente umana; di qui il riferimento alla produzione di senso, inteso come atto di nascita della cultura; la riscoperta dell'analogia, come di un vettore logico complementare al vettore dialettico; e il ritorno della retorica come regolatrice dei discorsi che oggi si tengono nell'agorà moderna, ricostruita appunto dai mezzi di comunicazione di massa, dove rifioriscono ritualità, miti, allegorie, favole, proverbi e paradossi, e dove i moderni "eroi" ricevono venerazione dai loro ammiratori e imitatori.

1. Semiotica e comunicazione

La semiotica, come scienza dei processi di significazione e comunicazione, è necessaria per capire e parlare il linguaggio dei media; si suole distinguere la *semiotica generale*, di natura filosofica, che studia le categorie generali della semiosi, dalla *semiotica specifica*, che è una grammatica, e dalla *semiotica applicata*, che rappresenta una zona, dai confini non sempre chiari, per la quale sembra opportuno parlare di pratiche descrittive e interpretative.

Per rispondere alle finalità del CICS, mi sembrano necessarie delle nozioni basilari di una semiotica generale, che poi servono anche per chiarire i processi culturali e la sperimentazione di alcune tecniche interpretative sia nella lettura dei prodotti (pagine iconiche della carta stampata, cartelloni e spot pubblicitari, ecc.) come nei tentativi di produrre quel tanto che è necessario, per capire il lavoro (difficoltà di passare dai principi ai prodotti, fatica, tempo, ecc.) dei comunicatori che operano nel campo. A tale scopo è necessario un corso di semiotica che si arricchisca anche con nozioni di retorica, di antropologia filosofica della cultura e dell'estetica[1]. Di qui, una breve presentazione di due temi fondamentali: cultura e retorica.

1.1 *Cultura*

È necessario elaborare una visione non monarchica della cultura: come si deve riconoscere pari dignità alle persone, così si deve riconoscere pari dignità alle culture. In forza di questo principio, giustificato da una concezione personalistica dell'antropologia e della comunicazione, la riflessione sulla cultura permette di riconoscere la dignità di tutte le culture. Inoltre, se l'atto di nascita della cultura è la produzione di senso, è impossibile elaborare una proposta semiotica, capace di favorire la comunicazione nella prospettiva della promozione umana, ignorando che la cultura stessa è un enorme bacino semantico, in cui i processi di significazione e di comunicazione trovano i loro percorsi già tracciati, poiché il segno si radica nel simbolo, e il simbolo emerge dagli archetipi.

Si comprende così come tra le culture esista una profonda comunicazione sotterranea, realizzata dagli archetipi e cioè da quelle immagini che sono cariche dei valori profondamente umani e universali, come espressioni della stessa natura umana. È importante stimolare i futuri comunicatori a scoprire questi valori, presenti e funzionanti nelle loro culture, e poi a valorizzarli nell'uso dei media, per favorire un dialogo interculturale, che è poi la comunicazione tra le culture. Si giunge a tale risultato, ordinariamente, mediante l'analisi dell'immaginario umano, comune a tutti gli uomini, dal quale emergono gli archetipi, che sono simboli generatori di altri simboli. Con ciò si può scoprire, successivamente, come si formano i simboli, che sono le "pietre" che edificano una determinata cultura, e i segni, che realizzano i processi comunicativi interculturali e presiedono alla traduzione delle lingue e dei linguaggi, nonché alle strategie comunicative della tecnica e dell'informatica.

Il comunicatore infatti non può ignorare che l'immagine è forza e quindi possiede una capacità di convinzione, che è più forte della parola. Comprendere questo principio, operativo soprattutto nelle strategie di persuasione, significa acquisire uno strumento di critica (di disincanto) e di persuasione, che è prezioso qualora si vogliano annunciare i valori umani e cristiani. Su questo solco è possibile porre, in modo corretto, il problema del rapporto tra etica e comunicazione, evitando soluzioni estrinseciste che non convincono nessuno oppure che convincono coloro che non ne hanno bisogno[2].

1.2 Retorica

Ci interessa la retorica come la stilistica, che nell'uso individuale delle strategie di comunicazione gode di una creatività senza limiti; e questa creatività trova la massima espressione nei segni linguistici per la loro doppia classificazione. La retorica aiuta soprattutto a capire il carattere metonimico dei desideri umani, i quali giocano un ruolo determinante nella comunicazione; i desideri umani sono metonimici, nel senso che si allargano indefinitamente. Di questa caratteristica usufruisce tutta la pubblicità; e proprio sui desideri umani si fondano il valore di scambio delle merci e tutti i processi di mercificazione.

Con l'aiuto della retorica possiamo comprendere meglio l'analogia tra segno linguistico e segno visivo e l'efficacia di ogni disegno nella schematizzazione dei discorsi, nei fumetti e nelle illustrazioni satiriche. Per questa via possiamo pure comprendere come ogni notizia diventi prodotto e come questo rischio riguardi anche la comunicazione dei valori, soprattutto quando si fa con strategie o strumenti poco rispettosi della capacità d'intendere e della libertà di scelta dei destinatari. Si ripropone così nuovamente il problema del rapporto tra etica e comunicazione; problema che diventa ancora più acuto, quando è in gioco la fede. Quello che mi sembra comunque necessario è che si promuova la capacità critica nei fruitori e la conversione della comunicazione dei media in una comunicazione sempre più interattiva.

2. Comunicazione e fede

La comunicazione umana è certamente legata alla parola e all'istituzione intenzionale dei segni. Già sant'Agostino sosteneva che il fine principale del parlare, per gli uomini, è "significare ad altri tutto quello che meditano in cuor loro (*quaecumque animo concipitur*)" (S. Agostino: 78-79). In questo "significare ad altri" prendono forma differenti processi comunicativi, in corrispondenza di "quello che sta nel cuore". Per comprendere meglio questa varietà e scoprire quali percorsi può seguire la comunicazione della fede, mi sembra utile richiamare i due vettori fondamentali della comunicazione umana, secondo la classica distinzione posta da Kierkegaard: il vettore diretto e quello indiretto.

La comunicazione diretta avviene tra uno che parla (*loquens*) e uno che ascolta (*audiens*), come nel caso emblematico del maestro che istruisce il discepolo. Si sa che per insegnare bene si deve conoscere ciò che si insegna e colui al quale si insegna, però questo non richiede al maestro, e tanto meno al discepolo, di manifestare esteriormente tutto ciò che sente o pensa nel suo animo. Questo significa che si intende comunicare nozioni o ragionamenti; pertanto la comunicazione diretta è intenzionale e concettuale. Kierkegaard, cui interessa chiarire come si comunica la fede, lega la comunicazione diretta al pensiero oggettivo[3]; e la comunicazione è diretta, anche quando "si dà un segno per effondere e trasferire nell'animo di un altro ciò che ha nel proprio animo colui che dà il segno (*ad depromendum et traiciendum in alterius animum id quod animo gerit qui signum dat*)" (S. Agostino: 76-77). In breve, la comunicazione diretta privilegia le conoscenze e le informazioni e perciò si può verificare e valutare.

La comunicazione indiretta si attua invece con il coinvolgimento personale dei comunicanti, senza usare la chiarezza delle nozioni e la forza dei ragionamenti: è l'espressione di una interiorità che si lascia dire, con l'unica attenzione a pronunciare parole vere, a riflettere su quanto si dice o non si dice, non solo avendo attenzione ai protocolli di comportamento o alle reazioni dell'interlocutore (prima riflessione) ma anche a quello che si vive e si pensa interiormente (seconda riflessione); e questo significa accogliere le esigenze di una doppia riflessione[4]. Impossibile quindi una comunicazione indiretta senza quella diretta, come è impossibile una seconda riflessione senza la prima riflessione; e, a proposito della fede, si dovrebbe precisare che non è possibile una fede di fiducia (*fides qua*) senza una fede di contenuto (*fides quae*).

In altre parole, il vero parlare è un dire che si lascia dire; un lasciarsi dire reso possibile da una riflessione, che va oltre l'espressione verbale e verifica continuamente il rapporto esistente tra quello che si dice (*verbum oris*) e quello che resta da dire (*verbum mentis*). Perciò la parola è vera (autentica), quando il parlante concede all'interlocutore la possibilità di entrare nel santuario della sua interiorità; e quando si toglie questa apertura, il parlare diventa recitare; e gli interlocutori normalmente avvertono quando chi parla recita.

Come nella comunicazione i vettori diretto e indiretto sono inseparabili, analogamente le dimensioni didascalica e mistagogica sono inseparabili; vedo però necessario individuare un giusto equilibrio nella loro compresenza. Qui può esserci utile il riferimento all'equilibrio che raggiunge, nel rito funzionante, la compresenza della parola e del gesto: come la parola non riduce al minimo il gesto (né il gesto, la parola), analogamente l'intento catechetico (didascalia) non dovrebbe ridurre al minimo l'elevazione dell'animo (mistagogia). Mi sembra che, nella vita di fede comunitaria e individuale, ci sia questo giusto equilibrio, quando la parola che illumina è accompagnata dal comportamento che realizza la parola; è la mancanza di questa testimonianza, nella vita dei farisei, che fa dire a Gesù: "fate quello che dicono, non fate quello che fanno" (Mt 23,3).

Il perfezionamento e la moltiplicazione dei media costituiscono certamente una grande opportunità per comunicare la fede, però presentano anche il grande rischio di "socializzare" la fede senza testimoniarla, rischio chiaramente presente ñelle trasmissioni radiofoniche e televisive; per evitarlo, è urgente e necessario che l'immagine (o sequenza di immagini) televisiva e la parola radiofonica siano vivificate dalla luce interiore del conduttore e dall'energia spirituale della parola: si percepisce se uno è o non è convinto di quello che dice. Questa forza interiore di convincere, senza violenza verbale, nasce mediante una fede vissuta (*fides qua*, la fiducia in Dio cui si fa credito) e coltivata (*fides quae*, le verità da credere).

3. Conclusione

Non si può capire in profondità la comunicazione, senza riferirsi ai tentativi d'inserimento simbolico che ogni uomo compie quando viene alla vita. D'altra parte la comunicazione, per una sua intrinseca tendenza, spinge alla comunione; e la comunione nasce dalla comunità di vita e porta a convivere la comunità. In questo modo sono identificati diversi momenti d'un procedimento unico, che è l'aspirazione dell'uomo ad unirsi con i suoi simili: informazione, significazione, comunicazione, comunione e comunità. Tutti questi tentativi prendono corpo in un contesto relazionale, che in qualche modo li unifica; perciò sembra lecito considerarli tappe di un coinvolgimento di vita; e, in una prospettiva sociale, possiamo vederli compiersi dinamicamente, in modo che il massimo di informazione coincida con il minimo di significazione, e così via. Ciò che conferisce motivazione e forza a questi processi comunicativi, diversi per natura e funzione, è sempre il *logos*, il quale opera, ora analogicamente ora dialetticamente, come la diastole e la sistole del cuore umano. Così vediamo, alla fine, comporsi le diverse esperienze ed espressioni di vita con quelle esigenze di razionalità che sono richieste da ogni tentativo di capire qualcosa, in una produzione di senso globale che conferisce motivazione e orientamento alla vita d'ogni uomo.

Note

[1] I testi usati furono quelli di filosofia, con continui adattamenti per i comunicatori: *Piccolo lessico di semiotica* (2003), *Produzione di senso* (1999), *Semiosi e Comunicazione* (1999) e *L'uomo e il suo volto* (2000). Per la lettura delle pagine iconiche, si veda: Babolin, 1989: 123-143.

[2] Per questo preciso problema rinvio a Babolin, 2004: 29; Babolin, 2005: 229.

[3] "Il pensiero oggettivo è completamente indifferente verso la soggettività e con ciò anche verso l'interiorità e l'appropriazione: la sua comunicazione pertanto è diretta. Di conseguenza esso non ha affatto bisogno di essere facile; esso è diretto, non ha l'astuzia e l'arte della riflessione doppia, non ha quella sollecitudine nel comunicare, umana e piena di timor di Dio, propria del pensiero soggettivo, si lascia capire direttamente, si lascia recitare a filastrocca. Il pensiero oggettivo è pertanto attento soltanto a se stesso e perciò non costituisce comunicazione alcuna, almeno nessuna comunicazione in senso tecnico, nel senso in cui sempre si esige di pensare a colui che riceve e di badare alla forma della comunicazione rispetto al fraintendimento del ricevente" (Kierkegaard, 1995: 192).

[4] "La riflessione doppia si trova già nell'idea stessa della comunicazione. Questa assume che la soggettività esistente nell'interiorità dell'isolamento vuole comunicarsi, e quindi vuole a un tempo avere il proprio pensiero nell'interiorità della sua esistenza soggettiva e tuttavia comunicarsi. Questa contraddizione non può trovare la sua espressione in una forma diretta [...]. Un innamorato, per esempio, per il quale il suo amore è propriamente la sua interiorità, può certamente volersi comunicare, ma non direttamente, precisamente perché l'interiorità dell'amore è per lui la cosa principale" (Kierkegaard, 1995: 192-193).

Riferimenti bibliografici

BABOLIN, S. (1989), "Campo semiotico dell'icona", in *Icona e conoscenza*, Padova: Libreria Editrice Gregoriana.

BABOLIN, S. (2004), "Etica e comunicazione", in *Cultura e libri*, n. 145-146.

BABOLIN, S. (2005), "Hacia una fundamentación ética de la comunicación", in *Producción de sentido*, Bogotá: Universidad Pedagógica Nacional & San Pablo.

KIERKEGAARD, S. (1995), "Postilla conclusiva non scientifica", parte 2ª, cap. 2°, § 1, in *Opere*, II, a cura di C. Fabro, Casale Monferrato: Piemme.

S. AGOSTINO, *De Doctrina christiana*, tr. it. *L'istruzione cristiana*, a cura di M. Simonetti, Verona: Mondadori, 1994.

"And they have seen his glory": aesthetic communications
David Eley, SJ

L'articolo espone i fondamenti estetici dell'atto comunicativo alla luce degli studi contemporanei sulla comunicazione. Viene offerta una breve rassegna circa la teoria estetica classica. L'autore suggerisce inoltre che la valutazione estetica influenzi ogni forma di comunicazione e che il tipo di piacere che si rende disponibile nell'uso dei media non dovrebbe essere sottovalutato. Attraverso tre esempi – il Credo, la Croce e la persona di Cristo – viene sviluppata una riflessione sul ruolo dell'estetica della comunicazione in teologia. Ognuno di questi tre esempi rappresenta una modalità diversa di relazione estetica con la persona umana.

Contemporary electronic media have been developing at a rapid pace in nearly every cultural community on earth. Society itself and forms of social interaction are being changed with the introduction and development of the media. The Church before and particularly since the Vatican Council II (*Inter Mirifica*) has stressed both the study and the use of contemporary communications because they have so much to do with the core activities of the Church: handing on of the faith; communal celebration of the Risen Lord; theological reflection on the faith through different periods of history; evangelical proclamation in other cultures; social mission to the poor; and so forth. In short, it is imperative to study communicational activity and its interrelationship with theology.

This study can be approached in a variety of ways but this paper will concentrate on one aspect which is the aesthetic component. Media aesthetics is central part of the study of the communication phenomenon but this assertion is not so self evident. An explicit course in media aesthetics has been offered from time to time at the Interdisciplinary Centre for Social Communications (CICS), whose 25th anniversary we mark with this publication, but more often than not the concerns of this discipline are treated tangentially in other courses such as Theories of communication, History of film, and Analysis of video and sound. But I will propose in this paper that the concerns of aesthetics are foundational to the study of social communication and to a larger Christian anthropology which is foundational to the study of theology.

Aesthetics traditionally has concerned itself with three issues contiguous with the realities of beauty and taste. It has attempted, first, to identify special types of experiences of designed objects which are termed aesthetic experiences. So the intent here is to identify and distinguish different types of human experience, particularly sense experiences: what the eye sees, what the ear hears, and distinguish them from other experiences, of hunger for example, or of knowledge. Another concern of traditional aesthetics is the quality in objects or of objects that allows them to be perceived as beautiful: aesthetic qualities. What harmonies, proportions, inventions, rhythms and so forth are embodied in works of art, literature or architecture that allow one object to be affirmed as beautiful or even a masterpiece and another as ordinary, one more pleasing and of profound meaning and another even ugly and mundane? The third zone of concern in traditional aesthetics has dealt with the judgments that are made in the evaluation of these objects and experiences: aesthetic judgments. This activity is in the cognitive realm. How are valid judgments made and under what conditions? How do our experiences and feeling lead to an assessment of value? The origin and status of these judgments is what is at issue here. Are they a matter of personal taste – "I like it" or "I do not like it" – or are they culturally lodged values in the works and perceived by the individual or group which are identified in the judgments, "This is the baroque expression of God's glory", and the like? The more objectively grounded a judgment is, the more we can talk of social and cultural realities. If everything is subjective as relativists like to tell us about religion as well as art, then one reaction is as valid as the next.

Although the ancients, Plato and Aristotle, dealt with questions of beauty and our experience of the arts, as did Thomas and Bonaventure in the Middle Ages, it was not until the 18th century that the word "aesthetics" was used as a branch of philosophy by Alexander Baumgarten (1714-1762); then thinkers such as Hume, Kant and Hegel took up these concerns in an explicit way. It was the compelling clarification of reason and the possibility of repeatable and verifiable science that forced thinkers to examine anew the role and evaluations of art, beauty and cultural objects. "Knowledge" of art objects seemed non-scientific, non-predicable and unclear, exactly the opposite of what scientific knowing should be. They, of course, affirmed that literature, particularly, painting, sculpture and the other arts embodied meanings and values, but they were unable to put that form of "knowing" in the same category as mathematics and physics. And so, they strove to identify in a coherent way the knowing that did take place in the producing and experiencing of the arts. This was the beginning of the great divide of the arts from the sciences. Concern for beauty had been repositioned from among the transcendentals to be a part of the phenomenon of knowing.

Much reflection was applied to the role of the arts in society and their relationship to history and morality (Hegel). The culture itself was ever productive during the romantic and post romantic periods and the activity of criticism was ever increasing, too. New art forms and the new media were developed at the beginning of the 20th century and aesthetic reflection kept pace with their enhancement and was in turn used as the grounds of further creative invention.

When we study the mass media which admittedly are not high art, or at least not most of them, we find, perhaps surprisingly, that all the classic aesthetic concerns still apply. Further, it can be postulated that the principle attraction that audiences have for the media, be it film, radio or television is the pleasure of perception that its use offers, and that pleasure, that enjoyment is centrally an aesthetic concern. Debates about the intentions of the makers and if they are relevant to the interpretation of the work still abound. Debates about the preconceived cultural conditions of the audiences as determinative beyond the initial purposes and intents of the makers are still present. The connection of art-making to life is still a core issue. And although each of the classical arts, painting, music, architecture, dance and the rest had its own aesthetic particularities, when the new and culture shaping contemporary media, the press, the radio, film and television and now the Internet have found their place in present day commerce and culture, they too draw upon the aesthetic range of approaches as did their culture bearing predecessors.

Theories abound. Whether imitationalism (mimesis), emotionalism and formalism offer the most appropriate approaches, they are as applicable to the new media as they were to the older arts. Some contemporary post-modern approaches to media analysis sidestep the aesthetic concerns by focusing exclusively on meaning in a linguistic and cognitive sense and even semiotics which deals with sign systems tends to de-emphasize the more purely phenomenal aspects of sense perception and the role they play in over all communicative event. But from "*gemütlichkeit*" to the "grotesque" aesthetics plays an important role in any study of communication. Social and political contexts, epistemic communities, rhetorical practices, economic conditions, faith traditions all brings tools and language to the study and production of contemporary communications. But the core zone of examination and explanation is the sensuous territory between the media presentation and the experiencing of the viewing/hearing participant.

Some might object that it is not appropriate to use the classic tools of aesthetics on such everyday objects as the mass media. But I will assert the opposite. We should not treat a piece of high art, a "Pietà", in the same way as a piece of say, advertising which is commercially motivated. True. But we must seek adequate explanation to do them credit which means treating advertising and the Coke can as culturally-designed objects which embody messages and values which make direct appeal to the sensibility of people. We are speaking here not just of high art, but a broad-based media aesthetics which concerns presentation and appearance and all the culturally designed ways in which "messages" come to us, and how we use them and make value and meaning with them. Insight into the media has led us to the realization that what used to be thought of as specific to high art is in fact an integral component of all communicative activity.

The main theoretical point is this. Every communicative activity takes place through a medium; every meaning and value when communicated is embodied. The model is clearly incarnational. One of the its clearest examples was enunciated by Ferdinand de Saussure (1857-1913), the Swiss founder of modern linguistics, when he hypothesized that every sign had two components, a signifier and a signified (de Saussure, 1966) and that this combination offered the clues to an interpreter for the use and meaning of the sign. It is the signifier which is the bearer of the meaning, the physical bearer in sound or in image which is perceptible to human sensibility. In the case of spoken language the bearer is combinations of audible sounds, as phonemes and in the case of written language it is combinations of alphabetic elements which stand in for sounds. The signified, the meaning, is other than this; it is what is apprehended by interior imagination and intellect. But this meaning can never be communicated without its collectively-constructed system of codification we are calling the signifier. (I will not here take up the case of direct divine inspiration or grace or intuitions and premonitions. But I think their communicative explanation will still come in terms of signifiers but in the interior imagination.) What I do want to stress here is that aesthetics attends to the signifier particularly and the rich world of sensibility which is part of the communicative experience but not the totality of it. So I am not taking about style or preferred cultural fashions but the necessary embodiment involved in all communicative acts, be they educational, liturgical, commercial, interpersonal and so forth. It is part of currency of being human and living in a human body. It is incarnational.

An adequate explanation of communicative activity is not as self evident as it sounds. We all speak; so we assume we understand what speaking is. We all can see our environment and images, so we assume that we understand all the paintings and films we see. But this is not the case. To understand communication we need to move to the explanatory level and seek a rather complete understanding of the human person, cognitive structure and the teleologies which condition human living, in short, a Christian anthropology. So, it is very important to get it right, particularly when our central interests are in communicating the faith, evangelical mission in diverse cultures, spirituality in commercially dominated societies. Communication theorists have often not got it right either, settling for some direct transfer of meaning and value packages, or cognitive theories which could not distinguish between seeing and knowing – Bernard Lonergan's staring point in the "*Verbum*" articles (Lonergan, 1997). And the issue is further complicated, as Marshall McLuhan has often pointed out when he insists that there has been a cultural re-weighting of the communicative sensorium. The "linear" culture in which the eye found most of its learning opportunities through texts is slowing being replaced by a culture in which the ear and image-eye is our most frequent and trusted contact with information, a difference, if you like, between reading the newspaper and watching the news on television. This has become the basis of a generational divide. Walter Ong's studies of new orality confirm and document these changes in cultural context (Ong, 1982). Thank God our catholic liturgy is not a linear and solely textual experience. It is culturally old enough that the full sensorium of colour, music, sounds, voice, movements, eating and drinking are all a part of it. So, an adequate explanation of human communication must take into account its full aesthetic dimensions.

I mention above that the principle pleasures of communicating were to be found in its aesthetic dimension. The joy of finding the truth and finding a community of truth is not just a cognitive joy. It is also the actual irreducible experience of being communicated to and communicating with others. Music is a fine example of this. The experience of hearing music and the joy it brings us is an irreducible aural experience. Learning about music or a particular piece of music, understanding what a piece of music expresses or refers to, the technical reproduction and the market of disks... are all related matters. But the experience of hearing the music ourselves, in our lived time, of giving it our attention cannot be condensed or replaced. The pleasure we find in this experience begins here. It is true that this pleasure is augmented with familiarity and with appropriate knowledge of the composer, the times, for the form of the work; this is part of the interactivity within the human being. We are not seeing or hearing for the first time every time. If that were so we would not make much more of our experiences that a new born child does. Our seeing and hearing is influenced and guided by our previous experiences, by our level of knowing and by our needs and desires. (Advertisers, of course, know this.) And the pleasure that is part of these communicative experiences is incremented accordingly.

One of the central pleasures of communication – always mediated, as we have already asserted – is the sharing in the experiences, meaning and values of another. Experiencing and knowing that we are not alone, that what we live through, we live through with others and that in certain cases we are part of a community of shared meanings and purposes. This experience of sharing is based not only on the collective nature of language systems but also on the interactive experience of leaning a language and participating, as it were, in a language community. The practice of living with others in a world of meaning and values is the ground of this communicational pleasure, let us call it, and the study of this experience is aesthetics.

Now I would like briefly to explore some of the relationships between aesthetics – media aesthetics in particular – and theology. Theology is not only a form of knowing, it is also a form of communicating and, at times, of teaching. Bernard Lonergan suggests that theology is eight different specialties, each of which is interdependent on the others. Theology struggles to find appropriate and adequate expression for its findings and articulations and the uses theology makes of images and analogies in general, for example, can lead us to examine the aesthetic dimensions of the theological enterprise. Let us consider the parables in the synoptic gospels. They are stories and sometimes extended images with which we are invited to uncover some other reality which is more obscure: "the Kingdom of God is like...". The parable provides us with an image model, as it were, a vehicle of knowing something that would be difficult to know otherwise. Often the narrative of the parable has an unanticipated twist at the end. For example, the person who worked one hour will get the same wages as the person who worked twelve. No parable explains itself or exhausts all the possible meanings it embodies and offers. It invites explanation, interpretation and application. The parable is a communicative model, a form of theological thinking. All human understanding uses questioning, imagination and articulating with language what we are learning. So, in a more specific way, theological understanding is done with image models and language structures.

The roles that models play in our understanding, and the process of modeling in theological discourse present themselves as one of the zones where aesthetics principles are at play. Theology aspires to be a work of art in this way. Let me propose two examples, the Creed, the explanatory formula or *Symbolum* of the Church, and the Cross. Both are the fruit of concepts and theories; both are the products of human creation. They have been shaped by traditions, styles and sensibilities; they had origins and developments. But their very expression requires the retaining of elemental meanings which include affect and feeling. Put another way, rhetorically they remain permanently at the symbolic level. As in the parables, their meanings are not fully explained or exhausted, but they endure as symbols of the faith. Imbedded in them are many doctrines and their inter-relationships. Their main communicative purpose is to give common ground to the community of Christ's followers, to provide a depository of individual and communal commitment and to express in a multivalent way the faithful tradition of Christ's believers. They provide, in short, aesthetic experience.

They are models in that sense of vehicles to a greater mystery. In a cognitive way they are not all that different from the models a physicist or biologist would use to explain an unseen atom or an unseen sting of DNA. The aesthetic component encompasses the model, the experience and the unseen reality to be discovered. In this we can examine the work of theology or some of the work of theology as a work of art or as a communicative event.

Bernard Lonergan (1972) in his *Method in Theology*, as I mentioned above, exposes eight functional specialties in theology. Communication is the eighth and as all the others imbues the other seven with its determinations. The relation of form and content, for example, the personal and social contexts, the intentional drive of a contribution in its historical setting are all appropriate apparatus. All these elements are ordered to the imperative that the findings of the investigation be presented in a way which is communicable within a specific culture and at a specific time. They therefore rely on common language and common interpretative codes. Models are made, not given or already there to be discovered. The Trinitarian formulations of Nicaea are a crowning achievement of creativity as well as gathering of earlier expressions of belief. They are a concise concentration of years of debate and consensus and they provided for future centuries a base for further reflection and articulation. In that sense, the paradigms of expression are also the contexts for continuing theological learning.

The symbol of the Cross provides another node of reflection for the functioning of aesthetic practices in the realms of belief. It is not a textual example as the Creed is and so it sheds another kind of light on these aesthetic processes. It is a work of art in its first ontological setting. One remembers the carved wooden door of Santa Sabina in Rome and from there, so many other manifestations through so many centuries. The Cross has become the symbol of christianity itself in the eyes of the entire world. It objectively embodies aesthetic qualities. It expresses abject execution, a "broken" human body, a victory, life, death and resurrection, love and hate and so much more. As Hans Urs von Balthasar (1982) points out, the Cross is not beautiful as an aesthetic focus, rather it is horrible, but it expresses through this the most beautiful reality, which is the saving love of God. So much persecution and brokenness in the human condition have led many generations of Christians embrace the Cross.

But like other expressions of faith the Cross does provide a lasting impression of a lived reality. It is like a thumbprint to the thumb. It is the signifier, the bearer of meaning. Von Balthasar's view is that so many of the sacred forms of expression, the psalms, the gospels, the parables and so forth provide the "shape" of divine revelation, again the thumbprint of God's presence throughout history and through to the present day. And each of these expressions has a communicative intent.

When looked at the Cross in this way or other symbolic modes of expressing faith, we are not only doing art history but we are doing theology with an aesthetic method; not to do so would be to miss crucial elemental meanings. We would be settling for a thin cognitive elucidation in contrast to a much richer and more evocative comprehension of the range of meanings and values expressed. Our faith is interlinked with our aesthetic, theologically aesthetic judgments.

My final example in this reflection is that of the Incarnate Word, Jesus Christ, made human for us. When God chose to reveal Himself more definitely that he had in creation and through the prophets, he chose to do so in the person of Jesus, His Son. Jesus is the image of the unseen God. Through his life, his words, his actions, he not only instructs but effects the purposes of God's love. He is the sacrament of God's commerce with every being. It is through him that all things were made and through him that all will be brought together in fullness. This is a high christology and the starting point of Christian theological reflection. And it is fundamentally aesthetic in its nature. The personal experience of the apostles and early followers was a complete aesthetic knowing. The texts reflect this. It is through the person of Christ that Christians have their relationship with God. The role of the Holy Scriptures and the unfolding of the tradition are subsequent to this.

The first aim is that God chose this way to express Him- (Her-) self. We can give God our most positive assumptions that He has chosen the preferred way to make His self revelation, His self communication. Secondly, it is also the preferred way for the "hearer", the receiver of the revelation to perceive. Whatever is received, is received according to the mode of the receiver, the Scholastics have taught us. God chose the mode of the human being to communicate with human beings. Much can be said about creation as a mode of God's speech as the psalms say and as Paul writes to the Romans. Speaking though creation is an aesthetic mode. Much can be said of the prophetic voice and the poetic voice of the psalmist in aesthetic terms. But the fullest aesthetic is the person of Jesus Christ, Son of God. His "language" is the human vocabulary. This is the irreducible elemental meaning, first the experience and then the understanding and the living out of the experience.

In this paper I have investigated the aesthetic foundations of the communicative act, enlightened by contemporary communication study and through three examples, the Creed, the Cross and the person of Christ, I have reflected on the role of communication aesthetics in theology.

Bibliographical references

VON BALTHASAR H. U., (1982), *The Glory of the Lord: Theological Aesthetics*, Vol. 1, Edinburgh: T. & T. Clark.
LONERGAN, B. J. F. (1972), *Method in Theology,* London: Darton, Longman, and Todd.

LONERGAN, B. J. F. (1997), *Verbum, Word and Idea in Aquinas,* Collected Works of Bernard Lonergan, Vol 2, ed. F. E. Crowe – R. M. Doran, Toronto: University of Toronto Press.

ONG, W. (1982), *Orality and Literacy: The Technologizing of the Word,* New Accent Series, New York: Methuen.

DE SAUSSURE, F. (1966), *Course in General Linguistics*, ed. C. Bally – A. Sechehaye in collaboration with A. Riedlinger, translated by Wade Baskin, New York: McGraw-Hill Book Company [original 1916].

Media accountability challenges in sub-Saharan Africa: the limits of self-regulation in Tanzanian newsrooms

Bernardin F. Mfumbusa

I problemi di credibilità sofferti dai sistemi giornalistici nell'Africa subsahariana di solito vengono attribuiti alla difficoltà di riprodurre nelle sale di redazione i modelli occidentali di responsabilità. C'è stata, nella recentemente liberalizzata industria giornalistica africana, una tendenza generale a favorire l'auto-regolamentazione tramite l'uso di codici deontologici. Ma i problemi di mancanza di responsabilità persistono. Alcuni studiosi africani propongono di aggiungere valori specificamente africani ai codici deontologici, nella speranza di farne strumenti più efficaci di responsabilità nelle sale di redazione. Tuttavia la ricerca condotta in due redazioni della Tanzania dimostra che, al contrario di ciò che si pensa, i valori africani sono in gran parte sconosciuti nelle redazioni stesse dei giornali africani.

1. Introduction

The neo-multiparty media[1] that emerged in the wake of political democratization in much of sub-Saharan Africa in the 1990s is often accused of mediocrity, sensationalism, and political activism (Kasoma, 1996; Nyamnjoh, 1999). And media professionals are alleged to indulge in corrupt practices and conflict of interest undermining the credibility of the media in the process (Kilimwiko, 2002; Grösswiller, 1997). Apparently, the existing media accountability systems such as journalistic organizations, media councils, and codes of ethics patterned on the Western models meant to promote self-regulation are not working as they should. As a result, Kasoma (1996) has called for the return to the African ethical roots as the answer to accountability problems facing the African media. And Traber (1989b) has characterized the African media as "foreign bodies in the cultural fabric of Africa".

2. Framing the question

Many people in sub-Saharan Africa, decades after independence, still rely on foreign sources of information such as the British Broadcasting Corporation (BBC), the Voice of America (VOA), and Deutsche Welle for what Kasoma (1995) has called "real news". The local media are seen as inept and partisan in their coverage of sensitive local issues like elections. Generally, trust in the Tanzanian media is low and dwindling. The popular word for journalist in Kiswahili, the national language, is *mwandishi,* which is now synonymous with lying. Journalists are often beaten or thrown into jail but there is no groundswell of sympathy towards them. The credibility of the media could hardly sink any lower. It has hit a nadir.

Naturally, the sense of euphoria that accompanied the advent of the neo-multiparty press has proved to be evanescent (Sturmer – Rioba, 2001). And the so-called democratic postulate (Herman – Chomsky, 1994: xi) – the contention that the media are independent and are committed to discovering and reporting the truth – is increasingly called into question. For the media often put sectarian interests and even vendetta first not truth or objectivity as the professional ideology would suggest (Kasoma, 1997).

2. Historical context

Until the late 1980s, the Tanzanian media were part of the civil service. The government contained and controlled them, among other things, through the use of "ideologically correct" editors and reporters[2]. Alternative viewpoints to those of people in power rarely got space. To some extent the liberalization of the media industry in the 1990s diminished the government's role in the media industry by ushering in a vibrant private media system. FM radio stations mushroomed almost overnight exhausting the Frequency Modulation (FM) spectrum in some major towns[3]. Newspapers are now published not only in Dar es Salaam, the capital city, but also in provincial towns like Arusha and Mwanza. Television stations, which were unheard of in Tanzania as recently as 1990, are now commonplace.

Characteristically, however, media outlets are concentrated on the hands of a few individuals and companies. These are: Industrial Products Promotions (IPP), Sahara Corporation, and Business Times Limited, which have access to donor funds through links with powerful political patrons. The Industrial Products Promotions (IPP), for example, controls more than ten newspapers, one television station, and one radio station.

3. Media pluralism: a blessing or a bane?

While media pluralism has injected variety and vibrancy into the media landscape, it has also unleashed media characterized by intolerance, fanaticism and extremism in much of sub-Saharan Africa (Nyamnjoh, 1999). The media quality is said to be uneven, presentation poor, and newspapers are said to contain more gossip and speculation than news analysis (Gadzekpo, 1996).

Kasoma (1997) has intimated of the existence of widespread unprofessionalism among journalists in the African independent (private) media. Like elsewhere in sub-Saharan Africa, media excesses came to a head in Tanzania in the 1990s. The Tanzanian government in 1993 tried to check the excesses through creation of a government controlled Media Council tasked with licensing and regulating the media. The move was resisted by stakeholders including media owners, editors, journalism educators, and media related NGOs. It was felt that only self-regulation, not statutory control, could guarantee the freedom of expression provided for in the Fifteenth Amendment of the Constitution of the United Republic of Tanzania, 1977, article 18(1).

But the question is: are the media professionals capable of effective self-regulation given the existing normative ethical framework? Though Enlightenment ideas of freedom of expression, the Fourth Estate, individual liberty, and the ideology of objectivity pervade the operational philosophy of the media professionals in Tanzania, often these very ideas are used to justify or gloss over media excesses whenever it suits the purpose.

4. Evolution of the private press: democratic imperative

The private press[4] (sometimes called free press) became an institution only after Tanzania became a multi-party democracy in 1992. Existence of private media is seen as an important indicator of democracy. Before then the media were owned by the government and the ruling party save for a few government-friendly media outlets. Journalism training was not encouraged, and journalistic organizations were non-existent. When the media industry was liberalized, therefore, fewer than 400 qualified journalists existed in Tanzania[5] and most were imbued with socialist ideology. As a result, people with little or questionable credentials were often employed as journalists in the thriving private sector. As Okigbo (1994) notes, literally an army of "bare-foot reporters" equipped with pens and notebooks swarmed the streets.

Mediocrity in reporting became phenomenal. Many newspapers began producing lurid articles pandering to the public thirst for the sensational to gain a market foothold. News articles were, and often still are, shallow and poorly researched (Kilimwiko, 2002: 64). Quickly, a cynical public dubbed these fledgling newspapers *magazeti ya mitaani* (street newspapers), implying that they are unreliable and rely on innuendo[6]. When a bill titled "Media Professions Regulation Bill" (Kilimwiko, 2002: 34), seeking to introduce mandatory registration for journalists was withdrawn in the face of criticism from local and international stakeholders, codes of ethics were touted as the ultimate "key" to media accountability among media professionals in Tanzania[7].

The first formal code of ethics was adopted in 1992 by the Tanzania Journalists Association (TAJA). The independent Media Council of Tanzania (MCT) (created by stakeholders themselves in 1995) adopted a code of ethics in 1996 that was revised in 2001[8]. This code is now accepted as the industry standard. The basic assumption in adopting codes of ethics is that by summarizing core values and professional taboos codes would act as benchmarks for acceptable professional behaviour (Sanders, 2003).

5. African ethics (*Afri-ethics*) perspective

Okigbo (1989), Kasoma (1996), and Moemeka (1997) believe in the existence of an African ethics with distinct values. These values include truth telling, ethnicity and tribalism, the supremacy of the community, and the sanctity of authority and they are considered as foundational African values[9]. Meanwhile, Traber (1989a) has argued that the half-truths, misinformation, disinformation and lies contained in the contemporary African press "are culturally alienating because honesty and truthfulness are highly valued African values". Despite the hype, the so-called African ethics is essentially communitarian ethics, its prevalence or effectiveness in the modern African newsrooms far from established.

Nyamnjoh (1999) suggest that codes of ethics adopted in most of Anglophone Africa lack "creativity" and fail to "reflect the concerns and interests of the majority of Africans". One weakness of the existing codes of ethics is the hastiness with which have been strung together to meet the Western standards of acceptability. Whether lacing codes of ethics with African values would improve compliance remains to be seen.

Kasoma (1996) maintains that the fundamental problem with the existing codes of ethics is failure to take into account the African view of man and society, the worldview in which "the dead and living" are said to interact in complex relationship and the former are said to have an influence over the later[10]. This worldview is simply anachronistic in the modern African newsrooms, however. Though the call for the return to the African ethical roots seems tempting, its allure lies in an as yet untested hypothesis that African journalism could have African ethical roots and yet maintain its global validity and appeal.

6. Media accountability as self-regulation

Media accountability is a multi-dimensional concept with legal, public, and professional dimensions. Normally, the legal accountability is enforced through Courts of Law, that is, erring journalists are indicted for specific infringements of law in court[11]. Public accountability is enforced through consumer boycott among other ways. Professional accountability is enforced largely through moral sanction enforced through peer pressure (Sanders, 2003). The cases of Janet Cook, a *Washington Post* reporter whose Pulitzer prize was withdrawn in 1981 for inventing a source, and Jayson Blair, a *New York Post* reporter who was dismissed for plagiarism in 2004, are classic examples of such peer pressure.

Professional accountability, therefore, is defined largely as disapproval for morally questionable activities achieved through the process of self-regulation. It is a peer centred process. Accountability through self-regulation is preferred by media professionals to other forms such as regulatory control because self-regulation is believed to preserve what Merrill (1989) calls "editorial determinism". Moreover, Belsey and Chadwick (1995: 465) say "neither legal rights for journalists, nor legal restrictions on the media, will in themselves produce good journalism". Good journalism would be guaranteed only when members of the profession themselves find it necessary to act in a responsible manner.

7. The scope of the study

This study sought to do two things: to replicate Boeyink's 1994 study[12] to see whether the conditions necessary to make codes of ethics effective exist in the Tanzanian newsrooms, and to test the African ethics (*Afriethics*) claim that a return to the African ethical roots would make codes of ethics more effective tools of behaviour regulation in the newsrooms.

Regarding methodology, in data collection the researcher used two research methods: interviews and participant observation. The study was done in two newsrooms in July and August of 2003. A total of seventeen reporters and editors were interviewed. Memoranda, codes of ethics, and letters to editors were collected and analyzed. The researcher observed newsroom activities and attended news postmortems for a total of fourteen days. The researcher also accompanied at least one reporter in each newspaper in a news beat as part of participant observation. Both newspapers are published in Dar es Salaam; so community level factors like the level of pluralism[13] and local political culture[14] important in explaining journalistic behaviour were constants. The units of analysis were: newsroom events, observable newsroom behaviour, news articles, and documents such as memoranda, letters to the editor, and press releases.

Five questions guided the research: what is the role of codes of ethics in media accountability? Are codes of ethics used to resolve specific cases? How does the newsroom climate influence the use of codes of ethics? How does the newsroom leadership influence the use of codes of ethics? Do values enshrined in the existing codes of ethics reflect values in the wider Tanzanian society? The data was analysed the used of thematic coding, sequential analysis, and the use of vignettes.

Two main limitations influenced the study. First, lack of research in media ethics in general and codes of ethics in particular in Tanzania forced the researcher to invoke a pan-African framework, hoping thus to shed some light in the Tanzanian situation. The assumption is that in most of sub-Saharan, Anglophone Africa the situation is similar in many ways to justify a certain amount of theoretical and methodological generalization (Mytton, 1983). Second, the study explores the concept of accountability on only one dimension, that is, professional accountability. Other dimensions of accountability such as legal accountability and public accountability were not explored.

8. The findings of the study

Conditions mentioned by Boeyink (1994) as necessary to make codes of ethics effective are non-existent at *The Guardian* and only partially found at the *Daily News*. In both cases, contextual factors such as bad working conditions, *laissez-faire* newsroom culture, cronyism and publisher interference influence both the perception of conflict of interest and reporting practices[15].

In both newsrooms there was no evidence of the direct use of codes of ethics (defined as any written ethical guidelines) to resolve specific cases. Although the newsroom conversations were often peppered with references to "our policy" and "codes of ethics" no physical evidence of either was seen. In both cases, no ethics audits or seminars were organized to address ethics problems. At the *Daily News*, an archaic motto and a mission statement reflecting an ideological slant characteristic of the socialist State of the 1970s are still in place. The mission statement says, among other things, that the role of the *Daily News* is "promote Tanzania's socialist ideology".

In the two newsrooms, ethical decisions appeared to occur on several levels: reporters during news generation and writing made basic ethical decisions largely on the basis of group norms[16]; newsroom leaders make most professional decisions supposedly abiding by the codes of ethics, and the level of policy.

The policy level at the *Daily News*, is symbolized by the existence of a mission statement, and a managing editor, both being embodiments of the government's authority in the newsroom. At *The Guardian*, in the absence of any motto or mission statement, the closest thing to a guiding policy was a constant reference of the interviewees to "*mzee*"[17].

In both cases, the newsrooms' leadership commitment to codes of ethics as institutional standards showed a gap between theory and reality. Though editors said they were professionals bound by codes of ethics, indicators identified by Boeyink (1994; 1998), any concrete signs of such commitment were absent[18].

The evidence gathered in the two newsrooms hardly supports the African ethics (*Afriethics*) claim that values such as sustaining social order, ethnicity, promotion of national development, tribalism and promotion of national integration are foundational African values with pervasive influence. The *Afriethics* basic claim that, if the so-called African values were integrated into codes of ethics, they would become more effective is undermined by lack of evidence as to whether the African values have preponderant influence in the newsroom decision-making. The interviewees mostly suggested that they acted according to professional, not African values.

Commercial interests appear to be the most important driving factor in the Tanzanian journalism enterprise. Journalism success is defined largely in material terms as reflected in the Kiswahili popular word for success, *kuukata*[19]. The word carries a connotation of easy success obtained through trickery, not hard work. *Kuukata* is also a philosophy of life epitomized in a popular cartoon character called *Pimbi* featured in a weekly tabloid *SANI* for the last two decades. *Pimbi's* view of life is one of easy success without hard work, without toil[20]. Some of the *Pimbi's* favourable antics include stowing away in ships bound to Europe and to the United States, returning with tons of money. *Pimbi* has become an embodiment of the *laissez-faire* culture pervading the contemporary Tanzanian journalism. Reporters tend to seek easy material success not through commitment to professional ideals and hardwork, but through intimidation of sources, and corruption.

9. Conclusion

Three conclusions have emerged from this study. First, African ethics (*Afriethics*) is a mere theoretical red-herring, diverting attention from problems facing the contemporary African journalism such as corruption, conflict of interest, plagiarism, and lack of a moral imperative to excel. Though calls for the return to African ethical roots have become insistent, the Africanization of values in codes of ethics would not necessarily make them effective any more than they are now. This is due to the fact that the conditions noted by Boeyink (1994) as necessary for codes of ethics to be effective are largely non-existent in the newsrooms.

Second, a *laissez-faire* newsroom culture[21] hampers recourse to codes of ethics as instruments of professional self-regulation. The *laissez-faire* newsroom culture is characterized by reporters' and editors' tendency to gloss over ethical problems, by lack of sustained outrage in the face of ethical violations by publications or individual reporters, by lack of adequate institutional mechanisms to address quality problems, and by a sense of entitlement among journalists that encourages aversion to hard work.

The lack of code compliance is not so much the result of the failure to Africanise values in the codes of ethics, as proponents of *Afriethics* suggest, but the existence of a *laissez-faire* newsroom culture that encourages a disregard of professional standards. Most reporters interviewed suggested that they could accept "freebees" and "junkets" and still maintain objectivity, a position that contradicts the conventional journalistic wisdom.

Third, contextual factors undermine the effectiveness of codes of ethics in the two newsrooms studied. These include weak peer-pressure that makes it hard to express collegial disapproval for morally-unacceptable actions by individuals and poor working conditions that tend to encourage violation of tenets enshrined in codes of ethics. For example, poor and irregular pay encourage moonlighting and acceptance of "junkets". Journalists are some of the worst paid professionals in Tanzania[22]; sometimes it takes up to six months for correspondents to get paid for their articles. There is also the issue of job insecurity that feeds on editors and reporters native fear to cross publishers.

More empirical research is needed if the value of African values in newsroom behaviour regulation can be properly understood. Most of the existing literature is philosophical and offers only general theoretical assumptions (Kasoma, 1995; 1996; Moemeka, 1997; Okigbo, 1989).

Notes

[1] The neo-multiparty media (a neologism coined by Kasoma) are characterized by donor dependence. See Kasoma, 2000.

[2] Ideological indoctrination of reporters and editors in Tanzania occurred largely through periodic mass media seminars organized by the ruling party. Four media seminars were held between 1973 and 1983. See Nordenstreng – Nkwabi, 1987: 40-54.

[3] The Friedrich Ebert Stiftung (FES) report names at least 28 radio stations. See *Tanzania* (2005): 117-120.

[4] The words "press" and "media" are used interchangeably in this article.

[5] At independence in 1962 there were only three qualified journalists in the country. See Hamelink, 1988: 48.

[6] The so-called street newspapers are characterized by stories that quote anonymous sources, carry no by-lines or fictitious ones, and carry large cry-wolf headlines not supported by story contents. And most of them are not regular; they tend to surface when important news events like elections are afoot. See Ochieng, 1992; Kasoma, 1997; Kasoma, 2000.

[7] Self-regulation can produce responsibility without impingement on journalistic freedom. The self-regulation mechanisms include post-mortems, press councils, journalism reviews, and codes of ethics. See Sanders, 2003: 143; Frost, 2000.

[8] "Codes of ethics come under the aegis of self-regulation". See Sanders, 2003: 141.

[9] Ethnicity and tribalism are said to be the strongest factors in shaping political opinions in Africa. See Okigbo, 1989: 126.

[10] African ethics is said to be primarily anthropocentric and has theo-centric dimensions, which have not been sufficiently considered. See Bujo, 1997.

[11] Legal accountability (also known as government accountability) is said to undermine press freedom. See Christians, 1989: 41.

[12] Two conditions are necessary if codes of ethics are to be effective: (1) newsroom leadership committed to codes of ethics codes as institutional standards, and (2) continuous discussion of controversial cases. See Boeyink, 1994: 894.

[13] See Tichenor – Donohue – Olien, 1980, quoted in Pritchard – Morgan, 1989: 936.

[14] See Kincaid, 1982, quoted in Pritchard – Morgan, 1989: 936.

[15] Boeyink said codes of ethics contain two types of precepts those involving conflict of interest and reporting practices. The former standards protect independence of reporters and editors; the latter standards protect their credibility. See Boeyink, 1998: 173.

[16] Group norms are defined as a set of understood conventions that govern behaviour. In the context of news generation, group norms guide everything from whether to use the name of sources or whether to accept some gifts from sources. See Elliott-Boyle, 1985-1986: 25.

[17] The Kiswahili word *mzee* rendered into English means boss, that is, big-man in a deferential, minion-like sense. Mzee here refers to the proprietor who usually have a final say in the newsroom affairs.

[18] Ethics visibility in the newsrooms is low: no display of core values in the newsrooms, no relevant mission statement summarizing the *raison-d'être* of the newspapers existence, no memoranda addressing ethical concerns, and no ethics seminars. See Boeyink, 1998: 173.

[19] *Kuukata* roughly translated means "to make it".

[20] *Pimbi* has become part of the *Kiswahili* lexicon, as a verb it means not being serious.

[21] Culture is defined as "a total way of life. It embraces what people ate and what they wore; the way they walked and the way they talked". See Rodney, 2001: 34.

[22] Basic salary in Tanzania is roughly the equivalent € 55 per month. Teachers get a minimum of € 77, doctors' salaries range from Euro € 74 to € 600, and most civil servants get upwards of € 70. But most reporters in the private press draw around € 50 and are lucky if they receive it regularly and on time. These figures were obtained through interviewing various professionals in the summer of 2003.

Bibliographical references

BELSEY, A. – CHADWICK, R. (1995), "Ethics as a vehicle for media quality", *European Journal of Communication* 10/4, 495.

BOEYINK, D. E. (1994), "How effective are codes of ethics? A look at three newsrooms", *Journalism Quarterly* 71/4, 893-904.

BOEYINK, D. E. (1998), "Codes and culture at The Courier-Journal: Complexity in ethical decision-making", *Journal of Mass Media Ethics* 13/3, 165-182.

BUJO, B. (1997), *The ethical dimensions of community: The African model and the dialogue between North and South*, Nairobi: Pauline Publications.

CHRISTIANS, C. G. (1989), "Self-regulation: A critical role for codes of ethics", in E. E. DENNIS – D. M. GILLMOR – T. L. GLASSER, ed., *Media freedom and accountability,* New York: Greenwood Press.

ELLIOTT-BOYLE, D., (1985-1986), "A conceptual analysis of ethics codes", *Journal of Mass Media Ethics* 1/1, 22-26.

FROST, C. (2000), *Media ethics and self-regulation,* Harlow: Longman.

GADZEKPO, A. – al., ed. (1996), *Going to Town: The Writings of P.A.V. Ansah,* Vol. 1. Accra: Ghana University Press.

GRÖSSWILLER, P. (1997), "Changing perceptions of press freedom in Tanzania", in F. ERIBO – W. JONG-EBOT, ed., *Press freedom and communication in Africa,* Asmara: Africa World Press, 101-119.

HAMELINK, C. J. (1988), *Cultural autonomy in global communications: Planning national information policy,* London: Centre for the Study of Communication and Culture.

HERMAN, E. S. – CHOMSKY, N. (1994), *Manufacturing consent: The political economy of the mass media,* New York: Random House.

KASOMA, F. P. (1995), "The role of the independent media in Africa's change to democracy", *Media, Culture & Society* 17, 537-555.

KASOMA, F. P. (1996), "Foundations of African ethics (Afriethics) and the professional practice of journalism: The case for society-centred media morality", *African Media Review* 10/3, 93-115.

KASOMA, F. P. (1997), "The independent press and politics in Africa", *Gazette* 59/4-5, 295-310.

KASOMA, F. P. (2000), *The Press and Multiparty Politics in Africa,* Tampere: University of Tampere Press.

KILIMWIKO, L. I. M. (2002), *The fourth estate in Tanzania,* Dar es Salaam: Colour Print (T) Ltd.

KINCAID, J. (1982), "Dimensions and effects of America's political cultures", *Journal of American Culture* 5, 84-92.

MEDIA COUNCIL OF TANZANIA (2001), *Codes of ethics for media professionals,* Dar es Salaam: Ecoprint Ltd.

MERRILL, J. C. (1989), "The marketplace: A court of first resort", in E. E. DENNIS – D. M. GILLMOR – T. L. GLASSER, ed., *Media freedom and accountability,* London: Greenwood Press, 284-290.

MOEMEKA, A. A. (1997), "Communalistic societies: Community and self-respect as African values", in C. CHRISTIANS – M. TRABER, ed., *Communication ethics and universal values,* London: Sage, 170-193.

MYTTON, G. (1983), *Mass communication in Africa,* London: E. Arnold.

NORDENSTRENG, K. – NKWABI, N. (1987), *Tanzania and the new information order: A case study of Africa's second struggle*, Dar es Salaam: Tanzania Publishing House.
NYAMNJOH, F. B. (1999), "West Africa: Unprofessional and unethical journalism", in M. KUNCZIK, ed., *Ethics in journalism: A reader on their perception in the Third World*, Bonn: FES, 31-81.
OCHIENG, P. (1992), *I accuse the press*, Nairobi: Initiatives Publishers.
OKIGBO, C. (1989), "Communication ethics and social change: A Nigerian perspective", in T. W. COOPER – C. CHRISTIANS – F. F. PLUDE – R. WHITE, ed., *Communication ethics and global change*, London: Longman, 124-136.
OKIGBO, C., ed. (1994), *Reporting politics and public affairs*, Nairobi: ACCE.
PRITCHARD, D. – MORGAN, M. (1989), "Impact of ethics codes on judgments by journalists: A natural experiment", *Journalism Quarterly* 66, 934-941.
RODNEY, W. (2001), *How Europe Underdeveloped Africa*, Dar es Salaam: EAEP.
SANDERS, K. (2003), *Ethics and journalism*, London: Sage.
STURMER, M. – RIOBA, A. (2001), "Watchdog in chains: Media regulations in Tanzania from their colonial beginnings to the era of democratisation", in S. BRUNE, S., ed., *Neue Medien und Öffentlichkeiten, Schriften des Deutsche übersee Instituts*, Hamburg (at *http://www.msimulizi.com.download/16November/01*).
Tanzania (2005), *Political Handbook & NGO Calendar 2005*, Dar es Salaam: FES.
TICHENOR, P. J. – DONOHUE, G. A. – OLIEN, C. N. (1980), *Community conflict and the press*, Beverly Hills: Sage.
TRABER, M. (1989a), "African communications: Problems and prospects", *African Media Review* 3/3, 86-97.
TRABER, M. (1989b), "The stories people tell: Are they part of the democratic process? *Africa Media Review* 2/2.

A social psychology of communication
Augustine Savarimuthu, SJ

Per valutare l'interazione tra persone, serve un approccio proprio della comunicazione. Di solito lo studio della comunicazione si focalizza sui bisogni e sulle capacità del comunicatore oppure sull'impatto di strutture o regole esterne, ma molto raramente si concentra sull'interazione stessa. L'autore mette in questione il modello strumentale e lineare della comunicazione e propone un modello transazionale che vede la comunicazione come costruzione della realtà sociale. Adoperando un assunto conversazionale, l'articolo conclude che è solo tramite la comunicazione che gli interlocutori possono generare, mantenere e rivedere se stessi e i propri rapporti, e che solo una psicologia sociale della comunicazione che colleghi microrealtà e macrorealtà può davvero aiutare a capire la persona e la natura dei suoi rapporti.

"This evening I want to go to the movies but not with you".

The above statement is a communication event that takes place in a domestic context between "Brian", who says the words, and "Lucy", to whom Brian has been married for several years; they have two little children. A cursory consideration of Brian's statement gives rise to a number of questions. Is Brian angry with Lucy? Is he being indifferent or insensitive to her and her needs? Or is he perhaps simply being honest? Is he a determined and balanced person? Is he a person who communicates his feelings or opinions accurately? Is he, perhaps, trying to be cautious because he was hurt in the past? Or is he arrogant and rusty who lacks social graces? This line of questioning offers some clue to the personal and interior reality of Brian, it suggests some of the psychological aspects of the person that Brian is.

Looking more deeply into the situation, Brian's comment can lead to a horde of other queries. Is Brian a loner and a misanthrope who prefers being alone and without the responsibilities of a relationship? Is he purposely trying to avoid showing affection to Lucy? Is he perhaps reminding Lucy indirectly that she has household chores to do? May it be that Brian does not have enough money to take Lucy to the movie?

Has Lucy done something wrong for which Brian wants to avoid her? Perhaps Brian already has a companion for the movie and neither needs nor wants another? Maybe he thinks that Lucy lacks social graces and will not make an acceptable companion in public. Some of the issues raised by these questions about Brian and Lucy are related to external and demographic dimensions of their relationship, and to the complex context of their their interaction. The line of questioning illustrated above highlights the relational aspect of the two interactants and suggests how they are affiliated.

1. Communication perspective

Often in academia, it is predominantly on psychological or sociological terms that a communication event, such as that of Brian and Lucy, is evaluated. It is studied only rarely from a communication perspective. A quick browse through the "Programma degli Studi" of communication institutions may show that communication has been studied in academia often either psychologically (dealing with the interactants inner capacities and needs) or sociologically (dealing with the impact of external structures and rules) but very rarely in terms of communication itself (using rules of interaction).

More often communication studies have taken an informational path by indexing or labelling a social event rather than taking a transactional one by describing and creating it. Most communication studies consider communication as an instrument of message transfer rather than as the substratum on which social realities are generated and sustained. However a transactional path focuses on the construction of interaction and its meaning. A transactional perspective evaluates Brian's statement as a piece of communication within intimate relationship and highlights how they create and recreate themselves and their relationships in communication. In this paper we assume such an approach to communication and concentrate on how Brian and Lucy in interaction offer a clue to their personalities and a clue to the quality of their relationship. This paper also assumes that in communication the interactants keep generating, maintaining and repairing themselves and their relationship. Social psychology of communication operates on the fundamental assumption that every communication event creates, maintains, and repairs self-identity and social bonds.

2. Social psychology

As the term suggests, social psychology combines two perspectives, namely that of sociology and of psychology. Social realities are both social and psychological and that it is in communication that they find their connection. The individual factors of psychology and demographic data of sociology find their link in communication. In it, individual identity, social relatedness, and almost all social activities are constituted and maintained. Social psychology assumes that social reality is a dialogical process, an intersubjective phenomenon, constructed in conversation among people. Knowledge is actively constructed by the individual in language interaction with others, and is not passively received. "Ideas, concepts and memories arise from social interchange and are mediated through language" and "all knowledge [...] evolves in the space between people" (Hoffman, 1992: 8). Communication that mediates the space among people offers clues to the nature and quality of the relationship among them (cf. Lederman, 1996). In interpersonal situations, like the statement above, talk among people provides evidence concerning the nature of the relationship among them (Goffman, 1967, 1959). Communication, therefore, is said to be the constitutive basis for speculation about the self and social relationships. Social psychology focuses on the self in relational mode in and through interaction.

3. The self is relational

Mead, Cooley, Goffman, and the Symbolic Interactionists question an objective, absolute, unitary individual self and recognize human beings as relational and as fundamentally social (sociological), emotional (psychological), and embodied (social-psychological). The relational nature of the person as constituted within human interaction has been the focus of many scholars across disciplines. Mead, Cooley, Goffman, Scheff, and Retzinger in sociology; Geertz and Bateson in anthropology; the MRI group of Palo Alto in therapy; Mechanic and Costello in medical sociology; and Deetz, Duncan, Fiske and Mokros in communication research – to name only a few – attempt to understand the self and social relationships as constituted in human interaction. Through an interdisciplinary effort, these scholars explore how human beings create and recreate their sense of self and society in interaction. Interaction is seen not as a tool of message transfer, but as the site in a communicative system "within which experience achieves a sense of coherence, structure and meaning" (Mokros, 1996: 4). From this perspective, the meaning of the concepts of the self and society are constantly negotiated in communication practices.

4. A psychological perspective

Communication is not the central concern of classical psychologists such as Freud, Jung, and Allport. They focus on an objective, unitary self and not its relationship to others or to society. Freud's conception of personality accepts the importance of society, but does not sufficiently recognize the relational nature of the self. In the case of our protagonist Brian, Freud (1915/1958) would be interested in discovering his hidden, unconscious self and the psychological impulses that compel him to exclude Lucy from his leisure activities; he sould not be interested in how Brian is affiliated to Lucy. Jung (1944) would have observed a genuine state of psychopathology in Brian's behaviour. However, since Jung does not acknowledge interaction between the self and society, he would explain psychopathology as an inner deficiency rather than as an interactional problem, an issue explored efficiently by Bateson later.

Some Neo-Freudians, such as Fromm, Erickson, and Horney, while adapting Freudian theory to new social and psychological insights, would focus on the importance of social environment of Brian as a determinant of his personality. Horney (1950) studying neurosis, might explain how inferiority feelings in women, and so in poor Lucy, can be constructed by society's attitude toward the sexes. However, in much psychological literature the communicative act of Brian would be viewed as an inner quality of unitary, rational, and autonomous human person. He would be seen as fully developed and pre-given and hence predictable. Thus, communication is explained using individual factors. Social, cultural, and historical changes are ignored in the development of personality. A social psychology approach to communication would challenge some of these assertions and would maintain that social acts could not be explained only on the basis of individualistic factors (Mokros, 1995). Human beings are social and relational and any human behaviour has to be viewed only within the Web of human interaction.

5. A sociological perspective

In classical sociological literature communication takes a central stage. For Durkheim (1893/1964) the quality of communication depends upon the quality of social solidarity, whether it is mechanical or organic. In mechanical solidarity the individual is conditioned by traditional forces through face to face communication and in organic solidarity by contract or free will through varied communication media. However, in both societies human relationship like the one that exists between Brian and Lucy is controlled and conditioned by external social forces. For Marx (1846/1978) who assumes a complete and comprehensive materialism to explain social phenomena, the communication interaction of Brian and Lucy is subjected to and determined by material conditions such as time, money, after-work fatigue, etc.. Although material conditions determine most social behaviour, great noble human ideals and enduring commitments in relationships cannot be explained by material conditions alone.

Weber (1904/1947) argues that using goal-oriented rationality, people make self-conscious and deliberate choices to achieve their goals (Coser, 1971). According to him, Brian might be driven by goal-oriented rationality when he wanted to go to the movie without Lucy. However, goal-oriented rationality may not always be the most desirable ethical state. One can be rational and legal but may be totally wrong. Brian's action might be justified as an example of goal-oriented rationality but can it be supported ethically? Simmel's (1908/1955) formal explanation of dyad in intimate relationships may be helpful to understand Brian's hostile behaviour towards Lucy because dyads are susceptible to enduring conflicts. However, external structure alone cannot account for Brian's statement; Brian and Lucy are not mere victims of external forms but they are willing and acting persons. Simmel appears to ignore the historical and dynamic nature of human persons in communication act.

Some recent sociological studies place communication at the heart of relationships. Communication as social action is studied in intimate relationship such as in marriage and family (Galea, 1996; Stiers, 1996; Cowman, 1995; Jenness, 1993) or in the context of business and organizations (Dadek, 1997; Park, 1996). Sociology considers communication as enhancing a bond, a tie between oneself and society. Every act of communication involves the development of identity and social bonds. In sociological thinking, the self is always viewed in relation to the society or social bonds (Mead, Cooley, Goffman) because to be is to be related. Social bond is the relationship of individual to the society and the primary motive of all social exchange (Scheff, 1990; Retzinger, 1991). Within such thinking, even emotions are considered social because they have significant function in society. Social emotions place the self in a relational mode. They index the state of the society and social bonds as Durkheim demonstrated in *Suicide* (1897/1951).

By removing the self from sociological analysis, Durkheim appears to have marginalized psychology and Marx, by reducing emotions to material conditions, seems to have ignored the complex quality of emotions. Communication can be adequately explored only when one recognizes the micro-macro reality of life world that is always revealed in self/other interactions. Mead, Cooley, Sullivan, and Goffman have come closer to understand the macro world by looking into the micro manifestations, namely, human communications.

6. From psychology and sociology to communication

A systematic assessment of communication of Brian and Lucy cannot be undertaken merely by studying the individualistic factors of psychology or the developmental and demographical data of sociology (Mokros, 1995). It has to be anchored in the interaction between individual and social factors, the micro-macro realities. Mead, a social psychologist, is one of the earliest social scholars who focused on the relationship between micro-macro worlds of psychology and sociology, and who recognized the importance of communication for such a relationship.

According to Mead (1934), communication is the primary condition of social life and of the development of individual self. Mead affirms that mind, self, and society are highly interdependent processes. In other words, each person requires the other, for people are connected through communication. The self is formed by the response of others. The ongoing, patterned, social activities that link the mind, the self, and the society are structured in communication. Like Mead, Piaget (1959) focuses on the communication games by which one grows in self-consciousness and self-reflection in an interwoven fashion. These games are microscopic reflections of the society and to understand the society one should understand the rules embedded in the social games. Piaget demonstrates empirically Mead's concept of interdependence of society, thought, and the self.

Sullivan (1964), a psychologist who concentrates on the interpersonal aspect of the self, strives to link psychology and sociology, the micro-macro concerns of the social sciences. He maintains that any understanding of the self has to include the analysis of the relationships and interaction that the self is engaged in. This relational aspect of the self, a being "with" another, is sustained and revealed in communication. Sullivan's understanding of the relational and interactional aspect of the self echoes the ideas of Mead, Piaget, and Cooley.

While Mead and Piaget focus on the phenomenon of interaction games, Cooley is interested in the motives of interaction. Cooley's (1902/1967) "looking-glass self" maintains that others act like mirrors to a person's sense of self imagination. The self-concept is formed as a reflection of others' perceptions. People change their interaction strategies according to other's response in whose mind they see themselves. Mead and Cooley viewed communication as a validation of the social self, that is, a person infers identity attributed to him or her from the responses of others. From this view, the actors appear passive recipients of random responses and the self appears as a victim, that is, as one who is acted upon. Hence it may follow that the self is not responsible for all its character traits. Goffman (1959) resolves this by placing in the self responsibility for its character traits and self-concepts.

Goffman (1983), in his microanalysis of social interaction, maintains that social situations are those in which two or more individuals are physically in each other's presence linked by communication. It is within such communication that identities and social bonds are created and maintained. Goffman (1959) observes further that the self is not passive in developing self-concepts, that is, accepting from others passively the responses that affirm the self, but is actively engaged in engineering favourable responses from them. Hence there is mutual communication between parties in the creation and maintenance of self-identities. In interaction, each participant is engaged in not only constructing his or her own identity (Goffman, 1967), but also in creating social bonds.

Seen from the above perspective, it is right to assert that self and social relationships are established, nurtured, and repaired in communication. It is a language game and a sacred ritual in which the partners put forth their best "line" through verbal and nonverbal codes to create a sacred bond. If, from the other end, it is accepted and responded to as it is intended, commitment to living improves. According to Goffman social life is a game and a ritual and participants are always out to manipulate each other. In such situations, commitment will be a way of engineering relationships to achieve one's personal goals. However, it is our experience that not all human actions are purposeful. Does Brian really know all the social and psychological reasons and impulses that compel and impel his action? Also, Goffman's theory seems to fail to recognize the institutional aspects of social behaviour.

The theories of Mead and Goffman have been extremely influential in inspiring research in microsociology that has focused on the interaction of human actors to make projection about larger social structures. These studies have taken a perspective that is now called "Symbolic Interactionism". An important tenet of this approach is that the self has a social origin, that is, it is a situated product of social interaction. Unlike in most traditional psychological theories, the self is not viewed as an intrapersonal phenomenon but as a constructed reality within interaction among people.

7. Communication as constructing and constructed concept

From Goffman's (1967) theory of interaction, the self, social relations could be viewed as constructed through interdependent and interactive processes. However, Foucault (1972) questions the very idea of thinking, acting, and interacting subject, the supposed basis of all social bonds. Foucault emphasizes the role of discourse in constructing the object, rather than the subject. White (1995) echoes this idea of Foucault when he asserts that "discourses, as practices, systematically form the object of which they speak" (p. 215). The ideas of Foucault and White seem to echo what Heidegger (1959) asserted earlier: "It is in words and language that things first come into being and are" (p. 13). From this perspective, there are no stable concepts of the self or society outside discourse or language (communication). The postmodern scholars (Gergen, 1982, 1985; Bruner, 1986; Foucault, 1972) look at communication as an ongoing, unending, created and creating reality. Giddens (1976) suggests that it is impossible to study construction of the self without looking at how the self and societal institutions mutually influence both the structuration of the self and the structuration of society. Giddens suggests that rather than looking at the self and society as a dualism, we should consider them as a duality of structure. Giddens offers a way of linking the micro-macro, the self-society, subjective-objective concerns in our analysis of the communication act of Brian and Lucy.

8. Communication as social matrix

Bateson (1956) extensively uses communication theories to treat mental patients because he is convinced that communication is at the heart of mental health. To deal with mental health, he does not turn to Freud or Gestalt psychologists, but to Mead and Sullivan. Studying schizophrenic patients, Bateson and colleagues (1956) focus on their pattern of communication because they maintain that communication is the matrix of psychiatry. Bateson's (1951) book *Communication: The Social Matrix of Psychiatry*, written with Juergen Ruesch, highlights the importance of feedback and information in communication and defines all human communication as being simultaneously a report and command, that is, descriptive and functional.

Bateson (1996) seems to take the position of Sullivan that mental processes are communicational and interactional rather than internal and individual. Bateson seems to agree with Freud when he maintains that nothing that is expressed happens by accident. This is a kind of interpersonal determinism that seems to be the highlight of Bateson's position in the communicational aspect of therapy. Bateson insists that every word or nonverbal cue expressed is part of the interpersonal process. Communication in certain cases provokes the behavioural characteristics of schizophrenia. In his now famous "double-bind theory" Bateson (1956) demonstrates how the mental health of a person is violated when two contradictory and incongruent messages are enforced by punishment.

Following the lead of Mead, Bateson (1996) assumes that the response we get from the other tells us about the state of the other once the other has received the signals we have emitted. It is only by the response of others that we know the import of the signal that we have sent. "For every human being there is an edge of uncertainty about what sort of message he is emitting, and we all need, in the final analysis, to see how our messages are received in order to discover what they are" (1996: 56). Sending signals and understanding messages presuppose certain common rules which are constantly created and recreated by interactants. The status quo in which interaction takes place also keeps changing every moment and hence at every moment the message is created anew.

In *The Natural History of an Interview*, Bateson focuses on the communication rules that seem to be happening constantly in every interaction: "This dialogue is not only between persons and about the pacts that they form, it is also and more strangely a dialogue that governs what each person is [...]. In everyday language we say that a person's self-esteem is enhanced or reduced by the responses of others. Or we say that 'he sees himself differently'" (Bateson, 1996: 60). In communicational terms, we may translate this into a statement that the very rules of self-perception, the rules governing the formation of a self-image, are modified by the way in which others receive our messages. Bateson's thesis highlights what communication of response or feedback coming from others does to one's self esteem.

9. Social psychology of communication

Social psychology places emphasis on communication as the constitutive substratum of all social reality, that is, as the ground on which all understanding of social reality including the self and social bonds is anchored. From this perspective, communication is not viewed as indexical, that is, labelling external concrete reality, but seen as symbolical, that is, creating the reality it signifies (Sapir, 1958). Knowledge is actively constructed in communication among people and not passively received and the function of cognition is to organize the life-world rather than discover an objective ontological reality. This approach considers human experience as dialogue, that is, always in a relational mode with others. From this perspective, knowledge is viewed as semiotic, hermeneutic, and narrative (Deetz, 1994; Mokros, 1993, 1995, 1996; Mokros – Deetz 1995). Even though these two approaches are distinctly different in their ontological and epistemological assumptions, they are not mutually exclusive.

The social psychology of communication views the self as a dialogue, a language-game constantly created and maintained within interaction. This perspective denies the possibility of acquiring an objective "true representation" of reality because human communication is symbolic representation and there is always a gap between the sign and the signified. There will always be a gap between what Brian intended and how he was perceived by Lucy. From this perspective, communication is an intersubjective phenomenon, a game, and a ritual, whereby the personalities of Brian and Lucy and their relationship are created and reviewed constantly. The reality of Brian and Lucy and their relationship is not a finished product but are constantly developing in interaction. Social psychology recognizes this ongoing ever generating aspect of relational communication. Therefore communication study has to move away from the positivist concerns of control and strategy (the focus of psychology and sociology) to a position informed by semantics, narrative and hermeneutic (the focus of social psychology).

10. Conclusion

Social psychology of communication maintains that social reality is a dialogical process, an intersubjective phenomenon constructed in conversation among people. The self and social bonds are social constructions, created so in and through interaction. Communication is at the centre of the creation, maintenance, and repairing of individual identity and social relatedness. Ideas, concepts, and memories arise from social interchange and are mediated through language. All knowledge evolves in the space between people. By maintaining the social and relational character of the self and keeping communication at the centre of that relationship social psychology preserves the sacred link between the self and social bonds and the micro-macro realities embedded in every lived human interaction. Therefore communication research should begin with the lived experiences of people as revealed in their communication acts not on the assumed inner impulses or external demography.

Bibliographical references

BATESON, G. (1996), "Communication", in H. B. MOKROS, ed., *Interaction & identity*, New Brunswick: Transaction Publishers, 45-70.
BATESON, G. – REUSCH, J. (1951), *Communication: The social matrix of psychiatry*, New York: Norton.
BATESON, G. – JACKSON, D. – HALEY, J. – WEAKLAND, J. (1956), "Toward a theory of schizophrenia", *Behavioral Sciences* 1, 251-264.
BRUNER, J. (1986), *Actual minds, possible worlds*, Cambridge, MA: Harvard University Press.
COOLEY, C. H. (1967), *Human nature and social order,* New York: Schocken Books (original work published 1902).
COSER, L. (1971), *Masters of sociological thought, ideas in historical and social context*, New York: Harcourt.
COWMAN, D. A. (1995), *An investigation into marriage commitment formation through the analysis of narrative accounts: Marriage is a story*, Unpublished doctoral dissertation, York University, Canada.
DADEK, W. (1997), *The effect of organizational decline on organizational and occupational commitment,* Unpublished doctoral dissertation, Nova Southeastern University.
DEETZ, S. A. (1994), "Future of the discipline: The challenges, the research, and the social contribution", in S. A. DEETZ, ed., *Communication Yearbook*, 17, Thousand Oaks, CA: Sage Publications, 565-600.

DURKHEIM, E. (1951), *Suicide: A study in sociology,* New York: Free Press (original work published 1897).
FOUCAULT, M. (1972), *Archeology of knowledge,* New York: Pantheon.
FREUD, S. (1958), *The unconscious,* in S. FREUD, *Standard edition XIV,* London.
GALEA, P. (1996), *Development and validation of the commitment to partnership scale: Applying psychological constructs to pastoral issues in marriage,* Unpublished doctoral dissertation, Loyola College in Marymount.
GERGEN, K. (1982), *Towards transformation in social knowledge,* New York: Springer.
GERGEN, K. J. (1985), "Social constructionist inquiry: Context and implications", in K. J. GERGEN – K. E. DAVIS, ed., *The social construction of the person,* New York: Springer-Verlag, 3-18.
GIDDENS, A. (1976), *New rules of sociological method,* New York: Basic Books.
GIDDENS, A. (1979), *Central problems in social theory,* London: Macmillan.
GOFFMAN, E. (1959), *The presentation of self in everyday life,* New York: Anchor.
GOFFMAN, E. (1967), *Interaction ritual: Essay on face-to-face behavior,* New York: Panthers.
GOFFMAN, E. (1983), "Interaction order", *American Sociological Review* 48, 1-17.
HEIDEGGER, M. (1959), *An introduction to metaphysics,* New York: Yale University Press.
HOFFMAN, L. (1992), "A reflexive stance for family therapy", in S. MCNAMEE – K. J. GERGEN, ed., *Therapy as social construction,* London: Sage.
HORNEY, K. (1950), *Neurosis and human growth.* New York: Norton.
JENNESS, A. (1993), *Families: A celebration of diversity. Commitment, and love,* Madison, WI: Demco Media.
JUNG, K. (1944), *Psychology and alchemy.* New York: Pantheon.
LEDERMAN, L. C. (1996), "Internal Muzak: An examination of intrapersonal relationships", in H. B. MOKROS, ed., *Interaction and identity,* New Brunswick, NJ: Transaction Publishers, 194-214.
MEAD, G. H. (1934), *Mind, self and society,* Chicago: University of Chicago Press.
MOKROS, H. B. – DEETZ, S. A. (1995), "What counts as real? A constitutive view of communication and the disenfranchised in the context of health", in E. B. RAY, ed., *Communication and disenfranchisement:*

Social health issues and implications, Mahwah, NJ: Lawrence Erlbaum, 29-44.

MOKROS, H. B. (1993), "Communication and psychiatric diagnosis: Tales of depressive moods from two contexts", *Health Communication* 5/2, 113-127.

MOKROS, H. B. (1995), "Suicide and shame", *American Behavioral Scientist* 38, 1091-1103.

PARK, D. L. A. (1996), *Common fire: Commitment in a complex world,* Boston: Beacon Press.

PIAGET, J. (1959), *Judgment and reasoning in the child,* Littlefield, NJ: Adams.

RETZINGER, S. M. (1991), *Violent emotions: Shame and rage in marital quarrels,* Newbury Park, CA: Sage.

SAPIR, E. (1958), *Selected writings of Edward Sapir in language, culture and personality,* Berkeley and Los Angeles: University of California Press.

SCHEFF, T. J. (1990), *Microsociology: Discourse, emotion, and social structure,* Chicago: University of Chicago Press.

SIMMEL, G. (1955), *Conflict and the Web of group affiliation,* New York: Free Press (original work published 1908).

STIERS, G.A. (1996), *From this day forward: Love, commitment, and marriage in lesbian and gay relationships,* Unpublished dissertation, University of Massachussettes.

SULLIVAN, H. S. (1964), *The fusion of psychiatry and social science,* New York: W. W. Norton & Company.

WHITE, M. (1995), *Re-authoring lives: Interviews and essays,* Adelaide, South Australia: Dulwich Centre Publications.

THE SOCIO-CULTURAL DIMENSION

Communalistic approach to communication with examples from the Yorùbá of Nigeria

Joseph Oládèjo Fáníran

L'autore indaga su come i popoli africani comunichino nel mondo odierno. Adoperando una teoria innovativa del rituale che proviene dalle filosofie africane, l'articolo mostra come un certo orientamento verso le strutture comunitarie della comunicazione possa essere appreso grazie a rituali di socializzazione che celebrano le fasi della vita. Basandosi su osservazioni personali dell'autore e su interviste rivolte ad alcune famiglie della tribù Yorùbá, lo studio fa un confronto tra le diverse modalità di realizzazione dei suddetti rituali di socializzazione, con speciale riferimento a quattro diversi gruppi sociali nigeriani: famiglie dei villaggi rurali, famiglie nel contesto semi-urbano di Ìbàdàn, famiglie nella metropoli di Lagos, e alcuni discendenti di ex schiavi che sono tornati dal Brasile a Lagos e ad Abéòkuta. Lo studio afferma in conclusione che il modo di comunicare degli Africani è comunitario, anche se in forma ibrida.

1. Introduction

The present social, political and economic crisis confronting the African continent causes people to question the commonly-accepted assumption that the African culture is basically communalistic. Some scholars argue that although communalism describes the way the people in rural areas of Africa communicate, the same cannot be said about, for example, youth in urban areas. These are rejecting communalism and opting for the rugged individualism of the West (Moemeka, 1999, 1998, 1997). This essay carries the argument a step further by asserting that despite the continuous penetration of the African world by modernisation and its attendant crisis, African culture and communication, whether in the urban or rural context, will continue to be communalistic, albeit in a new hybrid form.

2. Method

The position taken in this essay is the fruit of an ethnographic study, carried out by this author between January 2001 and January 2002, of the way people communicate among the Yorùbá of the south-western part of Nigeria. The south-western part of Nigeria is presently divided into six states – Ekiti, Lagos, Ogun, Ondo, Osun and Oyo. Twenty-five families were interviewed. Seven of those interviews were done in the rural areas of Ekiti and Osun states, while fourteen were in the urban areas of Lagos, Oyo, Osun, and Ondo States. The remaining four families were descendants of the returnees to Nigeria from Brazil, Cuba, and Sierra Leone. One of them was interviewed in Ibadan, while the rest were interviewed in Lagos. The geographical and socio-cultural spread of the interviewees justifies the claim that they represent the sampling universe of the research.

In the process of the interviews, the five indices of communalistic culture, proposed by Moemeka, were studied in seven rituals of life-transition in three different socio-cultural contexts, namely, the rural families, the urban families who are still in contact with the rural culture, and the urban families who have only minimal contact with that culture. The five indices used are: the supremacy of the community, the usefulness of the individual, the sanctity of authority, the respect for old age, and religion as a way of life. The rituals of life transitions are childbirth and naming ceremony, interaction within families, the use of oríkì, adulthood attained by marriage, human habitation, politics and mobilisation, and finally death/funeral ceremony. Before discussing the results of the research, we shall briefly review the elements of the communalistic approach to communication.

3. Elements of communalism and communalistic communication

As a vision of totality in which beings are perceived as distinct and yet ontologically and intimately related with one another (Nkemnkia, 1999: 172), communalism embodies the basic African concept of history and the fundamental values and symbols that are narrated in myths and celebrated in rituals. One of its indices is the supremacy of the community and closely related to this is the usefulness of the individual. The first is expressed in terms of kinship relationship, while the second emphasises the importance of the individual. Brought up on the basis of kinship relationships, an individual cultivates an intimate sense of obligation and belonging to the community (Wiredu, 1998: 21). His or her primary motivations are not of personal, individual success, but of the whole community. Though a being-in-relation, the individual is not swallowed up by the community, but is considered useful and valuable. Kwame Gyekye sums up this second element, saying that "the individual cannot develop outside the framework of the community, but the welfare of the community as a whole cannot dispense with the talents and the initiative of its individual members" (1996: 50). Thus, the focus is on the interaction, the in-between, the social relations or the commitment to the well-being of all. Here nurturing, service, and interdependence are highly prized.

In this context, the primary purpose of the communicative act is to confirm, solidify and promote the communal social order, while its secondary purpose is to maintain and improve interpersonal relationships. As noted by Moemeka, the high pedestal on which the community is placed imposes limitations and demands on what the individual can say about the community, to whom, when and how. Thus, vertical communication follows the hierarchical socio-political ranks within the community, while horizontal communication is relatively open and usually occurs among people of the same age, those who work together, live within the same proximity, or belong to the same ethnic group (Moemeka, 1998: 133).

This brings the discussion to the next two but related indices of communalistic culture, namely, the sanctity of authority and the corresponding respect for old age or the elderly. Here, the principle that young people are subordinate to older people and should show deference to them underlies and gives coherence to the whole kinship relationships (Redfield, 1963: 39). Since elders are seen as the repositories of wisdom and knowledge, they are accorded honour, dignity and respect. They also enjoy the cultural right to guide the community from their font of wisdom and have the final say or pronounce judgement on actions or events or on the collective decision arrived at. This often takes place in meetings, moonlight storytelling sessions, impromptu village-square discussions, one-to-one conversations along the streets and footpaths, and during the settlement of disputes (Ansu-Kyeremeh, 1998: 178).

Among the Yorùbá, this hierarchical social order and the asymmetrical role position are reflected in the reverential style of speaking and the vocabulary of respect employed when addressing an elder or someone perceived to be older or holding a higher position than the person communicating. He or she is expected to use the plural "you", "e" or "èyin" and not the singular "you", "ìwo". Another form in which respect for seniority and age is communicated is the way elders are greeted. A young man greets a person perceived to be older or holding a higher social position by prostrating himself, while a young woman in the same situation kneels. When he or she encounters a person to be his or her junior, he or she automatically expects to be greeted with the same gestures of respect. The communication, given and received, facilitates social interaction and contributes to peace and harmony among the interlocutors.

The last of the five indices of communalistic culture is the recognition of religion as a way of life. Religion permeates the whole of life and is used to safeguard the social order, and protect the social norms and communication rules. For instance, before the Yorùbá do anything of importance, like choosing a life-partner, contemplating a journey, at the birth of a child, or when starting to build a home, they would first consult If, a coherent and self-consistent system of their belief and worldview. Nothing is done or said except l'ágbára Olórun, i.e., by the power of God. Thus religious rituals assume and carry out a relationship of harmony. Indeed, rituals in general, involve people as members of a community, uphold their common social order, purge their community of disorder and restore its integrity (Wolf, 1966: 98).

Since rituals socialise people into communicative relationships and sustain these relationships, they constitute the entry point into understanding how the people communicate and the norms that govern its process. This is why the present research centers on the seven rituals of life transitions: childbirth and naming ceremonies, interaction within families, the use of oríkì, adulthood attained by marriage, human habitation, politics and mobilisation, and finally the death/funeral ceremony. These rituals were studied among families in the three sociocultural contexts mentioned above.

4. The findings: in the rural context

The analysis of the data gathered from families in the rural areas reveals that the communalistic values of the supremacy of the community, the usefulness of the individual, the sanctity of authority, the respect for old age, and religion as a way of life are still being inculcated through ritual communication. The communalistic values also form the basis of the social reality into which they are socialising their children. This is evident in the naming ceremony, the performance of the praise song (oríkì) and in the day-to-day interaction within the family till they attain fifteen years of age and later in life through the rituals of marriage, housing, politics and funeral ceremonies.

* Eight days after the birth of a child, the members of the lineage and their friends come together to welcome the child and create, share, and

celebrate its identity in the extended family by giving it its names and oríkì. These root the child in the past and the present history of its immediate family and by extension the entire society and signal some anticipated benevolent characteristics or heroism of the child in the future. The derivation of the names primarily from the circumstances surrounding the birth of the child shows the importance of the community in the process of identity formation. Thus from the very beginning of the child's life, it is made clear to the child that it is not an entity unto itself, but a being-in-relation with the community as a whole. Other items used to pray for the child during the naming ceremony include sugar, salt, sugar cane and honey, which signify joy and sweetness of life; kola signifies long life; ataare or alligator pepper points to fruitfulness and unity.

In addition, the data of the survey show that as the rural areas come more and more under the influence of such modernising agents as Western education and Christianity, the people are refining their culture in the light of the new by incorporating the symbols of the new religion and culture into the rituals of their life cycle. For example, even in the village context items like a pen, which is a symbol of Western education, and the Christian symbols like the Cross, the Bible or the Rosary beads, are included in the materials used to pray for the child during the naming ceremony. One of the interviewees relates how she creatively inserts the symbols of the Christian practices of her grandparents into the praise song (oríkì) of her family. The way the grandparents used to walk down to the Church every morning, their closeness to things sacred, and their celebrative mood, demonstrated in the way their flowing garments used to fly in the wind on Sundays, all these have become symbols of their dedication to the new faith, worthy of emulating by the oncoming generations. She thereby uses the expounded form of the oríkì of her family to pacify her born-again children who want to kick against its usage. In short, through the creative process of meaning making that is going on even in the rural areas, the rural dwellers are coping with the disruption that is taking place in their culture.

5. The findings: among urban families still in contact with rural culture

The data analysis here shows that as the Yorùbá families in the modern urban sector are experiencing the pressures of the socio-cultural change, those of them who are still in contact with the rural way of life are grafting the new demands onto the communalistic root paradigm of their culture. The city of Ìbàdàn is a typical example of a place where the old blends with the new. The indigenes have devised an unwritten rule that makes it mandatory to have the ritual of the naming ceremony of the first child take place in the traditional family compound in the old part of the city. Thus, the supremacy of the family as the foundation of the life of the young urban couple and their child is preserved, the bond of communion between the members of the extended family is renewed, and as those present at the ceremony return to their separate ways of life they carry with them the sweet memory of the unity of their family. On the whole, the ritual powerfully preserves the extended family, and ultimately, the community, from falling apart.

In addition, during the naming ceremony, the priest, the catechist, or the imams and alfas now direct the affairs, a role that is traditionally played by the eldest in the family. This signifies the shifting of the locus of the "holy" out of the family into the religious institutions. Besides, the religious institutions are beginning to redefine the ritual items. For example, the Muslims reduce the items to money; the Pentecostal Christians accept only water and the Bible, while the Catholic Christians add the Rosary, the Cross and the Bible onto the traditional items of water, honey, salt, kola and bitter kola.

Another area where the new is being blended with the old is in the relationship between a husband and a wife. Due to their exposure to Western education, the two are beginning to see and relate to each other as interdependent beings. They are prone to use the language of mutual respect instead of that of the hierarchical order. This does not mean that wives no longer respect their husbands; the respect between them is rather reflected in the pet names they invent to address each other. However, tension remains in the area of the choice of the language to use at home. In most cases, husbands prefer and encourage the use of Yorùbá, while their wives favour English. This suggests that, being more conservative than their wives, the husbands want to continue with the ritual language that preserves the hierarchical social order and the asymmetrical social role between husband and wife. The preference of the wives points to their desire to assert their self-identity, and English, a tool of modern culture, becomes a convenient way of expressing themselves without the cumbersome necessity of having to use the subordinate vocabulary of the plural "you", "e" or "eyin", each time they want to address their husbands.

A similar trend is noticeable in the organisation of marriage. The young couples are blending the interdependent self of the individualistic culture with the dependent self of the communalistic root paradigm. In the former, they choose their life partner and in the latter, they allow their parents to have the last say in the process of their marriage.

The traditional physical coming together to work in rotation for one another as members of the same egbé or age group is now being replaced by the symbolic giving of money. In addition, the socio-economic situation of the modern urban life transforms the egbé from a collection of people of the same age to that of the same occupational or professional associations. In the busy modern situation, the modern communication technology, like telephone and Internet, is replacing the mandatory physical presence that characterises interpersonal communication in the rural communities.

6. The results: among the modern urban families with little contact with rural culture

The families interviewed here, the descendants of the Yorùbá returnees from Brazil, Cuba and Sierra Leone, constitute the control group of the study. Historians have narrated how their grandparents

> spoke no African languages and tried to learn none, but carried out their cultural activities in English. In Lagos, they assiduously imitated and improvised upon the little European ways they had imbibed before returning to Nigeria, setting themselves up as models of civilization for the "bush natives" to admire and mimic (Ogundele, 1999: 71).

The assumption is that since their grandparents occupied the front seat of the modernisation drive into Nigeria, and since they were brought up with little contact with the agrarian way of life, the present generation of the descendants of the returnees would be noticeably different from the urban families who retain their contact with the rural culture. One would expect them to lead the rejection of the communalistic culture for the rugged individualistic culture of the West.

The data show that the present generation of the descendants of the returnees have moved away from the position of their grandparents. Not only do they identify themselves as Yorùbá, they also socialise their children in the first fifteen years of their lives into the communalistic Yorùbá worldview and ethos. Like in all other Yorùbá families, they insist on bringing up their children to respect their parents, the elders and their seniors by prostrating or kneeling and by using the vocabulary of respect that reflects the hierarchical social structure existing all over Yorùbá land. Like the urban families in contact with the village life, they too have stopped the asymmetrical relationship between husband and wife that is prevalent in the families with strong communistic tendencies.

The culture of cooperative system of coming together to work freely in rotation for one another is alien to these families. This is rightly so, because the logic of the modern urban culture does not provide for that type of social relationship. Cooperative ventures are carried out in such fora as egbé, i.e., the old students' associations, clubs, descendant unions, professional associations, and the various societies in the Church or Mosque. The meetings serve as a forum for reliving their togetherness and for expressing the communion that exists among them. At times, these fora also serve as channels for political mobilisation. In the area of building a house, the transaction is no longer based on family but on the professional relationship by which a service is provided according to the terms of the agreement. The other members of the family, relatives and friends are brought in only for the àríyá or the get-together that marks the completion and occupation of the building.

7. Conclusion

The findings from the three sets of families confirm the basic argument of this study, namely, that African cultures are communalistic and will continue to be, albeit in a new way. The new way is expressed in hybrid form. In other words, as an institution with individualistic logic but communalistic advantage is introduced, those involved are pulled towards the individualistic obligation. But because they have been socialised in the traditional communalistic ethos, they give a new symbolic meaning to the individualistic obligation, just as they graft the new on to the old root paradigm. The following direct quotation from one of the interviewees sums it up well:

> In fact, one of the major things that make me survive in the West today is that aspect of the strength of the community, of community that I bring to my work, even as I look at my work from the contemporary context within Western world... I think in Yorùbá and speak in English. So, I think in Yorùbá and choreograph in contemporary form, in the sense that we do not, if you respect someone, if he is older than you, you do not call him by name; you pluralise them. E ka aro o (good morning); E pele o (I salute you); that is my thinking. If I am addressing my father, I would say E nle, Sir (I salute you, Sir), or something like that. But when I am choreographing, if I want to choreograph the position of my father, I would find a way of making that particular subject or that phenomenon or that philosophy

larger than what it is, which is not the problem of Western choreographer because his father is "you"... So, when I choreograph, I choreograph from my understanding of my own culture or my language Yorùbá and then translate it (Badejo, 2001).

Thus, when the phenomenon of communication among the Yorùbá is examined in terms of their worldview, ethos, and the rituals of their everyday life and at the peak moments of their life, the conclusion can be drawn that at the beginning of the third millennium, communalism forms the basic root of the way they communicate. Given the complexity of the modern urban society and their interaction with people of varying backgrounds, they are flexible in their selection of symbols and organisation of rituals. Since communalism forms the kernel of the primary socialisation given to every child in the first fifteen years of its life, it remains the root paradigm that continues to inform their cultural and communicative action irrespective of their geographical location. Instead of rejecting one culture for another, they are creating pathways to new meaning, order and community.

Bibliographical references

ANSU-KYEREMEH, K. (1998), "Indigenous Communication in Africa: A Conceptual Framework", in K. ANSU-KYEREMEH, ed., *Perspectives on Indigenous Communication in Africa*, Vol. 1: *Theory and Application,* Legon, Ghana: School of communication Studies, 1-12.
BADEJO, P. (2001), Interviewed at Ayétòrò, Òsogbo on January 12.
GYEKYE, K. (1996), *African Cultural Values: An Introduction,* Accra: Sankofa Publication Company.
MOEMEKA, A. A. (1997), "Communalistic Societies: Community and Self-respect as African Values", in C. CHRISTIANS – M. TRABER, ed., *Communication Ethics and Universal Values,* London: Sage Publications, 170-193.
MOEMEKA, A. A. (1998), "Communalism as a Fundamental Dimension of Culture", *Journal of Communication* 48/4, 118-141.
MOEMEKA, A. A. (1999), "Communalism versus Modernism: The Struggle between Ethics and Convenience in Africa", Presented at the Third International Conference on *Media, Religion and Culture*, Edinburgh, Scotland, July 20-23.
NKEMNKIA, M. N. (1999), *African Vitalogy: A Step Forward in African Thinking,* Nairobi: Paulines Publications Africa.

OGUNDELE, W. (1999), "Western Education and Alienation in Contemporary African Cultural Affairs" *IFE: Journal of the Institute of Cultural Studies* 7, 66-78.
REDFIELD, R. (1963), *The Little Community and Peasant Society and Culture*, Chicago: The University of Chicago Press.
WIREDU, K. (1998), "Our Problem of Knowledge: Brief Reflections on Knowledge and Development in Africa", in O. OLADIPO, ed., *Remaking Africa: Challenges of the Twenty-First Century*, Ibadan: Hope Publications, 17-23.
WOLF, E. R. (1966), *Peasants,* Englewood Cliffs: Prentice Hall Inc.

La educación para los medios en tiempos de secularización *
José Martínez de Toda, SJ

Secularization is growing in Europe. It means to put God aside in daily life, to keep Him outside of the public sphere, and to have Him only for the inner personal world of each one. This is one of the worst things that can happen nowadays to Christianity. Mass media are one of the factors that contribute to secularization. Certainly a lot can be done with them to fight this disease. But what to do when they spread secularization? Media education will help students to develop six dimensions within themselves: to be media literate, conscious, critical, active, social and creative. Thus they will defend themselves against those mass media that promote secularization. But they can provide also new positive inputs in behalf of faith and Christian life. Different media education activities can be done to foster the students relationship with God. Examples for media education can be taken especially from the Gospel. It only depends on the faith, the zeal and the apostolic interest of the teacher.

1. La creciente secularización de Europa

La secularización es hoy el desafío más importante para el cristiano europeo. El *Informe sobre el estado y la situación del sistema educativo 2003/2004*, elaborado por el Consejo Escolar del Estado Español, informa que por primera vez en España, la mayor parte de los alumnos de Educación Secundaria Obligatoria (ESO), es decir, de la escuela pública, *prefiere no recibir religión* en sus estudios (*El Mundo*, 20 de Octubre de 2005, p. 18).

Estamos asistiendo a una descristianización progresiva de la sociedad a nivel público y privado. Es un proceso de secularización. La secularización es un prescindir de Dios. Es la dificultad en percibir la presencia de Dios en la vida cotidiana. Es un virus que ha invadido las familias y toda la vida pública. La secularización en la era postmoderna

---

* Conferencia durante el Simposio celebrativo de los 25 años del CICS sobre el tema "Comunicare e (è) partecipare – Dai mass media alla comunicazione partecipativa: quali sfide per la Chiesa?".

ha vaciado de *jóvenes* las iglesias, de *vocaciones* los seminarios y casas de religiosos/as, de *misioneros* los puestos de misión...

Mons. Fernando Sebastián, Arzobispo de Pamplona y Vicepresidente de la Conferencia Episcopal Española dice: "*La sociedad es cada vez menos y menos cristiana. Es triste ir muriendo en muchos ambientes*". Pero también en toda Europa. No fue accidental que no se incluyeran las "raíces cristianas" en el documento de la constitución europea. Y poco a poco está llegando también la secularización al Tercer Mundo.

La secularización trata de *desbancar* a Dios. Según Benedicto XVI para la secularización "Dios *nos estorba*, o se hace de Él una frase devota, o se le niega todo, *desterrándolo de la vida pública*, hasta que de este modo deje de tener significado alguno [...]. Sólo se admite a Dios como opinión privada" (Benedicto XVI, 2005). Esto no es nuevo. En dicha homilía sobre la parábola de los viñadores homicidas, el Papa subraya que "los arrendadores no querían tener un patrón". Eso ocurre hoy. Hay increencia, indiferencia, escapismo al tema de la fe, relativismo...

Los obispos de Pamplona-Tudela, Bilbao, S. Sebastián y Vitoria escribían al comienzo de la última Cuaresma (de 2005):

> [Hay una] creciente debilidad de la Iglesia [...] Una parte notable de nuestra gente cree que la Iglesia no va bien. Su experiencia personal, la opinión recogida en su entorno, la imagen recibida a través de la mayoría y de los medios de comunicación le confirman en esa percepción. El presente es crudo: el futuro es sombrío. El pesimismo prevalece. La autoestima colectiva decrece [...] Por primera vez en la historia a partir del s. IV la Iglesia católica y las demás iglesias viven en muchos regiones de Europa una situación de minoría cada vez más próxima a la diáspora, al estilo de las minorías judías [...] con riesgo de desdibujarse en una sociedad que va dejando de ser cristiana. Algunos analistas apuntan que el rápido avance de la increencia y la desafección religiosa en nuestra tierra pone en cuestión la propia pervivencia y persistencia de estas iglesias como realidad públicamente relevante en el futuro [...] Es triste ir muriendo en muchos ambientes.

Los obispos mencionados creen padecer un "descrédito generalizado", vivir en una "intemperie religiosa", y soportar "la crudeza de gran parte de la opinión pública".

Los principios ideológicos del laicismo programático se basan en el *racionalismo absoluto*, que considera a la razón como única fuente y medida de la verdad; el *inmanentismo radical*, que niega toda realidad transcendente; y en la *libertad llamada "absoluta"*, que sólo queda limitada por la libertad de los demás (Editorial de SIC, Caracas, agosto 2005, p. 291-292). El libertinaje individual es algo que se aprecia mucho hoy.

La ideología laicista, bajo una visión *atea o agnóstica*, pretende confinar la religión al ámbito privado, a la iglesia, a la sacristía, no sacarla a la calle, negarle todo espacio y expresión pública, especialmente cuando se trata de personas con función política. Este laicismo con ingredientes *ilustrados* es heredero de un viejo *anticlericalismo*, que hace alarde inclusive de su irrespeto a todo tipo de autoridad religiosa. Está también el *relativismo* y peor aún el *nihilismo*, para el que no hay verdades perennes. El fenómeno de la secularización forma parte de la cultura *postmoderna* con la caída de modelos pasados y la "vuelta al sujeto" (*turn to the subject*) con el *pragmatismo y el consumismo*.

¿Qué pensar de la situación actual? Aceptamos la laicidad, pero no el laicismo agresivo e intolerante. "Allí donde el hombre se convierte en el único dueño del mundo y en propietario de sí mismo, no puede haber justicia. Allí sólo puede dominar el arbitrio del poder y de los intereses" (Benedicto XVI, 2005). Si aun creyendo en Dios andamos tan mal, ¿qué será andar sin Dios?

2. ¿A qué factores se atribuye esta secularización?

2.1 *Factores externos a la Iglesia*

En décadas pasadas los factores que influían más sobre el individuo eran: la familia, el párroco, el maestro y los partidos políticos. Entonces la familia era la célula de la sociedad, se decía. Ahora no. Era una sociedad más cerrada, especialmente en los pueblos, donde vivía la mayor parte de la población.

Hoy día lo más común es echarle la culpa a *los medios de comunicación social*, precisamente llamados "escuela paralela" por los docentes y la Iglesia, pues sienten celosos que les han quitado el liderazgo en la transmisión de valores. Pero hay otros factores. Algunos en España le echan la culpa *al actual partido de gobierno* y a los poderosos medios de comunicación afines a él. Pero el problema viene de atrás. Con mucho de *anticlericalismo vengativo y revanchista*, quieren desenterrar viejas memorias. José Casanova (1994) ha escrito un libro en que muestra que el anticlericalismo ha sido en varias naciones consecuencia de situaciones, en que la Iglesia estaba asociada a situaciones hegemónicas. Seguramente no se podrá generalizar fácilmente, cada situación será muy distinta a otras, y esta interpretación se deberá matizar.

Habría que añadir la *globalización de las transnacionales*, que establecen como prioritarios sus productos con un énfasis materialista, consumista y de confort, etc. Asimismo el laicismo supone que sólo la *Escuela Pública*, administrada por el Estado, debe ser mantenida con fondos públicos, por cuanto sería pluralista y desideologizada, y no pretendería imponer, como las escuelas católicas, valores y creencias religiosas. Y, siendo éstas privadas, no deberían ser financiadas por el Estado ni directa ni indirectamente.

En el caso de los adolescentes y jóvenes se halla sobre todo el influjo de sus *coetáneos*. Algunos dicen que el primer elemento de socialización es la TV. Ciertamente estos factores son más importantes que la familia. El influjo de los medios y de los coetáneos ha eclipsado el influjo de los factores tradicionales: la familia, la escuela, la Iglesia... Por otra parte un estudio reciente de Estados Unidos ha descubierto una coincidencia: el grupo de alumnos que consigue mejores notas en la escuela secundaria es el que cena con sus padres en familia (por supuesto con la TV apagada). Ahí tienen tiempo de contar, hablar, escuchar y opinar responsablemente sobre el quehacer diario. Seguramente irán a la cama pronto dejando la TV y el Internet.

La primera responsable de la transmisión de valores en los niños, adolescentes y jóvenes debía ser la familia. Pero ésta se siente desasistida, derrotada y carcomida por la secularización. También lo está por la estructura económica de la sociedad, pues continuamente los dos padres trabajan fuera de casa, dejan a los hijos solos en casa con la TV, los videojuegos y el Internet, y llegan demasiado tarde para estar tranquilamente con los hijos.

2.2 *Factores internos a la Iglesia*

La *Iglesia* también tiene sus problemas internos. Los cuatro obispos mencionados antes indican algunas causas para la secularización de sus diócesis: la Iglesia católica tiene dificultades para *acertar con la palabra adecuada a su mensaje*; falta de *adaptación*; falta de *agresividad* para actualizaciones profundas; falta de *valentía* para renovaciones de calado. El hombre y la mujer de nuestro tiempo *han cambiado*, no en su estructura más profunda, pero sí en su sensibilidad, sus criterios, sus actitudes, su escala de valores... Jamás ha habido un cambio tan rápido en el mundo. La sociedad actual está en crisis, precisamente por la profundidad y la rapidez de los cambios sobrevenidos. Ellos constituyen tal vez la más severa y rápida ruptura cultural que se ha dado en la historia. Estamos cambiando de mundo y de sociedad. Un mundo desaparece y otro está emergiendo. *La Iglesia se encontraba bien insertada en el mundo que desaparece y permanece desconcertada en el que se está alumbrando...*

¿Cómo hemos llegado a esta situación?, se preguntan los obispos: por la *mediocridad de los cristianos*; los *escándalos* de personas y grupos eclesiales; la *visión corta* de sus pastores.

Efectivamente, los valores han cambiado. Y el valor que más ha cambiado es lo prioritario de lo religioso.

Quizá se pueda añadir algún otro factor. Un excesivo *clericalismo* en algunos sectores y en casos concretos, que todavía no dejan suficiente participación a los seglares, inclusive en parroquias, etc. Esto, además de ser anticonciliar, va en contra del movimiento actual cultural a favor de los derechos de todos, de la libertad de acción, de la democracia, del deseo de hacer algo y de ser activos y responsables. Falta mucho por recorrer en la paridad de géneros, sin tener que tocar lo ya establecido. Esto es parte de la cultura actual, que no se puede dejar de lado. Falta coherencia entre lo que se dice y lo que deja hacer. Esto es quedarse atrás de los tiempos.

3. Soluciones a la secularización

Prerrequisitos:

1. Conviene estar en un *alerta militante*. Si la secularización se caracteriza por prescindir de Dios, lo último que habrá que hacer es refugiarnos cómplice y cobardemente en el *ostracismo intimista o en la mudez*. Tampoco sirve quedarse en *meras denuncias y críticas contra el mundo moderno* (Editorial de SIC, agosto 2005, p. 292). "Ese es el reto más grande que tenemos: el de responder a una sociedad en la que Dios está cada vez más ausente, donde impera la ley del mercado que censura el deseo religioso, relegándolo al ámbito de la conciencia privada y sin que contribuya a la vida personal, familiar y social de las personas" (Monseñor Juan Antonio Raig Plá, obispo de Cartagena-Murcia, España; Agencia Veritas; cf. *Zenit*, Octubre de 2005).

2. *No desanimarse. Hay motivos de esperanza.* Antes Juan Pablo II y ahora más Benedicto XVI están insistiendo en responder a la secularización. Precisamente la intención papal del Apostolado de la Oración para este octubre de 2005 en su versión italiana salió al paso de una de las características de la secularización: el no dar la cara por la fe. Dice

así: "Para que la secularización no nos desanime en nuestro testimonio" ("Perché il secolarismo non ci scoraggi nella nostra testimonianza"). El mundo actual vive dolores de parto. Termina una época, hay decadencia (Anderson, 2005). Pero también se constata que hay hambre y sed de Dios. Estamos en el albor de una nueva época. Seguro que el Espíritu Santo nos encontrará una solución.

3. *Más bien luchar.* Debe hacerse todo lo contrario al desánimo: hacer presente el elemento espiritual. Paolo Coelho, brasileño, el escritor más vendido hoy día, por cierto católico practicante, escribe en *El Zahir* (2005): "Lucha por tus sueños, o los demás te impondrán los suyos". Contra la secularización creciente en Europa se necesita: luchar para mantener lo que tenemos; dar un nuevo empuje a la cristianización con una nueva evangelización.

4. *Buscar soluciones.* Pero no es fácil hallar soluciones. Quizá lo sea a nivel teórico, pero no en la práctica. Los mismos cuatro obispos mencionados confiesan su dificultad para responder al problema: *"Es penoso comprobar que nadie sabe con claridad qué es lo que tenemos que hacer* ni exactamente cómo se genera un cristiano en las actuales circunstancias. Nuestra Iglesia es altamente rica en los medios de que dispone, pero es profundamente pobre al diseñar sus propios fines". Mons. Fernando Sebastián, Arzobispo de Pamplona y Vicepresidente de la Conferencia Episcopal Española dice:

> Nuestra Iglesia necesita clarificarse más, diferenciarse más en el conjunto de la sociedad española que, aunque conserve muchos elementos cristianos, ya no es cristiana de corazón [...]. Estamos lejos de los niveles indispensables de comunión y confianza. Mientras los cristianos no recuperemos la confianza en nosotros mismos, no seremos creíbles ante el mundo (Sebastián, 2004: 46).

La nueva evangelización es más difícil que la primera. En ésta generalmente había que tener en cuenta otras religiones y convencer a las personas que la cristiana era la mejor, más aún la única verdadera. Uno de sus modelos sería S. Francisco Javier en el Asia. Lo peor de hoy día es que no hay religiones diversas, sino un alejamiento, falta de interés y aun desconfianza de todo lo que se presenta como espiritual y religioso. Predomina el nihilismo, que achaca de fanatismo a todo lo religioso.

5. *La solución más importante es profundizar la fe.* Nos quejamos de que no se transmite la fe en las parroquias, en las familias, en los cole-

gios, etc. Pero esta crisis viene precedida de otra, que se puede considerar como su causa: es la crisis de la misma fe. Para transmitir la fe, hay que estar antes lleno de ella. ¿Cómo se puede comunicar la fe, si no hay fe? ¿Podemos decir con S. Pablo: "Mi vida es Cristo"? ¿Podemos hacer lo que Jesús nos pide: "Buscad *primero* el Reino de Dios..."? ¿De cuántos cristianos Cristo es el centro de sus vidas? Por eso el primer paso en la nueva evangelización debe ser *reforzar la vida de fe*: la fe personal, familiar, grupal, comunitaria, social... Se necesita aumentar nuestra fe, hacer crecer nuestro amor a Jesús, seguirlo. Por ejemplo, a través de los Ejercicios Espirituales personales y grupales, al menos los de la Vida Ordinaria (EVO), que ya algunas parroquias están iniciando. De ahí la comunicación de la fe vendrá espontánea. La *Evangelii Nuntiandi* (1975: nn. 21, 41-48, 76) y la *Redemptoris Missio* (1990: n. 41) nos han indicado los prerrequisitos pedagógicos, los medios / métodos de evangelización y las dimensiones de la evangelización. En todos ellos aparece con fuerza la importancia de la comunicación-comunión, e inclusive el uso de los medios de comunicación social. Aquí nos vamos a fijar especialmente en la comunicación social.

4. ¿Qué hacer en el campo de la comunicación?

Hay cuatro aspectos importantes:

1. *La comunicación debe ser comunión.* No se trata simplemente de "transmitir" la fe. Hay que "comunicarla". Comunicación es compartir un significado, es crear algo en común. Y el grado supremo de comunicación la logró Cristo, cuando en la comunicación-comunión se dio a sí mismo, y nos participó su vida divina. Así debemos comunicar. Esta nuestra donación a los demás tendrá muchas ramificaciones. Una de las consecuencias será la credibilidad, prerrequisito indispensable de la evangelización. Lo más importante para evangelizar a través de los medios no es el dominar sus técnicas, aunque no se puede prescindir de ellas, sino contar con una *personalidad*, que llegue a generar confianza y credibilidad en la audiencia. Esto es especialmente difícil en los medios omnipresentes con informaciones de todo tipo, que nos saturan y tratan de apoderarse de nuestra atención y nuestro tiempo. Por eso ellos "a priori" suscitan desconfianza entre la audiencia europea. Por eso los mensajes religiosos se deben dar con sinceridad y con coherencia de vida. Es lo que logró Juan Pablo II, como Papa mediático. Todo el cariño que generó y se manifestó en su funeral, lo obtuvo gracias a los medios. El mundo lo conoció gracias a ellos. Y su mensaje

caló hondo. Por ejemplo, su oposición a la guerra a través de los medios...

2. *Establecer puentes de comunicación y comunión.* Se indicó que hay división dentro de la Iglesia, falta de comunión y de confianza, lo que dificulta la evangelización. El individualismo ha entrado también en la Iglesia. Hay muchas islas dentro de ella. Hace falta establecer puentes de comunicación y comunión. La fe del cristiano es comunitaria. La experiencia de hoy nos muestra que no basta con tener mucha información. Hace falta más comunicación. Se requiere también tender puentes con "el mundo de la cultura y la gestación de valores". Así daremos mejor testimonio del amor y de la unión que predicamos.

3. Y la fe se debe *comunicar a nivel personal, familiar, parroquial, escolar, social, artístico, público, etc. Debe ser total.*

4. *También hay que comunicar la fe a través de los medios.* El fenómeno de la comunicación social es un hecho cultural, que forma y condiciona en gran medida la mentalidad del hombre moderno. El influjo de los medios es grande. Ellos son agentes de cambio. Los medios de comunicación social ocupan un lugar preeminente en la lucha contra la secularización, precisamente porque actúan en el ámbito público, que es lo que preocupa a los laicistas. En ellos se deben desvelar abiertamente las intenciones de los laicistas, que quisieran silenciar lo religioso. Conviene sacar la temática religiosa a la calle, al foro público, hacer manifestaciones públicas de fe, hacer presente el elemento espiritual... Pero son también efectos del cambio cultural. La teoría de los efectos con sus diversas etapas históricas (McQuail, 2000: 417-420) cayó. Para los años 1970 tal modelo linear de los efectos dejó de ser dominante en el mundo académico. Porque los efectos directos sólo se dan en condiciones psicológicas y socio-económicas especiales.

5. El aporte de la educación para los medios

De todas formas conviene enseñar a usarlos bien. Esto lograría reducir su influjo negativo sobre los niños y jóvenes especialmente en el área de la secularización, y al mismo tiempo ellos aprenderían a hacer un uso positivo de ellos. Nosotros podemos influir en la forma de usarlos. También podemos influir en ellos. Es lo que se llama *"educación para los medios".*

La educación para los medios es distinta de la educación *con* los medios, es decir del uso de subsidios didácticos audiovisuales para las ciencias, la historia, etc. La educación para los medios ayuda a conocer los medios en todos sus aspectos, a saber defenderse de sus aspectos negativos, a recibir provechosamente sus mensajes y a usarlos creativamente produciendo otros mensajes en beneficio propio y de los demás.

Una descripción más completa de la educación para los medios comprende *seis dimensiones.*

Educación para los medios es un proceso que busca formar en el sujeto estas dimensiones educativas: que sea *alfabetizado mediáticamente, consciente, activo, crítico, social,* y *creativo,* pero entendidas según las teorías más recientes. Tal educación le permitirá participar más plenamente en la cultura popular contemporánea, tal como es presentada en los medios masivos (Martínez de Toda, 2003).

Todos los documentos de la Iglesia sobre medios de comunicación recomiendan la educación para los medios: *Inter Mirifica* (1963: n. 16), *Communio et Progressio* (1971), *Orientaciones para la formación de los futuros sacerdotes sobre los instrumentos de comunicación social* (1986), *Pornografía y violencia en los medios de comunicación social: una respuesta pastoral* (1989), *Aetatis Novae* (1992), *Ética en la publicidad* (1997), *Ética en las comunicaciones sociales* (2000), *La Iglesia e Internet* (2002), *Ética en Internet* (2002), los documentos del CELAM (Conferencia Episcopal LatinoAmericana).

El Cardenal Martini planteó la educación para los medios en tres de sus cartas pastorales, cuando era Arzobispo de Milán (Martini, 1990; 1991b: 102, 111-115; 1991a: 102, 104s, 111). Asimismo Mons. Rosario Mazzola, siendo obispo de Cefalú (Sicilia), escribió dos cartas pastorales sobre los medios, y una de ellas expresamente sobre la educación para los medios (Mazzola, 1993, 1996). Me detengo en la importancia de la educación para los medios para contrarrestar la secularización, pues nos encontramos en un momento de emergencia, en que se deben usar todos los medios para combatirla.

6. ¿Por qué la educación para los medios?

El objetivo general de la educación para los medios es ayudar a las personas a ser libres y responsables con criterios propios concretos de acción ante los medios. Es ayudarles a reflexionar y a tener pensamientos propios bien pensados y razonados, que los defiendan de las filosofías e ideologías avasallantes, que los rodean. Es una educación para los valores. Es el momento de hacer frente a las filosofías, que están detrás de la secularización, y que se mencionaron al principio. La educación para los medios da una gran oportunidad al docente de hablar y discutir sobre valores. Es un instrumento educativo excelente. Lograr este objetivo representa una gran ventaja a la hora de relacionarse con Dios en privado y en público. Ayudaría también a frenar los avances de la secularización, si el docente se lo propone.

La educación para los medios comienza a usarse en los años 1960 por la UNESCO y otros. En América Latina se usó especialmente en los años 1970 contra la ideología capitalista con su "lectura crítica". Ahora la debemos enfocar además contra la secularización. Para responder más ordenadamente a la pregunta, se va a seguir el esquema completo de las seis dimensiones. Este camino permite también indicar lo que se debe enseñar.

6.1 Para ser alfabetizados mediáticamente, y conocer así mejor el lenguaje y el mensaje de los medios

La educación para los medios está diseñada para ayudar a niños y jóvenes a *entender* el *mensaje* de los medios. Para ello necesitan conocer su *lenguaje*. Así podrán beneficiarse más de los aspectos positivos de los medios, y su capacidad crítica no quedará ofuscada para no ver sus aspectos negativos. La mayor parte de la gente entiende menos de la mitad de lo que se comunica a través de los medios masivos. Por ejemplo, si preguntas a algunos por el significado de un film determinado, no saben qué decirte. Ven imágenes que se mueven. Han entendido algo de la acción, pero no han entendido el mensaje real y los valores que encierra.

Por otra parte los medios no presentan la realidad, sino *representaciones subjetivas* de ella. Conocer esta distinción en cada producto mediático es lo más importante en la educación para los medios, según Masterman (1985: 2). Esto ayuda a mantenerse críticamente distante de la TV. Una vez que se ha conseguido esa distancia crítica, el telespectador ya no está tan subyugado por la TV. Ello ayuda a evaluar, reaccionar, elegir. El ciudadano se convierte en un telespectador activo. Estos conocimientos permiten que el usuario *se sienta dueño* de los nuevos alfabetos; esto le da seguridad para no dejarse someter por los medios. Es un factor psicológicamente positivo. Se ha generalizado el uso de los nuevos medios. Los medios han entrado en el tejido social. Los mensajes mediático-masivos pertenecen ya a la vida cotidiana. Son como cualquier otra experiencia. Por ello el niño debe aprender a deconstruirlos y construirlos para prevenir sus impactos negativos y aprovechar sus elementos positivos. Los niños pasan demasiado tiempo con los juegos inteligentes. A veces se enseña Internet, pero no cómo usarlo, con qué criterios. Al enseñar Internet, se da más libertad a los niños y jóvenes, pero hay que enseñarles también a usar bien esa libertad. Si no, la libertad se convierte en libertinaje. Como diría Freire, una educación para los multimedios debe ser una práctica para el ejercicio de la ciudadanía y la democracia.

6.2 *Para ser conscientes de cómo funcionan los medios*

Los medios son un gran negocio y buscan el poder. Su objetivo principal es utilizar todos los medios posibles (inclusive programas anti-sociales, como *violencia, sexo excesivo y prejuicios*) para aumentar la *audiencia* al máximo y así tener más *publicidad* (*o más influjo ideológico*) y ganar así más *dinero* (*y poder*). Es necesario conocer tales mecanismos.

Los medios son los *nuevos instrumentos del poder.* Por eso hay que saber cómo están hechos, quiénes están detrás de ellos, qué objetivos y qué intenciones tienen. Eso lo da la educación para los medios. El que ignora esto, queda fuera de la cultura contemporánea, se convierte en un excluso, en un marginado, está a merced de ser instrumentalizado, engañado y manipulado. La facilidad de acceso a la *información* de todo tipo hace necesario proteger a los más vulnerables, por ejemplo niños y jóvenes, especialmente a la vista del incremento del contenido de violencia, intolerancia y pornografía. A veces se invoca el derecho a la información. Pero... ¿los niños y jóvenes están preparados para ejercer ese derecho? ¿Tiene un niño derecho a jugar con fuego, con la electricidad, con un cuchillo afilado, con una pistola cargada, con un veneno, con el SIDA? ¿No debe ser guiado el niño? Se necesita desarrollar una capacidad para discernir la información recibida, dada la enorme cantidad de información disponible, un proceso que puede prosperar sólo donde hay una jerarquía de valores reconocida.

La educación para los medios pretende que el progreso de la tecnología lleve también al crecimiento de las personas en dignidad, responsabilidad y apertura a los demás. Un público bien educado en los matices y métodos de los medios visuales *exigirá mejor calidad* y será *menos manipulado* por ellos. Los pueblos tienen los políticos que se merecen. El público tiene también la TV que se merece. Una audiencia educada (consciente, etc.) exigirá y llegará a tener una TV mejor. Si en ese pueblo hay una auténtica democracia, se logrará esto mejor (Kubey – Csikszentmihalyi, 1990: 214).

6.3 Para ser críticos y saber defenderse de las ideologías de los medios

Los medios esconden ideologías y las tratan de imponer. Influyen como industrias de la conciencia y tienen una penetración creciente en nuestros procesos centrales democráticos. Hay presiones crecientes a nivel nacional e internacional para privatizar la información y someter la mayoría a los intereses de unos pocos. La educación para los medios capacitará al usuario para no dejarse influenciar tan fuertemente por ellos. Enseña a descubrir la ideología en los medios, a ver la falta de objetividad en ellos y a ver la manipulación en las campañas políticas. El verdadero problema ético, entonces, es el de dar a los niños la conciencia de la *ambigüedad de los medios*, en particular de los nuevos medios que, en su enorme posibilidad de simulación, pueden ofrecer modelos y simulacros que no se corresponden ni con la dignidad de la persona humana ni con los propios valores.

6.4 Para ser activos y aprovechar los elementos positivos de los medios

La audiencia re-elabora y negocia los significados, que vienen de los medios. La educación para los medios enseña a no ser teledependiente y a darse cuenta de las diversas interpretaciones de una imagen o escena. Los medios deben estar al servicio de la audiencia y no al revés. La educación para los medios enseña también a hacer una *selección correcta frente a la abundante información y saturación de los medios*, que refleje sus propias convicciones y valores. "Si tu hijo vive junto a la playa, es preferible que le enseñes a nadar en vez de hacer una pared frente al mar". Más que criticar la pasividad del telespectador, más que condenar y censurar, es más sabio enseñar a evaluar, a reaccionar y a elegir programas según su propia identidad. La educación para los medios ayuda a esclarecer su propia *identidad* y sus propios *valores*, y a crecer en el conocimiento de la *cultura* propia y en el desarrollo de su personalidad. Por otra parte es difícil hoy día captar la atención del niño y del joven, que se halla continuamente asombrado por lo nuevo y maravilloso. Los niños y jóvenes aman los medios. Se sienten atraídos por ellos, pues son entretenidos, les hablan de otros mundos reales o imaginarios, son interactivos y multimediales. Entonces conviene aprovecharse del atractivo de los medios para enseñarles a tener conciencia, a *valorizar*, a trabajar, a tener capacidad de análisis, de abstracción, y de capacidad crítica y creativa.

6.5 *Para ser más sociales buscando los intereses comunes prioritarios*

La interpretación de los mensajes depende también de las mediaciones sociales. Conviene ser consciente de cómo los padres, los coetáneos y los maestros pueden influir en la interpretación de los mensajes. Además la educación para los medios debe estar al servicio de los objetivos prioritarios de la sociedad: Educación para la Comunicación, para la Organización y para el Desarrollo (ECOD). La educación para los medios enseña a los estudiantes a enfrentar las demandas del futuro.

6.6 *Para ser creativos y creadores de cultura*

La educación para los medios enseña a desarrollar la capacidad productiva de los alumnos, a ser creadores de la cultura popular, y de estilos y modelos de vida. La tecnología parece aportar efectos positivos en el aprendizaje y en la productividad intelectual. La educación para los medios también permite ver la propia responsabilidad como usuario de tales medios, al preguntarse continuamente si es ésta la cultura que se desea crear. Como se ve, unas dimensiones ayudan a otras de una forma complementaria.

7. Cómo usar la educación para los medios contra la secularización

Al dar educación para los medios de una forma transversal en la clase de cualquier materia, se pueden poner ejemplos de temática religiosa. También se puede hacer en la clase de religión. Hay muchas palabras y frases del Evangelio, que pueden ser usados como ejemplos de educación para los medios. He aquí algunos ejemplos de actividades.

1. Jesús llama *"zorra"* a Herodes (Lc 13,32). Aquí se pueden explicar los conceptos de *"significante"* y *"significados denotativo y connotativo"*.

2. Jesús le dice a la Samaritana: *"Dame de beber"* (Jn 4,5-42). Es el momento de explicar el *doble sentido y* a Jesús como respuesta a las necesidades del corazón del hombre.

3. *La Misa por TV,* ¿es distinta de la Misa de la parroquia? Es el momento de explicar la Eucaristía. La Misa por TV no llega al ideal de la Misa verdadera, aunque es valiosa. En la de la parroquia participamos más y formamos comunidad, al menos con nuestra presencia, lo que es fundamental en la Misa. En cambio en la Misa de TV somos

meros espectadores, no participantes. Sirve también para explicar el concepto de "representación subjetiva".

4. Los *símbolos religiosos*: ¿Qué símbolos religiosos se usan más? ¿Cuáles prefieres? Ver los resultados de una encuesta en Martínez de Toda (2000).

5. *Valores cristianos.* ¿Qué personajes de los programas de TV o film tienen valores cristianos? Hay algunos personajes o escenas, que podrían ser como "imágenes" de Cristo? O también como símbolos de la acción del Espíritu Santo en nuestras vidas? Te ha ayudado este programa de TV o este film a descubrir a Dios en tu vida? La educación para los medios puede buscar el ayudar a la gente a ver los símbolos del Reino de amor de Dios en los medios. Estos símbolos son señales externas, que nos recuerdan el movimiento de la acción del Espíritu. Los símbolos y las historias de los medios me llevan a una relación con Dios.

6. Actividades de *Internet con los valores.* Manipulación de la información e inversiones éticas en los portales.

7. *El laicismo en los medios.* El cine, la radio y la TV europeas dan la sensación de que, o Dios no existe, o que no vale la pena creer en Él. Pocas veces aparece alguien rezando, asistiendo a Misa, o defendiéndose como creyente. A veces prevalece el reírse de lo católico, o lo que es peor, un silencio sospechoso de todo lo que a Dios se refiere. Sin embargo, una encuesta distribuida entre 200.000 europeos desmiente la imagen que se nos vende: el 71% afirma que la religión es una necesidad, el 69% asiste a servicios religiosos y el 68% reza (*Alfa y Omega*, 27-X-2005). Con estos datos se pueden comparar en tablas las veces que se habla positivamente de Dios en los medios y ver el porcentaje de quienes creen en Dios. Explicar el laicismo, que trata de reducir lo religioso sólo al foro interno.

8. Más ideas y actividades sobre *educación para los medios y religión* se hallan en Tricarico (1999: 142-150), Barcala (2000), Bazalgette (1989: 76s) e Imberdis y Tachet (sin fecha). Esta labor educativa debe hacerse a todo nivel: en las familias, en las escuelas y en las parroquias; especialmente estas son importantes para quienes asisten a escuelas públicas, donde no se enseñe religión. La secularización es el reto actual más grande que tenemos. La comunicación de la fe debe tener en cuenta esta realidad a la hora de establecer sus prioridades.

Referencias bibliográficas

ANDERSON, D. (2005), *Decadence: The Passing of Personal Virtue and Its Replacement by Political and Psychological Slogans*, London: Social Affairs Unit.

BARCALA CALVO, I. (2000), "Estudio de la publicidad desde el área de formación religiosa", en *Comunicación Audiovisual y Desarrollo de las Regiones,* Salamanca: Universidad Pontificia de Salamanca, 403-412.

BAZALGETTE, C., ed. (1989), *Primary Media Education*, London: British Film Institute.

BENEDICTO XVI (2005), "Homilía al comienzo del Sínodo de los Obispos sobre la Eucaristía"; cf. *Alfa y Omega*, 6-X-2005.

CASANOVA, J. (1994), *Public religions in the modern world*, Chicago.

IMBERDIS, P. – TACHET, D. [sin fecha], *Come realizzare un cartellone in Catechesi*, Cinisello Balsamo: Paoline.

KUBEY, R. – CSIKSZENTMIHALYI, M. (1990), *Television and The Quality of Life. How Viewing Shapes Everyday Experience,* LEA.

MARTÍNEZ DE TODA, J. (1998), "Las seis dimensiones en la educación para los medios (Metodología de Evaluación)", en *Comunicación. Estudios venezolanos de comunicación* (Caracas), n. 103, 33-47, http://www.ntedu.org/comunica/artimartinez.html.

MARTÍNEZ DE TODA, J. (2000), "Religious Symbols In Mass Media", 22nd IAMCR, International Conference, Singapore, 17-20 July 2000.

MARTÍNEZ DE TODA, J. (2002), "La responsabilidad de los ciudadanos en el uso de los medios", en J. Á. AGEJAS ESTEBAN – J. F. SERRANO OCEJA, *Etica de la comunicación y de la información*, Madrid: Ariel.

MARTINI, C. M. (1991a), *Camminare sulla seta*, Milano: Centro Ambrosiano.

MARTINI, C. M. (1998) *Comunicar a Cristo hoy*, Salamanca: Universidad Pontificia de Salamanca. Ahí se hallan traducidas sus cartas pastorales *Effatà, "Apriti"* (1990) e *Il lembo del mantello* (1991b).

MASTERMAN, L. (1985), *Teaching the Media*, London: Routledge.

MAZZOLA, R. (1993), *Nuova evangelizzazione e mass-media. Piano Pastorale Diocesano per le Comunicazioni Sociali*, Cefalù (Sicilia).

MAZZOLA, R. (1996), *Lasciare Babele! Lettera pastorale per il programma "Educare ai media"*, Cefalù (Sicilia).

MCQUAIL, D. (2000), *Mass Communication Theory*, New York: Sage.

OBISPOS DE PAMPLONA Y TUDELA, BILBAO, SAN SEBASTIÁN Y VITORIA, Carta Pastoral "Renovar nuestras comunidades cristianas", Cuaresma-Pascua, 2005. Un resumen en *El País*, 14 de Febrero de 2005,

39; *www.iglesianavarra.org/6105cuaresmaobispos.doc* (6 noviembre 2005).

SEBASTIÁN, F. (2004), "Conferencia en el Congreso Nacional de Apostolado Seglar", *ABC*, 13 de noviembre de 2004.

TRICARICO, M. F. (1999), *Insegnare i media. Didattica della comunicazione nei programmi scolastici*, Santhià: GS Editrice.

The "Media, Religion and Culture" perspective: discovering a theory and methodology for studying media and religion

Robert A. White, SJ

L'analisi degli effetti comportamentali e la correlazione della pratica religiosa o dell'uso dei media con le variabili demografiche hanno in genere dimostrato i propri limiti nel favorire la comprensione del ruolo dei media nello sviluppo spirituale e religioso. Lo sviluppo dei sistemi di credenza e l'organizzazione dei valori attorno a simboli centrali è un processo di costruzione soggettiva del significato ben più complesso, che comprende molti punti di riferimento. Sono di certo più utili una descrizione etnografica della costruzione del significato nei contesti olistici della vita, l'uso di forme multiple di informazione in risposta alle crisi personali, la formazione delle identità sub-culturali, lo sviluppo storico dei rituali e il confronto dei sistemi di credenza come singole unità. La tradizione della teoria e del metodo dei "cultural studies" è utile, dal momento che ha sviluppato una combinazione interdisciplinare estremamente ricca di forme di analisi, dalla semiotica all'economia politica.

The cultural studies analysis of the media has now become a dominant paradigm of communication research, and the "Media, Religion and Culture" focus is a central paradigm in research on religious media. For example, the biannual international conference on "Media, Religion and Culture" usually draws from 300 to 600 people from around the world, virtually all carrying on research on media and religion from a cultural studies perspective. The cultural studies approach recognizes the importance of so-called "administrative research" used by broadcasters to measure the reach and effectiveness of programming, but argues that quantitative effects research really does not answer the central questions of religious media.

Religion is a personal response seeking meaning in life and in one's universe. Religious expression is generally found within institutional religion, but the formal creed, rituals, devotions and moral codes do not exhaust the personal experience of religion. The central question of the cultural studies approach is concerned with how individuals in groups use media to construct religious meaning in life and how this religious meaning relates to many other aspects of human life. This approach typically draws its theories and methodologies, not from psychology, functionalist sociology or quantitative analysis, but from cultural anthropology, philosophy, literary studies, drama and history. The methods of research are no less rigorous, but these are much closer to a tradition of humanities than to behavioural sciences.

Until the 1970s virtually all research on media and religion was attempting to answer the questions of religious broadcasters as to what effects they were having. Most religious programs claimed to be having large audiences – impressed with what one can do with the media compared to the Sunday sermon – and they generally claimed to be "converting" many people. Others were sceptical, and the research was brought in to settle this kind of dispute. Gradually, however, researchers moved away from these "effects" questions to how people are creating meaning from media... and many other sources. How and why did this move to a new set of questions in research on religious media come about? To understand this change, one must go back to the early years of religious broadcasting.

1. The beginnings of religious broadcasting

Adventuresome priests and ministers began to use radio almost as soon as audible voice transmission was possible. A pastor in Oakland, California, was broadcasting to primitive crystal sets as early as 1912. When the first broadcasting station in the US was established in Pittsburgh in 1921, regular broadcasts from Calvary Episcopal Church were part of the programming (Armstrong, 1979: 19-20). By 1925 the US government had granted station licenses to 63 religious broadcasters (Erickson, 1992: 2), and in the 1920s there were already hundreds of regular religious programs in the United States. In the 1930s broadcast personalities such Fr. Coughlin, who offered a mixture of politics, economics and piety (and anti-semiticism!), were attracting millions.

In Britain, the BBC began broadcasting religious services from St.-Martins-in-the-Fields church in central London on January 6, 1924 (Wolfe, 1984: 9), and religious themes were part of the menu of the BBC's famous radio talks from the early 1920s. Liberal and Fascist governments in Europe were often hostile to religion, but the Vatican Radio, established in 1931, was one of the first fruits of the tenuous "reconciliation" between the Church and the Italian government under

Mussolini and was one means of consolidating Vatican independence (Matelski, 1995: xvi-xvii).

The religious personalities attracted to the use of radio and later television were persons deeply motivated to transform people's lives with the media and bring them to the moment of conversion. They were often dramatic speakers and preachers, and they felt that their words could have a powerful impact. This was an era of relatively gradual cultural change, and most religious traditions lived within their own institutional community. Religious communication was simply a matter of handing on the beliefs of the church or denomination from one generation to the other, and it was taken for granted that the young would accept the religious culture of the tradition simply by listening quietly and conforming. The culture of religious preaching, education and family socialization was simply a matter of finding the most persuasive form of communication that would get the effects desired.

The culture of religious communication in the 1920s was part of a general belief in the "power of the media". This was the era of the great newspaper barons such as Hearst in the US, Lord Rothermere and Viscount Northcliffe in Britain (Koss, 1984) and similar sorts of "kingmakers" in other parts of the world. The typical citizen was a much more political person, joining political movements and parties because they believed that politics could improve their lot and avidly reading newspapers. In almost all countries 70-80% of the eligible citizens voted. When radio news began to be important in the 1930s, people listened to radio as they read newspapers because the good citizen must be informed and the good member of a political party had to know the positions of that party. People were initially sceptical about radio information, but the directors of the BBC, other national public service broadcasting organizations, and the leading commercial networks in countries such as the USA made a concerted effort to have more accurate, faster, more live and more interesting news than the newspapers. Soon people were saying: "It must be true. I heard it on the radio". The general "authoritativeness" of broadcasting gradually spread its aura over the religious programs of radio, and many people became devoted followers and believers in the great personalities of religious radio programs.

Interestingly, the Church's were more concerned about the negative effects of film, radio and other media. The 1920s were a time of loosening of strict moral codes of family and sexuality, and film introduced a new culture of visual intimacy. Parents and religious leaders felt that the media were going over their heads directly to the youth. Film makers and radio producers knew, however, that some degree of sexual appeal and violence to heightened suspense was necessary to draw in the crowds. Every time representatives of churches, parent associations or teachers would complain, media producers would simply say that "you have no solid evidence that the media causes harmful effects". Finally, in the early 1930s, concerned religious leaders were able to convince the Payne Foundation in the US to fund a US$ 200.000 study to try to prove that film had a harmful effect on the youth (Black, 1994: 151-155). The study engaged the most competent sociologists in the United States and used the most rigorous quantitative methods in order to speak the only language that broadcasters and government legislators would accept: quantitative statistics.

When the report of the Payne Commission was published about 1935, the results could not prove unequivocally that film had a harmful effect on the morals of young people (Rowland, 1983: 94). There was no question that films had some portrayals that violated the norms of some religious groups. But there was little agreement on what was a moral violation. Baptists were strongly against any evidence of alcoholic beverages, while Catholics (especially Italians!) could not see any problem with a bit of wine sipping. Most important, when youth were interviewed, the responses about "effects" were ambiguous. What one young person saw as utterly lascivious others hardly noticed as an aggressive violation of their norms and sensibilities. What was violent to one person was simply an ordinary part of "our culture" to another. The overall conclusion of the Payne Study was that the "impact" of film depended very much on the family background, the subjective cultural background and other factors influencing the subjective interpretation of the *meaning* of the film (Rowland, 1983: 92-99).

From the time of the Payne Study, media researchers felt that they had to use quantitative, objective methods to show the positive or negative effects of media in order to get action by governments or other public institutions. One of the typical examples was the attempt to devise an "objective" measuring scale of violent content which rated violence from the low point on the scale of a strong discussion to the high point of a bloody murder. The researchers then attempted to show a direct correlation between the level of violent content and aggressive behaviour of audiences. Coders were instructed to mark exactly what they heard or saw whether it was a Bugs Bunny cartoon for children or a portrayal of the life of Christ. Not surprisingly, humorous children's cartoons, where rabbits, pigs and ducks were continually getting smashed about came out as horribly violent. If the quantitative interpretation of violence that some social scientists proposed were applied to the media, there obviously would be no further presentation of great works of art such as Shakespeare and even the presentation of the Bible would be questionable.

What soon became evident is that the *meaning construction* placed on a scene or particular action can vary a great deal (Newcomb, 1978). The portrayal of the crucifixion of Jesus can be seen as sickeningly offensive or as a beautiful sign of enormous love depending on the meaning that the beholder places on this. There might be wide agreement that the portrayal of explicit sexual relations is repugnant and morally offensive for many different reasons based on many different meanings. But in every case it is important to know the *meaning* not just for different audiences but for the writer, the producer, the actors and a host of others who are involved in some way with producing something that does have meaning (Newcomb, 1978: 279-280). It also became apparent that although the official practices of a religious tradition might define a devotion or action as religious, adherents of the religious tradition might have their own unique interpretations of the official practices and might have experiences which are generally consonant with the theological norms of the tradition but are completely unique for a given person.

2. Trying to find the "definitive" proof of effects of religious broadcasts

With the advent of television in the 1950s, religious television stars in the US, such as the evangelist Billy Graham and Bishop Fulton Sheen, began to gain top audience ratings. The mainline Protestant Church's felt that they were losing out and wondered if they could not find a Bishop Sheen in the Anglican or Methodist Church. There began to be considerable discussion of whether religious television personalities were really having a significant lasting impact, whether this was drawing people away from worship in the local churches, whether it appealed to young people, and other similar questions. In 1951 the National Council of Churches in the United States funded a major study of the "effectiveness of television" as a tool of evangelization. The director of the study was one of the great personalities of US religious broadcasting, Everett Parker, and the team included Dallas Smythe, who later became one of the leaders in the critical cultural studies school.

The description of the basic questions in the introduction of the published book reveals the classic concerns regarding research on religious media:

> In the absence of any study of *effects* (emphasis added) of religious programs, a number of questions of practical import have gone unanswered, or the answers have often been guessed at, often a very optimistic mood. Do religious programs on the air become a substitute for church attendance? Do they reach the non-churchmen (*sic*) and with what *effect?* Do they provide a valuable service for shut-ins? Do they help to build character, to improve society, to inspire reverence? Most important, do they convey the Christian Gospel faithfully, or is the Christian message distorted or falsified as it passes through these new media of communications? (Parker – Barry – Smythe, 1955: xiv).

The study was guided by one of the top sociologists in the US, August Hollingshead. A meticulously accurate quantitative sample was drawn, using carefully prepared questionnaires and in-depth interviews. The statistical analysis was the best of the time. The theory followed the then popular behaviourist social psychological models which bypassed any subjective judgements of meaning of religion to get "objective" data about the impact on the personality.

The study remains one of the classics of research on religious media, but, unfortunately, the authors themselves suggest that their methodology raised more questions than provide answers. The study confirmed what many other surveys had indicated and others would indicate: that the main users of religious broadcasting tended to be lower status, with less education, more likely to be women and more likely to be elderly. The major conclusion was couched in terms of the behaviourist psychology model, namely, that following religious broadcasts "reduced anxiety" (Parker – Barry – Smythe, 1955: 405). The researchers admitted that they discovered that their methodology (the behavioural psychology effects models used by media research at the time) was too limited to answer the real questions of the study, even in the simplest terms (*Ibid.*: 395). The study did not reveal whether users of these programs become more religious, more moral, closer to their local churches, or more inspired to be involved in work with needy people. The results could say little about the relation of the broadcasts to general belief systems? These are questions which deal with *meaning*. If one assumes, however, a model of religion that reduces all observable behaviour to projections of deeper, unconscious psychological urges, that religion is just a form of mild neurosis, then central questions about religious media could not be answered.

One must recognize that the researchers were using the available tools at hand in 1950. This was before the development of the sociology and anthropology of religion, before the major empirical work of Stark and Glock (1968) in the USA, before the great theoretical advances of sociologists of religion such as Peter Berger (1969) and Thomas Luckmann (1967) or of David Martin (1969; 1980) and Bryan Wilson (1982) in Britain and a host of other major theorists in Europe. It even predated the development of "parish sociology" (Fichter, 1954). The 1960s, however, brought a major shift in the focus of the human sciences and in the emerging field of mass communication research in particular.

3. The shift from a media effects paradigm to recognition of the importance of the cultural context of media use

In the late 1940s Joseph Klapper, for many years head of the research department at the CBS broadcast department and close associate of Lazarsfeld, did a definitive analysis (his doctoral thesis) of just what kind of effects one could expect from broadcasting. The surprising result of this analysis of hundreds of studies of media effects was that not a single study proved that the media had the powerful direct effects that broadcasters expected. The landmark book revealed that the influence of media is always limited by the subjective social context, knowledge, attitudes, motivation and *interpretation* of the receiver (Klapper, 1965). This suggested that broadcasters had to take into consideration the motivations, interests, enjoyments, cultural values and the subculture of the target audience of the particular audience that they wished to communicate with.

Klapper and others suggested that a better approach to audience analysis was not effects research but what came to be known as uses and gratification studies (Dennis – Wartella, 1996: 24). The central question was not what media did to people but what people did with the media. Peter Horsfield, in his comprehensive survey of the research on audiences of religious media in the early 1980s, found many doctoral theses and other research on religious broadcasting in the 1960s and 1970s using the uses and gratifications approach to document the now well-known patterns of religious media use (Horsfield, 1984: 118-124).

Another major influence was Marshall McLuhan's *Understanding Media* (1964) which argued that the most significant impact of media was not on individual psychology but on whole cultures and societies. McLuhan came to media studies from literary analysis which stressed the activity of the person in reading and interpreting a text. Different media touched different senses – the ear, the eyes, the whole consciousness – and the person responded by constructing the meaning of the text according to the major sense influence, thereby producing an "oral culture" or a "visual culture". The perspective of McLuhan and his student, Walter Ong, SJ, also helped to shift interest of religious communicators from broadcast effects to the *interaction* of a medium and religious cultural movements. The book culture was an integral part of religious modernity in the nineteenth century while electronic media were part of the contemporary religious culture (Babin, 1991). When the Jesuits established their centre for research on the mission of the Church in the field of communication, it was Walter Ong, SJ, who suggested that it be called "The Centre for the Study of Communication and Culture".

Berger and Luckmann, in their work on *The Social Construction of Reality* (1967) shifted the focus away from the systemic functionalism of Parsons which made the person the result of systemic forces at the intersection of the social system, the personality system and the economic system. The new focus made the starting point *culture*, defined now more cognitively as a system of meanings produced by persons in interaction.

All this was part of the great personalist movement in the late 1960s, inspired by thinkers such as Marcuse (1968) who emphasized the importance of responding to one's own identity and creativity, thereby rejecting conformity to powerful social controls. The countercultural movement of the late 1960s and early 1970s rejected the subjection of one's life to the mobilization of industrialization and mass consumption. World War II was carried on as a great crusade to vindicate human rights and this stirred movements of liberation and self-determination among colonized peoples. All this called into question the use of media for religious persuasion and manipulation. There was awakened interest in the use of media as a context for discovering personal religious values, religious cultural identity and an active faith expression.

4. The movements of "education for critical use of the media"

In the 1950s the dominant idea of the Church's use of the media was still a powerful, dramatic speaker using a persuasive rhetoric to convert audiences to a deeper religious practice. The logic of religious broadcasts was not much different than the political campaigns, advertising or radio talks. In the 1960s, however, there was a growing critique, especially in the churches, of the harmful effects on faith and morals of the manipulation of sex, violence, advertising and other forms of increasingly commercial, "hard sell" media. This set in motion a series of efforts to introduce "media education" which assumed that the audience was not simply a passive receiver of message effects. Audiences can be critical and have their own ideas about the media. Media education encouraged people to carefully select media use according to their personal values and to use this media to deepen one's value commitments. Media education has varied in its focus from a defensive view of media as highly manipulative to an appreciation of our benignly banal popular culture, but most approaches seek to strengthen the use of media from the perspective of one's own active interpretation and one's own cultural identity.

A more important contribution, in many ways, was the movement of education for freedom which emerged in the countries of the South, especially in Latin America. The churches in Latin America, Asia and Africa began a process of education of the rural and urban poor with a general educational philosophy of helping the poor and marginal form grassroots, participatory organizations to solve their own problems. These efforts incorporated the educational methods of Paulo Freire (1990; 1990), Badal Sircar's concepts of popular theatre in India (1978) and many other popular movements. In many ways this changed the perspective on religious broadcasting and research on religious broadcasting, in large part because this emphasis was adopted by international associations of religious broadcasting such as Unda (now SIGNIS) and The World Association for Christian Communication (WACC).

Firstly, these educational methods stressed not just new production techniques but the affirmation and promotion of the popular cultures. The media, especially small media such as group communication, popular theatre, and people's radio, were the sites where the poor and marginal could develop their cultural identity. Secondly, these methods saw as the reasons for poverty and oppression the passive dependences on the hegemonic culture which impose a self-concept of "natural inferiority" and need to depend on the governing elites. Thirdly, in the face of globalization of cultures, it is necessary for the poor and marginal to have their own media and to actively produce their own cultures. Thus, the concept of culture became central in religious broadcasting and in research on religious broadcasting.

Another very important emphasis coming from education for liberation was to develop the sense of dignity, creativity and freedom of the person through dialogue in community. These movements were far more aware of the dehumanization that comes from the concentration of power in societies and the use of media to impose that power. The ideal form of communication was a communitarian, participatory, dialogical communication, and this ideal became a central ethical and theological principle in the media, religion and culture perspective. This value position led many doing research on religious broadcasting toward theories and research methods of "cultural studies", with its different variants in the United States and in Latin America.

5. The cultural studies approach

Media studies began in the 1930s and 1940s in the US. There was virtually no communication research in Europe, at the time enveloped in total war. After World War II Europe began its own approaches to social studies and media. Public service broadcasting systems in Europe were much more concerned with national cultural integration and with the cultural quality of broadcasting. The effects of media that that commercial broadcasting in the US needed to prove to sell itself was not a major issue. Media researchers in Europe were concerned about the profound cultural transformations as the "welfare state" increased the incomes of the working classes and brought the working classes into a kind of broad middle status.

A decisive influence was the cultural studies approach that originated in France and which was picked up by the Centre for Contemporary Cultural Studies at the University of Birmingham in Britain. The centre began a programme of research on the factors influencing the profound cultural changes in Britain, especially among the working classes (Hall – Hobson – Lowe – Willis, 1980). Not surprisingly, in contrast to the behaviourist, functionalist dependence on psychological conceptions of the individual which lead to an emphasis on the blind behavioural effects of the media, the cultural studies approach borrows from the humanistic sciences of textual analysis, literary studies, semiotics, history, cultural anthropology, and cognitive structuralism. The focus was not on behavioural response but on the creation of meaning, or, more specifically, "signifying practices" which bring about "shared social meanings" in various "languages", especially mass media languages (Barker, 2000: 7). Contrary to views of institutions such as the BBC, the popular classes were not considered "cultureless" and passive consumers of media to be reshaped in the middle-class image, but active in the creation of a rich and strong culture (Hoggart, 1957, 1981; Thompson, 1963, 1980). Popular novels, films and television were sources of ideas and symbols that people used to create their own personal and cultural identities. The leaders in cultural studies were scholars formed in literary and dramatic criticism, and they saw the media as a text that both revealed and reflected the nature of the culture but that was also a source of symbols for the construction of the great variety of subcultures.

What was striking about the youth subcultures in particular was the use of popular music as a symbol of resistance to the dominant, hegemonic cultures (Hall – Jefferson, 1980; Frith, 1983). Rather than turn their backs on their poverty and working-class status, youth took from the media images that glorified their own popular class values. Postwar Europe was still struggling with the remnants of a rigid feudal class system, and much study of emerging cultures focused on the use of media, schools and a host of other institutions as means to get the working classes to accept their lower status as the inevitable and just reward for competence and hard work of those who made it to the top (Hall, 1977). Underlying the cultural studies approach was a strong commitment to the dignity, freedom, and creativity of all persons. The individual was seen, not as an object of culture and social systems, but as the author of culture. Although cultural studies has found Marxist analysis helpful for a critical understanding of the concentration of political-economic power in the formation of cultures, cultural studies rejected the economic determinism of classical Marxism. Instead they saw the person as a protagonist in the struggle with power to define the meaning of all economic products not as hegemonic ideology but as the affirmation of the cultural identity of the subaltern classes. Stuart Hall introduced the distinction of the concept of the encoding of the preferred, hegemonic meaning of media to support hegemonic power and the decoding of the message in terms of the identity of the media user. The studies of media fan groups have revealed how media users refashion the meaning of symbols of the media around their own person and cultural identities (Jenkins, 1992). Martín-Barbero's studies of the reception of telenovelas in Latin America suggested that the reading of media is a complex combination of seduction, rejection, resistance, and transformation of meaning (1993).

The American version of the cultural studies approach emphasized that media reception is a social, communitarian activity. The new religious, racial, ethnic and gender movements in the US and elsewhere, on the basis of their internal communication networks, *collectively* challenged the negative images in the media. Carey (1989), borrowing from cognitive anthropologist, Geertz (1975), introduced the ritual, communion notion of media, and Horace Newcomb (1983) used the anthropologist Turner's theory of ritual (1969) as the audience experience of the state between the world as it is and the world as the community would like it to become.

A turning point was the development of media reception theory in the late 1970s and 1980s, analysing how audiences take media narratives, role models and symbols as materials for constructing their own life histories (Morley, 1992; Fiske, 1987). From this came a series of new methodologies of audience analysis roughly described as audience ethnography and including life histories (Grodin – Lindlof, 1996), personal accounts through letters (Ang, 1985), observation of groups viewing television (Lull, 1988), observation of households using media (Silverstone – Hirsch, 1992) or participation in fan groups discussing programmes (Brown, 1994). What has characterised reception study is the analysis of the use of media as one source of constructing meaning in a "natural life context" and a whole meaning construction process: a whole life-time, an ongoing-friend group, a whole household, a whole community or church congregation. The purpose is to understand the role of media in a complex pattern of meaning relationships.

6. The beginnings of the Media, Religion and Culture approach

By the early 1980s, the study of media and religion had, at its disposal, a new set of tools that the authors of the 1950s study of the effects of religious television said were needed. Also emerging were new theologies of communication which defined the media as a process of bringing publics together to form dialogical communities. Evangelization was beginning to be seen, not as imposing a foreign religious culture, but as helping peoples discover and activate their best religious values. The reaching up to God is not something brought from outside, but is embedded in the nature of human existence and in human cultures. There was cross-fertilization of narrative theology (Shea, 1980), the life-history approach to moral development (Kohlberg, 1981 and

1984), concepts of faith as evolving through stages (Fowler, 1981), and the analysis of media reception as an interaction between media myth and narrative (Silverstone, 1981) and personal life histories (Fiske, 1987). Another very important influence was the new sociology of religion emerging in the 1970s and 1980s, which showed that religiosity could not be defined simply by the imposition of institutional religious affiliation (Beckford – Luckman, 1989; Beckford, 1989). It was evident that a new generations of seekers were building their own belief system from symbols from a variety of religious traditions (Roof – McKinney, 1987; Roof, 1999). An anecdote from the landmark book of Bellah and his associates, *Habits of the Heart* (1985), was symptomatic of this. When a lady named Sheila was asked in an interview what her religious beliefs were she paused and said: "Well, I take a little from this religion and a little from another to make my own belief system. I guess you would have call it 'Sheilaism'". This may always have been true, but the dominant paradigm of communication, a message-media-sender paradigm, had not been willing to recognize it.

By the 1970s and early 1980s the prominence of the televangelists began to stimulate many of studies of religious broadcasting, especially regarding the socio-cultural and political impact of new religious movements and the Pentecostals (Armstrong, 1979; Hadden – Swann, 1981; Frankl, 1987; Abelman – Hoover, 1990). Especially important were Peter Horsfield's *Religious Television* (1984), providing a summary analysis of research on religious broadcasting up to that point and the Gallup survey of audiences of radio and televison (Hoover, 1988: 63-70). All of these studies confirmed that audiences were largely the devout church members, the elderly, less well educated, more rural and tending to be heavier television users. Contrary to the claims of many religious broadcasters, television broadcasts made few converts among the un-churched, but television was most important in providing public symbols of identification for the new religious movements in the 1970s and 1980s.

The new studies of the sociology of religion in the 1970s and 1980s were confirming that a new religious configuration was coming into existence – more fundamentalist, intensely committed, more personalistic and spontaneous, more militant against liberal religious hegemony. No sociological study suggested that the religious broadcasters were an important cause of this, but broadcasting was part of the creation of a new culture.

In the mid-1980s Stewart Hoover, drawing on the many currents of thought about religious media described above, designed a new approach to the study of religion and media which focused on the role of media in the creation of personal religious meaning and religious cultures. Also important were discussions with the Centre for the Study of Communication and Culture in London which was encouraging a cultural studies approach and which published his book in its *Communication and Human Values* series. The central question in the study was: "What kind of religious culture are we creating in this era of great social and institutional change?" (Hoover, 1988: 12). Television was considered a cultural medium, a signifying practice. The study adapted the following aspects of the cultural studies approach: the focus was on the culture of a particular religious movement and the life context of people in this movement: their jobs, their families, the problems they faced, and their politics. The study focused on people involved with a televangelist movement, namely that of Pat Robertson, but looked at all the sources of religious meaning in their lives – their church, their political involvements, their general reading, their social affiliations, their many religious activities – and how they used these sources of meaning. The data were whole life histories and how these life experiences led up to the present searches for meaning in life, especially the precipitating factor that led to a kind of conversion to a deeper, more intense search for meaning. A particular focus was on the sources of meaning for their involvement in politics and other aspects of public life. The study revealed that following a particular televangelist was part of belonging to a particular religious subculture, in this case, a somewhat more fundamentalist and conservative religious, political and social culture. There were many sources of information that helped those associated with the movement to define the meaning of their life situation: interpersonal contacts, discussion groups, books and newspapers, and, since television was so important a part of these somewhat elderly and more sedentary people, various television programmes were important. All those interviewed felt that this movement had provided crucial help in defining how to make sense out of a central meaning problem in their lives: a death of a family member, a serious illness, loss of a job, family crisis or any of the many problems that could affect a person in modernity. Even though many did not regularly watch his TV programs, Pat Robertson was so much a public symbol of all that they believed in that they were ready to contribute relatively large amounts of money to make its voice heard. The networks of those associated with this movement included virtually all religious denominations: Protestants of all backgrounds and all social classes, Catholics and even some Jewish people, but the "meaning problems" were sufficiently similar that *all identified with what this media figure promoted and symbolized.* In the highly differentiated modern societies divided into single-value concerns and single-issue politics, people of different subcultures tend to identify with different public media figures. Moreover, those who identified with a particular media figure tend to be in contact with each other and to live in a particular value world.

Hoover's study showed that the way certain people come to be identified with certain media figures depends very much on the history of their social backgrounds and social networks. It also depends on life circumstances that present crises of meaning that make people move out of a particular routine and search for new meaning. Sometimes seemingly chance experiences lead people toward identification with a media figure, but almost always the social history of a person leads them toward certain types of media use. The social history also provides different resources of interpretative capacity, different "filters" and different interests. What became most apparent, however, is that religious media is an important provider of symbols that people can use to build their own system of meaning.

7. The formation of the "Media, Religion and Culture" network

In the 1980s and 1990s religion, which many had considered a phenomenon disappearing in the face of modernity, suddenly was recognized as becoming a much more central actor in political, economic and socio-cultural affairs of the world. The world-wide Pentecostal, evangelical movement was one dimension of this, but Pope John Paul II was another dimension and still other dimensions were the Islamic, Buddhist and Hindu socio-political-cultural revitalizations and the evident religiosity of the people of the new nations. The literally hundreds of new religious movements and "quasi-religions" came to be considered part of the "post-modern" culture. Many scholars began to speak of the "re-enchantment" of the world (Murdock, 1997).

The study of media also moved away from its administrative concerns to the recording of immensely varied ways of signifying to oneself and to others "who I think I am" (identity) or "what I would like to be", "with whom I and we want to be identified", and "what we think is important in life and in the world". Everything from billboards, to T-shirts, to horror films, to home decorations, to Internet – all are fitting identity signifying practices to be studied. They are religious because they were associated with what is called religious or because they deal with what the subjects involved consider to be matters of ultimate concern and what is considered to be "sacred". The preoccupation with signifying identity is due in part, on the one hand, with globalization and the confrontation of cultures and, on the other, the post-modern collapse of overarching cultural belief systems. The major institutions involved with providing signification materials are less and less the institutional churches and ever more the commercial marketing systems selling commodities that can be readily used to define and dramatize identities. The focus of study thus becomes the systems of persuasive selling that transforms everything potentially religious into commodities, from statues of Padre Pio to "I love Jesus" bracelets. The media – everything from the telephone to home video – have been a unifying focus in this because the media are what link us together.

The study of media, religion and culture also began to move out of a institutional religious base into a more secular scholarly context as it became evident that religion is a central *cultural* institution that is dealing with the signifying practices that link together areas of meaning. The institutional churches have ceded ground to popular culture signifying practices as the places of unifying the meaning of life. Indeed, religion is now studied more in departments and "centres" of the study of popular culture, although many of the centres that are part of the media, religion and culture network still have close links with institutional religion. This delinking of the study of religion from explicit connection with institutional religion makes it easier for the study of popular identity signifying practices to analyse critically the use of popular culture to establish cultural hegemony precisely through the commodification of objects of popular culture. In the view of some, the delinking of the study of religion from more explicit institutional definitions also helps to distance the study from more "essentialistic" conceptions of religion. Thus, the study of media, religion and culture retains the central humanistic focus of the critical cultural studies tradition and the defence of the freedom, creativity and sanctity of the person. The central question remains the same: what kind of culture are we creating in the context of mediated signifying practices and how do we evaluate this culture in terms of the meaning of human existence today?

The emphasis on studying religious media as part of a subculture, a life context and a life history, leads toward research on how different subcultures use media to build religious meaning: youth, women, the elderly, rural people and a host of other groups. This introduces another important premise, namely, that every person and group has its own concept of what is religious, often quite different from the variety of institutional religious creeds, and may project a religious meaning on to media. The focus moves beyond the institutional representations of religion to more poetic representations of personal spirituality, a sense of unity with personal identity and inspirations of others. This attempts to understand the experience of transcendent community in film, music and visual or plastic arts.

The study of the subjective interpretation of popular culture has led to a deeper understanding of how popular religious art, so often relegated to a marginal role by theologically dominated institutional religion, becomes the focus of stability of the emotional life in the life course (Morgan, 1999). The visual symbol often is a point of integration of meaning in life and a popular devotional icon becomes the organizing principle of personal identity. The study of religions, so limited to the analysis of print media and print-based messages, becomes more open to the role of the visual.

The study of media and religion as culture is also much more open to the processes of globalization and the "hybridized" reception of religious cultures as they travel around the globe (Asamoah-Gyadu, 2004). The ethnographic study of live rituals is able to catch the process of "hybridization" in the act of creation and to see the various roles and interaction of leading actors in the process of creating local cultures.

The study of religious conversion from a cultural perspective has moved away from a psychological reductionism and focuses more on the transformation of personal meaning systems and the integration of personal identities around central symbols. This has led away from understanding of religious and moral development or religious conversion as simply the result of "external" factors such as life crisis, new material opportunities or powerful persuasion and, instead, sees this as a personal search for the ever more profound integration of meaning in personal lives and in cultures (Ihejirika, 2004).

Also central to the study of media, religion and culture is the tendency in religious broadcasting to transform religion into an ideology which sacralizes and naturalizes the relations of exploitative power. The televangelists and many other religious broadcasters present themselves as the true national culture, sometimes under the guise of a "persecuted minority", thus drawing audiences into accepting and submitting to cultural hegemonies (Bruce, 1990).

8. Formulating a "Media, Religion and Culture" (MRC) research agenda

By the early 1990s there was gradually forming a network of individual researchers, research centers[1] and research programs which identified roughly with a cultural studies approach to the study of media and religion. The conceptualization of the contemporary relationship of media and religion of people in his network tended to follow the lines described above. The consensus that this focus represented an important area of research led to setting up a more formal structure of international conferences, publications and research groups. The book, *Rethinking Media, Religion, and Culture* edited by Stewart Hoover and Knut Lundby (1997) outlined the major concepts, arguments and issues in this area of study. My own chapter, "Religion and Media in the Construction of Cultures", was an attempt to provide a systematic theoretical explanation of the interaction of media, religious institutions and religious movements in the development of contemporary cultures (White, 1997: 37-64). The first International Conference on Media, Religion and Culture was held in Uppsala in 1993, and subsequent international conferences were held in Boulder, Colorado in 1996, Edinburgh in 1999, Jyvaskyla, Finland in 2003, Louisville, Kentucky in 2004 and in Stockholm in 2006. The *Journal of Media and Religion* was founded in 2002, and a book series with Routledge Publishers was initiated in 2003.

In 1996 the Porticus Foundation initiated the International Study Commission on Media, Religion and Culture made up of fifteen scholars and media producers to carry out a more focused study of the emerging shape of religion in the media-dominated age and how the institutions of religion should respond to these challenges. The commission has met with local religious leaders and scholars in Asia, Africa, Latin America, Eastern Europe and Australia to interchange perspectives on media and religion in those parts of the world.

In 1999, to encourage more research and scholarship on media and religion in countries of the South, the commission began a program of scholarships for Catholic doctoral candidates from Africa, Latin America, Asia and Eastern Europe. The scholarships are granted by the Porticus Foundation under the title "International Catholic Fellowships for Research in Media, Religion and Culture". The program does not simply pay tuition but attempts to bring together the approximately thirty fellows in roughly yearly meetings to discuss their research among themselves and with senior scholars in the field.

The commission has also been interested in reaching church leadership and leadership in seminary formation. For this audience Peter Horsfield has prepared a CD, *The Mediated Spirit*, that traces the role of media in the development of Christianity. The CD-ROM has proven to be a very useful resource for researchers, teachers, and youth leaders, or those simply interested in understanding the nature and reasons for the changes in religious faith and practices taking place today[2]. Peter Horsfield has also assembled a comprehensive bibliography of publications of the members of the comision which, when complete, will be found on the commission website (*http://www.iscmrc.org*).

Over the ten years of its existence the study commission has attempted to explore the following questions: (1) In what ways can we say that the media have come to occupy the spaces traditionally occupied by religion? (2) What is the relationship of religious authority to modes of symbolic practice? (3) How must we re-think the relationship between religion and media? (4) What does this new situation imply about epistemology? In the background of these questions is the emergence of global cultural and religious contact, the disappearing vestiges of collective nationalistic-ethnic definition of religious identity (the tradition of *cujus regio, ejus religio*), the personalization of religious choice, and the recasting of social relationships and information seeking in the moulds of communication technologies.

The book *Belief in Media* (2004) was in some ways a summary of the thinking of the commission about these questions, and my own chapter in the book, "Major Issues in the Study of Media, Religion and Culture" (White, 2004), was an attempt to summarize the thinking of the nearly ten years of discussions and research of the commission.

Perhaps a good way to close this chapter and to bring together more briefly the current thinking of the media, religion and culture approach is to sum up the evidence about the interaction of media and religion emerging from the numerous studies of people using the more open-ended ethnographic interviews of the cultural studies methods. In the background is the situation in which people are increasingly cut loose from the institutional religious framework which structured the parameters of their cultural beliefs and values. At one time an institutional religious framework structured the way people perceived their world, the standard questions about this world and the standard answers to these questions. These religious institutions were often closely associated with national and ethnic geographical territories. As people have moved out of these structured social contexts through globalization and physical and intellectual migration, they have had to piece together their own coherent world views, their own definitions of the key questions and their own answers.

Virtually all of the hundreds of interviews that one might consult in this research tradition over the last twenty years reveal people searching for answers to questions and solutions to the everyday problems of family unity, health, financial security, realizing lifelong dreams of personal aspirations, crises of personal friendship and affection, and a host of other problems. Virtually all the respondents have carried some degree of answers and coping mechanisms *in their own personalities* and either knew how or did not know how to relate their personal identities to the immensely varied situations that the extremely differentiated role situations of late modernity present. How well people responded to situations or found answers depended very much on how well their personalities were organized around central symbols that carried with them answers or coping mechanisms. For example, a young man whose personal identity came to be organized around the ideal of the successful businessman with the belief systems and values, including religious values, that this implies might move through life coping well with all the problems that life might present, including severe difficulties and reversals. Virtually all people had or were constructing some form of coherent world view or framework of ultimate explanation (Wuthnow, 1992).

Culture is understood most commonly in terms of Ann Swidler's concept of culture as a "tool kit", a pool of explanatory resource symbols that one might draw upon to make sense out of puzzling situations (Swidler, 1986). The religious in these studies is defined in terms of what the subculture considers religious, but this is most often experienced as what is at the very edge of structures of rational explanation but what underlies and is present in all explanations: the transcendent (Ammerman, 2004). For example, for people whose lives centre much on the experience of nature away from the congestion of cities, the transcendent sacred is the dynamic force of nature which is beyond explanation because it simply exists and at the same time underlies all of the power and beauty of nature. One of the best explanations of the basic theory of the MRC approach is found in the introduction to Lynn Schofield Clark's book reporting her research on the role of media in the religiosity of teenagers in the USA (2003).

When people meet situations of uncertainty, lacking in some degree coping mechanism in their personality organization, and begin to search for information, the most important sources are interpersonal contacts, and these contacts often lead into movements of cultural revitalization that provide a patterned explanation of life problems and patterned coping mechanisms. These movements of cultural revitalization carry with them a series of media sources that provided the continual feeding of information on how to cope with life's problems. Followers of the movement generally use continually the media associated with the movement because they know that it will provide solutions to questions and lead ever more deeply into the wisdom of the movement. Often, at the centre of these movements of cultural revitalization are prophetic founding figures whose messages seem to contain the answer to all the problems. In the recorded interview data, one finds members of the movements continually remarking that the prophetic figure seems to have all the answers, always makes sense to people, is a clear communicator, and is always accessible[3].

Regarding the question whether the media occupy the spaces traditionally occupied by (institutional) religion (*first question*), the closest answer is that the institutional churches were once based on a population much more homogeneous in terms of cultural background while today's societies are a mosaic of movements, leisure networks, associations and communities of interests. Each has its own world of media use and information sources. Each movement may have its own version of the broad umbrella institutional belief system of religion and politics. But the broader belief system of a church, a nation or a continental society such as Europe is mediated through an immense variety of subcultures each with its particularly strong religious symbols. For people who are attracted by the values of the ecological movement, for example, the relation with nature can be the major religious experience and their major form of responding to life's problems. Their media use will also centre very much around ecology issues. People vary in their closeness to the centres of the subcultural networks and they may be moving in and out of various cultural networks, but their religious symbols will be found in what these subcultural networks consider to be religious. If the symbols are somehow related to the institutional church umbrella and the major symbolic figures of the umbrella church are sympathetic to the values of their subculture, then they may draw on these symbolic resources.

Regarding the relationship of religious authority to modes of symbolic practice (*second question*), it is unlikely that the relationship is one of strict legal or doctrinal imposition. Everybody is picking and choosing from available ethical models what their experience tells them is a good way to act. Most tend to model their lives after persons known in interpersonal networks, but they would probably not identify them as "religious authority". Some may take as their religious authority the leader of their institutional identification, but most would select a person they know through the media whose life, writing and teaching is a model for what they think is a good way to act. The media tend to give prominence to institutional leadership such as a pope (Gans, 2004) and people tend to identify with the institutional leadership presented by the media to the extent that the media figure is a symbol of what they feel is the good life. Cultural revitalization movements engage followers at the point of "meaning gaps" in their lives and help to solve these meaning gaps by bringing followers to identify with central leadership symbols who "make sense", that is, they present a coherent pattern of meaning, making everything in their life "fit together". Virtually all central leaders in revitalization movements become mediated symbols, starting their own TV or radio programs, writing their own books or putting out their magazines. Sometimes the followers push the leaders into the media. Often the media seek out the leaders and offer them contracts. At times the leaders sense that they must become mediated for the sake of what they are trying to do. The media projection of leadership symbols gives them authority in "making sense" and the fact that many in the movement follow them gives them authority (Hoover, 1989; Ihejirika, 2004).

Berger pointed out in his sociology of religion (1969) that the public evidence of large numbers of followers, what he calls "massification", is an important source of the authority of the belief system. It is well known that the media give prominence in their reporting on the public appearances of leaders of institutions and movements such as a papal visit as a gauge of the authority of that leader as moral leader. Margaret Melady, in her study of the papal visits to the United States in 1987 (1999), reports that those planning the papal visit made sure that the Pope would make public appearances in those cities where there was assurance that a large public turnout of a particular kind of crowd, in this case Hispanics, could be mobilized. The supporters of canonizations of individuals whose symbolic power is being carefully created will make every effort to have a "record" crowd present overflowing out of St. Peter's square, and these supporters will make sure that the size and fervour of the crowd is vividly portrayed in the mass media.

The media prefer gigantic crowds because it also reinforces the importance of the media itself, that is, the size of the crowd justifies the media presence at the event and the fact that the media is where the great majority of the people are and where history is being made. Implied is the belief that the media themselves make history and that history cannot be made without the presence of the media. And the fact the media are present strengthens the identification of people with a symbol that the people feel sums up their belief system. The visual presentation of the media event draws out many iconic identifications that reinforce the strength of identification (Morgan, 1999).

Most great religious leaders who have made their way to the top intuitively understand all this, and their communicative charisma is often one of the criteria of their selection by followers who want to promote the institution. Great public religious figures, such as John Paul II, often have acting experience, that is, the experience of directly moving crowd response, and they – and their carefully chosen public relations managers – know how to mobilize public identification. In the election of the present Pope, Cardinal Ratzinger quickly outdistanced all other candidates because, in his celebration of the funeral of John Paul II, he showed that he had carefully learned the power of Vatican pageantry in developing symbolism in the public sphere.

Of course, all those who do not identify, in their personal experience, with the hegemonic public symbols, are part of what Kathleen Jamieson calls the "spiral of cynicism" (Jamieson – Cappella, 1997). They wait for their opportunity to mount a counter public symbolism and the clash of public symbolisms becomes the culture wars of today. The media almost certainly have intensified cultural conflict in the world today because the media works so much with stereotypes and a play on emotional prejudice. The media take the processes of social interaction out of the direct interpersonal context, where most conflicts can be mediated, and live off the drama of cultural conflict. The beginning of the resolution of culture wars are in favourable interpersonal contact where symbols are generated, but these unifying symbols must then be carried to the level of the public sphere which usually means the media sphere (Browning, 2000).

The *third question* which the International Commission for the Study of Media, Religion and Culture has posed is the need to rethink the dichotomies enveloping media and religion, the dichotomies of sacred and profane, good and bad media, media as either instrumental manipulation or idyllic communalistic participation. A list of these common and trite "culture wars" is found in my chapter in the book summarizing recent MRC research (White, 2004: 209). One of the most obvious ways that the MRC research breaks down the dichotomies is the study of the reception of the religious programs which shows a valid construction of religious meaning at times quite different from the official, institutional meaning of images. Implied in this is a distrust in classical "essentialistic" conceptions of religion and openness to ideas of what is religious emerging out of popular religious experience (White, 2004: 202-204). Another departure from the dichotomies is the MRC interest in popular culture expressed in the continually and rapidly changing tastes in popular media. Jolyon Mitchell's study of horror films in Ghana shows that what are seemingly garish and bizarre portrayals to Western canons of film are in fact serious religious reflections on the moral dilemmas of everyday life in Ghana, what one Ghanaian producer calls "moral parables" (2004: 116). The MRC program of international, comparative research in Africa, Asia and Latin America has helped to free the conceptions of media and religion from the fixed Western categories.

The *fourth question* raised by the commission deals with the epistemological practices implied in studies of media and religion. Has the MRC research helped to bring the way we think about media and religion closer to the experienced realities? Perhaps the most significant thing about MRC research is that it uses an ethnographic methodology that takes us into the everyday life of various subcultures and allows us to see the world through the eyes of the inhabitants of those worlds and how those inhabitants use the media to see that world. One of the best examples is Lynn Schofield Clark's five year study of youth and the media in the USA (2003). Another example is Ihejirika's study of the conversion experiences of Nigerian Pentecostals, the perception of a world inhabited by good and evil spirits and how they see Pentecostalism giving them greater control over this world (Ihejirika, 2004). One example of the attempt to theorize this new epistemology are Lynn Schofield Clark's essay on the move from an epistemology of institutional power over media and culture to an epistemology of increasing autonomy and reflexive awareness questioning our creating of culture in the media while we create it (2002). Another example is Jan Fernback's chapter exploring the epistemology of the ritualization of the experience of computer-mediated community (2002).

Finally, I would argue that the immense proliferation of the research on media and religion that has occurred in the last twenty-five years has brought us closer to answering the kind of questions that were posed by religious leaders in the study carried out by Parker, Barry and Smythe nearly sixty years ago in 1950. True, the way the questions are being asked has changed considerably. We now not only have a very clear idea of what groups listen to religious broadcasts and how the use of religious broadcasts contribute to patterns of religious development and spiritual growth, but precisely how religious broadcasts are likely to fit in a complex mix of many other communication sources. We can explain these much more complex processes because of more ethnographic studies of media use within the life context and life histories of people in very different social and cultural contexts.

The typical religious broadcaster or local parish priest wants to know how to help people grow spiritually, but spiritual growth is a transformation of the consciousness of persons. This means that we can know consciousness only as a particular kind of personal signifying practice, a cultural meaning-creating process.

Notes

[1] There are now some five or six centres in various parts of the world which generally follow the cultural studies approach to the study of media and religion. Some of the major ones are The Centre for Media, Religion and Culture, University of Colorado; Centre for Communication, Theology and Ethics, New College University of Edinburgh; Interdisciplinary Centre for Social Communications, The Gregorian University; The program of media and religion at Annenberg Centre at the University of Southern California; and the Centre for the Study of African Culture and Communication in Nigeria.

[2] The website for "The Mediated Spirit" is: *http://www.mediatedspirit.com*.

[3] I am particularly indebted to the interviews of Stewart Hoover in his study of the followers of televangelist Pat Robertson, the interviews of Lynn Schofield Clark with young people in the Denver area of the USA, but of great value more recently are the field notes of Walter Ihejirika studying converts to Pentecostalism in Nigeria, Columbanus Udofia studying youth and contemporary Christian music in Nigeria and Ray Debono-Roberts studying the life histories of members of the charismatic movement, the "Thy Kingdom Come Community" in Malta.

Biblical references

ABELMAN, R. – HOOVER, S.M., ed. (1990), *Religious Television: Controversies and Conclusions*, Norwood, NJ: Ablex Publishing Company.

AMMERMAN, N. (2004), "Religious Identities and Religious Institutions", in M. DILLON, ed., *Handbook for the Sociology of Religion,* Cambridge: Cambridge University Press.
ANG, I. (1985), *Watching Dallas: Soap Opera and the Melodramatic Imagination,* London: Methuen.
ARMSTRONG, B. (1979), *The Electric Church,* New York: Thomas Nelson.
ASAMOAH-GYADU, J. K. (2004), "Pentecostal Media Images and Religious Globalization in Sub-Saharan Africa", in P. HORSFIELD – M. E. HESS – A. MEDRANO, ed., *Belief in Media: Cultural Perspectives on Media and Christianity,* Aldershot, UK: Ashgate Publishing, 65-80.
BABIN, P. (1991), *The New Era in Religious Communication,* Minnealpolis, MN: Fortress Press.
BARKER, C. (2000), *Cultural Studies: Theory and Practice,* London: Sage Publications.
BECKFORD, J. A. – LUCKMANN, T. (1989), *The Changing Face of Religion.* London: Sage Publications.
BECKFORD, J. A. (1989), *Religion and Advanced Industrial Society,* London: Unwin Hyman.
BELLAH, R. – AL. (1985), *Habits of the Heart: Individualism and Commitment In American Life,* Berkeley: University of California Press.
BERGER, P. – LUCKMANN, T. (1967), *The Social Construction of Reality: A treatise in the sociology of knowledge,* New York: Doubleday.
BERGER, P. (1969), *The Sacred Canopy: Elements of a Sociological Theory of Religion,* Garden City, NY: Doubleday.
BLACK, G. D. (1994), *Hollywood Censored: Morality Codes, Catholics and the Movies,* Cambridge: Cambridge University Press.
BROWN, M. E. (1994), *Soap Opera and Women's Talk: The Pleasure of Resistance,* London: Sage Publications.
BROWNING, D. S. (2000), *From Culture Wars to Common Ground: Religion and the American family debate,* Louisville, KY: Westminister John Knox Press.
BRUCE, S. (1990), *Pray TV: Televangelism in America,* London: Routledge.
CAREY, J. W. (1989), *Communication as Culture*: *Essays on Media and Society,* Boston: Unwin Hyman.
CLARK, L. S. (2002), "The 'Protestantization' of Research into Media, Religion and Culture", in S. M. HOOVER – L. S. CLARK, ed., *Practicing Religion in the Age of the Media: Explorations in Media, Religion, and Culture,* New York: Columbia University Press, 7-34.

CLARK, L. S. (2003), *From Angels to Aliens: Teenagers, the Nedia and the Supernatural,* New York: Oxford University Press.
DENNIS, E. E. – WARTELLA, E., ed. (1996), *American Communication Research: The Remembered History,* Mahwah, NJ: Lawrence Erlbaum.
ERICKSON, H. (1992), *Religious Radio and Television in the United States, 1921-1991: The Programs and the Personalities,* Jefferson, NC: McFarland Publishers.
FERNBECK, J. (2002), "A Case Study of the Construction of Computer-Mediated Neopagan Religious Meaning", in S. HOOVER – L. S. CLARK, ed., *Practicing Religion in the Age of the Media: Explorations in media, religion and culture,* New York: Columbia University Press, 254-275.
FICHTER, J. (1954), *Social Relations in the Urban Parish,* Chicago: University of Chicago Press.
FISKE, J. (1987), *Television Culture,* London: Routledge.
FOWLER, J. W. (1981), *Stages of Faith: The Psychology of Human Development and the Quest for Meaning,* San Francisco: Harper and Row.
FRANKL, R. (1987), *Televangelism: The Marketing of Popular religion,* Carbondale, IL: Southern Illinois University Press.
FREIRE, P. (1990a), *Pedagogy of the Oppressed,* New York: Continuum.
FREIRE, P. (1990b), *Education for Critical Consciousness,* New York: Continnum.
FRITH, S. (1983), *Sound Effects: Youth, Leisure, and the Politics of Rock,* London: Constable.
GANS, H. (2004), *Democracy and the News,* New York: Oxford University Press.
GEERTZ, C. (1975), *The Interpretation of Cultures,* London: Hutchinson.
GRODIN, D. – LINDLOF, T. R. (1996), *Constructing the Self in a Mediated World,* Thousand Oaks: Sage Publications.
HADDEN, J. K. – SWANN, C. E. (1981), *Prime-Time Preachers: The Rising Power of Televangelism,* Reading, MA: Addison-Wesley Publishing Co.
HALL, S. – HOBSON, D. – LOWE, A. – WILLIS, P., ed. (1980), *Culture, Media and Language,* London: Hutchinson & Co. Publishers.
HALL, S. (1977), "Culture, the Media and the 'Ideological Effect'", in J. CURRAN – M. GUREVITCH, – J. WOLLACOTT, *Mass Communication and Society,* London: Edward Arnold in association with the Open University Press, 314-348.

HALL, S. – JEFFERSON, T., ed. (1983), *Resistance Through Rituals: Youth Subcultures in Postwar Britain*, London: Hutchinson.
HOGGART, R. (1957,1980), *The Uses of Literacy: Aspects of Working-class Life with Special Reference to Publications and Entertainments*, London: Penguin Books.
HOOVER, S. M. (1988), *Mass Media Religion: The Social Sources of the Electronic Church*. Newbury Park, CA: Sage Publications.
HOOVER, S. M – LUNDBY, K. (1997), *Rethinking Media, Religion, and Culture*, London: Sage Publications.
HORSFIELD, P. (1984), *Religious Television: The American Experience*, New York: Longman.
IHEJIRIKA, W. (2004), *Catholics Becoming Pentecostals in Nigeria*, Doctoral Thesis at the Pontifical Gregorian University.
JAMIESON, K. – CAPPELLA, J. (1997), *Spiral of Cnynicism: The Press and the Public Good*, New York: Oxford University Press.
JENKINS, H. (1992), *Textual Poachers: Television Fans and Participatory Culture*, New York: Routledge.
KLAPPER, J. T. (1965), *The Effects of Mass Communication*, New York: The Free Press.
KOHLBERG, L. (1981), *The Philosophy of Moral Development: Moral Stages and the Idea of Justice*, San Francisco: Harper and Row.
KOHLBERG, L. (1984), *The Psychology of Moral Development: The Nature and Validity of Moral Stages*, San Francisco: Harper and Row.
KOSS, S. (1984), *The Rise and Fall of the Political Press in Britain*, Vol 2: *The Twentieth Century*, London: Hamish Hamilton.
LUCKMANN, T. (1967), *The Invisible Religion: The Problem of Religion in Modern Society*, New York: Macmillan.
LULL, J. (1988), *World Families Watch Television*, Newbury Park: Sage Publications.
MARCUSE, H. (1968), *One-Dimensional Man: Studies in the Ideology of Advanced Industrial Society*, Boston: Beacon Press.
MARTIN, D. (1969), *The Religious and the Secular: Studies in Secularization*, London: Routledge & Kegan Paul.
MARTIN, D. (1980), *The Breaking of the Image: A Sociology of Christian Theory and Practice*, Oxford: Blackwell.
MARTÍN-BARBERO, J. (1993), *Communication, Culture and Hegemony*, Newbury Park, CA: Sage Publications.

MATELSKI, M. J. (1995), *Vatican Radio: Propagation by the Airwaves*, Westport, CN: Praeger Publishers.
MCLUHAN, M. (1965), *Understanding Media: The Extensions of Man*, New York: McGraw-Hill.
MELADY, M. B. (1999), *The Rhetoric of John Paul II: The Pastoral Visit as a New Vocabulary of the Sacred*, Westport, CT: Praeger Books.
MITCHELL, J. (2004), "From Morality Tales to Horror Movies: Toward an Understanding of the Popularity of West African Video Film", in P. HORSFIELD – HESS, M. E. – MEDRANO, A. M., ed., *Belief in Media: Cultural Perspectives on Media and Christianity*, Aldershop, UK: Ashgate Publishers, 107-120.
MORGAN, D. (1999), *Visual Piety: A History and Theory of Popular Religious Images*, Berkeley, CA: University of California Press.
MORLEY, D. (1992), *Television, Audiences and Cultural Studies*, London: Routledge.
MURDOCK, G. (1997), "The Re-Enchantment of the World: Religions and The Transformations of Modernity", in S. HOOVER – K. LUNDBY, ed., *Rethinking Media, Religion and Culture*, London: Sage Publications, 85-101.
NEWCOMB, H. (1978), "Assessing the Violence Profile of Gerbner and Gross: A Humanistic Critique and Suggestion", *Communication Research* 5/3, 264-282.
NEWCOMB, H. – ALLEY, R. (1983), *The Producer's Medium: Conversations with Creators of American TV*, New York: Oxford University Press.
PARKER, E. C. – BARRY, D. W. – SMYTHE, D. W. (1955), *The Television-Radio Audience and Religion*, New York: Harper & Brothers, Publishers.
ROGERS, E. (1994), *A History of Communication Study*, New York: The Free Press.
ROOF, W. C. – MCKINNEY, W. (1987), *American Mainline Religion: Its Changing Shape and Future*, New Brunswick, NJ: Rutgers University Press.
ROOF, W. C. (1999), *Spiritual Marketplace: Baby Boomers and the Remaking of American Religion*, Princeton: Princeton University Press.
ROWLAND, W. Jr. (1983), *The Politics of TV Violence: Policy Uses of Communication Research*, Beverly Hills, CA: Sage Publications.
SHEA, J. (1981), *Stories of Faith*, Chicago: The Thomas More Press.
SILVERSTONE, R. (1981), *The message of Television: Myth and Narrative in Contemporary Culture*, London: Heinemann Educational Books.

SILVERSTONE, R. – HIRSCH, E. (1992), *Consuming Technologies: Media and Information in Domestic Spaces*, London: Routledge.
SIRCAR, B. (1978), *The Third Theatre*, Calcutta: Badal Sircar.
STARK, R. – GLOCK, C. Y. (1968), *American Piety: The Nature of Religious Commitment*, Berkeley: University of California Press.
SWIDLER, A. (1986), "Culture in Action: Symbols and Strategies", *American Sociological Review* 51 (April 1986), 273-86.
THOMPSON, E.P. (1963, 1980), *The Making of the English Working Class*, London: Gollancz.
TURNER, V. (1969), *The Ritual Process: Structure and Anti-structure*, London: Routledge and Kegan Paul.
WHITE, R. (1997), "Religion and Media in the Construction of Cultures", in S. M. HOOVER – K. LUNDBY, ed., *Rethinking Media, Religion and Culture*, London: Sage Publications, 37-64.
WHITE, R. (2004), "Major Issues in the Study of Media, Religion and Culture", in P. HORSFIELD – M. E. HESS – A. MEDRANO, ed., *Belief in Media: Cultural Perspectives on Media and Christianity*, Aldershot, UK: Ashgate Publishers, 197-218.
WILSON, B. R. (1982), *Religion in Sociological Perspective*, Oxford: Oxford University Press.
WOLFE, K. M. (1984), *The Churches and the British Broadcasting Corporation 1922-1956*, London: SCM Press.
WUTHNOW, R. (1992), *Rediscovering the Sacred: Perspectives on Religion in Contemporary Society*, Grand Rapids, MI: Eerdmans.

Communication for education and development is key to formation: Development communication studies at CICS in perspective

Jacob Srampickal, SJ

L'autore offre una panoramica sul contenuto del corso offerto nel Centro Interdisciplinare circa il rapporto tra comunicazione e sviluppo. Dimostrando che la comunicazione per lo sviluppo è diversa dallo sviluppo e dalla comunicazione separatamente considerati, l'autore identifica due dimensioni concrete del tema in oggetto: il fatto che la natura partecipativa dell'atto stesso di comunicare possa promuovere lo sviluppo, e il fatto che i media tradizionali, di gruppo e moderni, possano agevolare il processo dello sviluppo stesso. Nella seconda parte dell'articolo, l'autore considera alcune situazioni degne di nota nel campo della comunicazione per lo sviluppo: la minaccia della globalizzazione, l'importanza della dimensione dell'identità sessuale, la sindrome divertimento-educazione, la ricerca partecipativa a base popolare e i movimenti popolari. Conclude infine con una sfida ad attivisti e teorici del Terzo Mondo, per l'elaborazione di una metodologia di comunicazione per lo sviluppo più adatta alla loro stessa situazione.

At the CICS I direct a seminar titled "Research in the field of development communication (DevCom)". In the seminar we go through the entire gamut of research from the 1940s to the present day in the area of communications for development and media for development: traditional, group and participatory. The seminar was developed at CICS in 1995-96, by Dr. Robert White, who studied the impact of radio on the development of farmers in Honduras in the 1970s. The course introduces the major authors both from the First World and the Third World on development communication (DevCom).

Although based in Europe, CICS has a sizeable number of students from the Third World, especially from Africa, Latin America and Asia. Being a centre committed to the well rounded development of humans at all levels, we at CICS envisage that clearer understanding of DevCom can help them in diverse ways. We believe that the students who have clear ideas on communication and media can assist in developmental action back in their home countries. Even students from the First World find the course useful as they get to know glimpses of the problems of development in the Third World, and a spirit of compassion and generosity is born in them. Clearly, total development which envisages social, spiritual, moral and economic development of the people is the all-pervasive aim of communication for development. One needs to study the role of communications and media in all these facets of development.

The major areas covered in this seminar are: theories of communication for development, colonization and its effects, cultural and media imperialism, the role of culture and traditional media in development, Paolo Freire's contribution to culture, education and development, the role of group media in development, the role of mass media in development, democratization of the media, the McBride report, New World Information and Communication Order, right to information, right to communication, human rights and the media, the poor and the media, digital divide to digital provide, Internet as a new medium in development, social movements, NGOs and people's movements, the participative dimension in development, the concept of empowerment, etc. The students present these themes in Powerpoint formats at the seminar, and then lead the group in a detailed discussion about their experiences and observations in their own country.

1. What is DevCom?

The expression "Development Communication", was apparently first used in the Philippines in the 1970s by Professor Nora Quebral to designate the processes of transmitting and communicating new knowledge related to rural environments. According to her, "development communication is the art and science of human communication applied to the speedy transformation of a country and the mass of its people from poverty to a dynamic state of economic growth that makes possible greater social equality and the larger fulfilment of the human potential" (Quebral, 1975: 3). In other words, it is an attempt at informing, creating awareness, educating and enlightening the people so that they can better their lives in every way. The concept of communication as sharing and exchange of meaning, defines DevCom in terms of participatory action for learning and sharing of powers: social (human rights and the emergence of the civil society), economic (egalitarian society) and political (democratization). The concept that communication always takes place in a specific cultural context has brought in culture as a major vehicle in carrying out development.

DevCom is a concept that stems from the belief that the recently developed communications media can be employed for the overall betterment of less privileged people living in underdeveloped countries. DevCom generally refers to the planned use of strategies and processes of communications aimed at achieving development. Unfortunately in most countries development seems to remain mostly with the upper layers in society.

Information flow and communication have important development roles. Without an adequate two-way flow of information and dialogue between periphery and centre, development is unlikely to take place at all levels. Communication in this sense is a process which links individuals and communities, governments and citizens, in participatory and shared decision-making. Seen from the instrumental point of view of communications, the media are essential supports to development. Here again research has shown that it is not the gigantic mass media conglomerates, but local participatory forms of group media that are more effective in convincing people to change attitudes and beliefs, and surge ahead with developmental ideologies.

Our seminar has revealed quite clearly to us that there is a confusion about DevCom. While it is easy to confuse or merge the two, one must distinguish the content and the purpose segments of DevCom. It is important to separate the two, although understanding the context and content of communications for development is necessary. It is our belief that the elements of communication like listening, feedback, participation, mutual sharing, empowerment, etc. need to be stressed in an actual study of DevCom. Communication actually is one of the independent variables like education, environment protection, natural resources, industrialization, co-operation, unity, national goals, planning, etc. for development, the dependent variable, in any country. Again, in some contexts there is also a mix-up of terms like DevCom and media for development: they are often used synonymously. Communication is a process that keeps on doing its function of creating awareness, constantly enlightening those involved in the process for the need for participation, sharing, education. Various kinds of media can be used to promote this process. Others mix-up terms like alternative, indigenous, group and traditional media, all of which have different emphases and assist in DevCom. In fact in DevCom one may, more or less, be concerned with how communication, and media of all sorts promote development.

A number of studies have been done on DevCom, from as early as 1940. It was first examined in the agricultural sector and the first DevCom agents were village level agricultural extension officers. The approach flourished from the 1950s onwards and roughly paralleled the de-colonisation experiences of many developing nations. To a great extent, DevCom was perfected, in the developing world. Our studies have also pointed that although the first concepts in DevCom like modernization came up in the context of research done by scholars from the First World; however, more and more research was gradually done in the Third World and some Third World theoreticians like Freire, Martín-Barbero, García-Canclini and others have contributed much to the expansion of the concept. Unfortunately today many theoreticians in this field from the Third World have migrated to the First World universities and use students from the Third World, who can afford to study in the First World, to continue the research. Obviously their findings are different from the observations of those working in the field close to local universities in the Third World. This approach to communication provides communities with information they can use to better their lives, and which aim to make public programmes and policies real, meaningful and sustainable at community level. Such information must be applied in some way as part of community development but it must also address information needs which communities themselves identify. However, we would often acknowledge with gratitude the contributions of theories like modernization, dependency, cultural actualization, etc. to the understanding of the concept of DevCom worldwide. Even now these theories are relevant and contributing to the understanding of DevCom.

2. The real role of media in development

Although there has been a lot of talk about media for development, the media in themselves are not the real remedies for development. In fact it is important to point out exactly what media can do. Media, as some one remarked, can only bark, and cannot bite. Information sharing, consciousness training, etc. can be done by the media; however, the real action for change has to come from enlightened people.

Nevertheless, the media can play a major role to fulfil the people's right to information. Moreover, developing village communities must be able to access information services from the various sources of government as well as a range of information products of government and other organisations, and they must also be able to communicate back to the government. Such a process of accessing services allows for an improvement in the quality of service delivery by the government. More importantly, interactive and participatory communication methods allow citizens to have their say and receive information and services in ways more suitable to their specific needs and requirements. As per the right to information, the government can be made more accountable, thereby giving the citizens a greater say in the governance.

The mass media, like radio, television, print, Internet, etc. can inform a large mass of people about developmental concepts, issues, programmes, etc. They can even educate people on these issues, in an appealing and convincing way. Precisely, the mass media are capable of providing information and creating a desire for better lives among the underdeveloped people. If these media are more focussed on communities or local needs, the people can be more intimately addressed and informed. In fact, after a number of empirical researches, DevCom scholars have come to believe that mass media in themselves do not help development but participatory media does (Hornik, 1988; Wilkins, 1988; Servaes, 1989; Jacobson – Servaes – White, 1996). Again in the fairly comprehensive study done by Fair and Shah (1997) of 209 development communication studies from 1958 to 1996, the authors have downplayed the role of media in either individual modernization or social change.

There has also been considerable research done in university circles on the impact of media in social change and development. Much of this research has contributed to the above-mentioned growth in understanding the phenomenon of development. With various UN bodies and other international developmental agencies getting into the fray, attempts have been made to develop a people-based participatory action plan to create awareness and eventual empowerment of the local people.

In sum, today theorists conclude that the mass media can only be trusted to provide a vast reservoir of knowledge. Taking a cue from the *two step flow*, several groups have realized the importance of participatory group media communication as the ideal tool to create awareness and lead to change of attitudes. DevCom is always in the process of further research.

The group media and other participatory methods, further, can educate, motivate and even gently encourage people to change for the better. Non-formal education rooted in the culture of the people using various indigenous media like popular theatre and other cultural programmes can help, as shown by Freire, in creating a civil consciousness and subsequent desire for development. Empowering the people through participatory forms of communication and action is key to development. This creates a kind of confidence, self-worth and dignity among people which are keen values in development. Group media or more precisely participatory indigenous media which allows for participant involvement in production, like street plays, puppetry, etc. can, through participatory action and the very process of making the presentation, help in creating an awareness that leads to action. "Theatre can be a rehearsal for revolution" (Boal, 1979: 122).

Education is clearly the key to development. It is an education that "helps people to read the world as they learn to read the book" (Freire), that can help one understand the causes of underdevelopment, the present day social system, and take action to change it. Present day education system is often meant to help students get a job and continue the oppressive system. In every developing country, those on the top echelons are often against this kind of education of the oppressed lot. Freire showed the best means of doing this kind of education. He says knowledge is perceived only when people realize that it is useful to their life. Communication, if it has to serve development, has to support this kind of education. A government that supports this people-based participatory action for development alone can induce development in any country.

Many rich conglomerates that own the media may not agree that the media has a responsibility to go beyond the sensationalism of headlines, to examine the underlying causes of the world's problems, and bring them to the public's attention. If six thousand children died of malaria in a country the media would not just report the disaster. They can and should look for signs of negligence, for culpability, failures of science and technology and governmental corruption. Media persons can create space in their schedules, to make sure they are covering the issues and using the power and reach of the media – embedding awareness of issues from human rights to AIDS in their services programmes. They can keep on putting pressure on governments to make a difference.

The world is crying out for change, and the media can be the messengers of that cry. It's the media's responsibility to hear it, and if it does, then it has a better chance of changing the world. Often important events like the death of 25.000 Africans daily due to poverty, hunger and malnutrition does not find front page importance.

In a Third World country exposing governmental and other forms of corruption on the media is already a development function. Thus media can play a role in the responsible functioning of major players in society. Normally, as Bruck and Roach observe, the tendency of the media to pick up on the sensational, dramatic, disastrous, and dangerous, on the negative in general, leads many peace activists to become generally sceptical, if not hostile toward the media. The media are consequently seen as one of the main obstacles to the creation of a culture of successful development stories (Bruck – Roach, 1993: 88).

3. Correct understanding of the causes of under-development

Development communicators need to have a correct understanding of the causes of underdevelopment and these needs to be explained powerfully and in an appealing manner through the media. It is through well written scripts on radio, television and other popular media that one can advocate that the causes of poverty are basically man-made. Poverty can be overcome by proper literacy, controlling rapid population growth, overuse of natural resources, and the degradation of the environment. However, the media in most developing countries is run by people with upper class interests, who care little about underdevelopment. There is an oft-quoted theory that underdevelopment is at the expense of development, i.e., because some people have developed much, others remain underdeveloped. In such a situation mass media is incapable of looking after development issues. A state that has the finer interests of the people as primary targets of development alone can help in such a situation.

4. Current concerns in DevCom

In this section some of the latest concerns in DevCom in the light of new developments in the world are looked at. Obviously there are no radically new movements; there are only certain modifications to the ideas of the secondary stage. Karen Gwinn Wilkins notes:

> In the field of development communication we now face a critical juncture. We are inundated with enthusiastic assessments of our shift from an industrial to an information age, where global knowledge takes precedence over national development. We hear about working with "partners", not "bureaucracies", to develop "people" in a global village, not "nations" through

"information", not "capital". Yet... serious problems such as poverty, malnutrition, over-population, inequality and environmental degradation remain. Despite being designed to resolve these social problems through the strategic application of communication technologies and processes, development communication programs for the most part have failed to achieve their objectives [...] The burdens of global commercialization and development privatization have weighed heavily on the potential of development communication to foster significant social change (Wilkins, 2000: 19).

From the days of modernization, dependency and Freire's cultural theories approaches which spoke of people participation, indigenous knowledge systems and empowerment of the marginalized, hardly any serious contribution has been made into the theories of DevCom. In fact as the following areas of current thinking show the above-mentioned concepts are being lived out in various ways and at different levels in the world today, with differing degrees of success.

a. *The threat of globalization*

Most development commentaries tend to agree that globalization process brings back the era of modernization theory with its concomitant dependence on the power of western technology. Clearly globalization is a phenomenon of the information\communication age. This concept could not have emerged earlier because the communication technologies that give it meaning, did not exist. Mass produced computers, commercially proven viable satellites for exchange of information and data, Internet and e-mail facilities, digital telephony, etc. have converged to make globalization possible.

Possibly it is in the area of globalization of cultures that DevCom would be most hit. A new inclusive, holistic, and universal concept of culture will emerge which will have at least 75% of the characteristics of the US tradition, because more than 80% of the global communication networks are US based or owned by companies that have their bases in the US. What was once called cultural imperialism is being brought anew through the media in globalization. It is essentially an uncritical participation in the consumption of commodities concocted by the media conglomerates to market their own commodities globally. The culture of globalization is a culture of conspicuous consumption, which in an earlier time was said to be the self-indulgent pastime of the leisure class (Brown, 2001: 71). Aided by international institutions like IMF and World Bank, the culture of globalization largely results from the deliberate strategy of the major actors in the international info-com industry, whose business revolve around the consumption of new info-com hardware and software that are mostly entertainment-dedicated and business-oriented. In such a situation communication seeking development of the deprived and less fortunate classes is almost absurd. The only solution is to empower the less privileged to the use of the very same info-com technologies for developmental purposes.

To cite a negative example, today several US development agencies fund major NGOs and bright-eyed youth with degrees in communications from developing countries, to make videos on developmental issues. Often these videos are hardly shown around and discussed. These end up as creative exercises for these youngsters. On occasion, the winning of an award will somersault them to higher levels. The funding agencies hardly ever make an evaluation of their contribution to rural development through such video productions. For if they did, they would realize that their attempts do not help development at all at the grass roots level.

A positive example is the growth of Call Centres. It is an interesting economic concept in the Third World made possible by information technology. Moving away from the former "brain drain" concepts, wherein the talented people were carried away to the First World, here the talented ones work in their own countries, on files transported across the Atlantic by information technology. In the end it breaks even for the owner and the labourer.

b. *The gender dimension*

Almost half the population of the world is feminine and so in every field of development their contributions have to be stressed. Today, termed *gender issues*, every funding agency is keen to ensure their participation in development. Often the developing world is male-dominated depriving itself of the marvels that women can perform. Earlier research focused on how to help women get into more central positions "in a man's world". Increasingly the emphasis is on the structural, institutional changing of the world so that all essentialist conceptions of gender, race, ethnicity, age and other identities are questioned and it becomes a more human world of equal citizens (Einsiedel, 2000: 175).

Since women are a major work force in agricultural production, small industries, improvement of health and education and other local community improvement programmes such as primary education, clean water, cleanliness, etc., research on ways to improve women's performance has to be a priority.

With women's involvement, a space is opened for a more participatory, dialogical, non-directive and horizontal communication which enables all in the group to gradually come into the decision making and contributing to collective action. In these groups, communication is not centred on the production of definitive messages that can be "transmitted" by a powerful source to passive receivers, but is seen as an ongoing process in which all are transmitters and all are receivers. Recent programs of community radio, community video production, and popular theatre have enabled women to reject hierarchical discourses and create a new mediated discourse in which their identities become part of the discourse. This can radically change accepted "media languages" (Rodriguez, 2001: 109).

Riano outlines three key areas of research and action on gender issues (1994). The first is to provide a space and a process for the articulation of women's competencies linked to their personal experience, their family experience and their experience in groups. Since women are so central in development at the community and regional levels, this experience has to be channelled into decisions at the community level and to linkages with development organizations. Secondly, women's media production competencies need to be developed in all media, from group and community to national and international media. Thirdly, women need to develop their capacities as socio-political actors both as protagonists in popular movements and in popular networking alliances and as representatives in governmental organizations. Steeves (2003) also argues for a more positive role for women in initiating developmental efforts, by recognizing their spiritual, moral, critical and feminist approaches.

c. *The entertainment-education syndrome*

In general, even in developing countries media is seen as a tool more for entertainment and wish fulfilment. The entertainment-education (E-E) concept is the intentional embedding of educational messages in entertainment media in order to change individual's knowledge, attitudes and overt behaviour. In recent years entertainment programmes have been made on television on wide-ranging issues as family planning HIV-AIDS prevention, female equality, environmental protection, etc. in Latin America, Africa and Asia.

If the merger of E-E in media productions is not clever enough, they tend to get preachy or patronizing, then even villagers and less educated people detest that kind of treatment. If they are cleverly done merging the message with the entertainment with certain subtlety these can peddle messages. But then often the producers aren't creative enough. Nevertheless, one cannot undermine the importance of entertainment in education. One should not consider entertainment merely as laughing matter. Anything deeply involving, gripping, captivating and capturing attention is capable of creating strong after-effects. People accept matters wholeheartedly, when said well in an appealing and entertaining manner. The power of rhetoric in languages has the power to convince people. Satire, understatements, irony, wit, reproaches and repartees are powerful means of communication. Thus, the call made by Singhal and Rogers (2002) to give more attention to the rhetorical, play and affective aspects of E-E connect with such findings.

Tufte has noted that the traditional concept of entertainment-education which has been the forte of using media for education can have powerful impact for social change if properly carried on through discussions. According to him, most of the women demonstrated a strong identification with the emotional television dramas. They confirm a point made by Fuenzalida: the fundamental emotional relation between media, culture and everyday life. Tele-novellas often proved more relevant to the Brazilian female audience than news broadcasts. Fuenzalida (1994) argues that we should take emotions seriously. Tele-novellas due to their widespread popularity in Latin American countries, constitute a much more important and relevant educational instrument than news programs or public service announcements. "The redundancy of the serials makes its attraction rationally inexplicable: but the interest is, precisely, emotional" (Fuenzalida, 1997: 25). This perspective also calls for modesty in expectations concerning the impacts of an E-E intervention: "The educational efficiency of the televised messages depends much more on the viewers' perception than on the intentions of the broadcasting station" (Fuenzalida, 1994). Tele-novellas increase dialogue and debate, and can break the silence around controversial or taboo issues. In Brazil, tele-novellas from the late 1980s onwards introduced taboo issues, be it a love affair between a married woman and a priest, or a love affair between two people who later in the story turn out to be brother and sister. Such issues question the norms and values upon which personal relationships in Brazilian society are based, and challenge the moral codes. When, embedded in identifiable settings and with realistic characters in a tele-novella, these issues are not normally rejected but get debated. In HIV-AIDS communication, taboo issues can be introduced, and discussing about these after seeing the programmes can help break the silence about, and the stigma concerning people living with HIV.

Despite portraying a material world far from the viewers' own lives, Brazilian tele-novellas touch everyday experiences which are highly recognizable for audiences. Tele-novellas articulate a sense of social and cultural membership and belonging to communities, both national, gendered and often across class, counter-balancing the many processes of socio-cultural and political-economic marginalization experienced by low-income citizens in Brazil. Accordingly, tele-novellas become an important way of exercising cultural citizenship in the sense of finding recognition of everyday concerns. Viewers recognize in tele-novellas the themes of striving to participate as members of different communities, transforming their use of tele-novellas into a process that promotes belongingness and citizenship. Given the massive presence of nationally produced fiction programmes in the lives of Brazilians and many other Latin American audiences, and increasingly elsewhere, this genre has an enormous potential for promoting public debates, thus exercising some degree of advocacy, in addition to articulating identities as citizens.

In other developing countries many watch serials or soaps as these have characters with whom the audiences identify intensely. The life-examples of the characters – their joys and sorrows, struggles and agonies – parallel those in real lives and hence the audiences draw confidently lessons from the way characters resolve their problems.

d. *People-based participatory research*

Research on the effect of media exposure to social change is also a major incentives in the popularization of media for development. Such research programmes involve the public at large and draw attention to the scope of a programme to create awareness among the target audience. For example doing research on the effect of an entertainment-education programme in a village on the target audience would show how much discussion and study of the issue at hand is happening at the village level. But it is possible that there may be no discussions or studies, yet people who watch the programmes get the message right and they change their lives accordingly. Participatory research as described by Rajesh Tandon (1983) is a process of liberation which begins with faith in the people, the beneficiaries of development, and in their capacity to take their own decisions. It believes that the rural poor are voiceless not because they have nothing to say, but because nobody cares to listen to them. More fundamentally, they constitute the silent majority because they have no say in the decision-making structures of society. In this perspective it is legitimate to say that development begins with listening to the people. To accept this in actual practice is not easy, even for voluntary agencies in development process. Participatory research tries to get the people involved in the cause-effect study of local problems.

Obviously, group action motivated by research teams have more efficacy as has been studied in the empowering role of local groups of micro-lenders in the Grameen Bank system of Bangladesh (Papa – Auwal – Singhal, 1995, 1997) and in the use of entertainment programmes for development over radio in India (Papa – al., 2000). It has been noticed that these groups involved in participatory research can also animate the villagers and motivate them for change. The role of the development communicators, planners and researchers as facilitators are derived from participatory research methodologies much prevalent today in developing countries (E. M. Rogers and W. B. Hart, in Mody, 2003: 270).

e. *People's movements and empowerment efforts*

In some countries the NGO movement has come together to form people's movements, that can highlight the kind of development that the people would really benefit from. Obviously this means tremendous communication at grass-root levels involving participation at every stage of decision-making, sharing, collaboration and final empowerment.

The recent research on people's movements and the use of media in such movements develops the idea of Servaes that movements are the major actors in the development process. Interestingly enough, these approaches are not particularly new. The model was clearly established in numerous institutions in the late 1800s and early 1900s in the form of the union movement, the cooperative movement and many other movements. Unfortunately, hegemonic interests which have controlled development institutions (such as the agricultural colleges and the rural extension systems) in the US and in some European countries opposed independent people's organizations from the beginning and propagated the modernization paradigm. Their primary interest was to continue to use the development bureaucracies as a form of hegemonic social control.

However, in the present context, what is lacking is the explanation of how groups come into existence and reach the stage of being ready for catalytic action from service providers. More important is the issue: how can local groups develop into large scale organizations aiming to transform the power structures around them? Often the presence of the NGO sector has only acted as a bottleneck in the formation of people's movements, as these prefer to work alone and manage their finances, daunted by one-upmanship and competition.

Empowerment has already been dealt with as a concern in the secondary stage of DevCom. Liberation from oppressive structures and empowerment of the people to take to action by themselves is in fact the real concern in DevCom. Ideologically these have been accepted conceptually, but in reality it is a long way off from realization. The struggle therefore continues. The power of group media like community radio, home-made videos, story telling forms, street plays, etc. in empowering people to take responsibilities and make calculated decisions have been proven beyond doubt in many of the developing countries.

Local groups can surely play an empowering role; even individuals in local areas too can play this role. Locals who have a high sense of awareness achieved through media exposure can also take to animation programmes among the rural folk to change attitudes, to force development issues. For example, in several villages in India, the practice of excessive dowry has been combated this way. Organizing for social changes has been done by several NGO groups. If these take on to larger, national proportions as people's movements, there is much hope for participatory media animating development.

5. The helplessness of development communication.
A Third World perspective

In our seminar sessions, for those from the Third World, certain issues become clear. An important challenge for those working in DevCom is the lack of human dignity among the receivers. Persons in the Third World, especially those living below the poverty line, need to feel that they too are human beings and that they need to live respectable human lives. Basic human rights like the right to live a decent life, education, drinking water, participation in the democratic process, etc. are denied to many people. These are caused due to corruption and systematic exploitation of the less privileged people. Media can surely highlight these issues. People can be made aware of these and prepared to take action against these oppressive structures. However, what happens if they are ruthlessly pulled down and massacred as it often happens in Third World countries where systematic oppression and exploitation have become the order of the day? Land reforms or any other ways to better the situation of the oppressed group is never allowed. Political structures are often hand in glove with oppressive structures. Media controlled by the ruling classes is often helpless in such situations.

Today one needs to say that the very structure on which nations are founded are faulty, state governments are not able to sustain steady development, and democracies are faltering. The basic human avarice and greed for power have debilitated the functioning of many positive development mechanisms. Will the upper class who indulges in all forms of research on development communication, really get to the action that will weaken people of their ilk in society? This is the big question that has pulled the plug on all attempts at realizing DevCom.

There are too many financial, political and technical problems in the Third World. It is easy to speak of plans and policies, but when it comes to implementation, there are no committed personnel ready to carry these out. Eventually it remains at the level of lip service. Several of the development agencies and plans set up by the government or non-government agencies aren't capable of withstanding the enormous challenges. Often many development communicators are trained as subject-matter specialists (agriculturists, anthropologists, environmentalists etc) and not as communicators, social activists, educators and animators, with a generous heart, who want to reach out in service.

6. Conclusion

In fact, the real causes of underdevelopment are the very structural system which is geared to the oppression of a group. Development of the upper sections is always seen at the expense of the lower sections. There is no sense of an egalitarian society in many of the underdeveloped countries. NGOs are not able to tackle this massive problem. Democratically elected or even a dictatorship government that aims primarily at an egalitarian society alone can bring about development of all in any country. In such a system of government mass media and group media can play major roles in development. If development is to be understood as the mobilization of all the human, social and economic resources to better the quality of life of all the people, certain attitudes and conditions need to be met in every country. These include:

1. Unity in the community: no in-fighting and self-satisfaction may be encouraged. These should be ruthlessly dealt with.
2. Selfless leadership, working only for the common good.
3. Making the government personnel responsible for developments in the villages: create awareness among the people so that they demand that the government machinery work. The NGOs need to work in tandem with the government with financial support only from the government. Based on these assumptions, let us see what the future holds.

However, today with worldwide forces of globalization, privatization, commercialization, entertainment and "informatization" dominating the media, the cry for human rights continues in several corners of the Third World. And it remains a major challenge for the development communicator.

Bibliographical references

BOAL, A. (1979), *Theatre of the oppressed,* London: Pluto Press.
BROWN, A. (2001), "Strategies for the globalization of culture in the 21st century", in M. RICHARDS – P. N. THOMAS – Z. NAIN, *Communication and Development, the Freirian Connection,* New Jersey: Hampton Press.
BRUCK, P. – ROACH, C. (1993), "Dealing with reality: News media and the promotion of peace", in C. ROACH, ed., *Communication and culture in war and peace*, Newbury Park: Sage.
GARCÍA CANCLINI, N. (1995), *Hybrid cultures: strategies for entering and leaving modernity;* transl. C. L. Chiappari – S. L. López; foreword by R. Rosaldo, Minneapolis; London: University of Minnesota Press.
EINSIEDEL, E. F. (2000), "Border Crossings: Gender, Development and Communication", in K. WILKINS, ed., *Redeveloping Communication for Social Change,* Lanham, MD: Rowman & Littlefield Publishers.
FAIR, J. E. – SHAH, H. (1997), "Continuities and discontinuities in communication and development research since 1958", *Journal of International Communication* 4, 3-25.
FREIRE, P. (1972), *Pedagogy of the Oppressed,* Harmondsworth: Penguin.

FUENZALIDA, V. (1994), *La apropriacion educativa de la telenovela*, Santiago: CPU.
FUENZALIDA, V. (1997), *Television y Cultura Cotidiana. La influencia social de la TV percibida desde la cultura cotidiana de la audiencia*, Santiago: CPU.
HORNIK, R. C. (1988), *Development Communication: Information, Agriculture and Nutrition in the Third World*, New York: Logan.
MARTÍN-BARBERO, M. (1993), *Communication, culture and hegemony: from the media to mediations*, transl. E. Fox – R. A. White; with an introduction by P. Schlesinger, London – Newbury Park – New Delhi: Sage Publications.
MODY, B., ed. (2003), *International and Developmental Communication*, Thousand Oaks, Sage.
PAPA, M. J. – AUWAL, M. A. – SINGHAL, A. (1995), "Dialectic of control and emancipation in organizing for social change: a multi-theoretic study of the Grameen Bank in Bangladesh", *Communication Theory* 5.
PAPA, M. J. – AUWAL, M. A. – SINGHAL, A. (1997), "Organizing for social change within concertive control system: member identification, empowerment, and the masking of discipline", *Communication Monographs* 64.
PAPA, M. J. – AL. (2000), "Entertainment-education and social change: an analysis of parasocial interaction, social learning, collective efficacy, and paradoxical communication", *Journal of Communication* 50/4.
QUEBRAL, N. C. (1975), *The making of a development communicator*, Laguna: University of the Philippines, Los Banos-College of Agriculture.
RIANO, P., ed. (1994), *Women in Grassroots Communications, Furthering Social Change*, Thousand Oaks: Sage.
RODRIGUEZ, C. (2001), *Fissures in the Mediascape: An International Study of Citizen's Media*, Cresskill, NJ: Hampton Press.
SERVAES, J. (1989), *One world multiple cultures*, Amsterdam: Amersfoort.
SERVAES, J. (1996), "Participatory communication and research in development settings", in J. SERVAES – T. JACOBSON – S. A. WHITE, ed., *Participatory communication for social change*, Thousand Oaks: Sage.
SERVAES, J. – JACOBSON, T. – WHITE, S. A., ed. (1996), *Participatory communication for social change*, Thousand Oaks: Sage
SINGHAL, A. – ROGERS, E. M. (2002), *Entertainment-education: A communication strategy for social change*, Mahwah, NJ: Lawrence Erlbaum.

STEEVES, L. H. (2003), "Development Communication as Marketing, Collective Resistance and Spiritual Awakening, A Feminist Critique", in B. MODY, ed., *International and Developmental Communication*, Thousand Oaks, Sage.

TANDON, R. (1983), *Participatory research and evaluation: experiments in research as a process of liberation*, New Delhi: Indian Social Institute.

TUFTE, T. (2003), "HIV/AIDS Communication-Beyond Marketing, Towards Empowerment", in U. CARLSSON – C. VON FEILITZEN, ed., *Yearbook 2003 of The UNESCO International Clearinghouse on Children, Youth and Media*, Göteborg: Nordicom-Göteborg University.

WILKINS, K. G., ed. (2000), *Redeveloping Communication for Social Change: Theory, Practice and Power*, Lanham, MD: Rowman & Littlefield Publishers.

FROM THE BEGINNING TO A FUTURE

Communicating with the world?
Maria Way

L'articolo esamina alcuni dei problemi e dei successi della Compagnia di Gesù nel campo della comunicazione, e suggerisce alcune strade da seguire per il futuro. Il contributo si basa sull'esperienza ventennale dell'autrice, e non intende offrire un resoconto storico completo, essendo disponibili ulteriori studi a cura di autori come John E. O'Brien, che scrive sull'apostolato della comunicazione nella Compagnia, e Alain Woodrow, con la sua storia della Compagnia di Gesù.

This article considers some of the problems and successes of Jesuits in communication and looks at possible ways forward. A complete history is not needed as O'Brien (1999) discusses the social communications apostolate of the Society and Woodrow (2001) the history of the Society.

For 20 years I have worked with Jesuits in the communication apostolate and the Centro Interdisciplinare sulla Comunicazione Sociale has been part of my life. I have worked with and for CICS' staff, visited, helped to organize events and even studied there. People have continually asked me the question: "Why Communication?", but without communication where would we be?

1. Church as medium

The Roman Catholic Church is herself a medium with many purposes, her main one being to spread the Gospel message. Since the Church's earliest days, she has used every means possible to tell her story. In the early centuries, when the Church was forbidden in the Roman Empire, disguised pictures were used, e.g., Christ shown as Apollo. Through plastic arts, the spoken and written word, the message was spread. For many who do not know the Society, Jesuits are known for three things – plots, intelligence and the Society's heritage to the world through scholarship, music, art and architecture. The Rome church of the Gesù was designed and decorated by two Jesuits, Tristano and and the better known Pozzo. Four centuries later it is still a building with the "Wow Factor". It was designed to be "awesome" in the word's original sense and to encourage an understanding of the Church's message following the Reformation. Despite the Society's attraction to artists and perhaps because wealthy patrons began to use those artists and architects to adorn "their private villas and palaces", as Fr. Arrupe suggests (Arrupe, 1972), artists who wished to join the Society began to be turned away. Today there seems to be a similar antipathy towards those who might choose the mass media as part of their apostolate.

The mass media are seen, in Chris Woodhead's words[1], as a "Mickey Mouse Subject" to study. He seemed to find no contradiction in using a media reference to describe these studies, which I believe only served to underline how important it is to study them. At my own university, the University of Westminster, London, we have a long tradition of teaching media going back to the 19th century. When the university was the Royal Polytechnic Institute, photography courses were instituted and the Lumière Brothers showed the UK's first commercial film there in February 1896. The number of students applying for media-related courses has grown exponentially and an early 2005 BBC Radio 4 programme advised that media studies students were the most employable British graduates. Studying media is not an easy option, as many seem to think. The media industries are big business and spread messages, for good or ill, to the world's people. While there is this growth in media studies, the number of Jesuits involved in communication and media has apparently dropped[2].

The Society deems writing an acceptable academic pursuit and Jesuits were noted for their theatrical productions in the 16th-18th centuries (O'Brien, 1999: 10; Arrupe, 1972), but despite Jesuit involvement in cinema, notably Fr. Lord's involvement in Hollywood, then as founder of the League of Decency and ghostwriter of 1936's first film encyclical, *Vigilanti Cura*, those Jesuits who go into the industry are often looked upon as odd. Yet many who do are good advertisements for the Church and the Society of Jesus, not always taken seriously within the Society, but bringing its charism to the world in ways many outsiders can understand. This is leavening of the type Biernatzki (1978: 6) discusses – bringing the Church into the media rather than making her own media product. Is this because the mass media are, on the whole, ephemeral? In a letter to Peter Favre, St. Ignatius writes that "one may write hurriedly out of the abundance of the heart, with or without a predetermined order. But this should not be true of the principal letter, which should always show signs of care, so that it can be passed about for the purpose of giving edification". While radio or television programmes may take weeks or months to make, once broadcast they cannot be withdrawn. The letter cannot be rewritten and so becomes possibly dangerous. The Society's Constitutions (Part 8)[3] believe communication results in union, unity encouraged by the letters, mentioned above, but para 675 does tend to suggest that communication is for edification only, while General Congregation Document 35 recognises that media are not just for relaxation but are also a means for expression and as part of the "culture of the image"[4].

2. The Centre for the Study of Communication and Culture and the Cavalletti conferences

Although I never had the honour of meeting Fr. Arrupe, he is a man I hold in the highest esteem. An article in *The Tablet*[5] describes Arrupe as visionary because he began the Jesuit Refugee Service in 1980. One of his visionary acts, I believe, was starting CSCC in the 1970s to act as a bridge between the Church and academia. Too often, it seems, those in Church communication try to reinvent the wheel. The Society and the Church do not have the funding to undertake enormous research projects like the recent USA "Faith and the Family in America" project. They can, however, provide expertise and assistance and be open to liaisons with academic institutes and personnel. This is exactly what CSCC did. I am now introducing CSCC's journal *Communication Research Trends* to a new generation of students – who, without exception, what ever their faith, praise it for its breadth of vision and scope. *Trends*, of course, is just one of the many journals Jesuits produce.

When I worked at CSCC, I met many academics with whom I am still in contact, all of whom regret CSCC's move from London to the USA and later into some form of cyberspace. The possibility of coming to London, one of the most multicultural cities in the world, hub for many airlines, to use CSCC's library and contacts, to stay in the house and interact with the Jesuits who lived there, was an admirable way for Jesuits to spread the Gospel in a non-combative way. This contact expanded with the institution of the Cavalletti seminars, where Church personnel working in media or teaching communication had the opportunity to interact with people from the industry and secular universities. The series' success was in no small part attributable to Bishop Peter Henrici, SJ and the charisma of Fr. Robert A. White, SJ, who is well known not only as a priest, but also as an academic of international renown. From the day that I met Bob White in the mid-1980s he became a sort of surrogate father. I am not alone in this. For many CICS students, he was the one to whom they turned for personal or academic assistance. From its early beginnings, with few students, CICS has grown enormously. While the number of Jesuits in communication may have dropped, the number of students studying communication and media in Jesuit universities has grown. Students come from around the world, Catholic and non-Catholic, lay and clergy. This is how it should be. It follows the tradition of the early society set up by St. Ignatius and, perhaps particularly, St. Francis Xavier in going out to the world, converting and training the "native" populations with whom they came into contact[6]. In this age of multiculturalism and plurality of religion, conversion is often considered one of the scandals of the early Society's activities. We are now more likely to enter into dialogue with other faiths. Even if students at Jesuit universities are not "converted", they will always be affected in some way by their experiences there. We should make every effort to ensure that those experiences are positive.

3. The Jesuit family

Religious communities are families and, as Ammerman says, "religion has always had a strong interest in the family, because families were seen as the way in which the next generation would be socialized into, taught the traditions of the religious community".

The Jesuit family does not consist of Jesuits alone, but their birth families and those on whom Jesuits have an effect. Communicating love of the Gospel, the Church's message and the Society's charism is vital. Too often it is difficult for Jesuits to communicate even with each other, but this is partly because they live in community with people with whom they have not chosen to live. Too often, clashes of personality disable the ability to view confreres for their abilities rather than their community presence. In his letter to Favre, St. Ignatius called for communication by letter, outlining the working and spiritual life of individual Jesuits, but realized such letters often contained irrelevancies which, although important to that Jesuit, were not for open consumption. In consequence, St. Ignatius chose those things which he believed would "give all of you some pleasure in our Lord and edification for those who hear them for the first time".

Inclusion in the Jesuit family may be the first time such edification is given to students. Particularly in the Western world, the number of priests is dropping. In my own diocese de Bortano (2005: 36) reports an increase in the number entering seminaries, but we still do not have sufficient priests being ordained to replace those who leave, retire or die. In the same journal, Hirst (2005: 28) reports that in every continent except Europe, the number of Catholics has grown in the 21st century, by 15 million in 2003 alone, to a total of 1.086 billion. *Fides*, who issued these figures, reports also that only in Asia has there been an increase in the number of young men training to be priests and that there are now 2.677 lay Catholics to every priest. Across the globe, the Church is responsible for 64.000 nurseries or daycare centres, 28.000 primary schools and 39.000 secondary schools and more than 55 million pupils attend these schools. The Church also manages 80.000 hospitals, clinics, homes of the aged and disabled, orphanages and counseling centres. It is evident that with a decreasing number of priests and, more particularly, the decrease in the number of sisters, the Catholic presence in many institutions will increasingly become a lay one. It is here that inclusion into the Jesuit family comes into its own. This brings me to the topic of hierarchy.

4. Hierarchy

Like most of the remainder of the world, the Church is an hierarchical institution. There are the Pope, the Curia, the clergy, the sisters and the rest of us. During John Paul II's reign, this was particularly noticeable as the Church became increasingly "popecentric". Anyone who has had dealings with the Church at a level above that of the parish, knows that the pope (who ever he may be) does not run the Church on his own, but with a cohort of assistants at the Curia and input from "the field". The continual presence on our screens (TV, computer and even cinema) of John Paul tended to underscore this notion of popecentricity. Too often, even today, the clergy tend to treat the Church's lay members as a lower order, one that does not quite understand the faith's intricacies. Yet it is these lay people who are the Church, who run parishes on a day to day basis, dealing with things that parish priests cannot (and should not) do alone. It is their hard-earned money that keeps the Church afloat. Without the laity, the Church would not exist. While many in the Church's upper echelons go out to parishes at weekends, as do some of those who teach in universities, they tend to be visitors rather than being deeply involved in parish activities. They have a tendency to lose touch with life's realities (there are evidently exceptions here). Communicating with the laity is a key factor in the Church's communication apostolate.

5. Formation for Communication

If, as mentioned above, there is only one priest to every 2.677 lay Catholics, then face to face communication, which should always be the ideal, becomes increasingly difficult. In Rome, this is difficult to comprehend when there seems to be a superfluity of priests. In some countries, or areas of countries, the ratio of priests to laity is even lower. The Anglican problem of having far too few clergy for far too many parishes has become a Catholic reality. How, then, does the Church and, more important in this context, the Society of Jesus, cope with this?

While St. Ignatius wrote of the Society's need for communication, Document 9, General Congregation [GC] 31, "Training of Scholastics", advised that the juniorate, in an attempt to have a "vital knowledge of man and of the modern world" should be trained not only in literature, history and sciences, but should also have their aesthetic senses developed since, "skilled in the arts of writing and speaking, they can become better preachers of the Gospel of Christ". Additionally, they should be given access to audiovisual media in order to use these successfully in their apostolate. The document recognizes that works of art exert great influence in the "growth and unfolding of human personality, or to the development of civil society, or to the mutual union of men, a union that paves the way to union with God".

Jesuits are encouraged to use arts to the best possible effect in the missions and have, it says, "achieved greatness in poetry, music, the theater, and architecture", while communication between Jesuits engaged in artistic activities is encouraged.

It is not until GC31 (1967) Document 15 that mass media are again mentioned. Their influence and presence, it says, "grow in intensity and extent in the modern world" [594] and are an important means of expression, "suitable aid[s] to our apostolate in many ministries of the Society". Here mention is made of the Second Vatican Council's decrees on social communication (as the Church tends to designate media) and suggests that Jesuits in formation should be media trained, both to take advantage of specific possibilities and for the purposes of training youth and preaching. It is, however, here that problems may be seen to arise. Para 602 puts forward the notion that Provincials should choose men "endowed with a religious spirit and other gifts" to train so that they can direct others and centres should be set up, where needed and possible, to make this possible. Here there is the idea that such formation should be undertaken "in house", so to speak, perhaps this is something that should be considered later.

Document 36, GC31 (1967), discusses the special objective of care of Vatican Radio, which since it began in February, 1931, has been entrusted to the Society. A Society commitment to the continuation of this work appeared in GC34 Document 15. Centro Televisivo Vaticano is similarly run by the Jesuits. Document 37 called for an internal Information Service to inform the Society at large and the historical preface to GC 31[7] notes that "not a few people" had asked that Jesuits and non-Jesuits be informed of the Congregation's actions, but also noted that some caution needed to be exercised and news issued was subject to a set of norms for delegates, established by the Father General, and regulations privately agreed by the delegate fathers. Such a document only encourages the notion of a "secret society", one of the prevalent views of the Society of Jesus. In interview, Archbishop John P. Foley, President of the Pontifical Council for Social Communications, stressed the need for transparency and truth from the Church. Notions such as those in this historical preface do not seem to fit into this notion. Nor does this fit with GC34, Document 15's call for freedom of the press and information. One acknowledges that any institution needs a certain amount of privacy in its internal dealings, but transparency is a vital need in modern society. The public relations disaster which ensued from the Church's lack of truth and transparency in relation to statements and decisions on the spate of abuse cases, which became public knowledge in recent years, only underlines this need. One cannot place the blame solely on the shoulders of those priests and/or sisters involved, nor on their superiors or bishops. Transparency must be evident from top to bottom of any organization if that organization is to be believed and respected.

By GC32 (1874-1875) Society regulations had been put in place for public information and a laudably international group of Jesuits was set up to produce bulletins in five languages. GC32's Decree 4 referenced four major apostolic directions (O'Brien, 1999: 35) including "Communication with 'vast number of people we cannot reach individually'" as well as Decree 6 on formation, which decreed that Jesuits be trained in modern communication "enabling the Jesuit to be one with the people to whom he is sent, capable of communicating with them" (O'Brien, 1999: 36). Evidently, such training would require that Jesuits be capable of speaking a number of languages, but also, one would suppose, able to utilize the mass media. It is now fairly normal practice for anyone in a business or institution who might be asked to deal with media to undergo some sort of training. Has this been done? I will return to this later.

To my mind, it is seriously worrying that Decree 1 of GC33 (1983) says that "the Society should promote the apostolate of the Social Communications Media which, like education and intellectual work, reaches large numbers of people and so permits a more universal service to mankind" (O'Brien, 1999: 36).

Why is social communication separated from education and intellectual work as though they are separate? Much of social communication's output is educational in nature. Lord Reith's intention that the BBC be "Educational, Informative and Entertaining" would seem to uphold this. As for intellectual input, there is a real need for research into media and communication. Programming without research enabling an understanding of the type of programme needed and/or whether it will be well received, is not acceptable. With exceptions, there are far too many religious programmes that appeal to only a small section of believers. Research seems to show that programmes are often chosen by pure serendipity.

By 1995 and GC34, Decree 15 recognised cultural shifts and the need for critical consumers and practitioners. It also outlined various areas which the Society should address (O'Brien, 1999: 36). While Document 15, GC34[8], looks to the future, the growth of the mass media and the information revolution, it has many sections which display an antipathy to media. Words like "negative", "ephemeral", "materialist" and "consumer-dominated" are used. I have already discussed the media's ephemeral nature, but we must look at the negative sides of the media and the media must be "consumer-dominated". It is only by appealing to those consumers that an audience is found. Unless high quality programming is produced it will not attract non-believers, nor even many believers. Serendipity will not come into play. Too much money is wasted on bad programming which can actually damage the Church and her message's transmission. Again, I will return to this later.

Fr. Rochford, SJ, Secretary of JesCom, has written that there have been various stages in the more recent development of the communications apostolate (Rochford, 2001):

- Pioneers and Early Adaptors – an emphasis on technology.
- Glory years when work was taken for granted – an emphasis on content.
- Discovering the audience and finding a two-way street – emphasis on communication.

He also suggests possible roles for the Jesuit and asks a series of questions about ways forward.

6. What can we undertake given our concrete talents and abilities?

- The Society can provide training and formation in its educational establishments and should also use these establishments to train lay people who can collaborate with the Society and the greater Church, either by working with them or by taking that charism into the main stream media.
- There will be men and lay collaborators who have talents in all three of Rochford's phases above and they should be allowed to use them.
- The Society can use those men who have an aptitude for the communications apostolate to work in media of various sorts. It should not appoint people to do work which is beyond their capacity or talent, just because they are Jesuits. Too often I have seen Church personnel (not just Jesuits!) appointed to jobs they would never have been given in the "real" world. Bad staff produce a bad product – just as bad teachers discourage students.
- Use the talent that is there and, above all, put the money and training in place to encourage and develop it. It may be that it is better, as was often the case in the past, to send a Jesuit to an "outside" institution to undertake training. In the long run, this may be a cheaper option.
- Rather than utilizing somebody to teach classes outside his area of expertise, it may be better to bring in somebody who (lay or clergy) can teach in his/her own area.

7. Where can we participate?

- The Society can participate in education, through teaching, research and in media companies. Only through working in mainstream media can Jesuits (and their lay collaborators) truly understand the industry's nature. Church media is outside the main stream.

- The Society should ensure that specialists (Jesuit or lay collaborator) are on the guest lists of media companies. The major companies are always looking for people who can really communicate their enthusiasm and give a well-informed "sound bite". It is irrelevant whether these people are actually considered part of the communication apostolate, not all good communicators work in this area. These people should be given at least a basic training in media appearance.
- The Society should be prepared to let, and indeed encourage, its men be used as "experts" for research purposes in both mainstream media productions and secular university projects, building on the work already done by some Jesuits.

8. What are we allowed to do by those in power?

The answer to this will evidently vary depending on which country is being considered or, indeed on the Society itself. However, the Society should take St. Ignatius' lead and push the boundaries to enable justice and truth to prevail.

9. What can we afford?

- Providing education is expensive, but this is bread that, cast upon the waters, will pay back a hundredfold.
- Developing the research profile of Jesuits in academic institutions is vital. Not only should they undertake research projects and publish through secular publishing houses, but they should also attend professional conferences, not just those arranged by the Church. Secular university staff have to publish through independent publishers and give papers at conferences and if Jesuits do not do this also, they will not be taken seriously academically.
- If the Society can provide staff who can make media productions or run media institutions that draw in an audience and, if possible, make a profit, then this should be encouraged. If not, then talented staff should be sent to work in secular institutions, thus encouraging that leavening Biernatzki (1978) mentioned. Bad programming, bad websites, reflect badly on the Church, the Society and their message,
- There have been a number of institutions based on the interests of one Jesuit. When he retires or dies, the institution also dies. This is

not only a bad economic move, but reflects badly on the Society. If something is started, continuation must be secured.

- Institutions that have proved their worth should be financially encouraged, but an office dedicated to fundraising for the communication apostolate should be developed. There are outside funding possibilities, but utilizing Jesuits to seek funding is a waste of manpower when this could easily be done by lay collaborators imbued with the Jesuit ethos. Such offices are fairly standard in universities.

- The Society cannot afford to consider social communications as separate from education and intellectual work. All are sides of the same coin, transmitting a message in the best possible way.

- The communications apostolate must be encouraged. Only by communication can bridges be built with believer and unbeliever, through face-to-face, one to many and electronic communication.

- The work of CICS must continue and develop, not just to provide diocesan directors of communication (there are often many people from the same diocese and so this is impossible), but also graduates to go into the world imbued with the Jesuit charism, prepared, like St. Ignatius, to be adaptable. CICS should continue to make it possible for the able student, from what ever country, lay or clerical, to develop his/her potential. Programmes need content, universities need staff and CICS students can take Jesuit-based culture learnt from both staff and other students, back to their own culture.

NOTES

[1] Chris Woodhead is the ex-Chief Inspector of Schools in the U.K.
[2] 2005 letter (n.d.) of Jacob Srampickal, SJ, Director, CICS, Università Pontificia Gregoriana, to Jesuit Communicators Worldwide.
[3] *Constitutions of the Society of Jesus*: Part Eight, "The Bonds of Union", http://www.sjweb.info/jescom/documents/Constitutions_PartVIII_eng.swf, accessed 10/10/2005.
[4] General Congregation 31, Document 35: The Mass Media Para 597, http://www.sjweb.info/jescom/documents/GC31_documents_eng.swf, accessed 10/10/2005.
[5] "Jesuit Jubilee", *The Tablet*, 29th October 2005, 17.
[6] See Woodrow (2001) for an account of this. "Native" is here not meant in a pejorative sense, but was the term used at that time. We would now probably use "indigenous peoples".

[7] *Historical Prefaces from General Congregations 31 and 32*, "General Congregation 31: note from the historical preface", http://www.sjweb.info/jescom/documents/GC31&32_historical_notes_eng.swf, accessed 24/10/2005.
[8] General Congregation 34, Document 15, "Communication: A New Culture", http://www.sjweb.info/jescom/documents/GC34_communication_eng.swf, accessed 24/10/2005.

Bibliographical references

AMMERMAN, N., Interview with Kim Lawton, http://www.pbs.org/wnet/religionandethics/week909/interview1.html, accessed 28/10/2005.
ARRUPE, P. (1972), "Art and the Spirit of the Society of Jesus: An Address to the Jesuit Institute of the Arts", a talk given at Mondragone, Frascati, Italy on June 16th, 1972.
BIERNATZKI, W. E. (1978), *Catholic Communication Research: Topics and a Rationale*, The Research Facilitator Unit for Social Communication: London.
DE BORTANO, I. (2005), "Upturn in Westminster vocations", *The Tablet*, 29th October, 36.
FOLEY, J. P., Interview with Maria Way, 17/05/2002.
HIRST, M. (2005), "More Catholics, but not in Europe", *The Tablet*, 29th October.
LOYOLA, ST. IGNATIUS, *Letter to Peter Favre I*, 236-238, Letter 58, Rome, December 10th, 1542, http://www.sjweblinfo/jescom/documents/ ignatius_to_faber_eng.swf, accessed 10/10/2005.
O'BRIEN, J. E. (1999), *Jesuit Apostolate in Social Communication*, Rome: JesCom.
ROCHFORD, T. (2001), "A Perspective on Communication", A Presentation to JesCom-Latin America in São Leopoldo, Brazil, August, 2001, http://www.sjweb.info/jescom/documents/Jescom_LA_eng.swf, accessed 24/10/2005.
WOODHEAD, C. (2004), Interview with Maria Way on Student Radio, University of Westminster.
WOODROW, A. (2001), *Gesuiti: una storia di poteri. Storia dei 450 anni dell'ordine più prestigioso della Chiesa Cattolica, a trent'anni dalla svolta che lo ha visto scegliere tra il potere di un tempo e le sue radici missionarie*, transl. A. Pavia, Roma: Newton & Compton Editori [originally published as *Les jesuites* (1984, 1990), Paris: Éditions Jean-Claude Larrés].

Some twenty-first century challenges facing Catholics in communication formation

William E. Biernatzki, SJ

Il compito del comunicatore cristiano è di proclamare il contenuto e le implicazioni della propria fede nel mondo contemporaneo. Per compiere questa missione, egli deve tener conto di diversi fattori, incluso lo sviluppo dell'insegnamento della Chiesa, soprattutto l'insegnamento morale. Deve dimostrare il coraggio e la formazione teologica e professionale tali da poter offrire al mondo odierno una chiave di lettura davvero cristiana. Questo compito richiede un alto livello di capacità professionale e un acuto senso etico. Richiede anche che il comunicatore mantenga una rete di contatti con altri comunicatori cristiani, condividendo con essi i medesimi fini. Apertura ed accoglienza verso le idee altrui sono essenziali.

The communication apostolate, for both clerics and lay people, depends on special training and preparation. It also bears a heavy burden of responsibility for professional integrity and courage. Those who share in the work of the Catholic communication apostolate automatically assume a degree of leadership, guiding others to accurately evaluate their experience of the world and how Catholic teaching should be integrated into that evaluation. That leadership brings with it the requirement to interpret the "signs of the times" correctly, with no concessions to worldly ambition or ideologies. The greatest challenge for Catholic communicators at the beginning of the twenty-first century is to be true to that requirement and to maintain that commitment throughout their careers.

The Centre for the Study of Communication and Culture in London (CSCC), with which Robert White was associated for many years, was intended to promote professionalism in the field by bringing the recent findings of communication research more easily within the reach of those actively involved in religious communication work. White was instrumental in determining the direction of the CSCC's research and publication from 1978 until he moved to the communication program of the Pontifical Gregorian University in Rome in 1988. Both at the CSCC and in the Gregorian's Interdisciplinary Centre for Social Communications (CICS) he has done much to shape the Church's response to the changing communication environment of the modern world by training Catholic communicators to use technology effectively to preach the Gospel and by establishing and maintaining links between those communicators and the latest research findings.

The CSCC collaborated with non-Catholic communication organizations with generally shared goals. This sharing, without compromising the Catholic identity of what the CSCC was trying to accomplish, helped give it an outreach to the wider world of communication researchers, and thereby greater depth and effectiveness in its work with Catholic communicators. The same spirit of outreach encouraged activities within the Church that looked to overcome provincialism. Provincialism has been a major threat to Catholic communication efforts since it tends to limit them to narrowly-defined spheres of action, hedged by diocesan or national boundaries or by those of their sponsoring religious orders, schools, etc., rather than reaching out to the whole world.

For some years after Vatican II the Church enjoyed a period of openness, in which communication studies and practice thrived. Pope John XXIII threw open the windows of the Church, allowing fresh air to circulate and fresh perspectives to replace sterile outlooks that not only had outlived their usefulness but were proving detrimental to the Church's ability to go out effectively to preach the Gospel to all nations.

A recent study in the United States, as cited by New York Times religion columnist Peter Steinfels and quoted by theologian Richard P. McBrien, found that only 10 percent of seminarians are "highly qualified" for their academic work, while just over half are "adequately qualified". More than one-third had poor educations or other disabilities. Even many of the "highly qualified" were found to resist "the learning enterprise because it threatens their preconceived ideas about theology" (Klimoski – O'Neil – Schuth, 2005). There is little reason to believe that the situation is any better in the rest of the world.

Catholics who want to work in Catholic media face certain challenges which must be met frankly and honestly if their work is to be true to the Gospel and to their vocation. Both anti-intellectualism and disparagement of the social apostolate must be strictly avoided if we are to be true to the Gospel.

The Catholic media in many parts of the world – like the secular media – are coming to be dominated by well-funded right-wing forces, which allow little voice for accurate representations of Catholic social doctrine as it has evolved since publication of the encyclical *Rerum Novarum* (1891). We must resist those forces that have not only hindered the full proclamation of the Church's social doctrine but have even backtracked on the implementation of the goals of the Second Vatican Council. The forces of laissez-faire capitalism are deeply implicated in this retrenchment and, despite the lure of their money, have to be recognized and condemned as being not only anti-Conciliar but as essentially anti-Catholic.

In recent times knowledgeable Catholics have come to recognize – in contrast to what they may have claimed fifty years ago – that Catholic teaching on some questions has changed over the centuries – 180 degrees, on some points! David Hollenbach, SJ, commenting on the new *Compendium of the Social Doctrine of the Church*, notes how it provides new theological depth for understanding "the link between Christian faith and human rights in the dignity of the human person as created in the image of God" (Hollenbach, 2005). The appearance of the *Compendium*, in itself, promises some hope for refocusing attention on the Church's social doctrine, even among those who may have felt the topic had come to be deemphasized by the Church itself during the past few years. Hollenbach warns that the *Compendium* should not be regarded as the "last word" on the subject but has to be considered as describing one stage in a line of historical development. He stresses, with John T. Noonan (2005), that "historicity and development need not be threats to the Catholic tradition. They can lead to growth in understanding of both the requirements of the Gospel and the demands of human reasonableness"(Hollenbach, 2005).

In dealing with controversial issues Catholic communicators should make sure the position of the other side is correctly represented. It does no good to create a "straw man" which bears little resemblance to what is really being said then knocking it down and claiming we have accomplished something worthwhile. We should follow the example of St. Thomas Aquinas in the *Summa Theologica*, where he stated the objections of his adversaries in full before replying: "I answer saying that..." (*Respondeo dicendum quod...*). We, in the twenty-first century, should be at least as fair in our argumentation as St. Thomas was in the thirteenth century!

These comments pertain to issues faced by the Church in general at the present time, rather than by Catholic communicators in particular; but the role of the latter is to express the faith in the most meaningful way not only to those outside the Church but also to fellow Catholics, lay and clerical at all levels. The internal issues mentioned above must therefore be grappled with in order to fill that role effectively. A communicator who has failed to develop a coherent posture regarding such fundamental questions would find it difficult or impossible to speak confidently about the very core of his or her message.

Reactions even to unjust situations have to be tempered, or run the risk of never being heard at all. Any communicator, but especially a Catholic communicator trying to work in a less-than-optimal intellectual environment, must respond by insuring his or her own intellectual preparation is well-informed, deep, balanced, and therefore adequate to the challenges. "Balanced", here, means uncompromisingly Catholic on essentials of the faith, avoiding all moral relativism but making sure that what are taken as essentials really are essentials, not simply rooted in nostalgia for superseded theological or philosophical theories or in remnants of discredited secular ideologies such as monarchism or laissez-faire capitalism. Those two ideologies, in particular, have been falsely accepted by some in the not-too-distant past as practically equivalent to *de fide* defined doctrines. This is where a good, modern education, both theological and secular, comes in.

Next to developing a thorough and accurate knowledge of the Church and what it teaches, the budding Catholic communicator must cultivate certain fundamental communication skills. The basic communication skill, even in this age of electronic media, remains the ability to write. Even the most sophisticated electronic technologies depend ultimately on the written word – as scripts for films or programs, etc. – so the aspiring communicator must learn to write effectively in his or her own language, and other languages if necessary. That can be difficult under any circumstances, but a certain fear of criticism or censorship may make some reluctant to write at all. The spoken word is transitory (unless electronically recorded), but writing makes one peculiarly vulnerable to criticism long after the words are put on paper. This is an old problem, and some of our most brilliant Catholic scholars accordingly have refused to put pen to paper for fear they will be misinterpreted and denounced to higher authorities.

The problem has been exacerbated in recent years by some Catholic critics who misunderstand, misinterpret and even misrepresent books and media productions that have sincerely tried to express Catholic approaches to the full complexities of contemporary problems. Often the productions thus targeted have been discarded, in spite of their quality. We can only speculate about what valuable insights and advances in theological thought and what developments in popular awareness of the Church have been lost to the Church because of such subversion!

Catholic communicators in most countries have relatively few overt external or legal barriers to overcome in communicating the faith. Exceptions to this general atmosphere of political freedom are found in countries with Islamic fundamentalist governments, in those with other intolerant forms of religious establishments, and in the few remaining hard-core communist countries. Efforts to surmount comparable obstacles have been made since the earliest days of Christianity, starting with handwritten Gospel texts and epistles passed clandestinely among Christian communities of the Roman world in times of persecution. More recently, radio has been used extensively, starting with Vatican Radio, in 1931. Satellite television has been tried, and even more recently the Internet. These technologies, particularly radio, are most effective on the local level where they can express their messages in ways closest to the people's hearts, although "feeds" from worldwide sources, such as Vatican Radio, give broadcasters a way to bring news of the worldwide Church to their more intimate local audiences.

Some of the instruments for effective communication have been mentioned in passing, above. Effective writing is essential to all communication. Effective speaking, of course, is also central to preaching, radio, television, and practically all electronic media. Some of our seminaries have, at times, allowed homiletic training to lapse, failing, for example, to challenge students to overcome their deficiencies in public speaking. Individual students can compensate for this by recognizing their courses' deficiencies and by taking steps, alone or with others, to participate in debate clubs, drama groups, or other occasions for overcoming their shyness or "stage fright", and working to perfect their public-speaking abilities. Those who do recognize defects in their courses – especially in the fundamental skills of reading, writing and public speaking – should call them to the attention of teachers or superiors, who may not be aware of problems.

Funding limitations may seem to be a cause for communicators to despair, in some cases, especially since many media undertakings can be very expensive. But much can be accomplished within even the most restricted budget. Sometimes, too, as the saying goes, "the best is the enemy of the good". At the same time, there is value in the phrase "God will provide". There is no set prescription for deciding which of these sayings applies in a particular case, but Ignatius of Loyola's formula for the "discernment of spirits" is a good place to begin making any serious decision by taking account of existing resources and opportunities for accomplishing a particular work or project and at the same time giving due weight to the real spiritual good it might accomplish, while praying sincerely and intensively that God's will be done.

Technological expertise is essential to make use of complicated modern media, but it can run the risk of confusing means with ends. We may sometimes become so enamoured with a particular communication technology such as film or television production that we forget that technologies are only means to the end of communicating our message. "The medium is the message" is a saying that points to the ways different media influence the messages they transmit. In secular media – most noticeably in advertising – the medium sometimes seems to take the place of the message. This may explain some of the effectiveness of modern secular media, but religious communicators and anyone else with serious content to communicate must not be satisfied with that slogan. The message is always at the heart of any serious communication. The medium must be the servant of the message, not its master.

Projects requiring large financial investment, such as film or television production, run the additional risk of having the message distorted by whoever provides the funding. Special care must be exercised in seeking funding for large-scale projects to ensure that the message – for example, social justice for the poor – is not distorted by donors with unsympathetic ideologies. The most important thing for the Catholic communicator to keep in mind is the ultimate value he or she is supposed to be communicating: the greater honour and glory of God.

When they look for ways to concretize this value in practice, communicators must find the contents of their messages by drawing on the whole spectrum of human experience. Every successful message must somehow involve both rhetoric and logic. In a real sense, emotions are primary, because they capture the attention of the audience and keep it while the logical argument also is being communicated. Psychologists have devoted considerable research attention to the functioning of emotion in communication in recent years. Much remains to be done in this field, but it is important for every kind of communication work. Werner Wirth and Holger Schramm, of the University of Zurich, have provided an introduction to research in media and emotions at the start of the new millennium with a valuable bibliography that can give the reader access to some of the most important recent research on the topic (Wirth – Schramm, 2005).

Some genres of communication media can provide insights that apply to all media. One of these is storytelling, a simple form of communication common to all cultures in its oral form, but reaching even into the most complex electronic media. Storytelling is attracting increasing attention from researchers, who recognize its universality and its power. Professor Sunwolf, of Santa Clara University, points out how the stories told in different forms in various cultures can have special power and relevance for communicating spiritual values (Sunwolf, 2004). Storytelling obviously plays a significant role in catechetical instruction, an indispensable sector of the Church's work that is woefully neglected in many places.

Catechetics obviously involves communication, and electronic media are becoming increasingly central to the ways children learn, but group instruction, and one-on-one dialogue must remain important parts of the process. Competition with flashy secular programming is a major stumbling block, here, and increasing resources need to be devoted to making catechetical efforts more competitively attractive to children.

The problem of world overpopulation is one that Catholics had earlier been slow to acknowledge, partly because it had not directly affected Europe or North America, but also because many of those who gave early warnings about it were too quick to propose immoral remedies such as abortion and contraception. Nevertheless, as the world's total population moves toward seven billion. Even the most optimistic must admit the growing pressures that are being exerted on food, fuel and other resources. Catholic communicators should carefully study the complex factors involved in this growth so they will not be tempted to give embarrassingly simplistic answers when the question is raised.

Some observers claim that Catholics, at least in the West, are declining very rapidly in their regular religious practice, to a level even below that of "mainline" Protestant churches. This trend is especially notable among young adults, precisely the age group upon which we must depend to transmit religious culture to the next generation. Mass attendance in most European countries is minimal. Ireland and Quebec, which long claimed to have the highest levels of Catholic practice in the world, have slumped in recent years until they now are among the lowest. Sociologists remain puzzled about the causes of this, but it is clear that any cure must involve Catholics working in the mass media. They should keep themselves informed about sociological studies being done on this problem in their own countries. They should also pay attention to media approaches that have proven successful in stimulating religious knowledge and practice, not only among Catholics but also among mainline Protestants and Pentecostals, and even among non-Christians, to find out what methods work in "gathering the flock".

Liturgists have long been working on this and related problems, so communicators are well-advised to exchange insights and ideas with liturgists, especially those working in their own cultures. The same can be said about religious composers, novelists, artists and others in the creative professions. Ideas do not limit their application to narrow disciplinary boundaries. Efforts should be made to recognize and publicize the products of those who are successful in expressing the faith in artistic works.

Peace is also a preoccupation of many, and it should be, since the prospect of nuclear war is unthinkable. Catholics share common ground with others on this question. But the means to effectively promote peace are so elusive that frustration blocks the way to any real answers, and we invariably fall into partisan arguments that become abusive and divisive, rather than seeking the common interests that might point toward genuine solutions.

The efforts of Catholic communicators should always seek to presume the good will of people with divergent views, on this and all other issues, rather than condemning them at first sight, and should try to work with them to achieve constructive solutions, for the good of humankind and the greater honour and glory of God.

Bibliographical references

HOLLENBACH, D. (2005), "Human Rights in Catholic Thought, A New Synthesis", *America* 193/13, 16-17.
KLIMOSKI, V. – O'NEIL, K. – SCHUTH, K. (2005), *Educating Leaders for Ministry*, Liturgical Press, as cited by P. STEINFELS, "Beliefs", *New York Times*, September 24, 2005, and by R. P. MCBRIEN, "Today's Seminarians", October 17, 2005, a paper circulated by the Fellowship of Southern Illinois Laity, Belleville, IL, USA.
NOONAN, J. T. (2005), *The Church That Can and Cannot Change*, Notre Dame, IN: University of Notre Dame Press. As cited in Hollenbach, 2005: 18.

SUNWOLF, J. D. (2004), "Once Upon a Time for the Soul: A Review of the Effects of Storytelling in Spiritual Traditions", *Communication Research Trends* 23/3, 3-19.

WIRTH, W. – SCHRAMM, H. (2005), "Media and Emotions", *Communication Research Trends* 24/3, 3-39.

Verso una comunicazione partecipativa.
L'opera del CICS in un'esperienza di vita e di insegnamento*

Robert A. White, SJ

The author comments on the idea of participatory communication and argues that if communication is not participatory it is not communication at all. Taking on from this point he focuses on Jesus' ideas on communication and then frames a theology of communication. The author then argues that a clear vision for participatory communication formation needs to focus on the idea of the human person, the social teaching of the Church, education for freedom, affirmation of cultural rights and models of socio-economic development based on networks of people's grassroots organizations. He goes on to comment on the importance of communication sciences recognizing the active, critical imagination of the audience, and then closes with the principle of social responsibility in public communication. The article throws up challenges to the future of communications formations.

La commissione organizzatrice mi ha chiesto di intervenire sul tema della "comunicazione partecipativa". Si tratta certamente di un argomento interessante. Probabilmente i coordinatori di quest'incontro, che celebra i venticinque anni del Centro Interdisciplinare sulla Comunicazione Sociale, avevano in mente il fatto che la comunicazione partecipativa sia stata centrale in ciò che il CICS ha cercato di fare nell'ultimo quarto di secolo. Se questo è vero, allora gli studenti, i professori e diversi altri partecipanti a quest'incontro dovrebbero conoscere la partecipazione comunicativa almeno quanto me, se non di più. La domanda centrale che vorrei innanzitutto porre è questa: che cosa intendiamo per "comunicazione partecipativa"? Suggerirei di tentare di costruire insieme ciò che questa espressione significhi e che tipo di azione/interazione essa implichi. Inizierei quindi con una descrizione di alcune delle caratteristiche della comunicazione partecipativa, per guidare il nostro

---

* Intervento tenuto in occasione del Simposio celebrativo dei 25 anni del CICS (17 novembre 2005), sul tema "Comunicare e (è) partecipare – Dai mass media alla comunicazione partecipativa: quali sfide per la Chiesa?".

dialogo verso una maggiore comprensione. È una comunicazione in cui:

- ogni individuo in un gruppo è invitato a contribuire liberamente all'opinione/consenso comune ed all'operato finale del gruppo stesso;
- viene dischiuso uno spazio di libertà che incoraggia tutti, specialmente i più emarginati e riservati, a scoprire ed esprimere i propri pensieri, portando alla luce le proprie risorse;
- le decisioni vengono raggiunte attraverso un processo di dialogo e di scelta comune;
- c'è un senso crescente di interdipendenza, di fiducia reciproca e di riconoscimento dei talenti di tutti;
- sono frequenti discussioni accese, ma tutti finiscono per (ri)conoscere le chiare posizioni degli altri e arrivano a capire come le differenze possano realisticamente ricomporsi in relativa armonia;
- ognuno si sente responsabile in ordine al consenso da raggiungere e all'operato finale, in virtù di un comune senso di responsabilità che lega ciascuno dei soggetti agli altri.

Personalmente, mi sembra opportuno individuare sette principali scaturigini del pensiero contemporaneo circa la comunicazione partecipativa, scaturigini che – tra l'altro – penso abbiano aiutato lo sviluppo della nostra "filosofia di vita" nella comunità del CICS:

- prima di tutto e anzitutto, le "nostre" teologie della comunicazione, con speciale riferimento a quelle fondate su *Communio et Progressio*;
- la ricchezza delle filosofie contemporanee – Buber, Levinas, Charles Taylor – ma anche la scuola filosofica viva presso l'Università Gregoriana;
- la filosofia sociale della Chiesa, emersa dall'azione sociale della stessa;
- le varie filosofie e i metodi di educazione per la libertà;
- gli sviluppi recenti nella scienza della comunicazione, specialmente la tradizione dei *cultural studies*;
- la teoria e la pratica dello sviluppo sociale;
- infine, il recente pensiero sull'etica delle comunicazioni.

1. Il punto di partenza: le nostre teologie della comunicazione

La teologia contemporanea della comunicazione, espressa così meravigliosamente in *Communio et Progressio*, è emersa da un grande rinnovamento teologico, e specialmente dal rinnovamento della teologia del mistero pasquale, condotta al livello dell'azione pastorale della Chiesa dal Concilio Vaticano II. *Communio et Progressio*, radicata specialmente in *Gaudium et Spes*, ha chiarito che il significato della comunicazione umana è quello di condurre tutti verso una comunità. La nostra interpretazione della "comunicazione per la comunità" è bastata direttamente sul mistero pasquale: Gesù Cristo è morto per amore nostro ed è risorto per riconciliarci tutti nello Spirito. Possiamo considerare tre livelli.

Innanzitutto, Gesù ha rivelato il significato di una comunicazione partecipativa attraverso la sua incarnazione: la Parola e l'Immagine del Dio Triuno è diventata uomo e, attraverso questo, ci ha riconciliato e ha ristabilito una comunicazione tra Dio e l'umanità. Per mezzo della morte e risurrezione di Gesù l'umanità è ricostituita come comunità. Uniti in Gesù Cristo, noi non siamo più un popolo di diversa razza, nazione e lingua, ma partecipiamo *allo stesso modo* della medesima vita e dello stesso potere d'amore. La vita e lo Spirito del Cristo risorto ci rendono capaci di riconoscere un unico Padre e un'unica famiglia di Dio. Lo spirito di Gesù ci rende "corpi interdipendenti", un'unica comunità. Proprio come il capo non può dire alla mano "io non ho bisogno di te", così ora ciascuno, riempito del carisma dello Spirito, ha bisogno di ogni altra persona. Per via del nostro battesimo in Cristo, noi diventiamo *partecipi* dell'azione di Cristo, con-creatori nell'azione creativa di Dio in Cristo.

In secondo luogo, tutta la comunicazione di Gesù con gli altri, la sua compassione, il suo paziente insegnamento, il suo farsi vicino ai peccatori, il suo aver cura del popolo che aveva perso la speranza, hanno rivelato l'amore del Padre, il suo amore *senza condizioni* per tutto il popolo. Soprattutto nell'accettare la morte, e soprattutto la morte sulla croce per amore del Padre e per noi, Gesù si è rivelato come "perfetto comunicatore". Nella sua vita, morte e risurrezione Gesù ci ha insegnato che la vera comunicazione non è solo trasmissione di idee; al contrario, come dice bene *Communio et progressio*, la comunicazione al suo più profondo livello è donazione di se stessi nell'amore. La comunicazione di Gesù è perfetta perché nessuno ha un amore più grande di colui che dà la propria vita per gli altri.

In terzo luogo, Gesù ha rivelato la natura partecipativa della comunicazione nel modo in cui ha insegnato, condotto conversazioni e annunciato il regno. Molto spesso Gesù ha portato i suoi discepoli a sviluppare un livello di comprensione comune, ponendo interrogativi aperti per sollecitare risposte attive e partecipative; in questa maniera ha orientato verso un consenso, ricomponendo insieme diversi livelli di risonanza. Ognuno poteva partecipare a questa costruzione condivisa. "Chi dice la gente che io sia?", ha chiesto. Quando Pietro risponde che egli crede che Gesù sia il Messia, Gesù riconosce la veracità di ciò che Pietro dice, ma non dicendo: "Pietro, finalmente hai trovato la giusta risposta, quella che io volevo che tu trovassi", ma piuttosto ascoltando, riflettendo e quindi richiamando il fatto che è stato il Padre di tutti che ha reso possibile per Pietro fare questa confessione.

Un'altra modalità tipica di comunicazione consisteva, per Gesù, nel raccontare una storia o una parabola che avesse un significato connotativo abbastanza aperto. Benché la storia venisse raccontata con una propria logica e un significato ben chiaro, ogni persona poteva accostarvisi personalmente, contribuendo alla qualificazione di ulteriori livelli di significato. Alla fine della parabola del Buon Samaritano, Gesù chiede chi di quei tre uomini sia stato il "prossimo": era sempre attestato, in altri termini, un *senso pleniore* che la comunità avrebbe potuto sviluppare ulteriormente. Molte delle azioni di Gesù, come i suoi miracoli, erano simboliche ed erano piene di significato esse stesse; erano piene di significati che tutti potevano trar fuori attraverso scambi partecipativi e che sono stati la sorgente dell'interpretazione condivisa lungo i secoli. Gesù presentava la buona novella in modo che tutti i suoi discepoli nella fede potessero continuamente partecipare nell'estrapolarne i significati più pieni, nel momento stesso in cui il Vangelo veniva annunciato in altri contesti culturali e in altri periodi storici. Ogni volta che viene tenuta un'omelia, Gesù ci invita a "contribuire" con qualcosa da attingere a partire dal livello profondo della nostra comprensione spirituale. La comunicazione partecipativa, quindi, non è mai una parola finale. Essa invita continuamente tutti a dare il proprio contributo alla crescita del Regno di Dio.

Certamente, molti potrebbero immediatamente far presente che esistono altri modi con cui Gesù indicava al popolo di partecipare. Tuttavia un altro aspetto della comunicazione di Gesù è importante: egli invita sempre ad una risposta *gratuita*. La risposta al Vangelo deve essere interamente libera, interamente personale, altrimenti non può essere una risposta nell'amore. La nostra risposta deve venire dal profondo della nostra piena convinzione, dal profondo del nostro cuore.

2. Il concetto di persona umana

Un'ulteriore sorgente per la comprensione della comunicazione partecipativa ci viene dalla nostra concezione della persona, dalla nostra antropologia filosofica. Per me una delle maggiori chiarificazioni in proposito è stata un articolo scritto da padre Henrici, fondatore del CICS, all'inizio del programma di studi del 1983. In *Toward an Anthropological Philosophy of Communication* (Henrici, 1983), padre Henrici ha affermato che l'unico modo per l'essere umano di diventare completamente umano è attraverso la comunicazione. La sua definizione di comunicazione è degna di essere citata integralmente: "si potrebbe quindi, con John C. Kelly, definire la comunicazione come opposta alla semplice trasmissione, come 'condivisione di significato', specialmente se consideriamo 'significato' nel suo valore pieno di senso ultimo". La comunicazione non dovrebbe così riguardare tanto lo scambio di informazioni e di conoscenza, quanto piuttosto il fatto di condividere un certo punto di vista sulla realtà e una certa comprensione del mondo. Questa concezione della comunicazione, condivisa da tutti noi che abbiamo lavorato con Henrici negli anni '80, è stata assai importante nel dar corpo alla prospettiva del CICS.

Nel suddetto articolo Henrici sottolinea che noi siamo nati incompleti e diventiamo veramente umani con il processo della comunicazione in comunità. La capacità dell'amore umano e della conoscenza giacciono all'interno di noi sin dalla nostra infanzia, ma tanto dipende anche dal contesto comunicativo in cui un bambino cresce. Il desiderio di sapere e di definire il significato è insito nel bambino, ma – ancora una volta – molto dipende da una comunità d'amore di adulti che lo ascoltino, lo incoraggino a scoprire i significati delle cose e a sviluppare un'espressione originale del loro significato. Educazione non significa inoculare i significati nel bambino, ma lasciar emergere da parte del bambino stesso la creazione del significato. Ciò richiede un ambiente di condivisione, partecipazione, in un senso e nell'altro. La comunicazione partecipativa sta esattamente ad indicare un processo di comunicazione in cui tutti – veramente tutti! – imparano continuamente a creare significato insieme.

È davvero indispensabile allontanarsi in maniera consapevole da una concezione behaviorista della persona, da quella concezione stimolo-risposta che soggiace a molta parte delle teorie contemporanee sulla comunicazione. È anche necessario prendere le distanze da una concezione dell'apprendimento come assorbimento psicologico passivo di esercizi continuamente ripetuti. Ancora più problematica per la comunicazione umana è infine la tradizione libertaria radicale dell'Occidente, che dà per scontato il fatto che la misura della verità sia nelle nostre idee e che sia praticamente impossibile raggiungere una comprensione comune del concetto di verità nella sfera pubblica. Ognuno ha infatti il diritto ad avere le proprie credenze e idee, ma esse sono e restano essenzialmente private. È impossibile condividere convinzioni comuni: il meglio che si possa fare è una specie di contratto sociale, laddove tu mi aiuti a raggiungere i miei obiettivi ed io aiuto te a raggiungere i tuoi. La sfera pubblica è una specie di libero mercato di idee dove ognuno può buttare ogni idea che gli piaccia e può prendere ciò che gli interessa, ma non è possibile – e in pratica non si può affatto – condividere alcun significato in quanto comunità.

Ciò che è condiviso dal punto di vista comunicativo è il *significato*, che io intenderei definire come la relazione di un esistente con altri esistenti. Henrici preferiva parlare del significato come "senso ultimo", relazione di un esistente con ogni altra esistenza. L'essere umano costruisce queste relazioni con gli altri, sempre in qualche modo arbitrarie – come costruzione sociale della realtà –, ma ha a che fare con la realtà stessa. Gli esseri umani vivono in un mondo di relazioni costruite e in un mondo di spiegazioni sul perché una data relazione sia importante. Noi non mangiamo soltanto, come fanno tutti gli animali, ma diamo anche al mangiare un nome e lo consideriamo una *relazione* verso cose che possono essere o non essere mangiate. Inoltre, gli esseri umani possono costruire una spiegazione sul *perché* mangiare sia importante. Così, mangiare non è solo uno stimolo che causa una risposta, come fa capire il classico esempio del cane di Pavlov. Al contrario, il modo in cui mangiamo è mediato attraverso il nostro significato del mangiare.

Ciò che Henrici voleva mostrare, dal punto di vista della comunicazione, è un concetto di persona che sia capace di riconoscere la possibilità, o in pratica la necessità imperiosa, di creare il significato insieme ad altri, così che si possano condividere vari significati nella sfera pubblica. Questo concetto considera la persona come un *essere in relazione* con capacità di relazionarsi espressa attraverso il linguaggio e la cultura. La specie umana è nata incompleta e non può diventare completa eccetto che nell'interazione. La comunicazione umana indica che la persona è capace di essere consapevole della propria identità "separatamente unica" come diversa e afferma la bontà dell'esistenza separata di ciascuno. Così, la persona può sempre comprendere e far proprie le idee degli altri, ma esse possono di fatto diventare consapevolmente *mie* idee. In secondo luogo, la mente deve essere capace di riconoscere, nell'alterità dei segni che mi giungono, la *similarità* tra le idee altrui e la mia personale recezione di queste idee, l'universale nelle idee particolari. Ciò è al cuore della condivisione del significato. In terzo luogo, il soggetto deve avere la capacità di far propria la similarità percepita dei significati degli altri e la comprensione di questo significato nella propria consapevolezza, *senza perdere la consapevolezza della propria unica identità*. Così, si può riflettere criticamente sulle idee universali nei termini della propria identità affermata come buona. Io posso guardare un programma televisivo e condividere i significati che ho recepito: lo posso guardare *criticamente*.

Assai importante è riconoscere che nella coscienza di ognuno c'è una profonda affermazione della bontà della propria esistenza e della volontà di vivere. Questo dinamismo è in ogni essere, ma appare come conscio e riflessivo solo nell'esistenza umana. Non importa quanto possano essere repressive le circostanze in cui si trova una persona e non importa quanto la cultura possa insistere sull'inferiorità e l'inutilità di un individuo: rimane sempre nella profondità della coscienza della persona l'affermazione del valore persona stessa. È questa volontà di esprimere l'affermazione conscia del proprio valore personale che un contesto sociale partecipativo lascia emergere chiaramente. Ciò che l'articolo di padre Henrici sottolinea è che questa volontà di esistere non è isolata nella coscienza del singolo, come buona parte della prima filosofia moderna sosteneva, ma nasce in comunità: si diventa consapevoli della propria bontà nell'interazione. Dunque, l'affermazione della bontà personale è sempre orientata verso l'altro e verso la comunità. Questa concezione della persona ci porterebbe a dire che l'orientazione verso l'altro e il desiderio di essere in comunità hanno le proprie radici nella coscienza prima che nel linguaggio, e sono condotti verso la propria fruizione dal linguaggio e dall'interazione sociale. Così, a partire dal modo in cui strutturiamo la vita della comunità e dal mondo in cui educhiamo, possiamo desumere che è possibile "compiere" l'umanità facendo sì che una persona contribuisca in qualche modo, attraverso un po' del proprio valore conscio, alla costruzione dell'interdipendenza nella comunità. È interessante che quando Clifford Christians, uno dei pensatori-guida nell'etica della comunicazione di oggi, volle stabilire un fondamento per una certa universalità delle norme morali nel mondo, dovette necessariamente fondare il proprio argomento su un campo non meno esteso dell'antropologia filosofica di Henrici (Christians, 1997). Christians considerava la volontà di vivere e il rispetto per la vita come proto-norma fondamentale che soggiace a tutti i sistemi dell'etica. Noi tuttavia scopriamo questo rispetto della vita in ciò che Henrici chiamava propriamente "comunità della vita".

3. L'azione sociale e l'insegnamento sociale della Chiesa

Forse la singola più importante fonte dell'idea di una comunicazione partecipativa è stata la scomparsa graduale della schiavitù, del feudalesimo e della dipendenza clientelare nello sviluppo delle organizzazioni volontarie dei lavoratori poveri e dei contadini al fine di risolvere problemi elementari di sussistenza. L'organizzazione degli artigiani nelle società auto-assistite risale al periodo romano nella civiltà occidentale e in quelle società che fiorirono nel Medioevo. Ovviamente, però, l'idea dell'organizzazione del popolo in una società industriale di massa è qualcosa che ha avuto inizio solo nel XIX secolo. I principi della libertà umana e dell'uguaglianza che emersero gradualmente durante l'Illuminismo e penetrarono nella "classe operaia" furono un'importante sorgente di queste idee. Lo sviluppo generale della democrazia popolare nel XIX secolo fu altrettanto importante in questo senso.

Alcune delle più importanti fonti dell'idea dell'organizzazione popolare furono i movimenti cooperativi, l'organizzazione delle unioni del lavoro e quelle dei piccoli contadini, insieme al diffuso movimento giovanile che si affermò come modello di educazione non formale.

Queste organizzazioni furono guidate da una serie di principi partecipativi:

- erano organizzate su base volontaria ed erano indipendenti da tutti coloro che detenevano potere politico, economico, religioso o di altro tipo all'interno di una comunità; avevano solo un obbligo: servire gli altri membri;
- l'opinione di ogni membro veniva considerata importante e la conduzione degli incontri doveva far sì che ogni opinione fosse ascoltata, rispettata e presa in considerazione, anche quando le opinioni opposte fossero state assai forti;
- ogni membro aveva un egual diritto di partecipare alle decisioni dell'organizzazione attraverso il voto e la parola; tutte le decisioni dovevano essere aperte alla discussione finché anche l'ultima opinione non fosse stata ascoltata;

- tutte le posizioni formali di guida del gruppo dovevano essere raggiunte per elezione e ogni membro doveva avere il diritto di essere eletto ad una posizione di leadership; in pratica, si dava per scontato che il ruolo di guida potesse essere a rotazione e che tutti i membri avrebbero occupato a tempo opportuno una certa leadership;
- ogni leadership doveva offrire al resto dei membri un rendiconto completo di tutte le azioni, specialmente dell'uso dei fondi;
- tutte le attività, inclusa la gestione della leadership, erano volontarie, in quanto contribuzione gratuita al benessere dell'organizzazione e della società.

Benché l'organizzazione dovesse rimanere libera dalle politiche ad ampio raggio o da altre organizzazioni, essa stessa venne considerata come un modo di articolare gli interessi della classe operaia e dei poveri.

In molte parti del mondo, la Chiesa cattolica vide in queste organizzazioni un riflesso del proprio principio sacramentale e comunitario e, mentre le manteneva indipendenti dalla propria gerarchia, le promuoveva come espressione dei valori cattolici nella vita pubblica. L'insegnamento sociale della Chiesa, nondimeno, emerse dall'esperienza pratica di queste organizzazioni popolari, specialmente quando le organizzazioni vicine alla Chiesa stessa si scontrarono con l'orientamento essenzialmente autoritario del movimento comunista e con i persistenti residui del feudalesimo. Molto spesso alcuni leaders cattolici di classi sociali ben affermate ostacolarono la promozione dell'organizzazione partecipativa del popolo, specialmente quando quelle classi erano collegate al fascismo in Europa o alle visioni tradizionaliste in America Latina e in altre parti del mondo. L'insegnamento sociale della Chiesa fu, in parte, un tentativo di definire il diritto della classe operaia di organizzarsi in partiti democratici e partecipativi, diritto considerato parte della dottrina cattolica stessa. Tale insegnamento continua ancora oggi a dare priorità ad alcuni principi chiave:

- il diritto del popolo, specialmente dei poveri, ad avere le proprie organizzazioni volontarie, democratiche, partecipative;
- la dignità e santità della persona nel contesto della società di massa, della legge del marketing che controlla il capitalismo internazionale e dell'enfasi funzionalista sul sistema piuttosto che sulla persona;

- l'importanza della comunità locale e delle organizzazioni locali, come contesto per lo sviluppo della libertà, dell'uguaglianza e della creatività della persona, specialmente del povero e di colui che ha meno potere.

4. L'educazione alla libertà, alla comunità e l'affermazione dei diritti culturali

In molte parti del mondo la maggior parte della gente continua a vivere in un contesto sociale dove un gruppo elitario auto-perpetuante controlla la ricchezza, i media, le opportunità educative e specialmente i simboli di prestigio. La cultura dominante continua a mantenere la considerazione delle classi popolari come intrinsecamente inferiori sulla base del loro stato sociale rurale o suburbano, della loro casta, razza, del loro background o della loro lingua. Questa gente vive in situazioni di dipendenza clientelistica: ognuno cioè dipende individualmente da un "patrono" che ha accesso ai circoli di potere, alle opportunità e al benessere, mentre l'interazione generale tra gli indigenti è considerevolmente bassa. Il sistema di comunicazione è controllato da un'elite dominante e quella parte di informazione che raggiunge il popolo ha assai poca rilevanza in termini di decisioni effettive. Il sistema di educazione si rifà particolarmente al valore della memoria, dell'unitarietà e del rispetto per la gerarchia. La modernizzazione rende questo contesto anche peggiore, dal momento che i poveri si trovano integrati nell'economia di mercato e il popolo diviene semplicemente una merce, privata persino della protezione delle relazioni familiari e paternaliste del sistema clientelare.

L'aspetto peggiore di questo sistema di comunicazione non è che il popolo resti per sempre in situazione di povertà: può infatti succedere, con la modernizzazione, che la gente riesca a guadagnare un certo tenore di vita e un certo grado di comfort, una migliore educazione tecnica e molti altri vantaggi. Potrebbe tuttavia continuare ad essere parte di un sistema di dipendenza, rimanendo almeno tanto disumanizzata e isolata quanto fosse in precedenza. L'unico cambiamento sarebbe in questo caso il livello di consumo: in definitiva, se la gente guadagna una posizione di potere, riproduce le stesse relazioni di sfruttamento che essa ha sperimentato.

Persone più sensibili, consapevoli di come questo contesto disumanizzi gli esseri umani e li ponga in conflitto l'uno con l'altro, iniziarono a sviluppare una filosofia educativa e un metodo che sottolineano peculiarmente lo sviluppo della persona. In pratica, molti di questi approcci educativi hanno ricevuto una forte influenza dalle filosofie personaliste di cui si è parlato prima. Paulo Freire è frequentemente citato come contributore in questo tipo di educazione per la libertà, ma è solo uno fra i tanti. Per esempio, Badal Sircar in India, Mandela in Africa, e Martin Luther King in America hanno sviluppato tanti degli aspetti di questo pensiero. È forse più corretto parlare di movimenti mondiali, piuttosto che di pensiero di un singolo in merito.

Possiamo di nuovo individuare un certo numero di caratteristiche comuni in questi approcci educativi:

- l'uso di una forma dialogica di discussione condotta da un "animatore", il cui compito primario è di guidare tutti partecipanti nella conversazione e incoraggiare il dialogo, ma non di iniziare temi specifici;
- il risultato della discussione non è definito in partenza: l'animatore rispetta e accoglie le idee che emergono dal gruppo;
- la discussione si sviluppa attorno ad una rappresentazione (o ripresentazione) del problema che il gruppo affronta: questo non per dare più informazioni del necessario, ma per ripensare criticamente le cause del problema stesso e valutare le effettive capacità di farvi fronte da sé;
- nel gruppo vengono messe a nudo, qualora vi fossero, le eventuali tendenze a dominare da parte di alcuni individui, oltre che la capacità positiva di sviluppare uno spirito cooperativo di ascolto e di lavoro comune.

5. I nuovi modelli di sviluppo socio-economico basati su una rete di organizzazioni base del popolo

Molti degli studenti della Pontificia Università Gregoriana vengono dal cosiddetto Terzo Mondo o vi torneranno dopo i loro studi. Tutte le attività della Chiesa, incluse quelle realizzate attraverso i media, stanno cercando di contribuire al processo di sviluppo dei loro paesi. Tutti cercano modelli di sviluppo socio-economico che rappresentino i propri ideali personali. Praticamente tutti dicono di volere una Chiesa partecipativa e comunitaria, e tutti dicono di andare in cerca di un modello di sviluppo che permetta ai popoli di assumere la responsabilità del proprio sviluppo.

È interessante notare come le teorie dello sviluppo abbiano progressivamente spostato il proprio ambito operativo da un modello di controllo statale verso modelli più partecipativi di comunicazione, tali da rendere ragione dell'esistenza di associazioni imprenditoriali, comunità, organizzazioni della società civile, istituzioni private come la Chiesa e associazioni professionali per diventare protagonisti nel processo stesso dello sviluppo.

6. La scienza delle comunicazioni riconosce l'immaginazione critica attiva dell'audience

Le prime emittenti radio cercavano disperatamente di condurre i comunicatori ad usare i media, e presentavano ai potenziali "clienti" la radio come un mezzo potente che avrebbe potuto persuadere e anche manipolare. Le stazioni di trasmissione promettevano ai politici che con la radio avrebbero potuto facilmente vincere le elezioni, ai preti che avrebbero potuto facilmente convertire la gente e ai commercianti che avrebbero potuto dischiudere vaste nuove aree di mercato con una pubblicità intelligente. I fascisti e i governi nazionalisti videro nei media un facile strumento di mobilitazione del pubblico per la guerra e l'espansione. Lord Reith della BBC vide nella radio un mezzo di educazione delle masse. I governi coloniali videro nella radio il mezzo per inculturare i nativi. I centri di ricerca sull'audience dovettero presto mettere in piedi metodologie quantitative per misurare le dimensioni dell'audience, il numero di ore di ascolto e il grado di cambiamento delle attitudini.

La definizione di Lasswell dalla comunicazione come trasmissione, derivata dai suoi studi sulla pubblicità, divennero il concetto standard di "comunicazione". Il punto focale degli studi sui media insisteva sulla formulazione di quel messaggio mediatico che avrebbe persuaso e modificato i gruppi "target". Un testo "chiuso": era questo che il comunicatore voleva raggiungere. L'audience non poteva partecipare, ma solo reagire.

Nel 1960 Joseph Klapper pubblicò un suo rivoluzionario volume che analizzava centinaia di studi sugli effetti dei media e dimostrava che quasi in nessun caso i media avevano avuto effetti diretti e duraturi sull'audience (Klapper, 1965). I messaggi dei media vengono filtrati dalle nostre attitudini culturali, dai contesti sociali, dal confronto con gli *opinion leaders* e da molti altri fattori intermedi che influenzano il modo in cui la gente pensa e agisce. Da qui iniziò un lungo processo di ricerca che rivelò gradualmente molti aspetti dell'attività dell'audience e della partecipazione.

La scienza delle comunicazioni iniziò negli anni '70 a concentrarsi di meno sul messaggio e sulle tattiche di persuasione degli emittenti e di più su come l'audience usi i media e tragga benefici da essi. Ancora più importante è stato lo sviluppo dell'approccio dei *cultural studies* alla ricerca sull'audience e lo studio della relazione tra i media e la totalità delle società e delle culture. I *cultural studies* nacquero dall'esegesi letteraria e biblica, e si interessarono a come l'audience "legga un testo", cioè a come il lettore o lo spettatore costruisca il proprio significato. La ricerca scoprì che indipendentemente da quanto persuasivo o anche coercitivo possiamo rendere un messaggio, ogni individuo nell'audience svilupperà una propria interpretazione del *significato* del messaggio secondo la propria *identità* personale e culturale. L'approccio dei *cultural studies* riconosce che gli interessi egemonici faranno sempre tutto il possibile per persuadere attraverso i media ad accettare la loro ideologia, ma questo nuovo approccio di ricerca riconosce che ognuno potrebbe e dovrebbe sempre proteggere la propria identità.

Per coloro il cui concetto filosofico dell'essere umano sottolinea l'importanza della libertà e della responsabilità nella costruzione della comunità, risulta certamente molto importante la scoperta che gli spettatori della TV, tanto per fare un esempio, sono sempre consapevoli della propria identità individuale in ogni uso dei media. Ciò offre il fondamento, in seno alla personalità individuale, per un'educazione all'uso dei media in modo da valorizzare l'identità personale responsabile e incoraggiare un discernimento critico nell'uso dei media stessi.

7. Il principio della responsabilità sociale nella comunicazione pubblica

All'inizio l'Europa moderna si trovava a confronto con la possibilità di tre diversi sistemi di moralità pubblica nella comunicazione: la continuazione della censura feudale e monarchica di tutte le pubblicazioni, la tradizione liberale individualistica – che frequentemente diventava avidamente interessata al proprio profitto – o lo sviluppo di un'etica della "libertà con un certo grado di responsabilità", al fine di servire la comunità. In pratica, il mondo scelse di sviluppare istituzioni di responsabilità libera radicate nella coscienza personale, nella consapevolezza dei propri doveri verso la comunità. Ancora una volta, abbiamo optato per un sistema etico che valorizzi la persona, la libertà, la creatività e la consapevolezza della nostra interdipendenza in comunità.

A livello delle nuove occupazioni nei mass media più recenti, tutto questo venne definito in termini di "professionismo". Il professionista assume liberamente la responsabilità davanti alla comunità a partire dalla percezione personale della realtà e dalla propria convinzione. Il codice etico non è definito dallo Stato, ma dall'associazione libera dei giornalisti, delle emittenti e dei pubblicisti. L'associazione si assume la responsabilità di educare e motivare i suoi membri per essere in grado di dirigere ogni pubblicazione secondo coscienza.

A livello del governo, la responsabilità è espressa nei termini della tradizione di trasmissione del servizio pubblico e della regolazione minima della legislazione.

A livello del pubblico, la responsabilità continua a risiedere nella libertà verso l'utilizzo dei media basata sugli imperativi di libertà delle coscienze. La responsabilità è basata sulle nostre tradizioni familiari, sui nostri sistemi educativi, sui media stessi, ma specialmente sulle nostre tradizioni religiose.

Dove l'etica della responsabilità sociale ha fallito è in genere nell'industria dei media, dove – sfortunatamente, penso io – si è finiti per ritenere che un sistema etico sarebbe stato prodotto dall' "invisibile mano del mercato", senza tenere in alcun conto l'ideale dell'etica radicata nell'essere persona.

8. Conclusioni

Uno dei tipici approcci del testo "aperto" è precisamente quello di non imporre una chiusura o una conclusione. La conclusione rimane aperta alla discussione dell'audience, non solo per annotare ciò che è stato omesso o non è stato detto bene, ma anche per portare avanti la storia della comunicazione partecipativa e la storia del CICS. Ora è il vostro momento!

Riferimenti bibliografici

CHRISTIANS, C. (1997), "The Ethics of Being in a Communications Context", in C. CHRISTIANS – M. TRABER, ed., *Communication Ethics and Universal Values,* London: Sage Publications, 3-23.

HENRICI, P. (1983), "Toward an Anthropological Philosophy of Communication", *Communication Resource: A Supplement of WACC Action,* March 1983.

KLAPPER, J. T. (1965), *The effects of mass communication,* New York: The Free Press.

CONTRIBUTORS

Sante Babolin, from Padova (Italy), is a Full Professor of the philosophy of Culture in the Faculty of Philosophy at the Pontifical Gregorian University. A number of his books are of particular interest to people in the field of communications: *Piccolo lessico di semiotica* (2003); *Produzione di senso* (1999 and, in Spanish, 2005); *Icona e conoscenza* (1989); *Semiosi e Comunicazione* (1999). Among his most important articles are: "Semiotica, base elementare per qualsiasi espressione gestuale, rituale e dottrinale", in *Comunicazione e ritualità* (1988) and "Telecamera sulla Messa: Criteri sul modo di svolgere la celebrazione", in *Rivista Liturgica* (1997).

Lloyd Baugh, SJ, from Quebec City (Canada), entered the Society of Jesus with a professional background of teaching University-level English Literature and Theater in Quebec. He was sent to Rome after ordination in 1984 to study at the Pontifical Gregorian University, where he obtained a Licentiate in Fundamental Theology and Film Studies, a Diploma in Social Communications and then a Doctorate in Fundamental Theology and Film Studies. He is now permanently assigned to the Gregorian where he holds the rank of Full Professor and where he teaches largely interdisciplinary courses, bridging the academic fields of film-studies and theology, philosophy, social sciences, spirituality and interreligious and intercultural dialogue. Author of *Imaging the Divine: Jesus and Christ-Figures in Film* (1996) and *Lux in Tenebris Lucet* (2005), he publishes widely on various topics: the representation of Jesus in film; the sacred and religious experience in film; religious themes in contemporary cinema; and theological and moral issues in the films of Kieslowski. He teaches regularly in Canada, the USA and the Philippines.

William E. Biernatzki, SJ, from the USA, has a PhD in Sociology and Anthropology. From 1969 to 1988, he taught at Sogang University (Seoul, South Korea). In 1989 he became research director of the Centre for the Study of Communication and Culture (CSCC) in London, and retained that position when the Centre moved to St. Louis (Missouri) in 1993. He has been general editor of *Communication Research Trends* since 1989.

Miriam Diez Bosch, from Spain, lectures in journalism in the CICS. She studied Information Sciences at the Universitat Autonoma of Barcelona and Ecclesiastical Studies at the Theological Faculty of Catalonia. Her research areas are Church organizational communication and religious journalism. She works as a Vatican correspondent for the international news agency *Zenit* based in Rome and for the Catholic newspaper *Catalunya Cristiana*. She is a regular contributor to several magazines both in Italy and Spain (*Jesus, Sir, Vida Nueva, El Punt, El Temps*). Diez Bosch is a WACC (World Association for Christian Communication) member and an ATE (Spanish Association of Women Theologians) member. She currently collaborates with the "Women and Christianity" Chair at the Pontifical Theological Faculty *Marianum*, in Rome.

Xavier Debanne, born in France, is a Senior Manager for the Siemens Corporation, based in Rome and works in the field of marketing and Communication. His educational background includes a Bachelor's Degree in Computer Science (1978) and a PhD in Artificial Intelligence (1984), both from the University of Paris VI. As an expert on Internet and its use within the Church, he taught courses in religious interactivity in Internet at the Gregorian, in the CICS, from 2002 to 2004. He is also responsible for the website "Anania in Rete".

Johannes Ehrat, SJ, from Germany, studied Philosophy and Theology at the Gregorian University, became a Jesuit and worked as a campus chaplain at the University of Karlsruhe, in Germany. He then studied communication sciences in Montréal (Canada), where he obtained his PhD at the Université de Montréal, in 1990. From 1989 to 1990 he lived and studied in the Centre for the Study of Communication and Culture (CSCC) in London, and from 1991 to 1996, he was Lecturer in semiotics and communications at the Hochschule für Philosophie in Munich. Since 1991, he has taught at CICS. He is the author of *Cinema and Semiotic: Pierce and Film Aesthetics, Narration and Representation* (2005).

Franz-Josef Eilers, SVD, from Germany, is Professor of social communication and missiology at the Divine Word School of Theology (Tagaytay City, Philippines), as well as at the Pontifical University of Santo Tomas (Manila) and at the Don Bosco Centre for Studies (Manila). He is also Adjunct Professor at the University of the Philippines in Los Banos and the Executive Secretary for the Office of Social Communication of the Federation of Asian Bishops' Conferences. He was a member of the preparatory commission for setting up the Interdisciplinary Centre at the Gregorian University and taught sessionally in the CICS from 1981 to 1996, offering courses in intercultural communication, development and communication. From 1971 to 1985, he was Director of the Catholic Media Council in Aachen (Germany) and is presently Consultor for the Pontifical Council for Social Communications.

David Eley, SJ, from Canada, teaches as a visiting Professor in the CICS since 1987. He has also taught communication in several Canadian universities. He moves freely among the fields of aesthetics, philosophy and theology of communications, advertising and the documentary film. He has done university administrative work and chaplaincy and presently he is Assistant to the Canadian Jesuit Provincial for social and international ministries.

Joseph Oládèjo Fáníran, from Nigeria, received his BA from the Pontifical Urban University (Rome), through the Seminary of S.S. Peter and Paul (Bodija, Ibadan). He has also completed a BA Honours in Communication from University of Ottawa (Canada), an MA in International Affairs from Carleton University (Ottawa) and a PhD in the Sociology of Communication from the Gregorian University (Rome), where he did his studies in the CICS (1998-2003). At present, he is a Senior Lecturer and the Director of the Centre for the Study of African Culture and Communication, Catholic Institute of West Africa, in Port Harcourt (Nigeria).

Bishop **Peter Henrici**, from Switzerland, was Professor and later Dean of the Faculty of Philosophy at the Pontifical Gregorian University. He was involved in developing the idea of an interdisciplinary approach to communications studies and became the Founder Director of the CICS in 1981. In 1993 he left the Gregorian to become Auxiliary Bishop of Chur, in Switzerland, and was later appointed also the Titular

Bishop of Absorus. Currently, he is the President of the European Bishops' Media Commission and actively involved in promoting media culture in the Church.

Nuno Brás da Silva Martins, from Portugal, is Professor in the Faculty of Theology at the Catholic University of Portugal. He completed his Doctorate in Fundamental Theology at the Gregorian University, where he also studied communications in the interdisciplinary Centre. For several of years he was Sessional Lecturer at the CICS in the area of theology and communication. Among other ecclesiastical responsibilities, he served as Rector of the Portuguese College in Rome for a number of years, and he is now Rector of the Major Seminary of Christ the King in Lisbon.

José Martínez de Toda, SJ, from Spain, worked in Venezuela for many years. He completed a Master of Education at Loyola University (Chicago), and a Master of Science in Economics at the University of Wisconsin. In 1988, he completed his Doctorate at the Pontifical Gregorian University with a thesis on "Metodología para evaluar la educación para los medios: la aplicación con un instrumento multidimensional". A Professor of communications for 22 years at the Universidad Católica Andrés Bello and for 12 years at the Universidad Central, both in Venezuela. In 1991 he began teaching in the CICS, and was Director of Interdisciplinary Centre from 2001 to 2004.

Giuseppe Mazza, from Italy, is Professor of Theology and Communication both in the Faculty of Theology and in the Interdisciplinary Centre for Social Communications of the Gregorian University. His major academic degrees are a PhD in Fundamental Theology from the Gregorian, a Diploma in Social Communication from the CICS and a Diploma in Mariology from the Pontifical Theological Faculty *Marianum*. He is a member of SIRT (Società Italiana per la Ricerca Teologica), and author of *La liminalità come dinamica di passaggio* (2005) and of various articles on different theological subjects. His research interests include theology and communication; postmodernism, semiotics and theories of the "limit"; liminal reception and theology of revelation; pastoral and religious communication.

Jim McDonnell, MA (Cantab), PhD (MCIPR), from Britain, was Assistant Research Director and Director of Projects at the Centre for the Study of Communication and Culture (CSCC) in London (1979-1990), Director of the Catholic Communications Centre in London (1990-2001), and now he runs his own public relations, consulting and training business, *McDonnell Communications*. He is President of the European Region of SIGNIS (World Catholic Association for Communication, earlier Unda/OCIC), Consultor to the Pontifical Council for Social Communications and an honorary visiting Fellow of Trinity and All Saints College (Leeds). He has written and spoken extensively on communications and broadcasting matters.

Bernardin F. Mfumbusa, from Tanzania, studied journalism at Nyegezi Social Training Institute (NSTI) in Tanzania and later completed the Licentiate and Doctorate in the Faculty of Social Sciences at the Gregorian University. He is currently the Acting Dean, Faculty of Humanities and Communications at St. Augustine University of Tanzania (SAUT) in Mwanza. His research interests include: newsroom socialization, media accountability systems, media policy and media curricula development. Dr. Mfumbusa is a recipient of Clement Mwila Award (1999) for excellence in journalism from Koinonia Media Centre (Nairobi) and has co-authored, with Professor Frans Wijsen of Nigmegen Catholic University, a booklet entitled *Seeds of Conflict: Religious Tensions in Tanzania*.

Joseph Palakeel, MST, from India, is Professor of Fundamental Theology and Communication at Ruhalaya Theological College (Ujjain, India). He is author of *The Use of Analogy in Theological Discourse* (1995) and editor of *Towards a Communication Theology* (2003). He is a specialist in theology and communication and conducts conferences, workshops and training in communication theology.

Paolo Prato, from Italy, has worked in the field of radio broadcasting for over thirty years. He collaborated with RAI, Radio Televisione Italiana (1982-2000) and was responsible of the programmes for Blu Sat (2000-2004). He teaches radio and music culture at CICS and is the producer of the program *Hola Mi gente/Ciao amici*, for Radio Vaticana and Radio InBlu.

Augustine Savarimuthu, SJ, from India, studied at Madras Christian College, where he obtained the MA in Language and Literature, and at the Gregorian University, with a Licentiate in Fundamental Theology. Then he pursued studies at the New York Institute of Technology, where he completed an MA in Communication, and at Rutgers University, where he obtained a PhD in Communication. Currently he is Assistant Professor of Communication in the CICS.

Michele Sorice, from Italy, is Professor of Sociology of Media at the University of Rome "La Sapienza" and of Media Studies at the University of Lugano, in Switzerland. He teaches Sociology of Media and Audience Studies at CICS. He's also Director of the Centre for Media and Cultural Studies (CRISC-CMCS) of the University of Rome. He has authored/edited several books published in Italy and abroad and he is coordinator of an international research group on Digital Terrestrial Television.

Paul A. Soukup, SJ, from the USA, has explored the connections between communication and theology since 1982. His publications include: *Communication and Theology* (1983); *Christian Communication: A Bibliographical Survey* (1989); *Media, Culture, and Catholicism* (1996); *Mass Media and the Moral Imagination* with Philip J. Rossi (1994), and *Fidelity and Translation: Communicating the Bible in New Media* with Robert Hodgson (1999). In addition, he and Thomas J. Farrell have edited four volumes of the collected works of Walter J. Ong, SJ, *Faith and Contexts* (1992-1999) as well as *An Ong Reader* (2002). A graduate of the University of Texas at Austin (PhD), Soukup teaches in the Communication Department at Santa Clara University in California and has served as a visiting Professor at CICS.

Antonio Spadaro, SJ, from Italy, graduated with a degree in Philosophy from the University of Messina and then obtained a Doctorate in Theology from the Gregorian University, and now he teaches in the CICS. Assigned to *La Civiltà Cattolica*, in Rome, he writes for that journal, mainly in the area of literature, music and the new technologies. He is the founder of an online school of creative expression, and is a regular contributor to several scientific and popular journals. He has authored *Tracce profonde. Il viaggio tra il reale e l'immaginario* (1993); *Radio on. Tra le colonne sonore degli anni '90* (1996); *Lo sguardo presente. Una lettura teologica di "Breve film sull'amore" di K. Kieslowski* (1999); *Pier Vittorio Tondelli. Attraversare l'attesa* (1999); *"Laboratorio Under 25": Tondelli e la nuova narrativa italiana* (2000); *Carver. Un'acuta sensazione d'attesa* (2001); *A che cosa* *"serve" la letteratura?* (2002); *Lontano dentro se stessi. L'attesa di salvezza in Pier Vittorio Tondelli* (2002).

Jacob Srampickal, SJ, from India, has a Doctorate in Development Communication from the University of Leeds (UK) and has authored several books, including *Understanding Communication* (1982); *Voice to the Voiceless, Power of People's Theatre* (1994); *Media Education, Emerging Perspectives* (1997); *Teaching Media Education* (2001); *Messages or Massages* (2001); *Babel to Babri Masjid and Beyond* (2003). President of Unda/OCIC, the international communication association of the Church, in India (1992-1998) and in Asia (1993-2001), he was the inspiration behind and the co-founder of the National Institute of Social Communications, Research and Training (NISCORT) of the Catholic Bishops' Conference of India in New Delhi, and he is presently the Director of the CICS. His areas of interest include media-religion-culture, media ethics, development communication, media education and pastoral communication.

Maria Way, from Britain, is the course leader of the BA (Hons) in Media Studies at the University of Westminster (London). She is now completing a research project on the Papacy in documentary and news film since 1896. Her area of specialisation is religion and the media. She has been associated professionally with the Jesuits for over twenty years, at the Centre for the Study of Communication and Culture (CSCC), in London, and at IKM, in Munich. Since 1994, she has worked at the University of Westminster and with a number of Jesuits on various projects. In the late 1990s she served on a committee set up by JesCom in Rome to consider the education of priests in communication and she is a visiting Professor at the Ateneo di San Bruno da Segni (Segni, Italy).

Mary Wilsey, from Britain, has worked as a journalist for three decades, first for *The Economist* in London and the United States, and then as a freelance political and economic journalist in Italy. In the mid-1980s she started a magazine for English-speaking foreigners living in Rome, which now has two websites, with a third in the making. She graduated with a BA from Sussex University and an MA from the London School of Economics. For almost twenty years she taught courses on journalism at the CICS.

Robert A. White, SJ, from the USA, holds an MA in Sociology and Cultural Anthropology from St. Louis University and a PhD in Development Sociology from Cornell University. From 1973 to 1978, he was Research Director at the Institute of Social Research in Honduras and carried out research on radio schools for the rural poor in various Latin American countries. From 1979 to 1989, he was Research Director at the Jesuit Centre for the Study of Communication and Culture (CSCC) in London, during which time he founded and edited *Communication Research Trends* and four book series including "Communication and Human Values" (Sage Publications), "Comunicación" in Spanish, "Communication, Culture and Theology" (Sheed and Ward), and "African Communication Studies". In 1981 he was appointed to the Advisory Council of the CICS, and in 1990 he became its Director. Currently he has been invited by the Nigerian Bishops' Conference to establish the Centre for the Study of African Culture and Communication in Port Harcourt, where he is now Professor and Project Director, and by the Tanzanian Bishops' Conference to assist in founding an MA and PhD program in Communication and an Institute of Development Studies at St. Augustine University of Tanzania.

STAMPA: Marzo 2006

presso la tipografia
"Giovanni Olivieri" di E. Montefoschi
ROMA • tip.olivieri@libero.it